INTERESTING HISTORICAL EVENTS RELATIVE TO THE PROVINCES OF BENGAL AND THE EMPIRE OF INDOSTAN

INTERESTING
HISTORICAL EVENTS,
RELATIVE TO THE
PROVINCES OF BENGAL,
AND THE
EMPIRE OF INDOSTAN

J. Z. HOLWELL

GYAN

Published by

GYAN

Gyan Publishing House
5, Ansari Road
Daryaganj, New Delhi-110002
Phone: 011-47034999, 9811692060
E-mail: books@gyanbooks.com

Distribution Network
gyanbooks.com
India, USA, Canada, UK, Australia

ISBN: 978-93-7014-183-4 (PB)

First Published, 1766

2nd Impression 2025

Printed at: Gyan Press, Delhi.

INTERESTING HISTORICAL EVENTS,
RELATIVE TO THE PROVINCES OF BENGAL,
AND THE EMPIRE OF INDOSTAN

Author: J. Z. HOLWELL

INTERESTING
HISTORICAL EVENTS,

Relative to the

PROVINCES OF BENGAL,

AND THE

EMPIRE OF INDOSTAN.

WITH

A Seasonable HINT and PERSWASIVE

To the Honourable

The COURT of DIRECTORS of the EAST INDIA COMPANY.

AS ALSO

The MYTHOLOGY and COSMOGONY, FASTS and FESTIVALS of the GENTOOS, Followers of the SHASTAH.

AND

A DISSERTATION on the METEMPSYCHOSIS, commonly, though erroneously, called the PYTHAGOREAN Doctrine.

By J. Z. HOLWELL, Esq;

PART I.

The Second Edition Corrected, with a Supplement.

LONDON:

Printed for T. BECKET and P. A. DE HONDT, near Surry-Street, in the Strand. MDCCLXVI.

To the Right Honourable

CHARLES TOWNSEND, Esq;

SIR,

LAST year you indulged me with an opportunity of communicating to you, ſome anecdotes (little known) relative to the Mogul Empire, and the ſtate of our *Eaſt-India* trade;——in the courſe of that conference, you manifeſted to me ſuch profound penetration, and ſuch a ready comprehenſion of theſe ſubjects, that I could not reſiſt cheriſhing a deſire, to ſubmit to the public my future labours on theſe intereſting matters, under the auſpices of your

your name. I lately intimated that wiſh and intention, when you moſt obligingly and politely favored me, with your permiſſion to dedicate to you *this Firſt Part* of a Work, which at preſent employs my leiſure hours: I now avail myſelf of the licence you have honoured me with; and beg leave to ſubſcribe myſelf, with true reſpect,

SIR,

Your moſt obliged

and moſt obedient

humble ſervant,

Mount Felix in Surry,
Auguſt 21ſt, 1765.

J. Z. HOLWELL.

TO THE PUBLIC.

PRELIMINARY DISCOURSE.

WHEN a man, excited by an irresistable and laudable impulse for the good of his country, *first speaks* before an August Assembly; he feels a certain kind of dread, awe, and trepidation, which he finds himself unable immediately to conquer; especially if he has not been much used to speak in public, or perchance possesses some share of modesty in his composition.——Thus, I conceive, it fares with every considerate author, on his first appearance before that *August Assembly* THE PUBLIC.

In this plight I felt myself in the year 1758, when I exhibited to you a scene of unparalleled horror and diſtreſs, which I judged not unworthy a place in our annals; ——juſtice, and the neceſſity of the times, lately urged my ſecond appearance, and obliged me to draw my pen in defence of injured worth and character: but now, by uſe and indulgence grown bolder, (a very common caſe) I preſent myſelf before you of my own voluntary choice.

Independency, and a pleaſing retirement, however *delectable* in themſelves, have yet their ſeaſons of *vacancy* and *leiſure*, that may want filling up.——And happy I ought that man to eſteem himſelf, who can employ thoſe *voids* and *blanks* in time to the emolument, or even literary amuſement of mankind.

Such is my ſituation, and ſuch are my motives, for taking up the pen again; motives, ſo laudable in themſelves, will, I truſt, engage the candor and indulgence of my readers for any defects in the following performance.

The *Eaſt-Indies*, and particularly *Bengall*, are now become ſo important an object and concern to *Great-Britain*, that every elucidation thereof, muſt, I think, be acceptable, that is founded on facts, just observations, and faithful recitals.

Through a course of thirty years residence in *Bengall*, my leisure hours were employed in collecting materials relative to the transactions, revolutions and occurrences of that invaluable country; and the religious tenets of its inhabitants, natives of *Indostan*; which I flattered myself, when reduced to form and order, might prove worthy your attention.

It is well known that at the capture of *Calcutta*, A. D. 1756, I lost many curious *Gentoo* manuscripts, and among them two very correct and valuable copies of the *Gentoo Shastah*. They were procured by me with so much trouble and expence, that even the commissioners of restitution, though not at all disposed to favour me, allowed me two thousand *Madras* rupees in recompence for this particular loss; but the most irreparable damage I suffered under this head of grievances, was a translation I made of a considerable part of the *Shastah*, which had cost me eighteen months hard labour: as that work opened upon me, I distinctly saw, that the *Mythology*, as well as the *Cosmogony* of the *Egyptians*, *Greeks* and *Romans*, were borrowed from the doctrines of the *Bramins*, contained in this book; even to the copying their exteriors of worſhip, and the diſtribution of their idols, though groſsly mutilated and adulterated. But more of this in the courſe of my preſent work.

I ſhould in the compaſs of one year more, with the cloſe application, I intended beſtowing on it, have accompliſhed a complete tranſlation of the whole *Shaſtah*; that would, I flattered myſelf, have been a valuable acquiſition to the learned world; had not the fatal cataſtrophe of fifty-ſix put it totally out of my power ever to attempt it again.

From that change in our affairs abroad, a new chain of purſuits engroſſed my time and attention; ſo that I could no longer devote either, to the ſtudies I had before ſo much at heart——however, during the laſt eight months of my reſidence in *Bengall*, being freed from the plagues of government, (thanks to my *very honourable maſters* for it) I reaſſumed my reſearches with tolerable ſucceſs; which, joined to ſome manuſcripts recovered by an unforeſeen and extraordinary event (that poſſibly I may hereafter recite) enables me to undertake the taſk I now aſſign myſelf.

It is true I intended a much nobler entertainment for my readers; but as that is now irrecoverably beyond my reach, without once more doubling the *Cape of Good Hope*, (to which I feel not the leaſt inclination) we muſt content ourſelves with the homely fare we have before us, ranged in the beſt manner our ſtraitened circumſtances will admit of——as it is eſſentially neceſſary at this intereſting period, that we ſhould be able to form ſome clearer ideas of a people, with whom we have had ſuch important tranſactions; and of whom ſo little is truely known.*

Having ſtudiouſly peruſed all that has been written of the empire of *Indoſtan*, both as to its ancient, as well as more modern ſtate; as alſo the various accounts tranſmitted to us, by authors in almoſt all ages (from *Arrian*, down to the *Abbé de Guyon*) concerning the *Hindoos*, and the religious tenets of the *Bramins*, I venture to pronounce them all very defective, fallacious, and unſatisfactory to an inquiſitive ſearcher after truth; and only tending to convey a very imperfect and injurious reſem-

* Here I would be underſtood to mean the *Gentoos* only, now labouring under *Mahometan* tyranny, but fated, I hope, ſoon to feel the bleſſings of a mild *Britiſh* government.

 blance

blance of a people, who from the earlieſt times have been an ornament to the creation—if ſo much can with propriety be ſaid of any known people upon earth.

All the modern writers repreſent the *Hindoos* as a race of ſtupid and groſs *Idolaters*: from the ancients indeed theſe people met with better treatment; although they too, as well as the others, were equally ignorant in the ſubjects they treated of.

The modern authors who have wrote on the principles and worſhip of the *Hindoos*, are chiefly of the *Romiſh* communion; therefore we need wonder the leſs that they (from a ſuperſtitious zeal inſeparable from that communion) ſhould depreciate and traduce the mythology of the venerable ancient *Bramins*, on ſo ſlender a foundation as a few inſignificant literal tranſlations of the *Viedam*; and theſe, not made from the book itſelf, but from unconnected ſcraps and bits, picked up here and there by hearſay from *Hindoos*, probably as ignorant as themſelves.

From ſuch weak grounds and evidence as this, and by the help of a few exhibitions of the *ſeemingly* monſtrous idols of the *Hindoos*. the *Popiſh* authors heſitate not to ſtigmatize

ſtigmatize thoſe moſt venerable ſages the *Bramins*, as having inſtituted doctrines and worſhip, which if believed, would reduce them below the level of the brute creation; as every reader muſt have obſerved, who has miſſpent his time in the peruſal of them. In the way of their proper calling and function, they were however right; as having been appointed to propagate their own ſyſtem of theology abroad; though ſtrictly ſpeaking, their own tenets were more idolatrous than the ſyſtem they travelled ſo far to ſtigmatize. On this miſtaken method and falſe zeal of propagating *any faith* at *any rate*, I beg to be indulged in making the following general reflections, which naturally ariſe from the ſubject before us.

In the firſt place, I obſerve, ignorance, ſuperſtition and partiality to ourſelves, are too commonly the cauſe of preſumption and contempt of others.——Secondly, That thoſe whoſe knowledge of ſtates and kingdoms extends no further than the limits of their native land, often imagine all, beyond it, ſcarce worth their thoughts; or at leaſt greatly inferior in compariſon with their own; a concluſion natural, though abſurd——Thirdly, If from clime and country, we proceed to individuals; we ſhall ſee the ſame unwarrantable prepoſſeſſion, and preference to ſelf take place; and proceeding ſtill further in our reflections, we may obſerve, the ſame confined way of thinking and judging, leads the multitude (and I wiſh I could ſay the multitude only) of every nation and ſect, to arraign and have in utter deteſtation and contempt, the religious principles and worſhip of all that happen to be out of the pale of their own church, or mode of faith.

That every nation and *ſect* ſhould have a high and even ſuperior opinion of the religious principles, under which they were born and educated, is extremely natural and juſt; provided they do not, from an intemperate zeal of religious vanity (now ſo much the faſhion) preſume to condemn, depreciate or invade the religious principles of others—this condemning ſpirit can proceed only from one of the three following cauſes; a defect in underſtanding; a want of knowledge of the world (in men and things;) or a bad (and reſtleſs) heart. The ſalvation of mankind, ſo much pretended, has no place in the wiſhes or labours of theſe zealots; or they would not go about ſeeking whom they can confound in ſpirit, deſtroying the peace and tranquillity of their *poor* fellow chriſtians.

Men

Men who have been conversant with foreign countries, and made proper and benevolent remarks on the manners and principles of their inhabitants; will not despise or condemn the different ways by which they approach the *Deity*; but revere it still as a divine worship, though they may piously lament it deviates so much from their own.

To rescue distant nations from the gross conceptions entertained of them by the multitude, of all other persuasions, is the true business and indispensable duty of a *Traveller*; or else his travels and remarks, can only amuse his readers, without conveying to them any useful instruction or solid satisfaction.

A mere description of the exterior manners and religion of a people, will no more give us a true idea of them; than a geographical description of a country can convey a just conception of their laws and government. The traveller must sink deeper in his researches, would he feast the mind of an understanding reader.——His telling us such and such a people, in the *East* or *West-Indies*, worship this stock or that stone, or monstrous idol; only serves to reduce in our esteem, our fellow creatures, to the most abject and despicable point of light. Whereas, as, was he ſkilled in the language of the people he deſcribes, ſufficiently to trace the etymology of their words and phraſes, and capable of diving into the myſteries of their theology; he would probably be able to evince to us, that ſuch ſeemingly prepoſterous worſhip, had the moſt ſublime rational ſource and foundation.

The traveller, who without theſe eſſential requiſites, (as well as induſtry and a clear underſtanding) pretends to deſcribe and fix the religious tenets of any nation whatever, diſhoneſtly impoſes his own reveries on the world; and does the greateſt injury and violence to letters, and the cauſe of humanity—How far the productions of moſt travellers may juſtly fall under this cenſure, I ſubmit to the public.

To the want of this attention and capacity in the traveller, we may aſcribe in a great meaſure, the deſpicable, and I dare ſay unworthy notion, we too aptly entertain of moſt nations very remote from us; whereas were we better informed, we ſhould find our minds opened; our underſtandings enlarged; and ourſelves inſpired with that benevolence for our ſpecies; without which, the human form becomes rather a diſgrace than ornament.

I am

I am ſorry to ſay, that in general the accounts publiſhed of the manners and religious principles of *the Eaſt and Weſt-Indies*, have been in the light and ſuperficial way before objected to: but as my knowledge extends only to the former, I ſhall confine my remarks to them; and endeavor to extricate them in ſome degree from the groſs abſurdities we have conceived of them: confeſſing myſelf amazed that we ſhould ſo readily believe the people of *Indoſtan* a race of ſtupid *Idolaters*; when, to our coſt, in a political and commercial view, we have found them ſuperior to us.

Having tranſiently mentioned the *Viedam* and *Shaſtah* (the *Gentoos ſcriptures)* it is neceſſary, I ſhould inform you——The book firſt named, is followed by the *Gentoos* of the *Mallabar* and *Cormandel* coaſts: and alſo by thoſe of the Iſland of *Ceylon*.—The *Shaſtah* is followed by the *Gentoos* of the provinces of *Bengall*; and by all the *Gentoos* of the reſt of *India*, commonly called *India proper*; that is to ſay—the greateſt part of *Oriſſa*, *Bengall proper*, *Bahar*, *Banaras*, *Oud*, *Eleabas*, *Agra*, *Delhy*, &c. all along the courſe of the rivers *Ganges*, and *Jumna*, to the *Indus*.

Both

Both theſe books contain the inſtitutes of their reſpective religion and worſhip; often couched under allegory and fable; as well as the hiſtory of their ancient Rajahs and Princes—their antiquity is contended for by the partiſans of each—but, the ſimilitude of their *names*, *idols*, and great part of their worſhip, leaves little room to doubt, nay plainly evinces, that both theſe ſcriptures were originally *one*.——And if we compare the great purity and chaſte manners of the *Shaſtah*, with the great abſurdities and impurities of the *Viedam*; we need not heſitate to pronounce, the *latter* a *corruption* of the former.——All that I need add here, is, that my remarks follow the *Shaſtah* only.

Taſte, in reading, differs as much as in the choice of viands. What proves a delicious morſel to one, is diſguſtful to another. I was never invited to a feaſt in my life, that I did not regret the abſence of a bill of fare:—Therefore to ſave you from the ſame regret, I here preſent you with a liſt of what is provided for your entertainment in the following Sheets, in eight courſes; ſo that if your ſtomach does not ſtimulate you to taſte the whole; you will be enabled to fall to, on that diſh, which may beſt ſuit your appetite.

I. Under

I. Under the First general head is contained—A short history of the succession to the empire of *Indostan*, from *Aurenge Zebe* to *Mahomet Shaw*.——This subject has been already touched upon by my ingenious friend Mr. *James Fraser*; but being foreign to his more immediate concern *(the invasion of* Nadir Shaw) he has touched it so slightly, as to convey a very imperfect idea of the *circumstances* attending the many astonishing changes that happened in this short and memorable period. These particulars I was favored with at *Patna, A. D.* 1733, by a sensible *Armenian*, who resided alternately at *Agra* and *Delhy*, in a civil post of some trust, under the Emperors; during the course of these transactions.

II. Transactions in the subahdaary of *Bengall*; from the period that *Jaffier Khan* ruled these provinces, to the usurpation of the government by *Aliverdi Khan*; with the extraordinary circumstances attending the rise of this last mentioned *Soubah*, and his brother *Hodjee Hamet**.

III. A

* The world has been already treated with this part of my subject, by a gentleman in his lucubrations, printed in *Edinburgh* 1761, under the title of "*Reflections on the government of* Indostan, *and a short* "*sketch,*

III. A ſummary account of the provinces of *Bengall*, (properly ſo called :) it's principal towns; their bearings and diſtance from each other, and from *Calcutta*; with an eſtimate of their revenues; and a ſeaſonable and perſuaſive hint to the gentlemen in the *Eaſt-India* direction.

"*ſketch of the hiſtory of* Bengall, *from the year* 1739, "*to* 1756." This little piece fell into my hands, about a year and a half after it was printed.——On peruſing it, I could not avoid being ſurprized at finding *The Author's* "Short ſketch, &c." was taken from part of *the Manuſcripts* herein before-mentioned, and makes from page 33 to 50, of his ſecond epiſtle——Theſe Manuſcripts were penned by me in the year 1750, in my paſſage to *Europe*, from materials collected abroad. I communicated them, during my ſhort ſtay in *England*, to my friends, Sir *William Baker*, Mr. *Mabbot*, Mr. *R. Drake*, Mr. *Davis* and Doctor *Campbell*.—— The orginal was loſt at the capture of *Calcutta*, but after my ſecond return in 1757, I learnt, a copy had been taken of it without my knowledge, by a gentleman to whom I lent it abroad—from this copy I was permitted to take another. How *the Author* of the Reflections came by it, he beſt knows——He honours me in tranſcribing from it, but he would have honoured himſelf more, had he acknowledged from whence he took it; and had not taken ſuch fruitleſs pains to diſguiſe his (yet obvious) plagiariſm; by mangling, maiming and curtailing my ſubjects in the manner I conceive he has done.

IV. A

IV. A ſummary view of the *fundamental*, religious tenets of the *Gentoos*, followers of the *Shaſtah*.

V. A ſhort account, from the *Shaſtah*, of the creation of the *worlds*, or univerſe.

VI. The *Gentoo* manner of computing time; and their conceptions touching the *age of the worlds*; and the period of their diſſolution.

VII. An account and explanation of the *Gentoo* faſts and feſtivals; with a repreſentation of their grand feaſt of the *Drugah*: compriſing a view of their principal idols, and the genealogy of their *ſubordinate deities*.——If the faſts and feſtivals of any nation are once clearly underſtood; there wants little more to convey to us a diſtinct idea of their religious principles; the *one*, being the only true criterion of the *other*.

VIII. A diſſertation on the *Gentoo* doctrine of the *metempſycoſis*; improperly called *Pythagorean*, by all who have wrote on this ſubject, hitherto ſo little underſtood.

Having

Having thus ſet forth my real motives for taking up the pen again, and opened the plan of my intended work; I ſhall here cloſe this preliminary diſcourſe: the favorable acceptance of my labors, by the candid public, is all the recompence hoped, or wiſhed for, by their

Obedient humble ſervant,

J. Z. HOLWELL.

CHAP.

CHAP. I.

The succession of the Mogull *Emperors from* Auring Zebe.

WHOEVER has attentively perused the histories of the rise of states and kingdoms, must have made this melancholy observation; that the approaches to usurped royalty, dominion and power, are *generally* founded, in the first instance, on the subduction of every virtue from the human breast; as, the sacred tyes of justice, natural affection, gratitude and *true* benevolence. A few exceptions may possibly subsist in the course of many thousand years, against our conclusion; but they are so *very few*, that we think they cannot in the least invalidate our general assertion.

The glittering prospects of a crown, so dazzle and dim the *eye* of cool reflection and reason, that it becomes *blind* to every other consideration of humanity.

Ambition, or a reſtleſs thirſt after power and dominion, has ever been the *bane* of the civil rights and liberties of mankind; and ſeems to be a paſſion implanted in the original nature and conſtruction of man:—if otherwiſe, his conduct is wholly unaccountable: for we ſee that every individual of the ſpecies, in every rank and degree, is graſping and labouring to poſſeſs that which every individual is ſo materially concerned to prevent; *neither* of them adverting to this invariable truth: That *he* who invades the liberty, rights and property of *another*, gives, at the ſame time, a leſſon and juſt cauſe for diſpoſſeſſing *himſelf*.——Why this eternal warfare and contention for dominion between man and man, collectively or ſeparately, (from his creation to this hour) was originally implanted in him, we may, in a future diſſertation, attempt to ſolve: here we will only lament, that ſo it undeniably is.

The miſerable effects of this fatal paſſion for *rule*, is no where more ſtrongly exemplify'd, than in the ſhort recital we are going to make of the ſucceſſors of *Auring Zebe* to the throne of *Indoſtan*; to which he himſelf did not arrive without wading through a ſea of blood, and a continued chain of almoſt unparallel'd religious fraud,

 per-

perfidy and cruelty: leaving on record a flagrant proof, That no tyes, however sacred, can resist, or come in competition with, the charms of royalty. His bloody example was very exactly copied by his descendants.

Auring Zebe deceasing the 21st of *February* 1707, was succeded in the throne by his second son *Mahommed Mauzm*; for, notwithstanding the positive injunction in *Auring Zebe's* last Will, in favour of his son *Mahommed Azem Shaw*, *Mahommed Mauzm* adopting the successful example of his father, disputed the crown with his elder brother; who, in battle near *Agra*, was defeated and killed. *Mahommed Mauzm* was immediately proclaimed Emperor, and assumed (amongst other titles mentioned by Mr. *Fraser*) the title of *Shaw Allum, King of the World*. I have, in my collection, two gold Mohurs struck in this Emperor's Reign, *Anno* 1709, and 1711; on the first is impressed *Shaw Allum*; on the other, *Bahadr Shaw, The Valiant King*; which title he was, latterly, fondest of.

Anno 1707. *Auring Zebe.*

His reign, though extended to the term of six years, was unhappy and turbulent. The fortune of war gave him the succession to his father's dominions; but he succeeded not to his capacity and fame: perplexed *Shaw Allum.* with the reſtleſs ambition of his *four ſons* who in his life time ſhewed themſelves competitors for his crown, he died of diſcontent and grief, *Anno* 1713.

Their names were, *Mauz O'din*, *Mahommed Azîm*, *Raffeeil al Kaddr*, and *Khojiſta* Anno 1713. *Akhter*: they had been ſome years Governors of diſtinct provinces, and were each, at the death of their father, at the head of a puiſſant army to ſupport their ſeveral pretenſions to the throne.

Mahommed Azîm, being ſuperior in force, wealth, and reputation, to the other three brothers; they joined in league againſt him; taking the moſt ſolemn oath on *Khoran*, to be faithful to each other, and to ſubmit to an equal partition of the Empire, in thirds, as ſoon as they ſhould defeat and ſucceed againſt their brother.

In conſequence of this compact, the three brothers united their reſpective armies; and a general battle enſued; in the firſt heat of which, *Mahommed Azîm* was killed by the ſhot of an arrow, as he was gallantly charging, on his elephant, the center of his bro-Anno 1714. thers army; which he was informed was com-

commanded, in perſon, by his eldeſt brother *Mauz O'din*.

The treaſures of *Mahommed Azîm*, by the dexterity of *Zulfecar Khan*, an Omrah in the intereſt or *Mauz O'din*, fell into the hands of the latter; with which having privately bought over moſt of the troops of his two remaining brothers, he attacked them on the field of battle, in violation of his ſolemn oath,

The brothers being no ways prepared for this ſudden, unſuſpected and perfidious ſtroke; were capable of making but ſmall reſiſtance: the elder of the two, *Raffeeil al Kaddr*, was preſently killed; and, what is worthy remark, fell upon the body of his brother *Mahommed Azîm*. *Khojiſta Akhter*, the youngeſt of the four, collecting ſome few of his own and *Raffeeil al Kaddr*'s troops, fled towards the province of *Deccan*, his government; but being purſued and attacked by *Mauz O'din*, ſhared the ſame fate with his brothers..

Thus *Mauz O'din* became, like his father and grandfather, poſſeſſed of the throne of *Indoſtan*, by the perfidious deſtruction of his brothers; one circumſtance however might be pleaded in behalf of *Mauz O'din*,

 which

which neither of the other two could lay any claim to,—for he was the legal heir to the crown: but it may also justly be said, that he had waved and given up his legal right, when he entered into the voluntary compact with his brethren. He was proclaimed Emperor by the stile and title of *Mauz O'din Jehandar Shaw, The King who possesses the World*; and appointed *Zulfecar Khan* his Vizir.

Shaw Jehandar, Anno 1715. *Jehandar* was a weak Prince; and very soon after he thought himself in secure possession of the throne, he sunk and lost himself in the luxuries and debaucheries of the Seraglio: so wholly devoting his hours to a famed courtesan called *Lol Koar*, (better known in *Indostan* by the name of *Loll Kooree)* that he neglected every duty which ought to distinguish the Man, and the King.

This courtesan was of exquisite beauty, and highly excelled as a dancer and singer, in which profession she was originally bred; besides these qualifications, it is said, her conversation was engaging and bewitching. The Monarch, intoxicated with her allurements, had no will but hers: by her influence she filled all places of the highest trust and honour, with her base relations. This infatuated conduct, brought the Emperor

peror and Empire into the loweſt contempt; and gave univerſal diſguſt to all the Omrahs and great officers of the kingdom; who one by one, under various pretexts, withdrew themſelves from court; and meditated a favourable conjuncture to depoſe their ſovereign.

Amongſt the diſaffected, were two Generals and Omrahs of the court, of diſtinguiſhed character and authority; named *Haſſan Aly Khan*; and *Abdallah Khan*; brothers of the tribe of the *Seyds*, for whom *Mahometans* bear a religious veneration. Theſe, in concert with others of the Omrahs, determined to raiſe *Mahommed Furrukhsîr* to the throne; and ſuddenly, at the head of a choice body of troops, retired towards *Bengall*, where *Furrukhsîr* then reſided.

This young Prince was the ſon of *Ma- Anno*
hommed Azîm, already mentioned, and ne- 1715.
phew to the Emperor; he had reſided ſome years at *Dacca*, (then the metropolis of *Bengal*) by the appointment of his grandfather *Shaw Allum*, where he was ſo much beloved, that the inhabitants of that city, to this day, in their common ſongs lament his fate, with tears; and celebrate his memory.

When *Furrukhsír* first received advice of *Shaw Alum*'s death, and the fatal catastrophe of his father and uncles; he withdrew from *Dacca*; knowing his uncle, *Jehandar*, would never think himself secure on the throne, whilst so near a pretender to it was in being. Much perplexed, and irresolute what course to take, as he was at the head of an inconsiderable, but faithful body of horse, retiring out of the province, he was met by express messengers from the revolters; urging his immediate advance to *Patna* in the province of *Bahaar*; where on his arrival he was received by *Seyd Hossan Aly Khan*, *Seyd Abdallah Khan*, and other principal Omrahs and Officers; who instantly proclaimed him Emperor of *Indostan*.

On the first news of this revolt and competitor, the court was struck with a panick; but the Emperor, buried in the embraces of his beloved *Loll Kooree*, treated it as an impotent attempt hardly worth his notice; contenting himself with sending his son *Eas O'din*, at the head of 15,000 horse, to suppress him; with orders to bring the traitor's head.

Express after express arriving with intelligence that *Furrukhsír*'s party gained strength

ſtrength every hour; and that he was in full march towards *Agra*; the Emperor re-inforced his ſon with a large body of troops, under the joint command of his Vizir *Zulfecar Khan*, and his favourite *Gokuldas Khan*; between whom there ſubſiſted much private jealouſy and enmity.

Furrukhsîr had by this time drawn together a reſpectable army; and thought himſelf ſtrong enough to quit *Patna*: which he accordingly did, and by forced marches advanced as far as *Chivalram* in the province of *Eleabas*, where he was met by *Eas O'din*, at the head of his 15000 horſe. This young Prince, after a ſhort conteſt, perceiving the ſuperiority of the enemy's forces; thought it adviſeable to retreat towards *Agra*, which he did in good order; and in a few days was joined near *Agra* by the troops, ſent by the Emperor under the command of the Vizir and *Gokuldas Khan*, to reinforce them: here it was reſolved to wait the approach of the enemy, for which they did not wait long; and a general battle quickly enſued. *Anno.* 1715.

The Emperor's forces, by the advice of *Zulſecar Khan*, were formed into three diviſions. The center was commanded by

Eas

Eas O'din; the right by *Gokuldas Khan*; and the left by *Zulfecar Khan*.

Furrukhsîr obſerved the like diviſion of his forces. He gave the command of his center to *Seyd Hoſſan Aly Khan*; the right to *Seyd Abdallah Khan*; and led on the left himſelf; preferring this, as the poſt of the greateſt honor; becauſe it was the poſt of greateſt danger, as being oppoſed to *Gokuldas Khan*; who commanded the right diviſion of the Emperor's forces; and was juſtly eſteemed the moſt conſummate general and intrepid ſoldier in the Empire.

Mr. *Fraſer* in his ſhort narrative intimates, that the Emperor was in perſon in this engagement; but herein his intelligence deceived him: for it is a known fact, that he was never rouſed ſo far from the lethargic pleaſures he was immerſed in, as once to quit the Seraglio; and indeed the flattering informations that were hourly conveyed to him of the defeat of the rebels, by *Loll Kooree* (who dreaded his abſence) prevented his ever beſtowing a thought that way; until it was too late to think of it to any purpoſe. But to reſume our ſubject.

The

The battle was fought with great obstinacy and gallantry on both ſides—Wonders are recorded of the ſpirited actions and perſonal bravery of *Eas O'din* and *Gokuldas Khan*; and not leſs reported of the valour of *Furrukhsîr*, and *Seyd Hoſſan Aly Khan*; but the deciſive ſtroke of victory was given by *Seyd Abdallah Khan*: this General, obſerving the Vizir draw off and retire with his diviſion, wheeled and vigorouſly attacked *Eas O'din* in flank; whilſt he was hard preſſed in front by *Seyd Hoſſan Aly Khan*, *Eas O'din* at the ſame time learning that the brave *Gokuldas Khan* was killed, and his right wing defeated by *Furrukhsîr*; a general rout ſoon followed.——*Eas O'din* eſcaped with difficulty from the battle; and by a change of ſwift horſes reached *Delhy*, where in the preſence of his father, he died of his wounds in an hour.

Furrukhsîr prudently ordered the troops to be ſpared in the purſuit. This clemency, and the addreſſes of ſome emiſſaries ſent amongſt them, operated ſo ſtrongly on them; that, to a man, they revolted from the Emperor; and joined *Furrukhsîr*: whoſe triumph, on this happy ſucceſs, was greatly abated by the abſence and ſuppoſed death of *Seyd Hoſſan Aly Khan*. Short ſighted mortal! little didſt thou at that time know, that

that thou wert regretting the loſs and life of the man, who in a very ſhort period would deprive thee of thine own!— A large reward being promiſed by the Prince; and ſearch being made; *Seyd Hoſſan Aly Khan* was found amongſt the ſlain with ſigns of life, and his recovery effected.

The treacherous conduct of the Vizir *Zulfecar Khan*, it was ſaid, proceeded from cowardice, and reſentment at *Gokuldas Khan*'s being joined in the command with him (a ſource from which the greateſt deſigns have often proved abortive.) When he retired with his diviſion, he made the beſt of his way to *Delhy*; where, ſoon after, the arrival of the unfortunate *Eas O'din*, too plainly ſpoke the deſtiny of the Emperor his Father.

Some feeble attempts were made to raiſe freſh troops, and put the city in a poſture of defence; but the ſudden approach of *Furrukhsír* put a period to every hope. The Emperor, his uncle, fell into his hands without reſiſtance. His head was immediately cut off; and his trunk being fixed upon an elephant, was expoſed round the city. His Vizir, *Zulfecar Khan*, was tied by the feet to the tail of the ſame elephant, and dragged until he expired: a death cruel,

and

and esteemed the most dishonourable that can be inflicted upon a criminal; but scarcely severe enough for that minister who sacrifices the interest, and cause of his King, to his own private resentments. He was little lamented; for by his mal-administration, whilst Vizir, he had acquired the universal hatred of the people.

Anno 1713. Mahommed Furrukhsir.

Mauz O'din Jehander Shaw thus falling a sacrifice to love and indolence; *Mahommed Furruksîr* was proclaimed Emperor of *Indostan*, without opposition. The first acts of his government consisted, in rewarding those who had raised him to the throne. He appointed *Seyd Abdallah Khan* his *Vizir*; and *Seyd Hossan Aly Khan* his *Bukshi*, or Pay-Master General, with the title of *Emir al Omrah*; *(The Prince of Princes)* and bestowed upon him the government of *Deccan*; suitably rewarding the other Omrahs that had rendred him service.

But before we enter on the reign of *Furrukhsîr*, we beg to be indulged a few words on the late murdered Emperor *Jehander*; whose character very minutely resembled that of the unfortunate and licentious Roman, *Marcus Antonius*.

He

He was thought by his father, *Shaw Allum*, the only General capable of repulsing the dangerous annual invasions of the *Boluccais*; which threatned the Empire on the side of *Persia*. Prince *Mauz O'din* was sent against these warlike people, at the head of the choicest troops in the Empire; and in a continued campaign of five years, he had many and signal battles with the invaders; that gave him vast renown. In one of these, when the enemy was intrenched behind a strong and thick wood, on which side they could only be attacked, he cut a passage through the wood; forced their intrenchments sword in hand, and hardly any of the enemy escaped the slaughter. No sooner were the particulars of this action arrived at court, than the Emperor his father, gave him the title of *Prince of the Hatchets*; one of the *honorary titles* ever since given to the first Prince of the blood.

His disposition, before he came to the throne, was so engaging and amiable; that he became the idol of the whole Empire. This drew on him the jealousy of his father; who, to counterbalance his growing influence, heaped that partial power and favor on his second son, *Mahommed Azim*, (the father of *Furrukhsir*) which enabled him to make the stand he did against his brother's legal

legal right of ſucceſſion; at the demiſe of *Shaw Allum*; as before recited. In ſhort, if he could be defended from that perfidious ſtroke againſt his other two brothers; and had eſcaped the bewitching ſnares of that eaſtern *Cleopatra, Loll Kooree*; he moſt probably would have left a more ſhining character, (and a much more honorable one) on the records of fame, than that of his grandfather *Auring Zebe*.

Loll Koar had the honor of being condemned, for life, a priſoner in the royal priſon, or caſtle of *Selimgur*. Some of her baſe relations, who had been raiſed to places of high truſt, were cut off by the conqueror; and others degraded.

Furrukhsîr having obtained the diadem, as before related, peace *ſeemed* to be ſettled in the Empire: but the evil deſtiny of that Prince forbad its long continuance. During this period, the power of the *Seyds* grew enormous; and left the Emperor the name and trappings of royalty only: for they diſpoſed of all important poſts by their ſole authority; amaſſed immenſe wealth, and ſequeſtered the public revenues to their own private emolument; ſecuring thereby the attachment of the principal officers of the crown: who (with a very few exceptions) were intirely devoted to their intereſt.

Furrukhsîr very ſoon ſaw, and felt his deſpicable ſtate of dependance; but could not eaſily forget, how much he owed to the ſpirited conduct and friendſhip of theſe ambitious brothers. He patiently ſubmitted to the many indignities he labored under: without meditating any thing againſt them; the life and crown they had given him, he knew, ſtill depended too much on their will and diſpoſal: he dreaded their power, which indeed was greater than any ſubjects in this deſpotick government can poſſeſs, with ſafety to their Prince; or than can be conſiſtent with his honor.

Wearied at length, at finding himſelf this cypher of a King; he nobly determined to free himſelf from the ſhackles with which he had been bound ſo long; by having both the brothers aſſaſſinated at the ſame time: *Abdallah Khan* at *Delhy*; and *Hoſſan Aly Khan*, as he was upon his march to his government at *Deccan*; where he was going to diſpoſſeſs *Nizam al Muluck*.

A deſign, ſo complicated in its nature, could not be carried on without being communicated

municated to many; amongſt theſe the Emperor chiefly intruſted and depended on the two Omrahs, *Khondoran Khan*, and *Mhîr Jumla*, for the execution of it; they being almoſt the only two officers about the court, who had been neglected by the powerful *Seyds*. *Khondoran* was ſuſpected of betraying the whole to *Abdallah Khan*: whether this was the fact, is uncertain; but it is very certain, both the brothers had early intelligence of the deſign againſt them; and determined to have the ſtart, by depoſing the Emperor.

The Vizir immediately withdrew from court; ſent expreſs upon expreſs to recal his brother; and put himſelf at the head of a body of troops, whoſe commander he was by virtue of his poſt.

Furrukhsîr finding his intentions againſt the *Seyds* diſcovered; had recourſe to diſſimulation: He ſent his mother to the Vizir; charged with his ſolemn proteſtations of the falſhood of the information the Vizir had received; and with profeſſions of inviolable friendſhip and affection intreating, that he would return to court; and contradict any advices he might have diſpatched to his brother.

The Vizir having no room to doubt of his intelligence of the Emperor's projected aſſaſſination, returned for anſwer—That, as a mark of the ſincerity of his profeſſions, he ſhould diſcharge his guards and ſervants; and ſubmit to receive ſuch as he, the Vizir, ſhould think proper to place about him. This hard condition the Emperor abjectly and unadviſedly conſented to; and the Vizir, contented with this ſecurity, waited the arrival of his brother, without proceeding further. Theſe events fell out about the beginning of the year 1719.

Seyd Hoſſan Ali Khan returned at the head of a ſtrong body of horſe, immediately on the receipt of his brother's letters; and arrived at *Delhy* the 14th of *February* 1719; where after a ſhort conference with the Vizir, and *Ajeet Singh* (*Mahah Rajah*, and father-in-law to the Emperor) and with ſeveral principal Omrahs; they all proceeded to the apartment of *Auring Zebe*'s daughter in the caſtle of *Selimgur*; and demanded the delivery of *Raffecil al Dirjaat*, (ſon of *Raffeeil al Kaddr*, third ſon of *Bahadr Shaw*) a youth about 17 years of age; proclaimed him Emperor of *Indoſtan*; and ſwore allegiance to him.

Proceeding thence to the palace with their new King, as soon as they came into the presence of *Furrukhsîr*; the *Seyds* upbraided him with perfidy and ingratitude; and *Ajeet Singh*, with the breach of his coronation oath; in imposing the Jescrah (or poll tax) upon the *Hindoos*: they then divested him of his sword, and ensigns of royalty: and, with little ceremony, informed him they had raised *Raffeeil Dirjaat* to the throne; to whom they forced him to pay obeisance; and then imprisoned him in a tower over the principal gate of the citadel. *Anno* 1719. *Raffeeil al Dirjaat.*

The day after his imprisonment, he was miserably deprived of his sight. On the second, he attempted to finish his torments by a dose of poison; but it proved ineffectual; on the third day, the Vizir sent executioners to strangle him: but as soon as he felt the cord about his neck (still wretchedly desirous of life) he interposed his hands, and forcibly broke it; dragging on, thus, a miserable being, until the next day, the 24th *February* 1719; when he was at last strangled, after a reign of little more than four years. Mr. *Fraser* says, seven; but this cannot be; for, by his own account, *Auring Zebe* deceased in the beginning of the year 1707: his son, *Shaw Allum*, reigned six years; that is, to the beginning of the year 1713. *Fur-*

 rukhsîr

rukhsîr was murdered in the beginning of the year 1719; so that if his succession had been uninterrupted, it could have been no more than six years: but the intervening reign of his uncle, *Mauz O'din Jehandar Shaw*, who sat on the throne 18 months, reduces the reign of *Furrukhsîr* to four years and six months.

The *Seyds* finding they had mistaken the genius of the young Emperor *Dirjaat*, (whom they had raised to the throne in preference to his elder brother *Raffeeil al Dowlat*, as judging his youth would be more subservient to their views) took him off by poison; when he had reigned about three months: and raised to the throne his eldest brother, just abovementioned, who assumed the stile and title of *Shaw Jehan*, *(King of the World.)*

Anno 1719. *Raffeeil al Dowlat. Shaw Jehan.*

The brothers, intoxicated with their excess of power, began by various acts of oppression to create themselves enemies from all quarters: the universal hatred of the people, for their repeated murders, co-operating with the envy of the principal *Rajahs* and *Omrahs*, (who could endure no longer to see the *Seyds* engross wholly a power and authority in the Empire, which they themselves

ſelves wanted a ſhare in) a powerful party was now formed againſt them.

At the head of this confederacy were *Sa-vejee Jeet Singh*, (more commonly known by the name of *Rajah Jaij Singh) Gopaul Singh Bowderee*, and *Chivalram Roy*; all puiſſant Rajahs. The firſt named being hereditary governor of the fortreſs of *Agra*.— Here it is appoſite that we recite an anecdote of this empire, which is not generally known.

When the *Hindoo* Rajahs, or Princes of *Indoſtan*, ſubmitted to *Tamerlane*; it was on theſe capital ſtipulations: That the Emperors ſhould marry a daughter of *Rajah Jeet Singh*'s houſe: that the head of this houſe ſhould be, in perpetuity, governors of the citadel of *Agra*; and anoint the King at his coronation: and, that the Emperors ſhould never impoſe the jeſſerah (or poll tax) upon the *Hindoes*.

These three powerful *Rhaaſepoot Rajahs*, *Anno*
with ſome diſcontented *Omrahs*, withdrew 1719.
themſelves; and aſſembled together in the neighbourhood of *Agra*: and, on the firſt intelligence of the murder of *Raffecil Dir-jaat*, releaſed (from a forty years impriſonment in the caſtle of *Agra*) *Nicoſir*; a ſon

 of

of the great *Ekbbar*; and proclaimed him Emperor: and raiſed a reſpectable army to ſupport their election againſt that of the *Seyds*, in favour of *Shaw Jehan*.

On the firſt notice of this formidable competitor *Seyd Hoſſan Ali Khan* was diſpatched at the head of forty thouſand horſe towards *Agra*; and was met, within four miles of that city, by *Nicosîr*'s forces, under the command of *Jeet Singh*: who putting himſelf at the head of his *Rhaaſepoots*, intrepidly charged *Seyd Hoſſan Aly Khan*'s army. A long and bloody conflict enſued; wherein, at laſt, *Nicosîr*'s forces began to give way; when the *Rhaaſepoot*'s, by the example of their Rajah *Jeet Singh*, diſplayed the *yellow ſcarf*, (the *Rhaaſepoots* ſignal for conqueſt or death) by which means the battle had a ſudden turn. *Hoſſan Aly Khan*'s troops, ſtruck with terror at ſeeing that dreaded ſignal, and the fury with which the *Rhaaſepoots* returned to the charge, ſoon turned their backs and fled; diſregarding as well the heroic example, as menaces of their General; who, finding all endeavours to rally them fruitleſs made the beſt retreat he could with them.

Shaw Jehan wiſely profiting by the error which had proved fatal to *Mauz O'din*; in a ſitua-

ſituation ſimilar to his own; immediately took the field with the Vizir *Seyd Abdallah Khan*: and with a large and choſen body of men marched to ſupport and re-inforce *Seyd Hoſſan Aly Khan*.

This General, in his retreat, or rather flight, had been vigorouſly purſued by *Rajah Jeet Singh*, and his nominal Emperor *Nicosîr*; ſollicitous, if poſſible, to prevent his union with *Shaw Jehan* and his brother; who were (they had learned) on their march to his ſuccour.——In this judicious intention they failed; for *Hoſſan Aly Khan*, with his beaten troops, joined the Emperor before the Rajah could overtake him. Both armies being greatly harraſſed with their ſevere marches, the deciſive battle, which was to determine the poſſeſſion of this mighty Empire, was delayed until the next day.

Hoſſan Aly Khan, it was ſaid, ſelected the evening before the battle, a body of 2000 horſe; compoſed all of ſubaltern officers; to whom he gave ſtrict command, that they ſhould pay regard to nothing elſe in the approaching engagement, but the cutting off, or taking priſoner *Nicosîr*, or *Jeet Singh*.

The battle began ſoon after ſun-riſe the next morning; and was fought with incredible fury and obſtinacy, for the ſpace of three hours: but, at length, the party abovementioned ſo well executed what they had in charge, that they took *Nicosîr* priſoner; which being immediately known to his party, they were ſoon after defeated, or rather put to flight: for in theſe eaſtern battles, if the principal on either ſide is killed or taken priſoner, there is an end generally to the conteſt.—— The iſſue of this battle, which was fought about the middle of *June* 1719, on the plains of *Fatteabad*, put *Shaw Jehan* in tranquil poſſeſſion of the Empire.

The Emperor gave *Nicosîr* the choice of death, or loſs of ſight: he preferred the latter; which was executed on him in the field of battle; and he then was conducted back to his priſon at *Agra*; a melancholy victim to the ambition of others.

Savagee Jeet Singh, with a ſelect body of *Rhaaſepoots* by a well conducted retreat recovered *Agra*; and was ſoon after reconciled to the King and admitted to favour; conformable to the ſteady policy of this government: in keeping a good underſtanding with the principal Rajahs; and more eſpecially with the *head* of this houſe; who is ever capable of raiſing and fomenting a very formidable party, upon any intended revolution

lution in this despotic and precarious monarchy.

Shaw Jehan lived not long to enjoy his high dignity; for he died a natural death, soon after his return to *Delhy*, towards the latter end of the year 1719. Happy! we may say, in having made this quiet and easy exit; for had he discovered a wish to make himself a *King, indeed*; it is more than probable, he would have shared the same fate with his three predecessors.

His death, for some days, was concealed by the singular address of the *Seyds*; and *Hossan Ali Khan*, on the night that *Shaw Jehan* deceased, privately set out with a small, but select party of horse for *Agra*, where he published his death: and, with the participation of the *Mhaahab* Rajah, *Savajee Jeet Singh* immediately proclaimed *Mahommed Shaw* Emperor of *Indostan*; who was by the Rajah anointed accordingly. *Mahommed Shaw* was the only son of *Khojistah Akhter*, before mentioned; the youngest son of *Shaw Allum*. Soon after, the Vizir and the other great officers of the crown arrived at *Agra*, to pay their submission to the new Emperor; and were all confirmed in their posts.

Ma-

Mahommed Shaw, was ſoon convinced, by the firſt movements of the *Seyds*, that though he was raiſed to the poſſeſſion of the enſigns and exteriors of royalty; he was in effect little better than a priſoner of ſtate; whilſt the two brothers exerciſed the uncontrouled authority they had ſo long and ſucceſsfully uſurped. He did not want courage; but plainly ſaw their power was too great to be attacked by open force: he therefore wiſely, for ſome time, diſſembled his ſentiments and reſentments; until he could form a proper judgment who, amongſt the Omrahs and officers, were truſt worthy; and in whom he could with ſafety to himſelf put a perfect confidence.

It was not long before his penetration pointed out the perſons he ſought for. *Mahommed Amin Khan*, *Heydr Kuli Khan*, and *Kondoran*, all Omrahs of the firſt rank, he was well aſſured, were inveterate, though concealed enemies to the *Seyds*: to theſe Omrahs therefore he ventured to open himſelf, about the middle of *September* 1720; and moſt pathetically lamented his abject dependant ſtate, under *the tyranny* of *the Seyds*; imploring their aſſiſtance to extricate and free him; themſelves; and his people from their uſurped power.

This

This overture from the Emperor met with a warm reception from the Omrahs; they ſwore fidelity to him; and he, on his part, ſwore that *Mahommed Amîn Khan* ſhould ſucceed to the Vizirut; *Khondoran* to the *Mhir Bukhſpi*; and be created *Embir al Omrah*: and that *Heydr Kuli Khan*, (who was at this time General of the Ordinance) ſhould obtain the Soubahdary of *Ahmedabad*.

Theſe preliminaries ſettled; and the fidelity of theſe Omrahs ſecured, more by making it their own intereſt, than from any attachment to the royal family; a favourable occaſion was only wanting: and the *Seyds* themſelves contributed in ſome degree to their own downfal,—for now the meaſure of their iniquity was full,—too long had they reigned the oppreſſors of their Kings, and of the people.

The firſt act of the *Seyds* power, after the acceſſion of *Mahommed Shaw*, was to oblige him to declare *Nizam al Muluck a* traytor; and demand his appearance at court.

Nizam had been long obnoxious to the *Seyds*: the inſurrection raiſed by *Rajah Jeet Singh* in favour of *Nicosîr*, had prevented their

their looking towards him ſooner ; but now, having fixed *Mahommed Shaw* on the throne, they determined to ſuppreſs him.

Nizam well knowing there was no medium between death and the jealouſy of the *Seyds*, in place of paying obedience to the royal mandate, killed the gurſburdars (meſſengers) that brought it: advanced from his government of *Malva* to *Eugon*; where he ſeized the royal treaſure: from thence he penetrated into *Deccan*, the government of *Seyd Hoſſan Ali Khan*; attacked the capital of the province and took it; aſſumed the Soubahſhip; and ſending *his Niabs*, or deputy governors to every part, diſplaced thoſe of *Hoſſan Ali Khan*; and treated even his women with great indignities. After theſe exploits (to which it was ſaid he was privately inſtigated by the Emperor purpoſely to exaſperate the *Seyds)* he wrote the moſt ſubmiſſive letter to the Emperor; extenuating and palliating the neceſſity of a conduct, to which the tyranny and injuſtice of the *Seyds* had drove him.

On news of the outrages committed by *Nizam* in the *Deccan*, the Emperor put on a well diſſembled rage; and ſwore by *Mahomet*, he would take the field againſt the rebel himſelf. This reſolution was the reſult

of

of a private conference with his aſſociated Omrahs; it being judged, the firſt neceſſary ſtep for the reduction of theſe *dangerous brothers* was, to ſeparate them: accordingly the Emperor ordered the Vizir *Seyd Abdallah Khan* to return to *Delhy*, to ſuperintend the civil adminiſtration; and preſerve the peace of that city during his abſence: and himſelf, with *Seyd Hoſſan Ali Khan*, and the reſt of the Omrahs, took the field on the 28th of *September* 1720, with a royal and powerful army, for the pretended reduction of the rebel *Nizam al Muluk*.

The Emperor made a long march that day towards *Deccan*, and encamped late in the evening. Here the means for aſſaſſinating *Seyd Hoſſan Ali Khan* were adjuſted by the three Omrahs, to whom the King left the execution of this important event: they found it neceſſary now to diſcover their deſign to ſeveral other Omrahs, who they knew had been deeply injured by the *Seyds*, and were as inveterate as themſelves. Amongſt theſe, one *Hyddr Khan*, a ſmall Munſubdar of diſtinguiſhed courage, was pitched upon to perpetrate the deed; and as the attempt muſt be attended with apparent hazard to *Hyddr Khan*, *Mahommed Amîn Khan*, and *Heydr Kuli Khan*, to encourage him they ſolemnly engaged to be at hand

with

with a ſelect party to reſcue him from the rage of *Hoſſan Ali Khan*'s followers.

Early the next morning the ſignal was made for decamping, and *Seyd Hoſſan* went into the Emperor's tent to pay his obeiſance and receive his orders: all the Omrahs and officers, as cuſtomary, were round his tent: *Hyddr Khan* placed himſelf at the door with a petition in his hand: as ſoon as *Seyd Hoſſan* came out of his tent, and had ſeated himſelf in his pallenkeen, *Heyddr Khan* preſented his petition; and whilſt *Seyd Hoſſan* was attentively peruſing it, the aſſaſſin ſtabbed him with his kunjaar (dagger) between the neck and collar bone, of which wound he inſtantly expired.

Notwithſtanding the ſolemn engagement to reſcue *Hyddr Khan*, it was judged expedient to ſacrifice this daring man, that his death might blunt and ſatiate, in ſome meaſure, the wrath of thoſe guards who were in immediate attendance on the General's perſon; by whom *Hyddr Khan* was aſſaulted with the utmoſt fury; and though, drawing his ſcymitar, he defended himſelf with aſtoniſhing bravery for ſome time; yet, overpowered by numbers, he was cut to pieces. Neverthele ſs the tumult raiſed about the body did not ceaſe, until *Mahommed Amîn Khan*,

Khon-

Khondoran, *Heydr Kuli Khan*, and their troops came up to quell it. The Emperor mounting his elephant and causing proclamation to be made to the army, that the *Embir al Omrah* was killed by his order, the confusion subsided; except in one quarter; where five thousand troops, commanded by *Jieratt Khan*, nephew to the deceased General, breathed nothing but revenge: between these and the royal troops a sharp conflict ensued, in which many were killed (on both sides) amongst whom was a son of *Mahommed Amîn Khan*; but *Jieratt Khan* falling by an arrow discharged by the King, (who it was said emptied three quivers in the engagement) the rest called for quarter.

The Emperor proceeding to the tent of *Seyd Hossan Ali Khan*, sat upon his elephant and saw the soldiers, by his permission, plunder it of a khorore of Rupees *. The jewels, found there to an equal amount, were appropriated to his own use.

Mahommed Shaw, sensible that but half the work was done, whilst *Seyd Abdallah Khan* survived, immediately directed his march towards *Delhy*; declaring *Mahommed Amîn Khan* Vizir, and *Khondoran*, *Embir al Omrah*.

* One Million Sterling.

Abdallah Khan was not far from *Delhy*, when an expreſs from *Jieratt Khan* overtook him, adviſing him of the tragical death of his brother: he ſaw his own danger, and inſtantly diſpatched a truſty officer with a party of horſe to that city, with orders to return immediately with *Sultan Ibrahim*, younger brother of the Emperors, *Raffeeil al Dirjaat*, and *Raffeeil al Dowlat*. The officer executed his commiſſion with great celerity; and being returned with *Sultan Ibrahim*, *Abdallah* proclaimed that young Prince Emperor of *Indoſtan*: then putting himſelf at the head of a numerous army, he marched back to meet *Mahommed Shaw*.

The two armies met the latter end of *October*, *Anno* 1720, and a bloody battle enſued. *Victory* ſtood doubtful a long time, to which ſhe ſhould give the day; but when *Abdallah* was on the verge of ſnatching a certain conqueſt, a ſeaſonable re-inforcement turned the iſſue in favour of the Emperor: for during the heat of the engagement *Diabchadr* (nephew of *Chivalram* Governor of *Eleabas*) arrived with a freſh body of troops; theſe aſſaulting the rear and flank of *Abdallah*'s army with the greateſt intrepidity, a total defeat and rout ſoon followed. *Seyd Abdallah Khan* was taken priſoner; the *Emperor* ſpared his life, in con-

ſideration

ſideration of his owing him the crown he wore; but condemned him to perpetual imprisonment (as recited more minutely by Mr. *Fraſer)* ſequeſtring his vaſt poſſeſſions and wealth to his own uſe.

Thus fell the *Seyds Hoſſan Ali Khan*, and *Abdallah Khan*, by a reverſe of fortune too common to be very remarkable. The wonder is, that they ſhould have maintained themſelves ſo long (in this deſpotic and violent government) in a degree of abſolute power and authority, hardly equalled in ſtory; and that, during the reigns of five ſucceſſive Emperors, four of whom they *themſelves* had placed upon the throne.

The laſt deciſive ſtroke put *Mahommed Shaw* into the quiet poſſeſſion of the Empire of *Indoſtan*. A long peace enſued; and the Emperor gave a looſe to the indulgence of his natural propenſities, which centered only in the exceſſive uſe of wine, women, and hunting. To every thing elſe he became regardleſs: the reins of government in time ſlackened; confuſion in the Empire followed: every *Omrah* was planning for himſelf; and none thought of the *public*. Theſe univerſal *diſorders* endangered, in conſequence, the *health* and well-being of the ſtate; and paved the way for the invaſion of the Empire by *Nadir Shaw*, in the year 1738; (ſo accurately inveſtigated by Mr. *Fraſer*) which was brought about by the intrigues of *Nízam al Mulluck*. This miniſter, after the reduction of the *Seyds*, was ſoon taken into favour, and confirmed in the government of *Deccan*; or rather maintained himſelf there by his own ſtrength, as an independant ſovereign.

My readers will eaſily perceive, that in the foregoing recital I have followed the thread of Mr. *Fraſer*'s conciſe narrative; and have only deviated from him in thoſe parts, where my materials afforded me fuller intelligence; and in variety of tranſactions which he (obviouſly) thought lay out of the way of his *main object*: his intention being, very evidently, no more than to give a connected catalogue of the Mogulls from *Tímur Lung*; (*Tamarlam*) and at the ſame time to convey a ſlight view of the progreſſive ſtate and condition of the Empire of *Indoſtan*, as neceſſarily preparative to the period of *Nadir Shaw*'s invaſion of it; without embarraſſing himſelf with any more of the particular circumſtances attending the ſucceſſions, than were conſiſtent with, and immediately in point to his

his design. All that I wish or hope for from *this* production is, that it may be esteemed an illustration only of that ingenious and learned gentleman's work; comprised within the space, from *Auring Zebe*'s demise, to the reduction of the *Seyds*.

CHAP. II.

Tranſactions in the Subahdary *of* Bengal, *from the year* 1717 *to the year* 1750, *incluſive.*

OUR preſent ſubject calls us back to the reign of *Furrukhsîr*, when *Jaffîr Khan*, an *Omrah* of great conſideration and intereſt at court, ruled thoſe provinces with a rod of iron. His name, to this day, is remembered with deteſtation; to fill his coffers, he inflicted the moſt cruel puniſhments on the *Rajahs* and *Zimindars*, by ways and means unheard of, and unknown, but in this Eaſtern government. He alſo highly oppreſſed the *Europeans* ſettled in theſe parts; yet, notwithſtanding his very mal-adminiſtration, he had the addreſs to obtain the governments of *Bahar* and *Oriſſa*, united with that of *Bengal* in his perſon; which ever before had been diſtinct and ſeparate Nabobſhips.

With

With this new acquisition of power, he removed from *Dacca*; which, until that time, had been the chief residence of the Soubahs, to *Morshadabad*; and this city now became the *capital* of the provinces.

Jaffîr Khan had a favourite daughter, whom he married to *Soujah Khan*, a native of *Delhy* of some distinction; this person was appointed *Niab*, or deputy governor of *Orissa*, when *Jaffîr Khan* changed the seat of his chief residence, and quitted *Dacca*.

Soujah Khan, by his marriage with the Soubah's daughter, had two sons born to him; the eldest named *Mahommed Tukhee Khan*; the younger *Suffraaz Khan*. The first had constantly resided with his father at *Cuttack*, the capital of *Orissa*, and the other, with his grandfather at *Morshadabad*.

Jaffîr Khan's fondness for *Suffraaz Khan* was so prevalent, that when he obtained an order from court for *Soujah Khan*'s succeeding him in the Soubahship; he procured at the same time *Suffraaz Khan* to be appointed King's Dewan of the provinces, in prejudice to the just pretensions of his elder brother, *Mahommed Tukhee Khan*.

This ill-judged mark of affection and preference in the old *Soubah*, was the cause of declared and unabating enmity between the two brothers; though *this effect*, probably without *that cause*, would have naturally resulted from the difference of their genius and dispositions; actuated by the different examples they had long before them, in the father, and grandfather.——*Soujah Khan* was bold; rigid in government; but, withal, complaisant and affectionate.—*Mahommed Tukbee Khan* was brave and generous; delighting in the exercises of a soldier, and the art of war.——*Jaffir Khan* was inveterate; avaritious; and a monster of cruelty.——*Suffraas Khan* was impetuous, overbearing and vindictive; and as he had been a stranger to contradiction from his infancy, so in his more advanced age, he could not bear it in the least degree, even from the mouth of wisdom.

Anno 1725. In the year 1725 *Jaffir Khan* deceased, to the general joy of the provinces; and *Soujah Khan*, hastening to the capital, took upon him the government. In the journey, he was accompanied by *Mahommed Tukbee Khan*.

When the brothers met, the embers of disgust and hatred, which had been only smothered by absence, now burst into a flame,

flame, that had well nigh consumed them both; had not the prudence and authority of the Soubah interposed; who, finding it impossible to accomplish a reconciliation between them, resolved to part them; and immediately appointed *Mahommed Tukhee Khan*, his Niab of *Orissa*; with orders, to set out the next day for his government. There in a few months he died universally lamented. His death gave his father the deepest sorrow; for he loved him with a just and truely paternal tenderness.

On *Soujah Khan*'s succession to the government, he released all the *Rajahs* and *Zemindars* that had been imprisoned by his father-in-law; and eased them of sundry heavy taxes and impositions, that they had been loaded with. Calling them all before him, he enjoined them to attend carefully to the cultivation of their lands, and the improvement of the manufactures: assuring them that, in future, they should be exempt from the severities they had suffered under his predecessors: reminding them, that as they themselves had long felt the hand of oppression; he depended it would be a lesson to them, not to oppress the *tenants* dependant on them. Then with a peremptory tone telling them, that if any were found deficient in their annual payments, their lands ſhould be taken from them, and given to others; afterwards he graciouſly diſmiſſed them to their reſpect diſtricts.

Soujah Khan taking into conſideration the ſmall ſtanding force of the provinces, that until his time never exceeded the number of five or ſix hundred horſe; determined to enlarge it to as many thouſands, which he ſoon accompliſhed. He then made ſundry regulations reſpecting the trade of the provinces, both inland and foreign; caſting his eyes particularly on the *Europeans*; and attentive that they ſhould not clandeſtinely partake of greater immunities and advantages, than the terms of their *Fhîrmaunds*, or grants, gave them a title to.

To this end, he encreaſed the number of *Chowkee*'s (or places for the receipts of cuſtoms) to twenty, upon the ſeveral rivers; whereas, before his government, there were only *two*, *Buxſh Bundar*, and *Azimgunge*.

This wiſe and ſolid conduct, had it's natural and proper effects; the provinces ſoon wore a different face; commerce and manufactures flouriſhed; and in a very few years he was enabled greatly to increaſe the royal revenue, and ſtipulate to pay into the royal treaſury annually, one *Khorore*, one *Lac*, one thouſand

sand one hundred and one *sicca Rupees*; over and above forty *Lacs* of *Rupees*, annually remitted to court, to different *Omrahs* residing there, on account of their *Jagbir* lands. In consequence, his interest at court was strengthened; himself established in his government; and the succession, by *grant*, secured in his family. *Anno* 1730.

Having brought the Soubah *Soujah Khan* to this happy and honourable period; and given a general view of the state of these opulent provinces; we next propose to trace the causes, circumstances, and progress of an extraordinary usurpation of this government in the beginning of the year 1742.

Though the ambition, avarice, ingratitude, treachery and violence of two artful *adventurers*, were the *seemingly* apparent causes of this usurpation, yet, without other *co-operating incidents*, those (too common successful auxiliaries in the invasion of *right*) would have proved ineffectual.

The secret springs of the above-mentioned incidents, were known but to few; and we venture to aver, were never put together before the penning of the manuscripts, A. D.

1750;

1750; alluded to in the preliminary discourse to this work; from which manuscript the author of the Reflections, as before remarked, disingenuously took as his own, what he calls his "Short sketch of the history of *Bengal*, from the year 1739 to the year 1750*."

Aliverdi Khan, and *Hodjee Hamet*, were brothers; natives of *Tartary*; and followers of fortune. In this pursuit they arrived at the court of *Delhy* about the year 1721; and put themselves under the protection of the then Vizir *Khondoran*. In their genius and qualifications they differed extremely. The elder, *Hodjee Hamet*, was of a cowardly, but deeply intriguing disposition; well skilled in political learning; and a profound judge of the nature of mankind. With *these talents*, he possessed not a single moral principle, capable of impeding *them* in their full career; and therefore became every way qualified for the transactions of *this Eastern* (or indeed any other) court.

* For he recites the same chain of facts as they stand in the manuscript, with little variation, except the poor disguise of, here and there a different mode of expression; interspersed with a few *tri e reflections*, which are *purely* his own. We thought this note highly necessary, lest we should incur the undeserved censure of retailing, at second hand, the labors of another.

Aliverdi

Aliverdi Khan was bold and daring; bred to arms; and ſkilled in all the duties of a ſoldier; enterpriſing; of ready underſtanding; and naturally virtuous and honourable; until theſe amiable qualities were perverted and ſubdued, by the inſtigations and evil counſels of his brother; and his other talents were made ſubſervient to *Hamet*'s ambitious views of aggrandiſing their obſcure family.

Hodjee acquired this title from his having in his early years made a pilgrimage to *Hodge*, (or the tomb of *Mahommed* at *Mecca*.) A duty which the *Khoran* impoſes on every *Muſſelman* once in his life, either in perſon or by proxy; and he who performs it in perſon, thereby obtains, for life, the honorary appellation of *Hodjee*; and is much reverenced by the true believers.

It has been confidently aſſerted, and as currently believed in *Bengal*, that *Hodjee Hamet*, had been preferred at *Delhy*, to the poſt of maſter, or keeper of the crown jewels: with the moſt valuable of which it was ſaid he eloped, and afterwards ſanctified this theft by a pilgrimage to *Mecca*. But, upon the ſtricteſt enquiry, we pronounce this report an aſperſion of his enemies; having the beſt authority for ſaying, neither

of

of the brothers appeared at court before the year 1721:—but the improbability of the fact ſpeaks it a calumny—their original obſcurity is allowed on all hands; can it then poſſibly gain credit, that either of them ſhould be preferred to a poſt, which is uſually beſtowed on one of the firſt Omrahs of the Empire?

But if we ſhould admit (what alſo has been aſſerted) that *Hodjee* was for a ſhort ſpace in the ſervice of the *keeper* of the crown jewels; and might have it in his power to commit the theft alledged againſt him; yet the fact remains equally improbable: for can it be believed that after ſo atrocious a crime, both the brothers ſhould obtain the patronage and recommendation of *Khondoran?*—Which they certainly brought with them to *Cuttac* (the reſidence of the Nabob *Soujah Khan) Anno* 1722.

Anno. On their arrival, they were taken into
1722. the ſervice of *Soujah Dowla*, as immediate attendants on his perſon: *Hodjee*, in capacity of his firſt *Kiſtmutgar* (or valet) and *Aliverdi*, his *Chilum Purdaar* (dreſſer or rather keeper of his ſmoaking pipe) with the additional pay and denomination of a ſeapoy, or foot ſoldier.

Their

Their riſe from theſe menial ſtations was rapid, but not aſtoniſhing; in a country where ſuperior talents ever make their way to ſpeedy promotion.——The Nabob very ſoon diſcovered in *Hodjee* an extenſive genius and underſtanding in men and things; and *Hodjee*, as ſoon found out the great, and almoſt only foible of his maſter; which was an ungovernable appetite for *variety* of women.

Hodjee benefited himſelf of this ruling paſſion; and by indefatigable attention and induſtry out-ran even the Nabob's deſires. ——The compiler of *the Reflections* ſays, *Hodjee* proſtituted, "and made a ſacrifice of "his own daughter to his maſter's luſt:" we confeſs we never heard of it before; be this as it may, it is moſt certain that *Hodjee*, by indulging and feeding this paſſion, quickly gained an aſcendant over his maſter; and had the diſpoſal of all places of ſmall importance; and as he was obſerved to be the growing favourite, all ſuits and petitions were preferred through his mediation.

Aliverdi Khan's extraordinary military genius did not eſcape his maſter's notice. He was ſoon promoted to be *Jemmautdar* of the Nabob's foot guards; and not long after

after preferred to a command of horſe, at the interceſſion of his brother.—The ruling paſſion of *Hodjee* was an unbounded thirſt of riches; but whilſt he labored to extend his influence over his maſter, as conducive to the ſatisfying this vice; he was ever watchful and attentive, that his brother's intereſt went hand in hand with his own.

To theſe ends he daily made himſelf more and more uſeful to *Soujah Khan*; and being well verſed in the arts of financing, and the invention of *ways and means*, his importance was confirmed: (this being the moſt uſeful and eſſential duty of a miniſter in the *Eaſt*, as well as in the *Weſt.)* He was alſo an exquiſite and penetrating *ſpy* upon the actions of all the Niabs and other officers employed under the Nabob; with whom he ſecretly planted his own emiſſaries; ſo that nothing was tranſacted in any part of the province of *Oriſſa*, that his maſter had not the moſt early intelligence of.——

The government of *Indoſtan* is perhaps the only government in the world, where the character of a *ſpy* is not attended, with reproach and infamy: here it is honourable and dignified. The Emperor and all the Soubahs of the provinces entertain an officer

cer with this title, who is always a person of consideration: but like *Satan* he is more generally feared than loved. *Hodjee* possessed not the title of the Nabob's *Hircarrah*, (spy) but he virtually was so; and by this practice, did not a little gain upon his master's confidence, and thereby smoothed the way to designs, which about this time, *Anno* 1724, began to open upon him; though he yet concealed them even from his brother.

The influence and power of the two *Anno*
brothers acquired new strength every day; 1724.
in such sort, that at the close of this year they had gained a full dominion over the actions and inclinations of the Nabob: who at this period succeeded to the government of the three provinces by the demise of the Soubah *Jaffir Khan*, as before recited in the former part of this chapter. The brothers attended him to the capital, where the scene *Anno*
of action became enlarged and more ade- 1725.
quate to their different, though equally enterprizing spirits. *Hodjee Hamet* was soon declared prime minister; and *Aliverdî* promoted to a command of horse of the first distinction.

The first judicious movements made by *Scujah Khan* on his coming to the Soubahſhip, (already recorded) were, it was ſaid, the reſult of the ſalutary councils of *Hodjee Hamet*.—But if we admit the fact, let us not too haſtily conclude that this advice flowed from any principle of affection to his maſter, or regard to his honour; or from a commiſeration of the ſuffering *Rajahs*: no, theſe worthy conſiderations were foreign to his heart, as appeared from the whole tenor of his future conduct. The moderate councils and meaſures adopted by the Soubah, raiſed the credit of the *miniſter* only, who (by reports of his emiſſaries diſperſed about the city and country) had the ſole honour of clemency, ſtrictly due to the Soubah's goodneſs of heart; who always ſhew'd an averſion to the practices of his predeceſſor.

The miniſter by this artful procedure gained many friends; and by ſecret ſtipulations with the enlarged *Rajahs*, he filled his own coffers, to the injury of the public revenue. In the degree that the miniſter gained credit and influence in the provinces—the Soubah ſunk in the opinion of the people (a very natural conſequence) and reſting ſecure in the ſuppoſed integrity and extenſive abilities of *Hodjee Hamet*, he abandoned *himſelf* to the full enjoyment of his *ruling paſſion*; and the *government*, to the abſolute diſpoſal of the miniſter; who without

out controul, put in, put out; removed; displaced, and preferred to every post of profit, whomsoever he pleased. And by this traffic he soon acquired immense wealth: taking care to keep his master buried in sensuality; still supplying the flame that had possession of him with fresh fewel; ransacking the provinces, and obtaining (no matter at what price) the most beautiful women that could be procured to answer his purposes: and it was confidently (and we believe truly) said, that he carried his panderism so far, as never to appear at the Soubah's nocturnal levee, without something of this kind in his hand; formed to attract and engage his attention.

Whilst *Hodjee Hamet* was thus employed in establishing his own power and fortune, and blinding the Soubah during the first three or four years of his government; his brother *Aliverdî Khan* began to think himself neglected; but *Hodjee* soon convinced him of his mistake.

Hitherto *Aliverdî* had not, in his own person, acquired any considerable lustre, except from the light thrown upon it, by reflection, from his brother's being the minister. In his military capacity he had indeed a few opportunities given him of shining alone, both at *Orissa* and *Bengal*; just sufficient to gain the belief of his being an intrepid officer: but now the time was come to bring his talents upon the stage in a more conspicuous view: an occasion offering, for which his brother had with impatience long waited.

Anno 1729. Having for some time lost sight of the Soubah's only surviving son *Suffraaz Khan*, we here think it necessary to bring him to the remembrance of the reader, by a slight mention of him. His character has been already delineated: he possessed the post of King's *Dewan*, by appointment from court, and was successor apparent to the Soubahship: he had long looked with an evil eye on the growing power and influence of *Hodjee Hamet*, which he thought became pregnant with danger, both to his father and himself—but he had not the means of reducing it. The impetuosity of his temper burst forth sometimes in abuses, and in insults to the minister; who bore them with patient submission: but heavy resentment from the Soubah, against his son, always followed such abuse. The crafty *Hodjee* treasured them up in his memory, for a future reckoning; he daily instilled into the ears of the Soubah the many extravagancies his son was guilty of; which had too much truth

truth for the foundation; but if that had not been the caſe, the Soubah was too ready to liſten to any thing to his prejudice; for he loved him not—ever ſaying, that his unbridled inſolence occaſioned the loſs of his favourite and beloved ſon *Mahommed Tukhee Khan*.

Anno 1729, the Nabobſhip of *Patna* becoming vacant, *Hodjee*, without appearing in it himſelf, influenced the then reigning favourite miſtreſs of the Soubah (who was deeply in his intereſt) to ſolicit it for his brother; who was accordingly the next day nominated to that government. *Suffraaz Khan* upon this appointment had the courage to tell his father in public *Durbar*, "he was warming and cheriſhing two "ſnakes, that would ſting him and his fa-"mily to death." The Soubah ordered him immediately to be taken into cuſtody; but by *Hodjee*'s artful interpoſition he was appeaſed.

The following night, the brothers held a long and private conference; to which ſeveral Rajahs and officers in their confidence were admitted.——Here the wicked plan of *Aliverdi Khan*'s government was ſettled, and he departed the next day for *Patna*; where in a few days he arrived, and put in

 execu-

execution the political maxims and instructions he had received from his brother.

Anno 1729 to 1735. The exploits of the first six years of his government—that is from the year 1729 to the year 1735, inclusive, were these following. By force, treachery, craft and policy, he subdued most of the *Rajahs* of the province of *Bahar*; some, by the basest dissimulation and professions of friendship, he drew to *Patna*; where he murdered them and seized their possessions; as the brave *Sonder Shaw*, &c.——He then carried his arms against the *Chukwaars*, a brave and warlike *Gentoo* race, who possessed a tract of country opposite *Mongheer*; up the river *Samboo*: the prince or *Rajah* of this country had never paid tribute, or acknowledged any subjection to the Soubah of *Bengal*; or indeed to the Mogul himself. He laid every thing that passed on the river, by *Mongheer*, under contribution; and put the *European* settlements to an annual heavy expence of a large armament, to escort their trade to, and from *Patna*.

The old brave Rajah of these people (who had many times fought hand to hand, with the intrepid commander of our troops, Major *Hunt*) deceased, in the year 1730; and was succeeded by his son, a youth of seven-

ſeventeen. This young prince, intimidated by the examples made of ſeveral of the *Babar* Rajahs, after a ſhort reſiſtance ſubmitted; acknowledged allegiance to the Emperor; and ſubjection to the Soubah. An annual tribute was ſtipulated, and regularly paid for four years—a ſpot was fixed on, five miles from the mouth of *Samboo*, and thirty from the capital of the *Chùkwaars*; where the prince every year met the Nabob's officer on a certain day: the one to pay; the other to receive the tribute; and it was agreed that they ſhould have only thirty attendants on each ſide.

The twentieth of *October*, (*Anno* 1735) was the day of payment; at which time the *Engliſh* army, under the command of commandant *Holcombe*, lay encamped in *Mongheer* grove, with the company's trade for the *Patna* factory.——At eleven in the forenoon, we obſerved a boat, which had come out of *Samboo* river, making for *Patna*: the commandant detached two light pulwaars after her, with orders to bring her to——imagining ſhe had a cargo of fiſh——the boat being brought to, and laid alongſide the commandant's *budgerow* —Gueſs, reader, our aſtoniſhment! when in place of a cargoe of fiſh, it contained a

 cargoe

cargoe of human *heads!* five baſkets full; and a ſingle head in the ſixth.

On enquiry, we learnt that before day break, the officer who was deputed to receive the annual tribute from the Rajah of the *Chukwaars*; had, by orders from the Nabob *Aliverdi*, placed four hundred men in ambuſh, under the high banks of the river, near the place of meeting—that the prince and the Nabob's officer Fowzdar of *Bahar*, (whoſe name we have forgot) with their uſual attendants, met at nine of the clock; and after the common ceremonials, and the tribute received, when they were juſt upon parting; the ſignal being given, the troops in ambuſh ruſhed out, and ſurrounding the Rajah and his few followers, cut them off, one only excepted; who upon a fleet horſe eſcaped, and gave the alarm to the city—among thoſe killed were his principal general officers.——We further were informed by the officer who had the charge of the boat, that his orders were to make the beſt of his way to *Patna*; and lay his freight at the *Nabob's feet*; and that the head in the baſket by itſelf, was the Rajah's—he added that the Fowzdar with his troops were in full march to the city *Samboo*.—This was ſoon after verified; for we obſerved about four in the afternoon a

cloud

cloud of ſmoke over the city; and the ſame evening we received theſe other particulars; that on the firſt alarm and known fate of the Rajah, his wife, the young *Begum*, ſhut herſelf up with her ſon (about a year old) and her attendants, and ſet fire to her apartments—that the Nabob's troops meeting with no reſiſtance, entered the city, plundered it, and then ſet fire to it.

A body of the Rajah's troops retired, and for ſome time diſputed the poſſeſſion of the country with the Nabob's; but the Fowzdar being re-inforced from his camp, which then lay at *Durrîapoor*; a ſhort march from *Mongbeer*; the whole country was ſoon reduced, and theſe brave people ſubdued.

Theſe were the *exploits* that rendered the name of *Aliverdî Khan* a terror to the neighbouring diſtricts; and by *theſe* he amaſſed immenſe riches; part of which he regularly remitted to *Morſhadabad*, to preſerve his own and brother's credit with the Soubah; but the much greater part he reſerved, for a purpoſe, he now had in agitation, by the pernicious advice of his brother.

Whilſt *Aliverdî Khan* was carrying on theſe operations to eſtabliſh his power,

Hodjee Hamet remained unrivalled in the administration of the Soubahship; but a transaction which now manifested itself, opened the Soubah's eyes.

Anno 1736. *Aliverdî Khan*, forgetful of the duty and obligations he owed to his master, and urged by the continued persuasions of his brother, began about the beginning of the year 1736, privately to solicit at court for the government of *Patna*, and the province of *Bahar*, independent of the Soubah of *Bengal*. This negociation, however cautiously conducted, came to the knowledge of *Soujah Khan*. Rage on the instant took possession of him. *Hodjee* was disgraced, and for some time imprisoned—but by the most submissive and deceitful letters from *Aliverdî*, and the powerful intercession of the *Seraglio*, (*Hodjee*'s never failing resource) the minister was enlarged, and *seemingly* again taken into favor.

Aliverdî did not slacken his negociations on this discovery of his treachery; but availing himself of the favor of his patron Anno 1737. *Khondoran*; and by well placed considerable bribes, he obtained the latter end of the year 1737, a *phirmaund* and proper *sunnods* from court, constituting him independant governor of the province of *Bahar*.

This

This confirmation of the ingratitude and treachery of the two brothers ſtruck deeply to the heart of *Soujah Khan*. He had, however, the reſolution and prudence to diſguiſe his ſentiments; knowing their power was too great to be attacked openly; or capable of being reduced by any weapons, but thoſe of diſſimulation and craft. By the aſſiſtance of theſe, he planned, and was juſt on the point of executing, a ſafe and certain revenge on both the brothers; when death put a period to his intentions.——It *Anno* 1738.
is more than probable, that *Hadjee*, who ſtill preſerved his influence in the *Seraglio*, received intimation by this channel of the Soubah's deſigns; for his death was ſudden, and judged to be by poiſon.

His Son *Suffraaz Khan* immediately ſucceeded his father in the government of *Bengal* and *Oriſſa*: as well as in his reſentment to the brothers.

Independant power, only increaſed the bad qualities, which had already taken too deep poſſeſſion of *Suffraaz Khan*: his exceſſes in ſpirituous liquors and women, were beyond controul and example; his inſolence and impetuoſity of temper became intolerable to all about him; his principal officers were treated with inſults and

and indignities: moſt of theſe had been diſguſted with the family for the preference given to *Aliverdî Khan*, in the government of *Patna*; though *juſtice* could not lay this charge againſt *Suffraaz Khan*.

There then reſided at his court a *Gentoo* named *Allum Chund*, who had been many years Dewan to *Soujah Khan*; by whom he was much revered for his great age, wiſdom, and faithful ſervices. This miniſter was the only man who had courage and honeſty enough to attempt reſtraining the extravagances of *Suffraaz Khan*; a duty he thought owing to the memory of his late maſter. He accordingly, with the greateſt circumſpection and humility, and with tears in his eyes, repreſented to him the fatal tendency of his conduct, which if not changed, muſt inevitably eſtrange the hearts of the few remaining friends to his houſe; and at the ſame time favour and promote the evil deſigns of his enemies.

Suffraaz Khan, inſtead of profiting by this wholeſome remonſtrance and admonition, highly reſented his preſumption; and ever after treated him with great indignities and contempt; and thereby loſt the heart of the only man in the provinces, who by his ſincerity, capacity and authority, was

capable

capable of counteracting and frustrating the pernicious machinations of *Hodjee* and his brother.

Though *Suffraaz Khan* did not immediately degrade *Hodjee Hamet* from the post of prime minister; yet he took every opportunity of showing an inveterate hatred to him. In public Durbar he commonly called him by the appellation of, "His "father's pander," and treated him with such insults and indignities, that he seldom frequented the Durbar; being ill able to brook such treatment in a place where he had for so many years been accustomed to a degree of deference and respect, equal to his master. Nor is it much to be wondered at, that he should meditate vengeance, when a fair occasion offered: this he was not long without; for *Suffraaz Khan*'s own folly and rashness supplied him with the means, and gave him a nearer, and more encouraging prospect, of an *event* which he for some time past had in view.

A few months after *Suffraaz Khan* came *Anno*
to the government, he threw a disgrace on 1739.
Futtuah Chund's house, which laid the foundation of his precipitate fall. The fact, though well known to a few, was only whispered, out of respect to the power and credit

credit of that family, which had maintained, even from the reign of *Auring Zebe*, a character of distinguished consideration; from *Furrukshir*, *Futtuab Chund* received the title of *Jaggaut Seet*; and might be justly esteemed the greatest banker, and most opulent subject in the world.

Anno 1739. He had about this time married his youngest grandson, named *Seet Mortab Roy*, to a young creature of exquisite beauty; aged about eleven years. The fame of her beauty coming to the ears of the Soubah, he burned with curiosity and lust for the possession of her; and sending for *Jaggaut Seet*, demanded a sight of her——The old man (then compleat fourscore) begged and intreated, that the Soubah would not stain the honour and credit of his house; nor load his last days with shame; by persisting in a demand which he knew the principles of his cast, forbid a compliance with.

Neither the tears nor remonstrances of the old man had any weight on the Soubah; who growing outrageous at the refusal, ordered, in his presence, his house to be immediately surrounded with a body of horse; and swore on the *Khoran*, that if he complied in sending his grand-daughter, that

that he might only *ſee her*, he would inſtantly return her without any injury.

The *Seet* reduced to this extremity, and judging from the Soubah's known impetuoſity, that his perſiſting longer in a denial, would only make his diſgrace *more public*, at laſt conſented; and the young creature was carried with the greateſt ſecrecy in the night to viſit him. She was returned the ſame night; and we will ſuppoſe (for the honour of that houſe) uninjured. Be this as it may, the violence was of too delicate a nature, to permit any future commerce between her and her huſband.

The indignity was never forgiven by *Jaggaut Seet*; and that whole powerful family, conſequently, became inveterate, tho' concealed enemies to the Soubah.

Hodjee Hamet ſoon came to the knowledge of this raſh ſtep and violence committed againſt the *Seets*; he was alſo well apprized of *Allum Chund*'s diſguſt, and, as he was upon a friendly footing with them both, he determined to avail himſelf of their reſentment, and make it ſubſervient to his own intended vengeance for the repeated inſults he had received from the Soubah. Revenge however was not his ſole motive: he he was actuated by another, yet more prevalent one, the further aggrandising his family; the hopes of which he had hitherto only seen at a distance; but now thought the conjuncture favorable for carrying his long projected plan into execution: which was to cut off the son of his late *master*, *friend* and *benefactor*; and place his brother *Aliverdi Khan* in his stead.

Hodjee lost no time in procuring a private conference with the disaffected *Seets* and *Allum Chund*; in the course of which he represented in the most lively manner, the "oppression and extravagant government of "*Suffraaz Khan*; and that nothing but the "most deplorable consequences to the provinces could be expected from such an "unbridled and tyrannic disposition—— "that if he already treated with such insults "and contempt, those for whom his father "had the highest veneration and friendship—what might not others dread from "his future violences?"——He then expatiated on, and with bitter exaggeration painted their own particular injuries; which had all the effect upon them that he might naturally expect or could wish.

He suffered not their resentment to cool; but supported this conference with many others;

others: and the unanimous conclusion of the triumvirate was; "That none could "be secure in their lives, honour or pro- "perty, whilst *Suffraaz Khan* remained "invested with the Soubahship."——*Hodjee* managed the passions of these men with such art and address in the promotion of his own views——that they themselves first proposed, "his brother *Aliverdi Khan*, "as the only one capable of rescuing the "provinces from apparent and inevitable "ruin.——That he should be immediately "advised of their sentiments, and intreated "to concur with their hopes by preparing "for a speedy march into *Bengal*, to take "upon him the government."

Hodjee, with expressions of gratitude for their favourable opinion of his brother, consented to their proposal with a well dissembled reluctance; declaring "nothing but the "necessity of the time, and the peril of the "country could have influenced him to "meditate aught against the son of his late "master."

It being objected by *Jaggaut Seet*, that an intercourse by letter with *Aliverdi* was liable to accident and discovery; it was on further deliberation resolved, that *Hodjee* should repair to *Patna*, where he could better inform

inform his brother of the ſtate of things, and benefit him by his council at this critical period: but as his ſudden and private retreat from court would raiſe a ſuſpicion in the Soubah, that ſomething was in agitation againſt him, *Allum Chund* and *Jaggaut Seet* engaged to make his departure an act of the Soubah's own weakneſs.

The plan of operations being thus agreed on, their next ſtep was to engage in the conſpiracy the Soubah's *Tope Khonnah Derogher* (or maſter of his ordnance) with ſeveral other diſaffected officers, which was very ſoon accompliſhed.——It was a ſaying of a great and brave king, "that one drop "of honey caught and engaged more flies, "than a ton of vinegar." *Suffraaz Khan* in place of ſweetneſs of diſpoſition and affability, unhappily ſubſtituted a moroſe, ſevere and inſolent carriage to all around him: which (at this moſt important juncture) left him not more than two or three officers of any conſideration, who bore the leaſt attachment to his perſon, family, or government.

Matters becoming thus ripe for execution; *Hodjee* began to grow impatient for a[n] interview with his brother; and urged th[e]

promi[ſ]

promise made to him by *Allum Chund* and *Jaggaut Seet*, of procuring his dismission from the capital.

These embraced the first opportunity, when the Soubah was, according to custom, reviling *Hodjee* (then absent) in publick *Durbar*; to represent to him, "that it was a dis-"grace to his court the suffering *Hodjee* to "appear there, considering the infamous em-"ploy he bore under his father.——Drive "him (continued they) from your presence, "court and city; and let him go to his "ungrateful brother." This council being echoed and applauded by the *Tope Khonnah Derogher*, and others in the confederacy: the unwary Soubah instantly sent an order to *Hodjee Hamet* to quit the provinces; who, not thinking it prudent to wait for a second order, departed without delay; and made the best of his way to *Patna*, where in a few days he arrived with some of his faithful attendants.

Suffraaz Khan, by this false step, deprived himself of the great security he had in his hands; for the good behaviour of *Aliverdi Khan*, whose ambition, he had cause enough to think, would not stop with the Nabobship of *Patna*; depended upon the detention of *Hodjee*.

On *Hodjee*'s arrival at *Patna*, he painted the whole conduct of the Soubah in the most hideous colours: he employed his whole art and eloquence in the exaggeration of the indignities himself had endured: he told his brother that he might rest assured "*Suffraaz Khan* could never "forget, nor forgive his obtaining the go-"vernment of *Bahar*, independant of the "Soubahship, whereby so large a portion "of the revenues was lopt from himself "and family: that he was from good au-"thority convinced, the Soubah only wait-"ed a favourable occasion to cut him off, "and seize and reunite his government to "the Soubahship; to which purpose he "knew he had forwarded dispatches to "court—That he had gone too far to stop; "that *Suffraaz Khan* was universally de-"tested in the provinces; and finally that "no security for himself and family remain-"ed, but in assuming the whole Soubah-"dary, which he might do with very little "difficulty."

Hodjee then opened to his brother, the progress he had made in this necessary step below; recited the several conferences he had with the *Seets* and *Allum Chund*, and the result of their deliberations; recounting at at the ſame time the names of the Soubah's officers, who had declared themſelves wholly devoted to his promotion to the *throne*.

It was ſaid; *Aliverdi* expreſſed much compunction on this overture's being firſt made to him, to diſpoſſeſs the ſon of his maſter and benefactor: but if we form our concluſion from his *Actions*, both antecedent and ſubſequent to his period, we ſhall have no foundation to encourage our belief in that report: for if he really had at firſt any ſcruples to combat with; it is certain he very ſoon ſubdued them, and determined to march into *Bengal*; of which, full advice was immediately diſpatched to their confederate friends there.

It was however thought eligible, that *Suffraaz Khan* ſhould be lulled into ſecurity; to which end, *Aliverdi* (at the time he was levying additional troops) wrote the moſt ſubmiſſive letter to him,——" aſſuring " him he was as much the ſlave of his " houſe, as he was in the time of his " father: humbly intreating his permiſſion " to throw himſelf at his feet, and plead " the cauſe of his unfortunate brother; " who, he had with grief learned, had in-" curred his diſpleaſure; hoping by his

"personal supplications, his unhappy bro-
"ther would be restored to the Soubah's
"favor *."

He departed from *Patna* the latter end of the year 1741, at the head of about 30,000 horse and foot; leaving his brother *Hodjee Hamet*, his Niab, or deputy governor of *Bahar*. We will leave *Aliverdî* on his march, and return to the court of the Soubah.

Suffraaz Khan had *still* about his person three officers of distinction, that remained faithful to his interest——though from different motives: their names were *Mussat Khoolî Khan*, *Goas Khan*, and *Banteer Ali Khan*; (more commonly known by the name of *Baaker Ali Khan.)* The first, was married to a sister of the Soubah, and appointed Nabob of *Orissa*; for which government he was in a few days to set out, with a small body of troops.——His interest connected him firmly to the Soubah, on whose well being his own fortunes depended.

* This was the specious pretext publickly avowed for *Aliverdî*'s march into *Bengal*, which he began soon after the dispatch of the above letter, and before he could possibly receive any reply to it.

The

The other two had been proved faithful servants to *Soujah Khan*; and were attached to the present Soubah, more from principles of gratitude, honor, and affection to the memory of their old master, than to any love they could possibly bear to himself—they supported the character of brave officers; were in considerable commands under the Vice-roy; and, in truth, were the only persons in his court, for whom he observed the least respect or regard.

These officers, after the departure of *Hodjee*, had received imperfect intelligence of the frequent meetings of *Hodjee*, *Jaggaut Seet*, and *Allum Chund*; which they ventured to communicate to the Vice-roy: intimating, at the same time, their *opinion or sentiments*, that such meetings, composed of persons, which they feared were disaffected to his government, called for his attention; and advised the immediate seizure of the *Seets*, *Allum Chund*, and the commanding officer of the artillery. But *Suffreaz Khan*, doomed to destruction, hearkened not to these faithful admonitions, which he treated as idle apprehensions, without any real foundation; thinking them friendly endeavours only, to draw him from his pleasures;

 which

which *these faithful monitors* had before attempted, but in vain.

By this fatal delusion, the Soubah lost the only opportunity of exerting that power which might have saved him from approaching ruin: for the bold step advised by *Goas* and *Baaker Khans*, of seizing those heads of the conspiracy, would have struck terror into the whole party; and effectually put a stop to *Aliverdi's* intended invasion; and probably a period also to his hopes.

Aliverdî Khan followed the letter he wrote the Soubah, with such expedition; that he gained the pass of *Sicly-gully*; and entered *Bengal* before the least intimation of his departure from *Patna* had reached the court of the Soubah.

The pass of *Siclygully* divides the provinces of *Bengal* and *Bahar*; is of considerable length, and only about ten to twelve feet wide; situate on the top of a mountain, with a steep ascent both ways. The course of the pass is *North* and *South*; flanked to the *Westward* by an impenetrable wood; and to the *Eastward* by the principal branch of the river *Ganges*. Thus circumstanced it was capable of being defended

fended by a ſmall number of men; but it was left unguarded by the infatuated *Suf-fraaz Khan*; and without any defence at all.

Aliverdi knew the importance of this paſs; and therefore determined, by forced marches, to gain the poſſeſſion of it; before it could poſſibly be put in a ſtate of de-fence ſufficient to oppoſe his entrance into *Bengal*. This he accompliſhed as above, and found it neceſſary to halt for ſome days to refreſh his fatigued troops.

On the firſt advice that the Nabob of *Patna* had paſſed *Siclygully*, the court of the Soubah was ſtruck with the deepeſt conſternation; every one ſeeing further into the conſequen-ces of his approach, than the unhappy and ſhort-ſighted *Suffraaz Khan*: who having, at firſt, no conception, that *Aliverdi* was at the head of an army; expreſſed only high rage and reſentment at his daring to enter the province without his permiſſion.—But when, ſoon after, *Goas* and *Baaker Khans* informed him of the number of troops he had with him——and that they were con-vinced (by intelligence from ſpies they had placed near his perſon) the deſign of *Ali-verdi* was to depoſe him; it is impoſſi-

 ble

ble to paint his fury.——He immediately ſent for *Jaggaut Seet*, and *Allum Chund* and demanded of them; how they dared ſuffer ſuch a body of troops to enter the province, without giving early notice of it? averring that he knew ſuch a ſtep was not taken without their privacy and counſel.

The accuſed, who expected this attack, came prepared; having previouſly concerted their replies, leſt they ſhould have been ſeparately examined——They ſuffered the Soubah's rage to expend itſelf in words, and then ſubmiſſively aſſured him "That "had there been the ſmalleſt foundation "for the belief of the reports falſly ſpread "of *Aliverdî Khan*, they would have been "the firſt of his ſlaves to adviſe him of "his danger.—That the forces of *Aliverdî* "were greatly exaggerated by ſome evil "minded people near the Soubah's perſon, "who were declared enemies to *Hodjee's* "houſe.——That *their* intelligence (on "which they could depend) ſaid, he was "only accompanied by his common at- "tendants, and a ſmall guard to defend "him againſt the petty Rajahs, and free- "booters of the mountains.——That they "were themſelves perfectly ſatisfied, the

"conduct

" conduct of *Aliverdî* was greatly misre-
" presented; and that his only design was
" to throw himself at the Soubah's feet,
" and plead the cause of his unhappy dis-
" graced brother *Hodjee Hamet*.

To corroborate this specious and deceitful harangue, they each produced letters from *Aliverdî*, and from other seemingly indifferent persons in his train, calculated purposely to support the deceptions; which being compared with others, wrote to the Soubah from *Siclygully*, he was thereby again lulled into a stupid security; and was influenced so far by the combined traitors, as to censure *Goas Khan*, and *Baaker Ali Khan*; as aiming to stir up troubles and a war in the province, that they might benefit themselves in the confusion.

We left *Aliverdî Khan* to the *Southward* of *Siclygully* pass, halting to refresh his troops after their fatiguing march.——Here he met with an impediment, that was well nigh making his whole scheme prove abortive.

His principal Jemmautdaars, officers and soldiers, had been promised four months advanced pay, (besides their old arrears) and

a graa gratuity of three Lacs of Rupees, as ſoon as they entered the province of *Bengal.*—The Jemmautdaars, in a body, preſented themſelves before the Nabob; and demanded the promiſed pay and gratuity for themſelves and their people; declaring if it was with-held from them, they would not march a foot further.

This demand threw *Aliverdi* into the utmoſt perplexity, as knowing his inability to comply with it. For, what with the large bribes remitted to *Delhy*, for the purchaſe of his independant government of *Bahar*; and what with other conſiderable ſums juſt diſburſed, to corrupt and keep firm the principal officers in the ſervice of the Soubah; his coffers were drained, and at a very low ebb.

However, without diſcovering the difficulty he was under, he with his uſual dignity, and voice of authority, "order-"ed them to withdraw, and wait without, "and they ſhould be ſatisfied."——Then calling a private *Durbar*, conſiſting of his Dewan *Chinkumunny*, and a few of his chief confidants, he informed them of the demand of his Jemmautdaars, and repreſented in lively colours, "the riſque

"himſelf

" himſelf and they ran, of being deliver-
" ed up to *Suffraaz Khan*, unleſs ſome
" expedient was deviſed to raiſe to the
" amount of three Lacs, with which he
" doubted not to quiet them for the pre-
" ſent." To this the Dewan replied, the whole ſum in his hands did not exceed 45000 Rupees; and that he knew of no means of raiſing more.——

This unfavourable report of the Dewan, proved a ſevere ſhock to *Aliverdi* and his adherents.—Various alternatives were (as uſual in theſe caſes) propoſed, without any having the appearance of ſucceeding: amongſt the reſt, it was ſtrenuouſly urged by the Dewan, that an expreſs ſhould be ſent to *Jaggaut Seet*; but this was oppoſed by the Nabob,—who aſſerted, " ſuch a de-
" lay would prove fatal to the whole en-
" terprize."—And he was juſt on the point of reſolving to retreat with thoſe troops he could depend on; when the *evil genius* of *Suffraaz Khan*, in the perſon of one of *Aliverdi*'s followers, conciliated all matters by a device, which merits being particularly recited.

There were two brothers, merchants of *Patna*, well known by the names of *Omy Chund*,

Chund, and *Diep Chund*: the former of theſe now attended the camp, and was generally of *Aliverdi*'s private councils; and much in his confidence.

One of the occupations of this *Omy Chund* was, to advance occaſionally ready money to the officers and ſoldiers at a very high premium; this is an allowed practice in all Eaſtern camps, and poſſibly, at leaſt for aught we know, it may be the practice in the Weſtern alſo——however the greatneſs of the riſque certainly juſtifies the largeneſs of the premium; for the repayment not only depends upon the lives of the borrowers, but alſo upon their ſucceſs.

Omy Chund had brought with him only 20,000 rupees, for this game at hazard: he deſired the Nabob would order his Dewan to pay him immediately the 45,000 rupees, which were in his hands; which being complied with, he inſtructed the Nabob, "To call in the Jemmautdaars——and "order them to bring in an account of "their reſpective claims, and to tell them "that he would give them draughts on "*Omy Chund*; taking care to give billets "firſt to thoſe who had the ſmalleſt ſums to "receive; and that in the cloſe of the "evening

" evening he ſhould (on pretence of freſh " intelligence by his ſpies that *Suffraaz* " *Khan* was in full march towards him) " cauſe the *Nobut* to be beat, and iſſue his " orders for engaging the enemy early in the " morning, and leave the reſt to him."

The Jemmautdaars were called and ordered to bring in their claims, which they did in leſs than an hour: for they generally have them ready made up on a ſcrap of paper, which they conceal either in their girdle or turband. When all the claims were laid before the Nabob—he ordered his Dewan to give them billets upon *Omy Chund*; the Dewan, according to private inſtructions, made what delay he could, not to occaſion ſuſpicion; and gave thoſe firſt who had the leaſt to receive.

When the Jemmautdaars tendered their billets to *Omy Chund*, he paid ſeveral of the leaſt conſiderable ſums readily, and without any deductions: then, as he had accounts to ſettle with moſt of them, he prolonged the time by many artful blunders and deſigned errors, until the day was far ſpent, and not more than one eighth part of their accounts was adjuſted. Then excuſing himſelf on account of the great fatigue he had un-

undergone, he deferred the further payments until the next morning.

As ſoon as the day cloſed, *Aliverdi* ordered the *Nobut* to be beat; and iſſued out his commands to his *Jemmautdaars* to hold themſelves in readineſs for engaging the next day; telling them that *Suffraaz Khan*'s army was not far diſtant.

This unexpected alarm had the effect, which *Omy Chund* had foreſeen: thoſe who had received the amount of their billets, in all haſte returned it into his cuſtody; and the others depoſited their billets in his hands. In the morning the Nabob reſumed his match; took the rout to *Morſhadabad*, and kept up the alarm and expectance of a battle; until he, in reality, encountered the Soubah; to whom we once again return.

Baaker Ali Khan and *Goas Khan*, receiving hourly intelligence from their ſpies of *Aliverdi*'s motions, and the number of his forces, had ſtill the courage to repreſent to the Soubah, the danger his perſon and government were in—and humbly beſought him, "to provide for ſafety whilſt in his "power;" urging "that if the deſigns "of *Aliverdi* were honourable, the moſt

 "eligible

" eligible way to preſerve him in thoſe " ſentiments, was to let him ſee he was " in a condition and poſture to oppoſe and " cruſh him. That if on the contrary the " deſigns of *Aliverdî* were aimed againſt " the government; his ſupine conduct muſt " inevitably ſecure his ſucceſs. That from " the face of *their* intelligence, and the " whole procedure of *Aliverdî*, they had " no room to doubt the wickedneſs of his " intentions."

Theſe remonſtrances joined to advices the Soubah had himſelf received of the *real* number of *Aliverdî*'s troops, at laſt rouſed him from his ſtupor; and he directly ordered his Jemmautdaars and forces to take the field, and rendezvous in the plains of *Gyria*, about three miles to the North of *Morſhadabad*; himſelf following the next morning. He had hardly time to marſhal his troops in order of battle, when *Aliverdî*'s army appeared.

Their forces were nearly equal; each about 30,000 men; 20,000 foot, and 10,000 horſe. *Suffraaz Khan* had twenty pieces of artillery, from twelve to ſix and four pounders: *Aliverdî* had none.

Suffraaz

Suffraaz Khan planted his cannon in his front; with strict orders not to fire, until the enemy advanced within half musket shot: for confiding on his artillery, he rested secure of victory—*Aliverdi* ordered his troops to receive the discharge of the cannon, and then to rush in upon the Soubah's army sword in hand. He issued these orders with great security; for he and his troops knew that by the treachery of the *Tope Khonnah Droger*, the cannon were loaded with powder only. He also issued his instructions to his officers, to regard nothing but attacking those posts, which were commanded by *Mussat Khooli Khan*, *Baaker Ali Khan*, and *Goas Khan*: well knowing that none of the Soubah's troops or officers would engage, but those which were immediately under their command.

When the engagement began, all but five or six thousand of the Soubah's troops stood idle spectators of the battle. *Aliverdi's* best troops advanced without the least apprehension; stood the discharge of artillery; and vigorously attacking the division of *Baaker Ali Khan*, (behind which the Soubah was stationed) they were twice repulsed with much slaughter: but *Baaker Ali's* troops being over-powered by fresh numbers,

bers, this brave man was killed; and moſt of his party cut to pieces.

Goas Khan penetrating to the center of the enemy, with a few brave followers, was near killing *Aliverdî* with his own hand; when *Sedun Hazzaary*, commander of his *Burkundaſſes*, interpoſed and ſaved him; obliging *Goas Khan* to retire with his command; who, ſoon after being ſurrounded by *Aliverdî*'s troops, and diſdaining to receive quarter, were to a man killed.

Muſſat Khoolî Khan, and the troops under his command, for ſome time exerted themſelves with great courage and fidelity in defence of the Soubah's perſon; who being now, for the firſt time, informed of the treachery of the *Tope Khonnah Droger*, and the defection and perfidy of moſt of his officers and troops; and that he was betrayed on all hands; and learning alſo the fate of his two faithful generals —— he ordered "*Muſſat Khoolî Khan* to retire from the bat-"tle; to make the beſt retreat he could to "*Cuttack*; and ſave, if poſſible, the pro-"vince of *Oriſſa* from the traytor and "uſurper *Aliverdî*;" telling him "he ſaw "it was vain for him alone to attempt "ſtemming the current of his adverſe for-

"tune."

" tune." *Mussat Khooli Khan* obeyed, and with a small faithful party retired, and eluded the pursuit of the enemy.

The Soubah, thus abandoned, determined, it should seem, to efface by a glorious death the remembrance of his inglorious life—— At this juncture it was, that the leader of his elephant proposed to him to return to the capital, " telling him that he would engage, on the forfeiture of his head, to " convey him safe thither, where he had " still some friends that would be able to " make a stand for him;" but he nobly replied, " It never should be said that *Suf-* " *fraaz Khan* fled from rebels and traytors." He then ordered him to plunge into the thickest of the enemy; where, with a few of his guards, that still remained steady to him, he for some time maintained an obstinate engagement——like an enraged lion he fought to a degree of desperation: it was said he emptied a whole quiver of arrows; and discharged more than a dozen javelins; besides the execution he did with the fire arms he had with him, on the elephant. But at last being weary with slaughter, and not able any longer to lift an arm, a period was put to his life and fortune, by a musket ball from a distance; said to be discharged

discharged by one of his own people. With this wound he fell dead from his elephant; and with his death the contest ceased.——

Thus fell the son of *Soujah Khan*, testifying by his exit from life, that he possessed a soul capable of producing great actions, had the soil been early and properly cultivated.

Aliverdî Khan possessed himself of the late Soubah's tent and baggage; the plunder of which, amounting to between nine and ten lacs of rupees, he bestowed upon his principal officers and soldiers—He received *Suffraaz Khan*'s perfidious officers and soldiers into his service; and marching to the capital, entered it without resistance through the acclamations of the people. Proceeding to the palace, he seated himself upon the *Muzinud*, and received the submission of the Rajahs, Jemmautdaars, and other great officers, who acknowledged and saluted him Soubah of the *Three provinces*. *Anno* 1742

The fate of one of the three principal conspirators, having something remarkable in it, calls for our particular mention.—— *Allum Chund* returned from the investing *Aliverdî* to his own house; and being bit-

 terly

terly reproached by his wife, for his perfidy and treason to the son of his prince and master, and predicting "that he would "shortly receive from the *usurper* the reward due to every *traytor*," he was thereby so much affected, that he swallowed diamond powder, and in a few hours expired.

Aliverdi Khan entertaining no favourable opinion of the military prowess and capacity of the *Bengal* soldiery; and having so very lately seen a glaring proof of their natural perfidy, as well as cowardice, in the unhappy fall of his predecessor; determined to put no trust or confidence in them: and in order to guard against their treachery, which he knew might be easily purchased against him, as it had been for him, he entertained immediately in his service a select body of three thousand *Patans*, with their commander *Mustapha Khan*, a soldier of fortune; who about this time arrived in *Bengal* with recommendatory letters from court. He bore the character of a consummate general; and his subsequent actions verified the report.—These new troops the Soubah kept always on duty near his person; and their chief was admitted to his councils and favour.

His next ſtep was to diſplace all officers, throughout the provinces, that he had reaſon to think retained any affection to the late Soubah's houſe: and when he thought himſelf ſecure againſt all attempts that might endanger his newly acquired government, he appointed a Niab *pro tempore*, for the government of *Babar* and its capital; and recalled his brother *Hodjee Hamet*, that he might benefit himſelf of his counſel, and aſſiſtance, in his arduous ſituation.

Hodjee being arrived, all matters were debated and concerted relative to the government of the provinces. *Hodjee* was inveſted with the government of *Morſhadabad*, in the abſence of his brother; who without delay took the field, and directed his rout towards *Oriſſa*, on the thirtieth of *March*, 1742*.—We will leave the Soubah on his march, and for a few minutes attend on the Nabob of *Oriſſa*.

This fugitive, and unfortunate brother-in-law to the late Soubah, (with whom I was

* *Suffraaz Khan*'s defeat and death was on the twenty-eight of *January*, 1741 2, and not on the thirtieth of *March*, 1742, as the author of the Reflections erroneouſly ſays, confounding the date of one event with another.

 inti-

intimately acquainted) escaped from the battle with a few followers, as before recited. He in a few days reached the capital of *Orissa*, where many of the friends of *Suffraaz Khan*'s house resorted to him: he made some attempts to fortify, and enlist troops for the defence of the place: but being ill supplied with cannon and ammunition, and receiving certain intelligence of the usurper's approach, with a very superiour force to his own; he thought it prudent to provide for his own safety, by retreating out of the province with his family. He left *Kuttack* four days before the Soubah's van-guard reached it; and found an asylum in the *Deccan*, under *Nizzam Al Mulk*.

Kuttack opened its gates to the Usurper; but he had scarcely settled the government of *Orissa*, when he was alarmed with the news, that an army of 80,000 *Mahárattor* horse had entered the province of *Bengal*, by a passage over the *Bierboheen* hills; and had already penetrated into the *Burdomaan* country.

The Usurper received this unexpected shock with manifest astonishment: he immediately saw, not only his retreat, but every communication with his brother and his

his capital cut off. In this dilemma we will leave him for a while, and investigate as well the causes of this invasion, as convey some idea of the people called *Maharattors*; who for a few years last past, have been as much the dread and terror of the East, as the *Goths* and *Vandals* of old were of the West: with this essential difference however in their characters, that whereas *these* were the barbarous invaders of the rights and property of others; *those* are making justifiable efforts to recover *that*, which their ancestors had been, for ages, in peaceable and just possession of.

When the Empire of *Indostan* was invaded; and, in part, conquered by the Mogul *Tartars*, about the beginning of the fifteenth century; many of the Rajahs, or *Hindoo* princes of the country, submitted with little opposition to the invaders, on condition of holding their lands and principalities, paying a stipulated annual tribute. But others of them, disdaining this tributary state of slavery, retired to the southward; and possessing themselves of the most southern parts of *Deccan*, they remained unmolested, until about the year 1654; the latter end of the reign of the Emperor *Shaw Jehawn*.

His third ſon *Auring Zebe*, being at that period Soubah of the *Deccan*, (or ſouth) made a fruitleſs attempt on *Golconda*; inſtigated thereto by *Mhir Jemla*, who revolted to him from the then reigning Rajah of that famous city, and the adjoining country.

Auring Zebe, ſucceeding to the throne of *Indoſtan*, in the year 1659; purſued by his Generals his former deſigns againſt the independant Rajahs, on the coaſt of *Cormandel*; being guided chiefly by the counſel and inſtructions of *Mhir Jemla*; by whoſe valour *Golconda* was reduced; and the whole coaſt ſubdued, from *Ganjam* to *Coleroon* river, that is, from the latitude of 11°. 40′. to 19°. 30′. north.

The other promontory of *India*, called the coaſt of *Mallabar*, from the borders of the province of *Guzerat* to cape *Comorin*, was never conquered by the Mogul Emperors: but the independant poſſeſſion of it was maintained by various Rajahs; the chief of whom was the Ràjah of *Sittarah*.

To *theſe* independant princes, the diſtreſſed and diſpoſſeſſed Rajahs of *Cormandel* applied for ſuccour. *They*, alarmed at the

the rapid progreſs of the Mogul arms, immediately united themſelves under the banners of the Rajah of *Sittarah*.

Theſe united princes and people, are thoſe which are known by the general name of *Maharattors*; a word compounded of *Rattor* and *Maahah*: the firſt being the name of a particular *Raazpoot* (or *Rojpoot*) tribe; and the latter, ſignifying *great* or mighty; (as explained by Mr. *Fraſer*) a term we have had occaſion to make uſe of before; and frequently ſhall again.

The acquiſitions thus gained to the Empire, by the Generals of *Auring Zebe*, coſt ſo much blood and treaſure, that the diamond mines of *Golconda* hardly proved an equivalent: for the confederate princes made ſuch vigorous efforts to regain what they had loſt, as obliged *Auring Zebe* to keep up ſo large an armament, that the expence of preſerving his new conqueſt exceeded the whole revenues acquired by it. The glorious vanity, however, of havin carried his conqueſts of this Empire further than any of his predeceſſors, determined him not to abandon them; until finding at laſt, he ſhould riſque the loſs of the whole, he began to meditate coming

to

to a treaty with them: which resolution was hastened by several bold attacks, made on different parts of his dominions by the *Maharattors* at the same time.——On the side of his new southern acquisitions, they carried fire and sword sometimes into the province of *Dowlatabad*; and attacked the capital *Auringabad*; and from *Sittarah* they penetrated through the province of *Guzerat*; and sometimes alarmed even the court of *Delhy*; striking a panick wherever they came.

Auring Zebe, seeing, at length, no prospect of extending his conquests farther over these intrepid natives; thought it a wise measure to secure, and keep, if possible, what he had got.——To this end, he entered into a treaty with the confederate Rajahs; and by a secret valuable consideration given to the *Seboo* Rajah, King of *Sittarah*, a peace was concluded between them on the following terms. "That "*Auring Zebe* should remain in quiet "possession of his southern conquests as "far as the river *Colercon*, before mention-"ed, and the port of *Surat*; and that in "lieu thereof, the *Mabarattors* should re-"ceive, and be intitled to, for ever, a "*Chout* (that is, the fourth part) of the

"reve-

" revenues of *Deccan*;" to which *Soubahship*, these new southern conquests were annexed by the Emperor.

Thus a period was put to a war, that had chiefly employed the attention of near two thirds of *Auring Zebe*'s long and fortunate reign; by which, so important an addition of territory and revenue was obtained, that had it been duly and honestly governed and administred; and the treaty kept inviolate on both sides, would have yielded a perpetual source of riches to all succeeding Emperors, on every emergency of the state.

As long as *Auring Zebe* lived, the *Choût* was duely paid to the *Maharattors*; but on his decease the treaty began to be infringed, though it suffered no open rupture until the death of *Shaw Allum*; when the Empire falling into a state of universal confusion, (by the contentions that arose between his sons for the succession to the throne, and by the subsequent distractions during the despotic tyranny of the *Seyds*) little regard was paid to it, on the part of the government.

Things being in this situation, the *Maharattors* determined to pay themselves; by making

making incurſions on different ſides of the Empire; and laying the city of *Surat* under contribution: in which warfare they met with ſuch ſucceſs from the continued puſillanimity and diſtraction of the government, that at length, they extended their claim and demand, from the ſtipulated *Choût* of the revenues of the *Deccan*; to a *Choût* of the whole revenues of the Empire.

However, when *Mahommed Shaw*, by the overthrow of the *Seyds*, arrived to the ſecure poſſeſſion of the throne, *Anno* 1719; ſome check was put to their invaſion: and terms of accommodation being made to them, they for ſome years acquieſced in the terms of *Auring Zebe*'s treaty; and annually received the *Choût* of the revenues of the *Deccan*, by their agents out of the royal treaſury at *Delhy*; long after theſe revenues had loſt their way to court, by the uſurpation and independance of the traytor *Nizam al Mulk*.

In the year 1740, the deputies of the King of *Sittarah*, arrived as uſual at *Delhy* to receive the *Choût*; when they were given to underſtand by the *Mogul*'s miniſtry, "That "*Nadir Shaw* had lately ſo exhauſted the "treaſury, that the Emperor was rendered

" utterly incapable of ſatisfying their demands: the more eſpecially, as the revenues of the *Bengal* provinces had been witheld from the year 1738, by the rebellion of *Aliverdî Khan*; who in conjunction with his brother *Hodjee Hamet*, had uſurped the government of that Soubahdary: they requeſting at the ſame time that the deputies would intreat their maſter in the Emperor's name, to ſend an army of ſufficient force to exact the amount of the *Choût*, that was due to them; and alſo to take the heads of *Aliverdî* and his brother; and reſtore the family *Soujah Khan* to the Soubahſhip; as the then diſtracted ſtate of the Empire put it out of his power to ſend a force, ſtrong enough, to reduce the two rebels."

With this anſwer, and *actual powers* from the *Emperor*, the deputies departed for *Sittarah*.—A fact that fully confutes the aſſertion of *Aliverdî*'s having received a *Phirmaund*, confirming him in the government; as was publiſhed by beat of drum, and induſtriouſly circulated by the *Seets* the latter end of the year 1739 *.

The

* *Aliverdi* is reported to have ſat in ſtate a whole day to receive the ſham *Phirmaund*, with the uſual ceremonials

The *Maharatter* deputies arriving at *Sittarah*, reported the result of their deputation, and the Emperor's request. The King of *Sittarah* did not ruminate long what resolution to take: he now had obtained a justifiable plea to attack the Mogul's dominions with his own consent; therefore, without loss of time, he ordered an army of 80,000 horse to take the field, and march into *Bengal*; under the command of *Boschar Pundit*, a general of some reputation, and favorite of the *Sekoo* Rajah King of *Sittarah*. This general, and army, we left in the *Burdomaan* country between the usurper and his capital; to whom we

monials on such occasions; but this is a farce that has been *since* played in *some parts* of the province of *Bengal*, and laughed at, as much as it was then.—For the *Seets* could always *cook up* a *Phirmaund* from court whenever it was *wanted*. That *Aliverdi* was *never* confirmed in the government by a *real Phirmaund*, is a fact that admits of no doubt; and it is well known, that so late as *June*, *Anno* 1750, the Vizir *Monsoor Ali Khan*, (father of *Soujah Doulat*, the present Soubah of *Oude*) was advanced at the head of 100,000 horse, within eight days march of *Patna*, purposely to restore these so long dismembered provinces to the Empire, and punish the usurper:—but differences arising between the young Emperor *Amet Shaw* (son and successor to *Mahommed Shaw*) and Rajah *Jeet Sing*, the Vizir was recalled from this service; or, as others more probably said, his retreat was bought off by *Aliverdi*, at the price of fifty Lac of Rupees.

must

must again return; and point out the errors that drew him into the perilous situation and dilemma we left him in, before we shew how bravely he extricated himself from it.

Some short time before he departed from *Morshadabad*, a slight rumour prevailed of the intended invasion of the *Maharattors*; to which no credit was given, either by the usurper or his brother. But slight as the report was, it ought to have merited their attention at a juncture when he was departing with all the strength of the provinces to the most extreme part of his government: and as he must have known, no enemy could enter the province of *Bengal*, so as to cut off his communication with his capital, but by the western hills of *Bierboheen*; prudence dictated that he should have secured the fidelity of the Rajahs of *Bierboheen* and *Bisnapore*; who were alone capable of harrassing and retarding, if not of preventing the *Maharattor* army from entering on that side.

But (as if Fortune had purposed, that the neglect of this wise precaution should be conducive to the higher exaltation of the character of this her favorite son) so far were

were the brothers from adverting to the necessity of such a security in their rear, that both these Rajahs had been highly incensed by some acts of oppression exercised towards them soon after *Aliverdi*'s usurpation of the government; and were readily disposed, in place of obstructing the enemy, to give them a free entrance into the heart of *Bengal*; which they did without the least opposition: though in pursuing their resentment, they entailed a long series of heavy calamities on their unhappy country.

We left *Aliverdi Khan* at *Cuttack*, in deep astonishment at the news of this dangerous invasion. Without discovering the least apprehension or alarm, he withdrew for the space of half an hour; in consultation only with *Mustapha Khan*; and then ordered his people to prepare for marching. He quitted *Cuttack* the same day; and by forced marches arrived near *Burdwan*, the principal town of *Burdomaan*; (within five days march of the capital) two days after the *Maharattors* took possession of it. Here he intrenched himself; and was soon surrounded by the enemy; who though they had at least the superiority of eight to one, had not the courage to attack him.

Boschar

Boschar Pundit, however, sent *Aliverdi* a letter; explaining the nature of the powers he was invested with; demanding "three years arrears of the *Chout*; the "treasures of the two late *Soubahs*; and "that in future, an officer of their own "should have a seat in every Cutcherry "throughout the provinces; to collect the "fourth part of the customs, on their be-"half."

The usurper received these *terms* with the highest indignation and impatience; instantly commanding the messenger to leave his camp, without deigning to send any reply to *them*: and finding by the propositions made to him, that there remained small hope of effecting any accommodation with the *Maharattor* General; he determined to make one vigorous effort, to break through the enemy, and regain a communication with his brother. To this resolution he was stimulated, by observing an universal panic amongst his *Bengal* troops, many of which deserted him, by favour of the night.

In pursuance of this resolution, he issued the necessary orders; omitting nothing that could speak the consummate General; promiſing moſt liberal rewards to thoſe who maintained, in this exigency, the character of ſoldiers: and well judging that his principal dependance reſted upon the *Patans*, he beſtowed the higheſt encomiums and promiſes on that body; by whom he began to be loved and revered; for being themſelves brave, they admired thoſe intrepid qualities in *Aliverdî*, which ſo nearly reſembled their own.

All things being prepared, the uſurper directed that part of the trench to be leveled with the utmoſt ſilence, which looked towards *Cutwah*. Then putting himſelf with *Muſtapha Khan* at the head of the *Patans* half an hour before day break, he marched out; and with amazing courage charged that part of the enemy that intercepted his rout towards the laſt mentioned town.

His rear being compoſed entirely of his *Bengal* troops, (then eſteemed the worſt ſoldiers of the Empire) was ſoon ſurrounded and put to flight; but the *Patans* exhibited a glorious effort: theſe led on (as before obſerved) by the *Soubah*, and their gallant chief *Muſtapha*; and their rear commanded by the brave *Zeyndî Amet Khan*,

Khan, (*Hodjee*'s ſecond ſon) with much ſlaughter cut themſelves a paſſage through the enemy; and gained the *Cutwah* road: In the courſe of which, they maintained a moſt memorable retreat for near three days and nights: being often ſurrounded and attacked on all ſides, by the whole *Maharattor* army, and as often repulſing and forcing their paſſage until they arrived at *Cutwah*.

At this place the uſurper muſtered his troops, and found that of 25,000 fighting men, with which he departed from his capital, he had only remaining 2500 *Patans*; and about 1500 of his *Bengal* ſoldiers, including their officers: theſe laſt named troops, ſtimulated by the example of the *Patans*, and the intrepid behaviour of their Jemmautdaar *Jaffier Khan**, were kept firm to their duty.

At *Cutwah*, *Aliverdi* found it neceſſary to halt for a ſhort ſpace to refreſh his harraſſed troops; who, during the term of this aſtoniſhing retreat, had in a manner been ſtrangers to food; reſt; or ſleep.——Here *May Anno 1742.*

* Since better known by the name of *Mhir Jaffier Ali Khan* Soubah of *Bengal*.

they were again ſurrounded on all ſides except on that of the river; which *Aliverdi* was informed was in one place fordable; a circumſtance unſuſpected by the enemy.

It was now univerſally believed that the uſurper muſt ſurrender himſelf, or be cut to pieces with the few that remained with him. And indeed a report ran through the province that he was actually taken priſoner; but the actions of this handful of men, in their retreat from *Burdwan*, had ſtruck ſuch terror and amazement into the whole *Maharattor* army; that they gazed upon them as ſo many enraged tygers in a net, without daring to approach the toils that encloſed them; and contented themſelves with the proſpect of ſtarving them to a ſurrender; little dreaming that *Aliverdi* would attempt fording the river, with people nearly exhauſted by continued labour and watching.

The uſurper taking advantage of this viſible panic in the enemy, and unwilling to let the triumphant ardour of his own ſoldiers cool; reſolved to attempt the river without further delay: and knowing there was a defilè leading from the village to the river, through which the enemy might intercept

tercept his paſſage, he judged it neceſſary to ſecure it; thereby alſo to prevent his rear's being attacked before they could gain the river.

The defence of this dangerous poſt was given to *Muſtapha Khan*, ſupported by *Jeyndî Amet Khan*, and *Jaffîer Khan* with eighty *ſelect Patans*; who immediately departed to take poſſeſſion of the *Defilè*——As ſoon as they were poſted, *Muſtapha Khan* diſpatched a meſſenger to the Soubah to adviſe him, he might attempt the river whenever he pleaſed.

Aliverdî having previouſly made the neceſſary diſpoſitions, put himſelf at the head of the *Patans*; and gave the ſignal for marching to the river; which they entered without moleſtation, preceded by well inſtructed guides.

As ſoon as the enemy perceived him in motion, they inſtantly attacked the *Defilè* with great violence; hoping ſtill to circumvent him.——They at firſt ſeemed to deride and deſpiſe the ſmall number left for the defence of it; but ſoon found their error, in repeated repulſes with heavy ſlaughter; from this determined, though ſmall body of men:

each of their leaders, on this momentous occasion, giving proofs of valour worthy the greatest heroes of antiquity.

They maintained their post, for a full hour, against reiterated attacks of fresh troops; without giving the least way; and until they judged the Soubah had safely past the river. They then began to retreat by slow degrees through the *Defilè*, without turning their backs; and having gained about the middle part of it *, advice was brought to *Mustapha Khan*, that his rear was attacked by the enemy †.——This general, without hesitating a moment, committed the charge of his front to *Jeyndee Amet Khan*, and *Jaffier Khan*: and ordering the forty men that composed his rear to face about, he put himself at their head, forming two fronts to oppose the enemy; and sending orders to *Jeyndee Amet* to continue his retreat, he bravely charged his new antagonists, and forced them to retire with much loss. When the whole party

* The *Defilè* was about eighty yards in length and ten wide.

† This event happened thus—a body of the *Maharattors*, about one thousand men, forced an entrance into the town, and had made a fruitless attack upon *Aliverdi's* rear, as they passed the river, from which they were now returned.

had cleared the *Defilè*, he commanded his men to form in one line on the ſhore, with their backs to the river; and making a feint to give a general aſſault; the enemy, as he expected, was ſtruck with terror, and retired many paces. *Muſtapha* taking advantage of their diſtance, inſtantly commanded his troops to face about and take the river; into which they plunged, and gained the oppoſite ſhore, with the loſs, on the whole, of only fifteen men.

If we conſider the retreat of theſe Veterans (from *Burdwan* to the oppoſite ſhore of *Cutwah* river) in all its circumſtances; it will appear as amazing an effort of human bravery, as the hiſtory of any age or people have chronicled; and we think it merits as much being recorded and tranſmitted to poſterity, as *that* of the celebrated *Athenian* general and hiſtorian.

Muſtapha Khan, *Jeyndee Amet Khan*, and *Jaffier Khan* were received by the Soubah, with all the marks of the higheſt affection and eſteem. He beſtowed great encomiums on the valour of *Jaffier Khan*, who was ever after diſtinguiſhed by his favour. He ſaluted, and thanked by name, every one of the *Patans*, who fought under theſe com-

 manders

manders at the memorable defence of the *Defilè*: and having refreſhed his troops, proceeded on his march to the capital, where he was received with aſtoniſhment and reverence. His firſt acts were, to preſent *Muſtapha Khan* with ten lac of rupees; and proportionably to reward the reſt of his brave defenders.

Whilſt the uſurper was gaining everlaſting renown as a ſoldier, his brother *Hodjee Hamet* was employed in putting the city of *Murſhadabad* in a poſture of defence. With extraordinary expedition he ſunk a ditch round it; formed a rampart and parapet; and planted cannon in thoſe parts where the city was moſt open to the enemies attacks.——*Aliverdi* reproaching him, "with having abandoned him to the ene-"my; and with being ſolicitous only for "his own ſafety; by neglecting to ſend a "body of troops to favour his retreat"——*Hodjee* replied, "that concluding (from the "number of the enemy, his forlorn ſitua-"tion, and the repeated reports of his "being taken priſoner and killed) he was "no more; he thought it more adviſe-"able to ſtrengthen the city, than to wea-"ken the defence of it, by parting with "any of the few forces he had been able

"to

" to raiſe for its preſervation." And in truth, *Aliverdi* found it in a much better ſtate of defence than he expected.

Before the uſurper had ſet out on his expedition for the reduction of *Oriſſa*, he had ſent orders to his deputy governor of *Patna*, to levy troops in the province of *Babar*. But theſe forces being not yet arrived in *Bengal*, he was to the great mortification of his enterpriſing and military genius, reduced to the neceſſity of ſhutting himſelf up in his capital; and was employed in providing further for its ſecurity.

The *Maharattors* recovering from their conſternation and panic, and acquiring a better knowledge of the river, paſſed it with their whole force; advanced to *Morſhadabad*; and ſurrounded it without attempting to aſſault it. They detached parties into the environs; plundering and deſtroying wherever they came; they ſent ſome bodies of horſe into the iſland of *Coſſimbuzar*; who committed there the moſt horrid devaſtation and cruelties: they fed their horſes and cattle with mulberry plantations; and thereby irreparably injured the ſilk manufacture: in ſhort, after committing every hoſtile

hostile act, which plenitude of power licensed without molestation; they thought it at length prudent to retire with their plunder; lest the approaching rainy season (which sets in, annually, about the middle of *June*) should intercept their retreat.

June Anno 1742. With this necessary precaution they quitted the blockade of the city, and repassed at *Cutwah* early in *June*, 1742, with all their immense plunder.

From *Cutwah*, they penetrated through the *Burdomaan* country; detaching their parties into every district; still amassing greater booty, and striking universal terror round them; sometimes alarming even the *European* settlements. The rains at length setting in, about the middle of *June*, gave a flattering hope that the land would soon be delivered from these devouring locusts. But alas! this pleasing prospect had but a short duration; they retired it is true; and bent their rout towards the *Bierboheen* hills; irresolute whether they should quit the provinces intirely; or only lodge themselves in convenient quarters in that high country; where they would be ready to commence a new scene of destruction as soon as the rains broke

broke up (which they generally do about the latter end of *September* or the middle of *October.)*

It was by most believed that the enemy had taken their departure for their own country; and it is certain they had formed that resolution: when on a sudden, to the utter amazement of all, *Boschar Pundit* issued orders to march into *Bengal*;—so his ill destiny prompted him, that he might by his fall pay a sacrifice for the cruel enormities committed on all ranks, by those under his command. *July Anno* 1743.

They returned about the latter end of *July*, and pitched their tents on the highest parts of the *Burdomaan* country; and settled themselves there for the remainder of the rainy season.

On this event, a general face of ruin succeeded. Many of the inhabitants; weavers; and husbandmen fled. The *Arungs* were in a great degree deserted; the lands untilled; and the wretched fugitives who had escaped with nothing but their wives and children, and whatever they could carry in their hands, thought there was no safety for them, until they arrived on the *Eastern* shore of of the *Ganges*; to which they flocked in ſhoals, without intermiſſion for many days together.

The manufactures of the *Arungs* received ſo injurious a blow at this period, that they have ever ſince loſt their original purity and eſtimation; and probably will never recover them again. But it is neceſſary we explain what influenced *Boſchar Pundit*, to take the extraordinary and unexpected ſtep above-mentioned.

There was an officer employed in the receipts of the revenues at *Dacca*, named *Mhîr Hubbeeb*, who had embezzled a conſiderable ſum; and had otherways been guilty of mal-adminiſtration in the execution of his truſt. This man had been ordered, ſoon after *Aliverdi*'s ſeizing the government, to repair to the capital, and render an account of the branch committed to him.——He was bold and enterpriſing; of ſolid judgment; minutely acquainted with the ſtate of the provinces and courſe and nature of the revenues. To draw his character, in ſhort, we need only ſay, he was in *political virtue* the very counterpart of *Hodjee Hamet*.

Con-

Conſcious that his conduct at *Dacca* would not bear the teſt of examination, he availed himſelf of the preſent juncture of confuſion; and in place of repairing to the capital, he fled to *Boſchar Pundit*; and arrived in his camp, at the very period when that general reſolved to quit the provinces, and return to *Sittarah*.

His known character and abilities procured him a ready and welcome reception; and his miſchievous talents made him a dangerous inſtrument in the hands of theſe invaders; to accompliſh, in a manner, the utter deſtrúction of the country. He repreſented to *Boſchar Pundit*, "That in the "preſent ſtate of the provinces, he might "with facility and ſecurity aſſume the go-"vernment of the Soubahdaary himſelf; "that it would be inglorious for him *to re-"treat with the calf, when he could take the "cow alſo*; that the rains would ſoon break "up, and ſet his cavalry at liberty; and that "he had no cauſe to apprehend the uſurper "would ever have any power or force capable "of oppoſing them." *Boſchar Pundit* greedily hearkened to this pernicious advice; immediately changed his rout; and returned from *Bierboheen* to *Burdomaan*, as before remarked: and having fixed his head quarters

at

at *Burdwan*, he ſent proper officers at the head of ſmall parties to collect the revenues at every ſeat of cuſtom; and this they did for ſome time with as much tranquillity, as if they had been the natural ſovereigns of the country.

During theſe tranſactions the uſurper was not idle. As ſoon as he had certain intelligence that the enemy had repaſſed the *Cutwah* river, he quitted the city; and being ſoon after re-inforced by the *Patna* levies, and the number of his *Patans* being encreaſed from the Northward, he formed his camp in the neighbourhood of *Morſhadabad*.—— The *Engliſh*, *French* and *Dutch*, thought it neceſſary, during the rains, by various means to fortify alſo, and add to the ſtrength of their ſeveral ſettlements, at *Fort William*, *Chundernagore*, *Hougly*, and *Coſſimbuzar*; though they were hitherto unmoleſted in their perſons, or property, by the enemy.

Early in *October* the enemy, by the advice of *Mhîr Hubbeeb*, threw a ſtrong bridge of boats over the *Cutwah* river; the defence of which was given to him. By his aſſiſtance alſo the enemy was now ſupplied with ſome ſmall cannon; fire arms; and ammunition. He conſtructed for the defence of of his bridge two large boats; the one contiguous above; the other below the bridge, on the *Plaſſey* ſide. On theſe he threw platforms, on which he planted a few carriage pieces; forming effectual barricadoes with loop holes; for the ſecurity of his own people, as well as for the annoyance of the uſurper's troops, in caſe they ſhould prove hardy enough to attack the bridge; for the defence of which he embarked with him the beſt markſmen he could ſelect.—

This diſpoſition being completed the whole of the *Mabarattor* army croſſed over, and began their incurſions to different parts of the iſland, wherever the waters would admit their marching: ſometimes ſhowing themſelves in ſtrong bodies round the uſurper's camp; and inſulting him with opprobrious language, without daring to attack him.

The latter end of *October*, the rains broke up; the waters decreaſed hourly; and the roads ſoon became paſſable every where. It was now the enemy thought it adviſeable to recall their detached parties, and unite their whole force; which they drew up between the uſurper's camp and *Plaſſey* grove, ſecure of a retreat to their bridge. Here they

they halted three days; and reported they would wait there and give the ufurper battle.

Aliverdi, elated at this report, took the field, and advanced towards the enemy; not doubting but that if he could once bring them to a general engagement, it would prove decifive in his favor.——His whole force amounted to about forty-eight thoufand men; of whom barely twenty thoufand were horfe. Whereas the enemy's force was wholly compofed of cavalry; an advantage they had the wifdom fully to avail themfelves of, by the fagacious counfel of *Mhîr Hubbeeb*; through the courfe of this deftructive and long conteft.

As the ufurper advanced, they retreated towards the bridge, which they now refolved to repafs. This they could not effect without their rear's being warmly attacked and harraffed by *Aliverdi*; who, for this purpofe, advanced with a chofen body of horfe, fome hours before the main body of his army.

The enemy had gained the bridge, and paffed over three fourths of their army; when *Aliverdi* made a furious affault upon the remainder,

remainder, and threw them into confusion. But notwithstanding a heavy slaughter made amongst them, the greatest part of them recovered the bridge; and *Aliverdî* was obliged to draw off his people (who began to be severely galled by the fire from *Mhîr Hubbeeb*'s floating machine) and retire out of the reach of the shot, where he stayed until his heavy cannon was brought up to him.

Had *Mhîr Hubbeeb*, in obedience to *Boschar Pundit*'s orders, drawn off his party, and destroyed the bridge, as soon as the rear of the *Maharattor* army past it; and *Aliverdî* retired; he would have gained great reputation in the action. But not suspecting that the usurper's cannon could possibly be so near, as it really was; he was so rash as to remain on his post, until *Aliverdî* had, with astonishing expedition, opened a battery of three six pounders upon it.——*Mhîr Hubbeeb* stood one discharge from the battery; and now perceiving his error, attempted to escape with his party: but *Aliverdî* had posted a body of horse so advantageously, that immediately upon the discharge from his battery, they fell in pell mell with the enemy on the bridge; and a furious engagement ensued: in which *Mhîr*

Hubbeeb's party, three excepted, was cut to pieces. Himſelf and thoſe three gained the *Cutwah* ſhore; and by the advantage of a fleet horſe that waited for him, he eſcaped to the *Maharattor* army. A melancholy event cloſed the action: *Aliverdî's* troops crouding, in too great numbers, upon the bridge; it failed under them; and a thouſand brave fellows periſhed in the river.

The uſurper repaired the bridge with all poſſible diligence, and croſſed over his troops and artillery in purſuit of the enemy; who artfully eluded every attempt he made to bring them to a general action. Thus, by continual marches and counter marches, his troops, particularly his foot, were almoſt exhauſted by fatigue: whilſt the *Maharattors*, in detached parties, ranged the provinces at large; collecting the revenues without the leaſt interruption: the uſurper not daring to divide his army further than reinforcing the garriſon of *Bukchs Bunder* on the *Ganges*, with 500 horſe, and 1000 gun men; under the command of *Seraſdî Mahomet*.

Aliverdî, touched with deep chagrin at ſeeing his ſo lately uſurped dominions a prey to his enemies, without being able to protect

protect them, or bring the *Maharattors* to any decisive action; at last resolved to treat with *Boschar Pundit*. But that General was so elated with success, that he now added, at the instigation of *Mhîr Hubbeeb*, a new article to those already offered at *Burdwan*, *viz*. "that the usurper should also restore "the Soubahship to *Soujah Khan*'s family; "and resign the government he had so "wickedly usurped to *Suffraaz Khan*'s el-"dest son." *Mhîr Hubbeeb*, who knew that any treaty of peace would be fatal to himself, artfully threw this stumbling block in the way; which he foresaw would render the treaty of none effect: and to carry this point, he insinuated to *Boschar Pundit*, "that unless this article was insisted on, "the most essential and positive part of the "Emperor's orders would appear totally "neglected; and wished him, with great "humility, to reflect how he would answer "this neglect to his master, the King of "*Sittarah*."

This additional article produced the effect that *Mhîr Hubbeeb* expected; for it was refused by the brothers, with marks of resentment and disdain; and hostilities were immediately commenced again on both sides. ——Several skirmishes happened between

 them,

them, in which the ufurper's horfe always gained fome advantage; but thefe produced nothing decifive.

Hodjee Hamet, who never fuffered any fcruples of confcience to oppofe the fouleft means to accomplifh his views; in a private letter fent to his brother, urged the neceffity, in their prefent fituation, of attempting that by treachery, which they had failed in obtaining by every other means. *Aliverdî*, who faw the hazardous and neceffitous pofture of their affairs, as well as his brother, did not long oppofe the motion. *Hodjee* formed the plan; and it was executed in manner following.

A treaty was fet on foot by *Aliverdî*, who, under pretence of making it more conclufive and lefs liable to interruptions, propofed a conference with *Bofchar Pundit*. The overture was accepted by that General; contrary to the opinion of *Mhîr Hubbeeb* and the reft of his principal officers.

It was agreed that a fpacious tent fhould be prepared and erected by the ufurper, midway between the two armies, where the chiefs were to meet on a certain day and hour; attended each with eighty followers only; and

and that in the mean time hoſtilities on both ſides ſhould ceaſe.

The appointed time being come, and all things prepared for the reception of the chiefs; they advanced with the ſtipulated number of followers, conſiſting on both ſides of principal officers. When they approached near the tent, *Aliverdî* entered firſt, and was followed by *Boſchar Pundit*, without the leaſt ſuſpicion of treachery.

The uſual ſalutations and ceremonials being over, and both parties ſeated; on a ſignal given, two hundred ſelect men who had been concealed by *Aliverdî* between a double lining of the tent, ſuddenly ruſhed out; and cut the *Mabarattor* General and his party to pieces, before they were able to draw their ſcymiters; two or three only eſcaping in the confuſion.

At the ſame inſtant a ſignal was diſplayed from the tent (before agreed on) for the ſpeedy advance of the uſurper's army: this being obſerved by the *Mabarattor* army, they alſo began to be in motion, not knowing as yet what had happened. But being not long after joined by thoſe who had eſcaped the ſlaughter, and informed of the fate of their general and officers, they breathed nothing but fury and revenge.

In the first transports of their rage they advanced, and seemed resolved to avenge the treachery; by giving immediate battle to the usurper. But here, the wisdom and address of *Mhîr Hubbeeb* interposed: he represented to them, "that the only means to frustrate the great object the usurper had in "view by this treacherous assassination, "was, to avoid coming to a general action "with him." His arguments gained force and influence from the distracted state of the army; which was now under no head or any regular command: and observing the usurper advancing towards them in full march, they suddenly retired; to his great mortification and disappointment.

As soon as the disorder in the *Mabarattor* army subsided, they elected unanimously *Allee Bey* for their General; an officer that held the next rank to *Boschar Pundit*; and who bore a considerable degree of reputation amongst them. And now their conduct seemed to shew that they had resolved to execute that vengeance on the distressed country and inhabitants; which they could not execute on the usurper himself. To this

this end, they planted ſmall parties of obſervation about the ſkirts of his army to report his motions; and appointing *Nagur*, the capital of *Bierboheen*, for their general rendezvous, they divided their army, and carried fire and ſword in all their different routs.——They detached a ſtrong body to *Bukchs Bunder*, which they attacked; took; and plundered: perpetrating every where the moſt execrable cruelties that revenge and inhumanity could dictate; cutting off the ears, noſes, and hands, of any of the inhabitants whom they ſuſpected of concealing their wealth, or valuable moveables; ſometimes carrying their barbarity ſo far, as cutting off the breaſts of women, on the ſame pretence; neither ſex nor age proving any ſecurity againſt theſe enraged barbarians.

During theſe horrid ſcenes of deſolation, the uſurper left no ſtratagems uneſſayed to bring the enemy to a battle; but all his endeavours proved ineffectual. He was in continual chace of them from the beginning of *December* 1742, to the end of *February* 1742-3; and at length, with aſtoniſhing bravery and perſeverance, he obliged them to repair to their general rendezvous; and to retire out of the provinces over the *Bierbo-*

keer hills; from whence they ſoon took their departure for *Sittarah*, to render an account of their expedition—leaving many of their brethren behind them in the hands of *Aliverdi*, who had been taken priſoners in different actions. Amongſt the priſoners, was an officer of diſtinction, character, and authority, named *Seſſarow*, of whom we ſhall again have occaſion to make mention.

The uſurper had hardly time to breathe and form ſome hopes of receſs, and eaſe to himſelf; and tranquillity to his harraſſed and deſolate country; when he was again alarmed by advices from *Oriſſa*, that another army of *Mahrattors* had entered the provinces by the way of *Cuttack*, commanded by *Ragojee*: and to compleat his diſtreſs, and put his fortitude to the utmoſt proof, he ſhortly after received intelligence by expreſs from *Hodjee*, that a third army of *Mahrattors* had entered by the ſide of *Patna* commanded by *Ballerow*, and had already penetrated within a day or two's march of *Siclygully*. Theſe Generals led each an army of 60,000 horſe; the firſt had been diſpatched from *Sittarah*, to enforce the orders before given to *Boſchar Pundit*, and to ſupport him in the execution of them: the latter, marched out later from

the

the ſame city with inſtructions to join *Ragojee*, and avenge the murder of *Boſchar Pundit*; of which, advice had been received at *Sittarah*, by expreſſes ſent from *Bierbobeen* immediately after that event.

The uſurper thus beſet, and apprehenſive of being hemmed in by the two armies, and again cut off from his capital; directed his march with the utmoſt celerity to *Cutwah* bridge; which he gained; paſſed over his whole army; deſtroyed the bridge; and proceeded to his capital; with a mind greatly agitated and oppreſſed, by the reflection of being again forced to abandon his country to mercileſs enemies, whom he was not able to oppoſe with troops, enfeebled by continual labour and hardſhips.

The reader may remember of how great importance *the paſs of Siclygully* might have been to the unfortunate *Suffraaz Khan*, had it been properly put in a ſtate of defence. The uſurper well knew its conſequence; and therefore, ſoon after his poſſeſſing himſelf of the Soubahſhip, he ſtationed there a truſty officer with proved troops, and three pieces of cannon——depending that a vigorous ſtand would there be made againſt the invaders on the ſide of *Patna*; and their

en-

entrance into *Bengal* at leaſt retarded, if the *paſs* was as well defended as it was capable of: not ſuſpecting that there was a poſſibility of their obtaining an inlet by any other paſſage, unleſs they marched far to the Weſtward by the *Pachet* road, and entered by *Bierbobeen*; as *Boſchar Pundit* had done the preceding year; flattering himſelf, ſhould they attempt it, that by ſo long a march they would not be able to reach the province before the annual rains ſet in: but herein his foreſight failed him.

Ballajee Row, more commonly (though improperly) known by the name of *Ballerow*, on his arrival in the neighbourhood of *Boglypore*, received intelligence from thoſe who had joined him, and were declared enemies of the uſurper's houſe, that by his attempting to force the paſs of *Siclygully* he would hazard the loſs of a multitude of his men; and probably in the end be obliged to relinquiſh the deſign with diſgrace to his arms.——The *Pachet road* was propoſed, but he declined hearkening to it, urging "that thereby he ſhould loſe his "harveſt of plunder for that year; all "which would be appropriated by his "friend *Ragojee* to *fatten* himſelf and fol- "lowers; whilſt *he* and *his* people would "be

" be left to *ſtarve* on the *Padjee* (paltry) " contributions, he had been able to raiſe in " *Bahar*."

Whilſt he was under this difficulty, the evil genius of the uſurper (and of unhappy *Bengal)* dictated a meaſure, that extricated him out of it without danger to himſelf or followers. He ſent for ſome of the petty Rajahs from the neighbouring *Colgong* hills; and queſtioning them concerning a paſſage through the hills to *Bengal*, he offered them a large reward if any of them would ſupply him with guides to anſwer that purpoſe. The Rajahs, to a man, were well enough diſpoſed to comply with his wiſhes; for the uſurper's treacherous conduct, during the firſt ſix years of his government of *Bahar*, had rendered his name as hateful as dreadful to them all: yet none of them had knowledge enough of the three ranges of mountains that ſeparated *Bahar* from *Bengal*, to engage in ſo hazardous an undertaking.

The enquiry and reward being, however, bruited abroad, it came to the ears of an old peaſant an inhabitant of *Colgong* hills. This man came to the *Maharattor* camp, and deſired to be introduced to the preſence

of

of the General ; which having obtained, he boldly undertook, on the forfeiture of his head, to guide his army through ſecret paſſes into *Bengal*, for a reward of one Lac of Rupees, paid down to his family.

The General taking two of the Rajahs aſide, to whom the peaſant was known ; and enquiring of them touching the character of the man ; and what degree of credit might be given to his veracity and knowledge; he received ſuch encouragement that he no longer doubted ; and accordingly paid down the money, and iſſued his orders for marching the next day.

The guide, with faithfulneſs and dexterity, led the whole *Mabarattor* army ; at firſt Weſtward, a point or two Southerly ; until he found a *paſs*, which he ſought for about the center of the range of the *Colgong* hills. This paſs being found, it was his mark for the remainder of the expedition ; and he carried them through it by very practicable roads with much facility, until the mouth of it opened upon the level country between the *Colgong* and *Telliagurry* hills. From hence his courſe was due South, which led to the ſecond paſs through the laſt-mentioned hills : this paſs he accompliſhed with equal

equal eaſe; and from hence for two days he croſſed the level country, that lies between the *Telliagurry* and *Rajambol* mountains; ſhaping his courſe about South-Eaſt: at night he told the General he muſt halt until the morning ſun appeared.——In the morning he led them due South; and in the evening of the ſame day entered a paſs which guided them through the *Rajambol* mountains; and landed (if we may be allowed the expreſſion) the whole army, without the loſs either of man or horſe, in *Bengal*; on the plains, Weſt of the city of *Rajambol*, at a little town called *Banian Gang*. Having performed his obligation in ſix days, from leaving *Bogulpore* (more commonly by the Engliſh called *Boglypore)* through ways until this period deemed totally impaſſible; he was farther rewarded with handſome preſents by *Ballajee Row*, and departed to his home: his name was *Sittaram Roy*; a *Gentoo* of the *Raazpoot* tribe.—*Ballajee Row* reached *Banian Gang* the 13th of *March*, *Anno* 1742-3.

The uſurper, who had received expreſs intelligence of *Ballajee Row*'s departure from *Bogulpore*, and of the march of his army Weſtward; did not entertain the leaſt doubt but he was gone round the mountains

tains to enter *Bengal* by the *Pachet* or *Bierbobeen*; and was ſo much convinced of it, that he began to prepare again for taking the field; projecting that he might be able to bring the other army under *Ragojee* to an engagement, and defeat him before he could poſſibly be joined by *Ballajee Row*: but he had hardly formed this reſolution, when he was adviſed by a courier, from his Governor of *Rajambol*, "That *Ballajee Row* had en-"tered *Bengal* by paſſes through the moun-"tains, and was by that time, he believed, "joined with *Ragojee*."

This intelligence ſhocked the uſurper's preſent hopes, but not his courage and conſtancy: he laid aſide the project of repaſſing the *Cutwah* river——but determined not to coop himſelf up again in his capital; for the defence of which having made every neceſſary proviſion, he formed a ſtrong camp not far from the city; preſerving a ready communication with it.

The two *Mahar attor* Generals met in the *Burdomaan* country, the 17th *March*, 1742-3; and after a private conference, the following agreement was publiſhed, "that "an equal partition of the revenues and "plunder ſhould be made between the two

"armies,

“ armies, who neverthelefs were to act “ diftinctly under their refpective Generals “ and officers.” They then fettled the different routs of their detached fmall parties, and took intire poffeffion of the country. Then uniting the main bodies of their armies, they marched to *Cutwah*; conftructed a new bridge ; and paffed over with their whole force. Here they again feparated, and renewed the depredations every where, that *Bofchar Pundit* had begun the preceding year.

During thefe tranfactions, the ufurper kept himfelf within his entrenchments; yet he was not idle. Convinced he could not oppofe them by force, he had nothing left but to combat them with fraud and ftratagem ; weapons which he was as great a mafter of, as of arms. His firft movement was, to acquire a minute knowledge of the temper, genius, capacity, and characters of the two leaders of the enemy ; and how they affected each other. In all thefe particulars he obtained perfect fatisfaction, by the means of his prifoner *Seffarow* before mentioned ; whom he had diftinguifhed by every mark of favor and refpect from the time he firft fell into his hands ; forefeeing he might be of future ufe to him : and from the arrival of the two armies he had redoubled his careſſes; and of an enemy, had made him a faſt friend.

Divide and conquer, was one of the uſurper's favorite maxims in politics, as well as war. By the lights he had received from *Seſſarow*, he rightly judged the minds of the enemies Generals were fitly diſpoſed to take the impreſſion he intended to ſtamp on them——he learnt that *Ballajee Row*, was hot; inſolent; and withal avaritious to an extreme degree: that *Ragojee* was the braveſt ſoldier, but irritated and jealous at *Ballajee Row*'s being ſent equal in command with him, as he bore a ſuperior rank to the other. And more to flatter the uſurper's artful views, he was informed that already there ſubſiſted ſome miſunderſtandings between them and their reſpective troops; touching ſuſpicions of an unjuſt diviſion of their plunder on both ſides.

With theſe materials he began to work; laboring to enlarge a breach that was not yet wide enough for an attack. His plan was; by every means to promote the growth of thoſe ſeeds of diviſion and jealouſy which had already taken root amongſt them: to this end, he directed ſome capable emiſ-

ſaries

ſaries (fully inſtructed) to deſert to both armies; theſe executed his purpoſes ſo well, that they produced the effect he wiſhed: they prepoſſeſſed the enemy againſt themſelves; who accuſed each other of illicit practices in the diviſion both of the revenues and plunder; and the ſpies were ſo well prepared, that they produced proofs and vouchers of many inſtances of what they inſinuated (on both ſides) that would not admit of contradiction. This occaſioned mutual heats and animoſities between the two armies, and an open rupture ſoon followed; each reſolving to act in future on a ſeparate and independant footing. The uſurper ſeized this favorable occaſion; and knowing *Seſſarow* had an influence over *Ballajee Row*, (to whom he was related) he employed him to negociate, in the moſt ſecret manner, a ſeparate treaty of peace with that General.

Seſſarow exerted his power with ſuch ſucceſs, that he ſoon diſpoſed his relation to receive favorable impreſſions of the uſurper, and readily to hearken to a peace with him. To this he was the more eaſily induced, as thereby he indulged his ruling paſſion in the hopes of making his own advantage of the Uſurper, without the participation of his rival *Ragojee*.

The preliminaries of this treaty were ſoon adjuſted, " the uſurper was to cede " to *Ballajee Row* alone, the *Chout* of two " years revenues; and *Ballajee Row* engaged " on his part, to join the Uſurper with his " force, and aſſiſt him in driving *Ragojee* " and his army out of the provinces." It was further agreed, that to keep up the appearance of enmity and deceive *Ragojee*; *Ballajee Row*'s army ſhould advance nearer to the Uſurper's camp,—and make a ſhew of attacking it: this movement was not only made to amuſe *Ragojee*, but alſo to facilitate a perſonal conference between the Uſurper and the General; which was to take place on the thirtieth of *March* 1743, near *Plaſſey*.

On the twenty-ninth of *March*, the uſurper quitted his camp, and directed his march towards *Plaſſey*. He was not far advanced, before his ſpies brought him intelligence, that *Ragojee*'s army was in motion, as well as *Ballajee Row*'s: this raiſed a ſuſpicion in *Aliverdi*, that the treaty was only aſſented to, to amuſe him, and draw him out of his camp: therefore he immediately retired to it again; and the treaty was retarded until the motions of the two armies were explained to him.

Seſſarow,

Seſſarow, deeply chagrined at ſuſpicions which reflected on his own *ſincerity*, engaged on the forfeiture of his head for *that* of his couſin; which engagement being ſupported by a ſolemn oath (the *Ganges)* on the part of *Ballajee Row*, *Aliverdi*'s doubts ſubſided; the treaty was reſumed; and the conference appointed on the third of *April*: but the place of meeting was changed to midway between *Plaſſey* and *Burwah*; a few miles nearer his camp and capital *.

On the ſecond of *April*, the uſurper again quitted his camp, and began his march; having draughted off a ſelect body of 10,000 horſe; commanded by *Muſtapha Khan*; that moved on his flank, to be an occaſional check on *Ragojee*.

On the third, the chiefs met at the appointed place, in a tent (previouſly examined by deputies from both parties) about two corſe diſtant from each of their armies.——The condition openly inſiſted upon by the *Maharattor* was, " that twenty-five lac of

* The cauſe that gave riſe to *Aliverdi*'s ſuſpicions, was this.——*Ragojee* having heard that *Ballajee Row* intended to attack *Aliverdi*'s camp, and judging the city would fall a prey to him if he ſucceeded, he put his army in motion, that he might be near at hand, to come in for a ſhare of the plunder.

 " rupees,

" rupees, for two years Chout of the reve-
" nues, ſhould be paid down in gold ;"——
to this the Uſurper replied, " that howſo-
" ever unreaſonable the demand was, con-
" ſidering they themſelves had collected
" *the whole* of the revenues and cuſtoms
" for the laſt two years ; yet, he would
" not make any objection, provided that
" *Ragojee* could be brought to ſign the
" treaty ; otherwiſe he could not ſubmit
" to it :" This unexpected propoſal was highly diſguſtful to *Ballajee Row*, and had well nigh broke off the treaty ; but by the interpoſition of *Seſſarow*, he was at laſt prevailed on to ſend the overture to *Ragojee* ; but not until he had been made eaſy by the promiſe of a private gratuity for himſelf.

Ragojee immediately returned for anſwer,
" that he would hearken to no terms of ac-
" commodation, unleſs the payment of the
" Chout in perpetuity, was eſtabliſhed to
" them ; as a preliminary article for treat-
" ing at all *."

When the meſſenger returned with this laconic reply, the treaty ſeemed for ſome

* This preliminary was dictated to him by *Mhir Hubbeeb*, who joined *Ragojee* as ſoon as he entered the province of *Bengall*.

time

time ſuſpended.—However, by the addreſs and mediation of *Seſſarow*, a ſeparate peace was at laſt concluded with *Ballajee Row*, on the following terms—" That the Uſurper " ſhall pay down two years Chout, eſtimat- " ed at twenty-two lac of rupees in gold ; " and that *Ballajee Row* ſhould either ſatisfy " *Ragojee*, or join the Uſurper to drive " *him* out of the country." To the performance of which they both ſolemnly engaged themſelves by the moſt obligatory oaths ; this done, and mutual compliments and preſents made, they parted.

The Uſurper with great punctuality performed his part of the treaty in two days ; and *Ballajee Row* ſo far regarded it, that he drew off his army ; repaſſed *Cutwah* river ; and retired to *Burdomaan*, followed by *Ragojee* ; who thought himſelf no match for the Uſurper on equal terms.

Ballajee Row recalled all his detached parties ; and making a dividend amongſt his troops of part of the Uſurper's contribution, according to their different ranks, he quitted *Bengall* ; and marched by way of *Bierboheen* to *Sittarah* ; leaving (in breach of his ſolemn oath) *Ragojee* to make the beſt terms he could for himſelf.

 This

This General made the most of his time; and immediately took possession of those parts of the country, which had been lately evacuated by *Bãllajee Row*'s flying parties. He sent *Mhîr Hubbeeb*, with the title and authority of General, to take possession of *Orissa*; who accordingly seated himself at *Cuttack*, where he ruled as sovereign of the province.

The Usurper, called upon by the universal clamour of the people, and distresses of his country, once more quitted his capital, crossed over *Cutwah* river; and marched in pursuit of *Ragojee*: in which chace he was employed all the remaining part of *April*, and until the middle of *May*; without being able, by any art or stratagem, to bring him to a general action. And the rains setting in earlier than usual this year, and the roads becoming impassable, both armies were obliged to go into quarters, about the twentieth of *May*. At the close of this campaign the enemy remained in quiet possession of *Orissa*; and of all the country on the Western shore of the *Hougley* river; from *Ballasore*, to within a few miles of *Tanna*'s *Fort*, near the *English* settlement of *Fort William* *.

* *Aliverdi* retired with his army to *Morshadabad*, and *Ragojee* with his main body to *Beirboon* during the rains.

Though

Though the treaty of peace with *Ballajee Row* anſwered a preſent purpoſe, and relieved the Uſurper from the more immediate danger which threatened himſelf, his capital and family; yet it afforded no relief to the provinces. The partial execution of the treaty on the part of the *Mahurattor*, he could not be much ſurpriſed at; as himſelf had ſet them an example of perfidy and treachery.

Every evil attending deſtructive war, was felt by this unhappy country in the moſt eminent degree. A ſcarcity of grain in all parts; the wages of labor greatly enhanced; trade; foreign and inland, laboring under every diſadvantage and oppreſſion: ——and although during the receſſes of the enemy, from *June* to *October*, the manufactures of this opulent kingdom raiſed their drooping heads, yet the duration of their reprieves from danger was ſo ſhort, that every ſpecies of cloth at the *Arungs* was haſtily, and conſequently badly fabricated; though immenſely raiſed in its price; and from theſe cauſes came into diſrepute at all the foreign markets; particularly at the Weſtern ports of *Juddah*, *Mocha*, and *Buſſorah*.

The trade of the *Europeans* became greatly embarraſſed and injured; their effects were often plundered by the enemy; and theſe grievances were much heightened by oppreſſive exactions of the Uſurper. But in this they were not ſingular; for the whole of the people who ſtill remained within the reach of his graſp, ſuffered equally in this reſpect: even *Juggaat Seet*'s houſe, which ſo eminently promoted his uſurpation, was often fleeced; to the malicious joy of all, who were friends to *Soujah Khan*'s family.

For theſe oppreſſive meaſures the Uſurper had nothing to plead in extenuation, but *the neceſſities of his ſituation*: and in truth, had he not been the ungrateful traytor he was, they were ſuch, as would have merited the deepeſt commiſeration: for although by his uſurpation he became poſſeſſed of the treaſures of the three laſt Soubahs, yet ſo immenſe were his continual expences and diſburſements, that little of them remained; it being pretty well known, that he, notwithſtanding what has been ſaid of the treaty with *Ballajee Row*, did not buy the abſence and retreat of that General, for a ſum leſs than five *korore* of rupees*; although the twenty-two lac, for two years Chout only, were ſpeciouſly publiſhed to the world; to

* *Five Million Sterling.*

ſave

ſave the credit of the Uſurper, and to afford an opportunity to the *Mabarattor* of ſecreting from his followers all above that ſum; which he appropriated to his own uſe; beſides the lion's ſhare of the twenty-two lac: therefore he was well enabled at his departure to preſent to *Jeyndî Amet Khan*, *Hodjee*'s ſecond ſon, a ſingle compleat dreſs (for Seerpah) valued at two lac of rupees.

In *October* 1743, the next campaign opened; when the Uſurper again took the field: and *Ragojee* deſcending from the heights of *Bierboheen*, aſſembled his forces about *Burdwan*.—The ſucceeding months exhibited the ſame ſcenes of marches, countermarches, retreats and ſkirmiſhes, with various ſucceſs; but with uniform miſery to the people; who now for the firſt time, began to be plundered, and cruelly treated; as well by the detached parties of the Uſurper, as of the enemy: the former aſſuming the dreſs and accoutrements of the *Mabarattors*, to cover and conceal their villanies. *Anno* 1743.

In *March* 1744, theſe invaders entered the provinces in freſh ſhoals, by *Cuttack*, *Bierboheen* and *Patna*, excited by the immenſe booty carried off by their brethren, the two preceding years—and thus this miſerable *Anno* 1743-4.

ſerable country fell annually a prey to the depredations of the *Maharatters*, under various leaders, for the ſix ſucceeding years; receiving no effectual check, but from the ſucceſſion of the uſual rainy ſeaſons. During theſe intermediate ſpaces the country was left to fatten, that it might again be worth devouring. In the mean while, the Uſurper ſuſtained himſelf with amazing conſtancy, intrepidity and addreſs; though often reduced to the deepeſt diſtreſſes; parts of his capital being frequently attacked and plundered.

In the latter part of the year 1744, by indefatigable and ſudden marches he attacked and beat up all the quarters of the enemy; and obliged them to retire much ſooner than uſual. *Oriſſa* only remaining in their poſſeſſion; early in *December* 1744, he marched to that province; where with expedition hardly to be conceived, he retook *Cuttack*, and recovered the province; obliging the enemy to retreat to the hills. Then leaving forces for the defence of it, he returned, and arrived at the capital, the beginning of *February* 1744-5; crowned with laurels; and received with wonder. Here, revolving in his mind the confuſion of affairs in the province of *Bahar* and city of *Patna*; and

its

its importance to him, as being one of the enemies keys into his country; and determining to have a Governor there, whoſe courage, capacity and integrity he might repoſe a perfect confidence in, he fixed upon his nephew *Jeyndee Amet Khan* for this poſt of truſt, who poſſeſſed theſe qualities in a very high degree. He ſoon after ſet out for his government, eſcorted by a ſtrong body of horſe.

We ſhall omit entering more minutely into the particular occurrences of theſe annual invaſions, which would only exhibit an irkſome detail of murders, oppreſſions, and diſtreſſes, ſimilar to thoſe already recited: but as we cannot help viewing this Uſurper in an extraordinary light, we ſhould be inexcuſable in neglecting to lay before the public and poſterity thoſe ſtriking events, which were intereſting in themſelves; and which more ſtrongly mark the character and genius of this great, though wicked man, in the courſe of a deſtructive eight years war. With this intent only we again reſume our narrative from the cloſe of the year 1745; a period which gave birth to an *incident*, that eventually proved not only the deſtruction of his hither-

to

to favorite General; but alſo that of his brother and nephew.

It was, at the time juſt mentioned above, that the Uſurper firſt began to entertain ſuſpicions and jealouſies of the great reputation and power of *Muſtapha Khan*; who had, by his maſter's liberality and other means, at different times acquired great wealth; which he profuſely beſtowed on the ſoldiery, but chiefly on the *Patans*; thereby gaining a dangerous popularity, that bore too much the appearance of ambitious views. Whether he really had any deſigns againſt his maſter is not known; but his being the idol of the army was cauſe ſufficient to make him obnoxious; in a government where no ſubject can with ſafety to himſelf, or to his prince, be poſſeſſed of a ſuperior degree of power or renown.

The Uſurper had received intelligence from his brother *Hodjee*, that *Muſtapha Khan* was forming deſigns to his prejudice; and that he had actually concerted meaſures with the *Maharattors*, for cutting him off the enſuing year; and placing himſelf in the government.

Whether this intelligence had truth for it's foundation, or was only afterwards deviſed

viſed to cover the ſtep, that was premeditated againſt *Muſtapha Khan*, is uncertain. *Hodjee*, however, had the addreſs to produce vouchers for his ſuſpicions that approached to facts; and theſe acquiring weight from the brother's apprehenſions of that General's known talents, reputation, and popularity; it was reſolved at all events that he ſhould be aſſaſſinated the next time he appeared at court: aſſaſſins were accordingly provided, and ſtationed for his reception.

But *Muſtapha Khan* being generally beloved, the deſign againſt him could not be ſo ſecretly conducted, as to prevent his receiving hints to provide for his ſafety; and though theſe were imperfect, they were yet ſufficiently alarming to urge his immediate departure from the city, with 3000 *Patan* horſe. In about twelve hours after, he was followed by *Sumſeer Khan*, a *Patan* General next in command to him, with about 2000 more of their country-men. The whole being joined, by rapid marches, they arrived at *Siclygully*, before any ſuſpicion or intelligence of a breach between them and the Uſurper had reached the commander of that *paſs*; and by a well feigned ſtory of their being diſpatched to

join

join and re-inforce *Jeyndee Amet Khan*, they were permitted to advance into *Bahar* without interruption; intending to paſs through that province into the *Patan* country.

So great a defection of his beſt troops, with two officers of ſuch reputation at their head, ſtruck the Uſurper with the deepeſt apprehenſions, and this on a double ſcore. He had the greateſt cauſe to dread a union between the *Maharattors* and *Muſtapha Khan*; and by the ſecret flight of that General, he became convinced that ſome traytors were about his perſon: but ſtill himſelf, under every exigency and difficulty, he loſt not a moment—by large preſents, and larger promiſes, he ſecured the fidelity of the remaining *Patans*——ſent expreſs upon expreſs to his nephew *Jeyndî Amet Khan*, informing him of this untoward event, with orders "to take the field with what troops "he could get together, and endeavour to "intercept the fugitive *Patans*—and that "himſelf would go in purſuit of them, "and probably they might be hemmed in "between them."

The Uſurper immediately put himſelf at the head of a ſtrong body of forces, who

were

were beſt attached to his perſon and government; and with the greateſt expedition arrived at *Siclygully*; where he only ſtayed to ſtrike off the head of that commander, who had ſuffered the *Patans* to paſs his poſt.

Had the unfortunate *Muſtapha Khan* made the ſame expedition from the paſs of *Siclygully*, as he did to it; he would, in all human probability, have eluded the purſuit, and paſſed through *Bahar* before he could poſſibly have been intercepted by *Jeyndî Amet Khan*, or overtaken by the Uſurper. But for a particular reaſon, to be hereafter mentioned; and not ſuſpecting he was purſued, he proceeded through *Bahar* by ſuch ſlow marches, that the Uſurper came up with him between *Monghîr* and *Patna*; and ſent a meſſenger to him with offers of pardon, to himſelf and followers; if they would ſubmit, and embrace again his ſervice.

Muſtapha Khan, diſdaining all terms of accommodation, returned the Uſurper's meſſenger, with a brave defiance to him; and receiving intelligence at the ſame time, that *Jeyndî Amet* was within a few hours march of him, he thought it moſt adviſeable to face

face about, and fight the Usurper first; having learnt his troops were very little superior in number to his own; therefore without hesitation he distributed the necessary orders, and gave the signal for battle.

The conflict was bloody, but of no long duration. Valour and resentment took full possession of the soul of *Mustapha Khan*, and left no place for prudence or precaution: fired with the hope of executing his vengeance on the Usurper, he thought all else unworthy his sword; and attempting with too much impetuosity to penetrate to that part where *Aliverdî* fought, and not being well supported, he was soon surrounded, overpowered and slain—his head was separated from his body, and elevated upon a spear——his death being known to the *Patans*, *Sumseer Khan*, with those that survived the battle, made a speedy flight; and taking a rout different from that, by which *Jeyndî Amet Khan* was advancing, they escaped out of the province; notwithstanding the eager pursuit that was made after them.

The Usurper returned to his capital more dreaded, but less beloved by the people, for this last stroke of his policy. The jealousy, and (generally believed) unjust motives, for aſſaſſinating the *Patan* General were now blazed abroad; and the Uſurper became the object of deteſtation to ſome of his beſt friends, who drew a concluſion (from this act of baſe ingratitude to the man, who had ſo often preſerved his life and government)—very unfavorable, and alarming to themſelves; as the merits of their greateſt ſervices, might on the ſlighteſt ſuſpicions or fear, in the cowardly breaſt of *Hodjee*, only draw on their own deſtruction.

Hodjee, who had accompanied his brother in this expedition againſt *Muſtapha Khan*, advanced with the head of *the General*, to meet his ſon *Jeyndî Amet Khan*. With him he returned to *Patna*; and after beſtowing many indignities upon the head of that brave man, whoſe face he could not have beheld the day before, without ſinking into abject fear and terror; he had now the coward bravery, to order it to be carried in triumph three times round the city;——unworthy and indecent inſults! from which the remembrance of his former ſignal ſervices ſhould have defended his ſenſeleſs remains.——*Juſtice* ſeemed to intereſt herſelf in avenging the death of this gallant man, by favoring in an extraordinary manner the eſcape of her deſtined inſtrument

Sumſeer Khan: and the brave *Jeyndî Amet Khan*, at the ſight of the barbarous inſults exercifed by his father, could not refrain from tears; for great friendſhip ſubſiſted between him and the deceaſed; and his memory was dear to him.

We will leave *Hodjee* on his return to *Morſhadabad*; exulting for a ſhort time over the ſucceſs of his treacherous machinations; and advert to *Sumſeer Khan*.

This *Patan* General arriving ſafe with his few followers in their own country, began immediately to levy troops; and with ſuch ſucceſs, that in the year 1747, he was enabled to advanced towards *Patna*, at the head of 8000 choice horſe.

Here it is neceſſary to advertiſe the reader, that the two *Patan* Generals on their ſudden retreat from the city of *Morſhadabad*, had opened a correſpondence with *Mhîr Hubbeeb*, informing him "that they ſhould "return the next year, to attempt the cap-"ture and plunder of *Patna*; then march "by the hills and join the *Maharattor* "army; and with their united force at-"tack the Uſurper; declaring themſelves "juſtly abſolved from all allegiance to *the* "*aſſaſſin*."

" *assassin.*" *Mhîr Hubbeeb* improved upon this plan and advised " to encounter *Hodjee* " and the Usurper with their own weapons, " *craft* and *treachery*; for that, by address " and management, and a well feigned con-" trition for their former conduct, and a " fresh tender of their troops, they might " easily obtain an interview with the Nabob " of *Patna*; at which they should cut him " off: a circumstance that would much fa-" cilitate the taking and plundering that city " (which seemed to be their principal ob-" ject) as such an event must necessarily " cause the greatest confusion and conster-" nation in the place."

It was this intercourse of letters, that proved fatal to *Mustapha Khan*; by retarding his escape through *Bahar*, as already mentioned—but the counsel of *Mhîr Hubbeeb* was not lost upon *Sumseer Khan*; who was a man, possessed of every requisite, for carrying it into effectual execution. He was brave; artful; beloved and highly esteemed by his officers and soldiers; who, to a man, were united to him in a solemn vow, to take an exemplary revenge for the death and indignities of their late lamented commander; or perish in the attempt.

November 1747. With this determined view, *Sumſeer Khan* began his march; and being arrived within a ſew hours of *Patna*, on the oppoſite ſhore of the river, he diſpatched a letter to *Jeyndî Amet Khan*, couched in the following terms, "that his heart had felt the "deepeſt compunction for his paſt conduct, "to which he had been inſtigated by the "raſh counſels of his late commanding of-"ficer; that he appealed to *Jeyndî Amet* "himſelf, to witneſs for the approved fidelity "he had always ſhown for the ſervice and "intereſt of the Soubah his uncle; that he "had now raiſed a faithful and tried body "of officers and troops; who, with him, "were ready to devote their lives to his "commands, againſt the common enemies "of his houſe and country: hoping he "ſhould obtain permiſſion to viſit him; and "in a perſonal conference, give him more "convincing proofs of his attachment and "ſubmiſſion."

Jeyndî Amet Khan immediately communicated the contents of this letter to his father *Hodjee*, who was very lately arrived at *Patna*; brought thither by ſome informations the brothers had received of the concerted ſcheme between *Sumſeer Khan* and *Mhîr Hubbeeb*, for the plunder of that capi-

tal—

tal—*Hodjee*, without a moment's hesitation, ordered his son to encourage *Sumseer Khan*'s visit, and cut him off; telling him, he himself would direct the means.

Jeyndi Amet Khan, much averse to obey these orders, determined to wait those of his uncle to whom he wrote, and transmitted a copy of *Sumseer Khan*'s letter; and in the mean time he returned in civil terms a reply to the *Patan* General, telling him "he "had forwarded the purport of his request "to the Soubah, but that he could not give "any conclusive answer thereto, before the "Soubah's pleasure was known."——This soon reached him, in these few, but peremptory words, "Regarding the business "between us and *Sumseer Khan*, follow the "orders of your father."

Hodjee directed *Jeyndi Amet Khan* to write to the *Patan* General, "that he should "with pleasure receive his visits, and re"joice to embrace him; as the Soubah had "readily accepted the tender of his services, "and wished his speedy march to *Morshada"bad*."——To which purport the Usurper had likewise wrote to him in pressing terms; thereby intending to lull him into the greater security.

We have already hinted the method propoſed by *Mhîr Hubbeeb* to the two *Patan* Generals, for taking off the Nabob of *Patna*, and plundering the city. The intelligence the brothers had received extended only to the latter part of their ſcheme; of the intended aſſaſſination of the Nabob they had not the leaſt conception.——*Hodjee's* counter-plot for the murder of *Sumſeer Khan*, was concerted in manner following. A day was appointed for the General's viſit to *Jeyndî Amet Khan*, on a plain a ſmall diſtance North of the city; where a ſumptuous tent was prepared for his reception; in the floor of which a mine was ſunk, whoſe train extended ſome diſtance from the tent. The ſignal for putting fire to the train, was *Jeyndî Amet Khan's* withdrawing a certain ſpace from the tent.——Every circumſtance of which was betrayed to *Sumſeer Khan*, by a *Patan* in the ſervice and confidence of *Hodjee*.

On the receipt of the Uſurper's and the Nabob's letters, *Sumſeer Khan* paſſed the
May river with his troops, about two miles to the
1747. Northward of the city; and being advanced, on the day appointed, within a furlong of the tent; he received a polite meſſage from the Nabob, requeſting, "that he would "favor

“ favor him in ordering his troops to halt; “ that they might not in their conference “ be incommoded by the duſt; for that he “ himſelf was only attended by fifty fol- “ lowers.”——This requeſt was inſtantly complied with, and the *Patan* General proceeded to the tent with a few ſelected attendants only; all of whom were provided with armour under their coats.

They met in mutual embraces, and with the moſt affectionate compliments; theſe over they ſeated themſelves, and began to confer upon the operations of the war, againſt the common enemy the *Maharattors.*——After about an hour's diſcourſe, a ſervant came and whiſpered the Nabob, who ſoon after aroſe, telling the General “ that he was juſt going to give ſome ne- “ ceſſary orders for his reception and en- “ tertainment in the city, and ſhould at- “ tend him again in a few minutes.”—— When he had got half way to the door of the tent, *Sumſeer Khan* and his attendants drew their ſcymitars, fell upon *Jeyndî Amet Khan*, killed him, and all that were in the tent, before they had time to make any reſiſtance: ſome inſtantly flew to the head of the train, to which they were perfectly inſtructed, and prevented fire being put to

 it;

it; for on the alarm, thoſe who were on the outſide of the tent, and thereby eſcaped the ſlaughter, fled with all ſpeed to the city.

Sumſeer Khan made a ſignal for his troops to advance; and mounting his horſe gained the city almoſt as ſoon as the fugitives, and entered it ſword in hand with his ſoldiers; before *Hodjee Hamet* had received the leaſt intelligence of the unhappy fate of his beloved ſon.

He proceeded immediately to the palace, where, with little reſiſtance, he took *Hodjee Hamet* priſoner, at the very moment he was (in diſguiſe) making his eſcape; and after ſecuring him under a ſtrong guard, he went in ſearch of the principal *treaſures* of the city, (to which he was minutely directed by his ſpies) theſe he depoſited in the palace, and gave up the town to be plundered by the ſoldiers; who, for the ſpace of three days, committed every ravage and outrage that revenge and avarice, backed by uncontrolled power, could meditate and execute; except againſt the Engliſh, French, and Dutch factories; which alone remained exempt from ruin and unmoleſted.

Hodjee

Hodjee Hamet, after ſuffering the heavieſt reproaches and revilings from *Sumſeer Khan*, for his baſe ingratitude, treachery, and cruelty to *Muſtapha Khan*; and after undergoing a hundred and one laſhes from the ſevere diſcipline of the Khorah, was by order of the general ſet on an aſs, with his legs tied under the belly of the animal; and his face painted half black, half white; and thus led round the city, the ſame route himſelf had appointed for the head of the unfortunate *Muſtapha Khan*.—Returning from this diſgraceful progreſs, the diſcipline of the Khorah was again inflicted on him; not only as a puniſhment, but with a view to extort from him a confeſſion and diſcovery of a large ſum of gold and diamonds; which, it was ſaid, he had buried or otherwiſe ſecreted;——but he bore the laſh with amazing conſtancy; and made not the diſcovery that was aimed at.——After this he was chained to the leg of an elephant,—to that very elephant, on which the head of *Muſtapha Khan* was expoſed and elevated. *Sumſeer Khan* had doomed him to a cruel and lingering death; but one of his guards, touched with his great age; the high dignity he had born; his cruel ſufferings; and heavy lamentations for his murdered ſon; conveyed, in pity to him, a doſe

of

of poiſon ; which he greedily ſwallowed and put an end to his miſerable being.

Sumſeer Khan, after this exemplary vengeance, made a ſhort ſtay at *Patna*, and retired to his country with an immenſe booty; but without paying any further regard, at leaſt for the preſent, to the engagements that ſubſiſted between him and *Mhîr Hubbeeb*.

The fates of *Hodjee Hamet* and *Jeyndî Hamet Khan*, met a very different regard from the world; the latter being as much lamented, as the memory of his father was deteſted. But it may be very eaſily conceived that the loſs of both proved a heavy ſtroke of Affliction to the Uſurper ; who now became as eminently wretched as he was great. His grief on the arrival of the news was ſuch, that it was with the greateſt difficulty he was prevented following them.—However ; cool reflection ſoon took place; and his uſual fortitude ſurmounted, in a few days, the firſt violent impreſſions of his irreparable misfortune; and obliged him to attend the concerns of his government; to which he was rouſed and ſtimulated by the ſpirited, wiſe and affectionate repreſentations of his *Begum* ——A woman whoſe wiſdom, magnanimity, benevolence, and every amiable

able quality, reflected high honour on her sex and station. She much influenced the Usurper's councils, and was ever consulted by him in every material movement in the state; except when sanguinary and treacherous measures were judged necessary; which he knew she would oppose, as she ever condemned them when perpetrated howsoever successful,——predicting always that such politics would end in the ruin of his family.

Though the Usurper's critical situation called him to action; yet the death of his nephew ever after remained a heavy pressure upon his heart. He greatly loved him, and had designed him his successor in the government of the Soubahship, in preference to *Hodjee*'s eldest son; who then bore the title of the Emperor's Dewan, (to which he had just as much right as his uncle had to that of Soubah.) But this design being blasted by the untimely decease of *Jeyndî Amet*; and that occasioned by the pernicious policy of his brother and himself: the only amends in his power to make to the manes of his murdered nephew was, to transfer the affection he ever bore him, to *his* eldest son *Mhîrza Mahommed*; whom he immediately adopted as his own: and this

 youth

youth was, from that period, looked upon as his ſucceſſor.

October 1747. Until the rains broke up in *October* 1747, the Uſurper remained unmoleſted; but now the *Maharattors* re-entered the province of *Bengal* by the *Bierboheen* hills; and *Sumſeer Khan* having ſafely lodged his *Patna* plunder returned and entered *Bahar*; at laſt remindful of his engagement to *Mhîr Hubbeeb*, and hoping by an union with the *Maharattors*, *to ſhare* at leaſt the plunder alſo of *Morſhadabad*.

The Uſurper had taken the field very early—and on the firſt advice that *Sumſeer Khan* had entered *Bahar*, he advanced towards him by rapid marches; thirſting to revenge his brother's and nephew's deaths; and depending that he ſhould be able to engage and defeat him before the *Maharattors* could poſſibly join him. Whilſt he was in this purſuit, the *Maharattors*, who did not think it eligible to riſque an action with the Uſurper until they had joined their new allies, were on full march to the ſettled rendezvous at *Bogolpore*; near which place the three armies arrived about the ſame time in the night. The Uſurper encamped, and ſent out his ſpies for intelligence. They ſoon returned and informed him he was encamped between the enemies armies; the *Patans* a corſe to the Northward of him; and the *Maharattors* about the ſame diſtance to the Southward.—This perilous ſituation would have ſtruck any but this brave Uſurper with alarm and terror: ſome of his general officers propoſed his taking the advantage of the night, and attempting a ſilent retreat to *Siclygully*; but he rejected this overture with high indignation.—He was perfectly acquainted with the different genius and diſpoſition of the enemies he had to encounter; and from this knowledge formed his reſolutions; the only reſource left him was inſtantly obvious to this conſummate general and ſoldier.

At midnight he held a council of war, of three or four of his principal officers only. To theſe he opened his deſigns, and directed them to iſſue orders for the troops to be ready to march, half an hour before day break; without ſtriking their tents——ſtrictly prohibiting they ſhould encumber themſelves with aught but their arms; for that his own, his officers, and ſoldiers baggage ſhould be left in the camp; for which he himſelf would be accountable to them.

—Theſe

——These orders distributed he went to rest.

Before day break the Usurper put himself at the head of his troops, and marched to attack the *Patans*; leaving his camp standing——he found them prepared to receive him, not doubting but their allies, whose situation they had learnt, would attack his rear.——A bloody engagement ensued, in which the Usurper might justly say, with another great usurper, "that he had many "times fought *for Empire*, but in this bat-"tle, *for Life*."—After an obstinate contest *Sumseer Khan* was slain and the *Patans* put to flight—instead of pursuing them, he immediately returned in good order to his camp; where, as he had foreseen, he found the *Maharattors* plundering it, confusedly dispersed, and regardless of the commands of their General or Officers:—In this situation the Usurper fell upon them, and after a great slaughter gave them a total defeat and rout. After these exploits he returned triumphantly to his capital.

Notwithstanding these glorious successes, he was incessantly harrassed by, and forced to be ever in the field against the *Maharat-*

tors,

tors, until the year 1750; when he made a lasting peace with them on the terms recited in the "Short ſketch of the hiſtory of *Ben-* "*gal,*" before mentioned; tó which we beg leave to refer. There the reader may if he pleaſes follow this great wicked man, "*through the more pleaſing ſcenes of domeſtic* "*life, and public tranquillity.*" We ſhall content ourſelves in cloſing this chapter, and ſecond general head, with a few circumſtances which happened in conſequence of his natural demiſe, *Anno* 1756.——It is pretty well known, and has been by us ſeverely felt, that he was ſucceeded by *Mhirza Mahommed* his adopted ſon and grandſon (who aſſumed the title of *Surajad Dowla)* in the government: that after he had quelled an oppoſition that was made to his ſucceſſion by part of his own family, he directed his arms againſt our ſettlements; took, and deſtroyed them.——The *cauſes* for that invaſion of property, have been faithfully inveſtigated and preſented to the public in a ſecond edition of "India Tracts," publiſhed *March* 1764.——This ſhort recapitulation would have had no place here, but to introduce a circumſtance not ſo well known as the foregoing.

When *Surajad Dowla* declared his reſolution to attack and drive the Engliſh out of of *Bengal*, he was oppoſed by the affectionate remonſtrances of the deceaſed *Aliverdi Khan*'s *Begum*, already mentioned——with every argument which love and maternal authority could deviſe, ſhe laboured to diſſwade him from his purpoſe; but laboured to no end: for though the young tyrant preſerved ſome reverence for her perſon, yet her influence was not great: but when ſhe found him deaf to her entreaties, ſhe had the courage to tell him, "She ſaw his own "fate was blended with, and waited on "the deſtruction he was aiming to accom-"pliſh againſt the Engliſh; and that if he "perſiſted, his raſhneſs and injuſtice would "not only be the cauſe of his own death, "but the total ruin of his family." Her wiſdom and foreſight was ſo great and extenſive, that it was commonly ſaid by the Uſurper, "He never knew her judgment or "predictions fail."

We hope to meet with pardon for doing honour to the character of this extraordinary woman; eſpecially as we thereby embrace a favourable opportunity of diſcharging the tribute of ſincere gratitude particularly due from us,—the author owing life and liberty to her humane and ſucceſsful interceſſion.

CHAP.

CHAP. III.

HAVING in the preceeding chapter ſhewn from what cauſes, and by what gradations the provinces of *Bengal* fell under the uſurpation of *Aliverdî Khan*; our plan leads us next to convey a ſummary account of their produce; the diviſion of their principals; diſtricts; and towns; with their ſituation reſpecting each other; and their commonly eſtimated diſtance from our principal ſettlement of *Calcutta*.

Geographers have diſtinguiſhed theſe provinces by the title of *the rich Kingdom of Bengal*; an epithet it highly merited when conſidered in its original ſtate of opulence and tranquillity; in which point of view we intend to exhibit it; for this prevalent reaſon only; that we think it perfectly capable of being re-inſtated and improved; a circumſtance well worthy our *preſent* knowledge and attention.

To form a juſt eſtimate of the value and importance of theſe provinces, we muſt conſider them at the period, when they were governed by the younger princes of the Blood Royal; that is, ſome years before *Jaffier Khan*'s Soubahſhip; for in his time they firſt began to decline and decreaſe in their worth; from cauſes already inveſtigated in our laſt general head.

From his demiſe, the country for a few years recovered, and began to flouriſh, until within two years of the deceaſe of *Sujah Khan*; when, by the rapacity of *Hodjee Hamet*, the Rajahs and Zemindars were again cruelly oppreſſed and plundered; and were thereby diſabled from making good their contracts to the government.——Soon after this period, commenced the uſurpation of *Aliverdî Khan*; that drew on the *Maharattor* invaſion; which overwhelmed the country in miſeries of every kind for the full ſpace of eight years.

The peace which the Uſurper made with theſe invaders, *Anno* 1750; ſeemed, for four or five years, to promiſe the reſtoration of vigour to this haraſſed country: but its ſhattered conſtitution was ſcarcely beginning to revive, when the raſh conduct of the

ſuc-

ſucceeding young tyrant reduced it again to eminent peril. A juſt vengeance and neceſſity drew the Engliſh arms againſt him and his country; which produced a revolution fatal to himſelf and family;—neceſſity again, produced a ſecond revolution;—— wantonneſs a third; and when we ſhall ſtop, time alone can diſcloſe.—A few individuals may benefit by this ſhifting ſyſtem; but total ruin to the trade of the provinces, and to the Company, muſt manifeſtly in the end be the conſequence of this continued warfare, if not timely prevented; notwithſtanding the flattering fallacious ſucceſs of our arms.

The foregoing ſhort recapitulation we thought neceſſary, to vindicate our concluſion; that no perfect judgment can be made of the value of this ineſtimable country from any period of time within the laſt forty years; during which ſpace, with few and ſhort interruptions, it has been involved in war, and labored under difficulties that have impaired it's very vitals. Thence, the neceſſity of our giving a picture of it in a permanent ſettled government; when the lands were permitted to yield their produce unmoleſted; when the manufactures and every branch of trade flouriſhed; and when the rents, revenues and cuſtoms reſulting from

 that

that happy ſtate, prove it to have been as valuable a ſpot as any upon this globe; if not the moſt ſo.

To this deſirable ſtate, we repeat, from our perfect knowledge and experience, it is capable of being reſtored under a *proper government*; if it was not, our preſent labors were vain; and could anſwer no end or purpoſe. What eſſential end and purpoſe they are calculated to obtain, we ſhall now venture to open; and as I have no motive to influence me but ſincere gratitude to my former employers, and true love for my country, I truſt my endeavours will meet with candour and thanks—at leaſt from the public, if not from that *reſpectable body of men*, for whoſe benefit they are more particularly intended.

Notwithſtanding the plauſible face of ſucceſs, our affairs in *Bengal* may wear at preſent by late advices from thence; it is as demonſtrable as any propoſition in Euclid, that they cannot produce the great and eſſential end aimed at, *viz.* a laſting peace and ſettled government; without which, the Company muſt ſink under the preſſure of a long expenſive war; which not only ſwallows up their new acquired revenues;

revenues; but impedes and ſhackles their trade in every inſtance, ſhape and form. In proſecution of this war, the heads of their ſervants abroad are turned and bewildered; and their mercantile buſineſs (which only can ſupport the Company in the end) muſt ſuffer under unavoidable neglects and abuſes. The gentlemen at home in the direction of affairs, muſt labor under heavy embarraſſements in conducting the two branches of war and trade; either of which would fully employ their whole time and attention.

A trading and a fighting company, is a two headed monſter in nature, that cannot exiſt long; as the expence and inexperience of the latter, muſt exceed, confound, and deſtroy every profit or advantage gained by the former.—New *temporary* victories, ſtimulate and puſh us on to graſp at new acquiſitions of territory; theſe call for a large increaſe of military force to defend them; and thus we ſhall go on, graſping and expending, until we cram our hands ſo full that they become cramped and numbed; and we ſhall be obliged to quit, and relinquiſh even that part, which we might have held faſt; if bounds had been ſet to our progreſs:

which (upon the present system) we now see is utterly impossible; therefore a total change in our politics becomes indispensably necessary.

The gentlemen in the direction must surely see this fatal tendency of their affairs, and must tremble at it——but where's the remedy they will say?—it has been already pointed out and no regard paid to it—possibly, though convinced, they want the public sanction to a step they may think so extraordinary——though every day they are taking steps more extraordinary, in supporting their servants in a war against the Mogul, his Vice-Roys, and subjects, which on the present plan must unavoidably prove the ruin of the company.—We have a considerable concern in this stock, and therefore claim a right to speak—when private remonstrances fail, public ones may acquire a due influence.

Why we should wantonly persist in a state of destructive war, with a Potentate, whose alliance is so materially necessary to us; when we have it so much in our power to make a useful friend of him and his successors; is a conduct that surpasses human under-

understanding; and yet that such has been our conduct for five years past is most certain.

Let us have done with this ringing changes upon Soubahs; there's no end to it. Let us boldly dare to be Soubah *ourselves*; our own terms have been more than once offered to us by the Emperor; why should we longer hesitate to accept them? We have not scrupled to seize and possess part of his territory with violence; surely it would be more conscientious, and more consistent with the laws of nature and nations, to hold the whole of these provinces under him, by his own appointment.—That this would be readily assented to on his part, if a proper overture came from us, is not to be doubted: the consideration of his own great and obvious advantages, and the necessities of his situation would leave him no room for choice.

We have already convinced him, we are able, when we have a mind to set our own ruin and the lives of our fellow subjects at nought, to hold this part of his country from him, in spite of his strongest efforts against us: nay, possibly we might retain it under our subjection for some short time at least;

 but

but the consequence to him, and us, is obvious: a wanton expence of blood and treasure; while the object we are contending for is daily more and more desolated by this contention; and, bye and bye, will not be worth the possession of either——for every movement that does not tend to a lasting and firm peace by advantaging both, is fruitless; and can have no permanent or salutary effect: and most sure it is, that the plan we have hitherto pursued, and are still pursuing, cannot accomplish that desirable issue.

It is true, we have seen our forces in the East, under the conduct of an able and active commander, drive the Mogul's Vice-Roys out of the provinces. It is also true, that we have seen a spirited conduct and bravery in the Mogul's troops, that ought justly to strike us with apprehension of future consequences. The *Russians* when first attacked by *Sweden*, did not possess a tenth part of the courage and discipline that these our enemies have now acquired; and yet the event is known to the world.——Let us reason upon very probable suppositions; and not rest in a too great and flattering security, at a time when we have the greatest cause to be alarmed.

Sup-

Suppoſe the Mogul's Vice-Roys ſhould, from experience, at laſt evidently ſee; that the only way to conquer us, and render our courage and diſcipline of none effect, is to avoid ever coming to a *general action* with us: with the great ſuperiority of numbers they will ever be able to bring into the field, they may by this precaution and dividing their army (which conſiſts chiefly of cavalry) into ſmall bodies; cut off our proviſions and forage; beat up our quarters; harraſs our handful of men without ceaſing; and finally deſtroy us without danger to themſelves——and is it improbable they ſhould at laſt adopt this conduct? we pronounce, no; it is moſt probable they will, as the only reſource left for them.

Let us again, ſuppoſe a rupture with *France*, whilſt we are engaged in this war with the Mogul; our preſidency of Fort *William*, and our other factories in a manner deſerted; and the chief ſtrength of all our ſettlements acting at the diſtance of eight or nine hundred miles from the center of our poſſeſſions.——We will not ſuppoſe a rupture with *France* near; but let it come when it will, it ſets at nought the article in the laſt treaty of peace, which gave us an excluſive right to *Bengal*; and therefore

 ought

ought to be attended to: for it is not to be imagined, that they will neglect so favourable an occasion of attacking a settlement, which constitutes, in the East, the very essence of our being; when they find it left defenceless by the absence of our troops.

In short, every consideration calls aloud for a period being put to this unprofitable, and precarious war, by some other plan of operations; and we assert none is so eligible, honourable, or practicable, as that we have now hinted at.—We have nibbled at these provinces for eight years; and notwithstanding an immense acquisition of territory and revenue, what benefit has resulted from our successes, to the company? are their dividends raised to the late standard of eight *per Cent?* no——it is impossible they should, whilst this destructive expensive contest exists---and shall we thus go on, nibbling and nibbling at the *bait*, until the trap falls and crushes us?---but to come more immediately to the point.

Permit us, Gentlemen, most humbly to advise, that express orders be sent without delay to your President and Governor of *Fort William*; to make the following overture of peace to the Mogul; viz. " That on con-
" dition

" dition of his appointing and investing (to " all intents and purposes) your Governor " for the time being, Soubah of the Pro- " vinces of *Bengal*, *Bahar*, and *Orissa*; you " will engage on your part, that the sti- " pulated sum of one khorore of rupees, " shall be annually paid into the royal trea- " sury; free of all deductions."

As this sum nearly doubles the stipulation made by the usurper *Aliverdî Khan*, with the Vizir *Munsoor Ali Khan*, *Anno* 1750, (a tythe of which by the bye was never paid) and we venture to say, *re-doubles in one year*, any advantages the Emperors have received from the revenues of these provinces, for the space *of forty years last past*; we cannot entertain a doubt of his most readily acceding to the terms proposed; as thereby he would also secure a powerful ally, who could be occasionally of service to him on any emergency, in his government.

When we are invested with this sovereignty and empowered to display the Mogul's royal standard; the provinces will be easily governed and kept in subjection, at a less annual expence and force, than the Company are now from necessity loaded with——but suppose it double, the *stake* is amply sufficient, as we shall presently demonstrate.

Some

Some narrow minded people, ſtrangers to the nature of the country and government, will ſtart; and make the greatneſs of the object a bugbear to their hopes and wiſhes--- Was it poſſible, that the Company could unmoleſted enjoy what they have got, and purſue their trade without interruption; we ſhould be amongſt the firſt that might juſtly exclaim againſt their extending their views; ---but, that this was impracticable, we have long foreſeen and publicly declared;---and if we think at all, we muſt now be convinced there is no medium, or alternative, but this; that can be adopted with any appearance of ſecurity or permanency—— *aut Soubah, aut nullus*, muſt now be our motto.

We cannot enough applaud the ſeaſonable meaſure of ſending out Lord *Clive*, which we eſteem a happy event; notwithſtanding, what could be done upon the preſent plan of politics, has been done without him—— the weight of his Lordſhip's reputation and experience, in thoſe parts, will moſt eſſentially promote this our new plan: he is the beſt qualified to negociate it; the fitteſt to be firſt inveſted with that high power; and the moſt capable of fixing and leaving it upon a ſolid baſis.——That theſe are our

real

real ſentiments, flowing from a juſt regard to his Lordſhip's character, I think the public will not doubt; as they already know, we lie under no obligations to that quarter, that might excite our partiality.

We are very ſenſible, our rulers at home do not like to have the affairs of the Company, the ſubject of public diſquiſition. But as *they* and their affairs, are now truly become a very important national concern; and their own inteſtine quarrels have given a latitude to make their conduct the ſport of every pen; we think there needs the leſs apology for the liberty we now take; as one of our chief motives is, to extricate *them* from the difficulties, we imagine they muſt be plunged in at this period. And no drowning man will be angry at another, who ſtretches out a friendly hand to ſave him from ſinking?—The pointing out a meaſure to them that muſt, if it takes place, in a very ſhort ſpace, mount their ſtock in ſubſtantial real value to five hundred; will not hurt them or the proprietors.

But it may be aſked us, if theſe only are your motives, why not intimate the meaſure in private to our chairman or court of directors? Why not communicate it, and enforce

force it, at a quarterly general court? Why not call a general court *on special matters?* Why are our affairs and schemes to be canvassed by the public? Have patience, my friends, and we will answer these interrogatories by one prevalent reason that determines us, to adopt none of them.—*Private* intimations for *public good,* leave the *parties entrusted,* at large; and without public check, to concur with, or *reject* and lay aside, the means proposed; as caprice, want of comprehension, particular private views, or divided counsels, may chance to influence :---but when *publicly made, they* then become accountable *to the world.*——In assigning this reason, we must not be thought to insinuate any doubt, injurious to the honour and integrity of the present Chairman, or present court of Directors, whom, from the sincerity of our heart, we believe as much attached to the true interest of the *East India* Company, as any sett of gentlemen who ever sat at that board.

Our wish is, to promote the well being of the *East India* Company; and not intentionally to give offence to any; and if our proposed plan meets not the approbation and concurrence of those who will most benefit by the event, we can only lament

ment their loſs and our own.---It appears by a correſpondence laid before the public, laſt year, that we urged the neceſſity of *this meaſure* in the year 1760; Glorious! would have been the iſſue for the company, had it been then carried into execution; and happy for many unfortunate individuals, who ſince periſhed by a contrary ſyſtem of politics!---There would then have been no call or neceſſity for this Nabob-changing ſcheme; the provinces would have been eſtabliſhed in peace; and war, revolutions, murders, and maſſacres, without a being——however, from a thorough conviction we ſay, it is not now too late to regain the happy opportunity we then loſt: nay, ſubſequent events, rather encourage and afford a more favorable aſpect; as things may be accompliſhed now under leſs difficulties, than we ſhould at that period have had to encounter and ſtruggle with.---In this confidence we ſhall proceed, and by a rough ſketch of the produce of the revenues, ſhow the vaſt ſtake we throw for. If we win, the gain will be immenſe: if we fail in the attempt, we are but where we were; and at the worſt, ſhall have it in our power to reſume our *old Dog Trot* policy again.

— —

At

At *Natoor*, about ten days travel North-East of *Calcutta*, reſides the family of the moſt ancient and opulent of the *Hindoo* Princes of *Bengall*; *Rajah Rhaam Khaunt*; of the race of *Bramins*; who deceaſed in the year 1748, and was ſucceeded by his wife, a Princeſs named *Bowanny Rhaanee*; whoſe Dewan, or Miniſter, was *Diaram* of the *Teely* caſt, or Tribe. They poſſeſs a tract of country of about thirty-five days travel *; and under a ſettled government, their ſtipulated annual rents to the crown were ſeventy lac of *Sicca* rupees,——the real revenues, about one khorore and an half.

The chief towns of theſe diſtricts are *Malda*, *Hurrial*, *Seerpore*, *Balekooſhy*, and *Cogmarry*; all ſeparately famous for manufacturing the following ſpecies of piece goods, viz. for the *Europe* markets, coſſacs, elatches, hummums, chowtahs, ootally ſooſies, ſeerſuchers and raw-ſilk:——for the markets of *Buſſorah*, *Mocha*, *Judda*, *Pegu*,

* The *Gentoos* eſtimate diſtances by corſes, but more commonly by a day's journey, which they reckon five corſe, but as the corſe varies in different diſtricts, from one and a half to two and a half miles *Engliſh*, we take the medium days travel at ten *Engliſh* miles.

Acheen

Acheen and *Malacca*, the different ſorts of coſſa's, baftas, ſannooſe, mulmulls, tanjebs, ordinary kenchees, *&c. &c.*

This country produces alſo, copoſs, or *Bengal* cotton, with which the above ſortments of goods are in part manufactured; but the produce does not bear any proportion to the conſumption, ſo that they are indebted to foreign markets for this article; and chiefly to the port of *Surat.*

The towns of *Bowangunge*, *Siebgunge*, *Sorupgunge*, and *Jummaalgunge*, are all famous markets for grain; as their names imply *.

Contiguous to this laſt mentioned diſtrict, but ſtill more to the North-Eaſt, lie the lands of *Rajah Praunaut* of the Koyt, or Scribe Caſt. His diſtrict extends about fifty days travel; conſiſts moſtly of low-lands; and is in great part annually overflowed. His ſtipulated yearly payment is twenty lac; the real produce of his revenue, from ſixty to ſeventy---the chief products of his country are grain, oil, and ghee, (an article much uſed in *Indian* cookery) it likewiſe yields ſome ſpecies of piece goods and

* The meaning of *Gunge* being a grain market.

raw ſilk; alſo foole ſugar, lump jaggre, ginger, long pepper, and piplymol---articles that uſually compoſe the gruff cargoes of our outward bound ſhipping.

The principal towns of this diſtrict, are *Rungſore*, *Gooragat*; and *Santoſe Buddaal*, the capital reſidence of the head of this family: from theſe *Arungs*, the *Eaſt India* companies are ſupplied with ſannoos, mulmulls, tanjebs and raw-ſilk.

The great market of *Bugwan Gola* *, is ſupplied from this diſtrict, with the three important articles of grain, oil, and ghee:--- and now we have occaſion to mention this mart, it is not foreign to our purpoſe to dwell a little longer on it——it is ſituate on the *Ganges*, about a day and a half North from *Morſhadabad*; and two days South Eaſterly of *Rajambol*; and is the greateſt market for the above-mentioned articles in *Indoſtan*, or poſſibly in the known world. The cuſtoms on grain only, amount to three lac of rupees *per Annum*—all the cuſtoms and duties of *Bugwan Gola*, rank in the liſt of revenues, under the head of *Khoſs Mhol*, that is, duties which are kept in the government's hands; and not farmed out.

* *Gola* ſignifies a granary.

This

This place is defended on the land ſide by a ditch and palliſadoes; and is always, in troubleſome times, garriſoned by a thouſand horſe and a thouſand foot.——In the year 1743, it was four times attacked by the *Mabarattors*, under *Boſcbar Pundit* and *Alibeg*, who were as often repulſed—It is a place of ſuch importance to the Soubah, that the command of the garriſon is always beſtowed on the moſt experienced and truſt worthy officer he has in his ſervice: the whole of its revenues being uſually valued, in peaceable times, at thirty lac *per Annum*. In the beginning of the year 1750, it was again attacked by the *Mabarattors*; taken and plundered of an immenſe booty.

North-Weſt of *Fort William*, and about three days and a half diſtant, lie the lands of *Rojab Tilluck Chund*, extending twelve days travel. The ſtipulated rents of theſe lands are thirty-two lac *per Annum*; but their real produce and value, from eighty lac to one khorore. This is the principal of the three diſtricts, ceded in perpetuity to the company, by the treaty with *Coſſim Ali Khan*, in the year 1760.

The principal towns of this diſtrict are *Burdwan*, *Kirpy*, *Radnagore*, *Dewangunge*

 and

and *Ballikiſſagur*; theſe ſupply the *Eaſt India* companies with the following ſortments of piece goods, viz. doorcas, terrandams, cuttanies, ſooſies, ſoot romaals, gurras, ſeſterſoys, ſanton coupees, cherriderries, chilys, cuſtas and dooſoota's. The capital, *Burdwan*, may be properly called the center of the trade of the provinces. In tranquil times, this place afforded an annual large vend for the valuable ſtaples of lead, copper, broad cloth, tin, pepper, and tootanague. The *Puggiah* merchants from *Delhy* and *Agra*, reſorted yearly to this great mart; and would again, if peace was eſtabliſhed in the country:——they purchaſed the above ſtaples, either without money; or in barter for opium, tincal, ſalt petre and horſes.

This diſtrict produces raw-ſilk and coposs, ſufficient only for manufacturing their ſooſies, cuttanees and gurras.---The leſſer towns manufacture other inferior ſortments of cloth, as ſeerbunds, gollabunds, *&c.*——It produces grain, equal to the conſumption of the people only.

Burdumaan (the proper name of the diſtrict) is high; better peopled, and better cultivated than any part of the three provinces.

vinces. Bleſſings! that cauſed it every year, more particularly, to become a prey to the *Mabarattors*; as before recited.

The family of this Rajah farmed lands to the amount of four lac *per Annum*, contiguous to the bounds of *Calcutta*; and had a palace at *Beallab*, about ſeven miles South of it---the fort of *Buzbudjee*, on the *Ganges*, was alſo their property.

To the Weſt of *Burdwan*, ſomething Northerly, lie the lands belonging to the family of *Rajab Gopaul Sing*, of the *Raazpoot Bramin* tribe. They poſſeſs an extent of ſixteen days travel; this diſtrict produces an annual revenue of between thirty and forty lac; but from the happineſs of their ſituation, he is perhaps the moſt independant Rajah of *Indoſtan*; having it always in his power to overflow his country, and drown any enemy that comes againſt him: as happened at the beginning of *Soujah Khan*'s government; who ſent a ſtrong body of horſe to reduce him: theſe he ſuffered to advance far into his country; then opening the dams of the rivers he deſtroyed them to a man. This action diſcouraged any ſubſequent attempts to reduce him——but if the frontiers of the diſtrict were ſo inveſted, as to prevent the exit of the merchandize of his country, which might easily be done; he would be presently brought to obedience; and would be glad to compound for a tribute of twenty lac *per Annum*. As it is; he can hardly be said to acknowledge any allegiance to the Mogul or Soubah; some years deigning to send to him an acknowledgement, by way of salaamy (or present) of 15,000 rupees; sometimes 20,000; and some years not any thing at all; as he happens to be disposed.

But in truth, it would be almost cruelty to molest these happy people; for in this district, are the only vestiges of the beauty, purity, piety, regularity, equity and strictness of the ancient *Indostan* government. Here the property, as well as the liberty of the people, are inviolate. Here, no robberies are heard of, either private or public: the traveller, either with, or without merchandize, on his entering this district, becomes the immediate care of the government; which allots him guards without any expence, to conduct him from stage to stage: and these are accountable for the safety and accommodation of his person and effects.--- At the end of the first stage, he is delivered over, with certain benevolent formalities, to

the

the guards of the next; who after interrogating the traveller, as to the usage he had received in his journey, dismiss the first guard with a written certificate of their behaviour, and a receipt for the traveller and his effects: which certificate or receipt are returnable to the commanding officer of the first stage; who registers the same, and regularly reports it to the Rajah.

In this form, the traveller is passed through the country; and if he *only passes*, he is not suffered to be at any expence for food, accommodation, or carriage for his merchandize or baggage. But it is otherwise, if he is permitted to make any residence in one place above three days; unless occasioned by sickness, or any unavoidable accident.--- If any thing is lost in this district; for instance, a bag of money or other valuable; the person who finds it, hangs it upon the next tree, and gives notice to the nearest Chowkey or place of guard; the officer of which, orders immediate publication of the same by beat of tomtom, or drum.

There are in this precinct, no less than three hundred and sixty considerable Pagoda's or places of public worship; erected by this Rajah and his ancestors.——The worship of the cow is here carried to so

 great

great an extreme; that if that animal meets with a *violent* death, the city, or village, to which it belonged, goes into a general mourning and faſt, for three days; and all are obliged, from the Rajah to the meaneſt of the people, to remain on the ſpot, where they firſt heard the publication of the accident; and are employed, during that ſpace, in performing various expiations, as directed in the *Shaſtah*. But more of this under a ſubſequent general head.

Biſnapore, the capital, and chief reſidence of the Rajah, and which gives a name to the whole diſtrict, is alſo the chief ſeat of trade. The produce of the country conſiſt of ſhaal timbers (a wood equal in quality to the beſt of our oak) dammer lacca's, an inferior ſortment of raw-ſilk——and coposs and grain, ſufficient only for their conſumption: it is from this diſtrict that the *Eaſt India* Companies are chiefly ſupplied with the article of ſhell lacca.

North-Weſt of *Biſnapore*, contiguous lie the territories of *Buddeir Jamma Khan*, ſon and ſucceſſor to *Aſtoola Khan*, a Mogul, and Prince of *Bierbobeen*.——How this *Mahommedan* family, originally crept in among the *Hindoo Rajahs*, we never could learn

learn with any preciſion; but think it proceeded from it's importance to the Mogul government; as being the paſs into *Bengal*, from which moſt danger of invaders was to be apprehended; and therefore the Emperor judged it expedient to have the government of this paſs in the hands of a Mahommedan Prince: the conquered Rajahs not being deemed truſt worthy.

The lands formerly poſſeſſed by this family, equalled in extent thoſe of *Biſnapore*; and yielded nearly the ſame articles of merchandize, and about the ſame revenue: but as ſoon as *Aliverdî Khan* uſurped the government of the Soubahſhip, he diveſted this Rajah (for ſo he is commonly called) of a great part of his country, and otherways oppreſſed him; which he had afterwards cauſe to repent, as we have before ſhewn, but notwithſtanding that, he remained taxed at ten lac *per Annum*.

The fertile part of his country is in the center of the *Bierboheen* mountains. His chief reſidence is the fortreſs of *Nagur*; and his principal town of trade, is *Illumbuzar*; from whence the *Eaſt India* Companies uſually had the greateſt part of their gurras provided: but the *Maharattor* invaſion

ſion occaſioned, in a great meaſure, this branch of trade to be transferred to the town of *Cutwah*.

North Eaſt of *Calcutta*, diſtant about three days journey, lies *Kiſſnagur*; the fort and capital of *Rajah Kiſſen Chund*. He poſſeſſes a tract of country of about twelve days journey; and is taxed at nine Lac *per annum*; though his revenues exceed twenty five Lac. His principal towns are *Santipore*, *Nuddeah*, *Bouren*, &c. where mullmulls, coſſaes, and cotton yarn are manufactured for the Europe markets: the country produces copoſs and grain, but not ſufficient for exportation.

The revenues of the city of *Dacca* (once the capital of *Bengal*) at a low eſtimation, amount annually to two Khorore; proceding from cuſtoms and duties levied on cloths, grain, oil, ghee, beetlenut, chank-metals, ſalt, and tobacco, &c.

The foregoing inſtances of the value of the lands, in the province of *Bengal* only, held by the Rajahs, ſhall ſuffice; without our particulariſing thoſe held by the *Zemindars*, ſcattered through the province: ſome of whom are very conſiderable land-holders.

Theſe

These are generally taxed nearer the real value of their lands, than thoſe which are held by the Rajahs.

Time preſſes, and will not permit us to enter minutely into a detail of the other branches of the revenues of this opulent country, in times of ſettled peace; a bare mention of the principal remaining ſources will fully and amply juſtify the point we aim at, and ſhew the vaſt importance of the ſtake we are puſhing for.

Under this head are the revenues of the city of *Patna*, and thoſe of the province of *Bahar*—the government of *Purnea, a rich Nabobſhip*—the revenues of the capital of *Morſhadabad*; the city of *Rajahmbol*; the towns and diſtricts of *Coſſimbuzar, Cutwah, Mercha, Buxbunder, Azimgunge, Jilinghee, Baaker Gunge, Rajapore*; ſeveral petty Nabobſhips and *Fowſdaarys*, &c. &c. &c.——the governments and diſtricts of *Midnapore*, and *Chitygongh*, already ceded to us by the treaty of 1760—and the *Purgunnahs* ceded by the treaty 1757, all held by a moſt precarious tenure, whilſt this war with the government ſubſiſts.

We make no account of the province of *Oriſſa*, uſually eſtimated at one Khorore

 and

and a half, becauſe it is a moot point, whether the Emperor will engage in any equivalent plan of ſatisfaction for the *Maharattors* evacuating it. Be this as it may, if our general ſcheme ſucceeds, it would be worth *our* while to attempt the getting rid of them by fair means, as this province is greatly improvable, and conſtitutes a neceſſary frontier barrier to *Bengal* on the South. We ſay nothing neither of the *Jagghier* lands, which are not taken into our eſtimate, though theſe are objects may be worth a future conſideration.

To ſum up the whole, we venture to ſtake our credit and veracity on the aſſertion, that the two provinces of *Bengal* and *Bahar*, will fully yield a revenue of *eleven* Khorore *per annum*, or 13,750,000 pounds ſterling—if it yields this under a deſpotic and tyrannic government, in times of peace and currency of trade, what may *we* not more expect from it's improvements, under a mild and Britiſh one?—We beg leave to repeat, by way of concluſion, that

If we ſhould ſucceed in the attempt, great and glorious will be the Britiſh name in thoſe parts; and immenſe the gain to the company and nation—if we fail—nothing remains,

remains, but to obtain a laſting *peace* on almoſt any terms—for if this war continues much longer, on the preſent ineffectual and expenſive footing, the company, as a company, cannot poſſibly ſupport it; and therefore they muſt be reduced to the neceſſity of applying to our own government, for more powerful and potent aids then they hitherto have been indulged and favored with; though this has, we confeſs, been *pretty conſiderable already*. What right we have (I ſpeak as a proprietor) to claim or expect more—we leave to be reſolved by our honorable rulers.

With the above obvious concluſion, we cloſe this our third general head, and *firſt part* of our work; and ſhall proceed to the diſcuſſion of our remaining five general heads, in a ſecond part, as ſpeedily as leiſure and opportunity will permit.

POSTSCRIPT.

Having received intimation that a certain party intended again to make application to parliament, for an act to lay the *ſplitting* of Eaſt India ſtock under ſome reſtrictions; and having ſeriouſly conſidered this ſubject in, we think, a new point of view; we beg

beg leave to be heard a few words relative to this matter; and a few more, touching the present mode of governing this company.

It is extraordinary that in the course of so much altercation before the general election, last year, on the propriety or impropriety of splitting stock; two obvious considerations should not (as we remember) have been ever urged in defence of this practice: which, if duly weighed, we humbly imagine would determine parliament to discountenance, and throw out, any bill brought before them for the above-mentioned purpose.

That both parties, in the last year's direction, benefited themselves by this practice, is incontestable; notwithstanding the bold assertion and fallacious reasoning on one side; and the unmasked hypocrisy of *their champion Verax*.

It was asserted, "that neither the stock-"holder could split nor transfer, nor the "transfer accept and vote, consistently "with a good conscience as a christian, or "an honest man."—To examine the foundation of this heavy charge, let us consider the

the ſituation of every Eaſt India proprietor on the common plan of voting, at general courts or general elections.

The proprietor who holds 50,000 *l.* original ſtock, and he who holds 500 *l.* are, touching the government of this company, upon an equal footing. Strange! that a regulation ſo repugnant to equity and the nature of things, ſhould have ſo long ſubſiſted without amendment.

The *attachment* and *attention*, which every individual owes to the particular community he belongs to, will, nay, muſt be in proportion to the ſpecific *concern* and *part* he holds therein: therefore the proprietor who holds only 500 *l.* ſtock, will be leſs attached and attentive, and more liable to be ſwayed and influenced to join in bad meaſures with deſigning men, than the proprietor who holds 50,000 *l.* ſtock —— Therefore whilſt this inconſiſtent regulation ſubſiſts, and the letter of it is ſtrictly adhered to, what remedy or means has the proprietor of 80,000 *l.* ſtock, to obtain an influence in the government of this company on any critical emergency in their affairs, adequate to his *concern* and *riſque*, but this very method of ſplitting and dividing

ing his ſtock? conſequently, every attempt to deprive him of this only reſource is, beyond doubt, moſt unjuſt; and may tend to the deſtruction of the company, if they ſhould ever fall into the hands of a deſig ng, ſelf-intereſted, and wicked ſet of directors.

To refute the charge of diſhoneſty in the action itſelf, we need only conſider it in compariſon with a tranſaction much more common; yet, we conceive, ſtrictly ſimilar to it.

A. borrows 500 *l.* of B. *on note of hand payable in any ſtipulated time*;—will any man be hardy enough to ſay, that this money is not the property of A. to all intents and purpoſes, during the time of poſſeſſion?—and could not A. conſcientiouſly and honeſtly ſwear it was ſo?——where then is the eſſential difference between borrowing 500 *l.* caſh, or 500 *l.* ſtock?—*Verax* will tell you (though he laughs in his ſleeve at the ſame time) "that A. borrows the "500 *l.* caſh to convert it to his own pri-"vate occaſions: but that the ſtock lent "and transferred to A. is the conſequence of "a private compact and colluſion between "A. and B. to enable and qualify A. to "vote on that side of the question A. is to "point out to him."——Be it so—yet the moment B. transfers, and A. accepts, this individual 500*l.* stock becomes the property of A. it has every essential of property, that property can have annexed to it——he can sell, dispose of, give it away, and expend it in any manner he pleases; and though he determines to hold it, yet it remains totally in his own breast on which side he will bestow his vote, (as a certain party we believe found the last election, to their great disappointment and disgrace.)——*Verax* will again tell you, there is a counter obligation for A's replacing this individual stock. ---In like manner A. is obliged to repay his 500*l.* cash, and take up his note; if in either case he fails, B. has his remedy at law ---but A. may most truely swear either to be *bona fide* his property, whilst they continue in his possession; tho' he is accountable in the one case for payment, and the other for replacing.

Touching the mode of governing this company, we beg leave to say, it never was, nor ever can be *well governed* on it's present institution.---Would you have your court of directors respectable? reduce their number to fourteen; raise the qualification

 for

for a director to 10,000*l.* original ſtock; and their ſalaries to 600*l.* *per annum.* On this plan, the direction of your affairs would become an object worthy of being courted by men of the moſt diſtinguiſhed characters, abilities, and property: which the preſent great importance of this company loudly calls to be at their head---men who would not be ſhackled by their neceſſary attention to their own little concerns; and thereby, obliged to abandon thoſe of the company to the conduct and diſpoſal of one, two, or three members of their body; which unhappily has been the fate of this company from it's firſt inſtitution.

SUPPLEMENT.

To HENRY CRABB BOULTON, Esq;

CHAIRMAN,

AND THE REST OF THE GENTLEMEN

At present in the Direction of the Affairs of the *East-India* Company.

GENTLEMEN,

THE many years I resided in *India*; the many offices I bore in the Company's service; the natural bent of my genius to observation and inquiry, and the various occasions that called forth a particular exertion of it, with the fruits of all those taken together, having been, in every interval of leisure and retirement, the subject of much meditation and recollection; I have been induced to give to the Public my thoughts on the affairs of that Country in general, and of *Bengall* (with which I am best acquainted) in particular. My intention was surely laudable from its utility to you, to your Constituents, and my country; I say, for this reason my intention was laudable, whatever defects might be in the execution.

I was very conſcious of the difficulty of the undertaking, and not leſs ſo, that there were many gentlemen, who had merited and raiſed to themſelves both honours and fortunes in the ſervice, more able to have performed ſuch a taſk. Yet ſeeing their neglect, and well knowing that the greateſt capacity, the moſt unwearied diligence in a Board of Directors, could never ſupply them with thoſe lights, which experience only can furniſh, or open to them the large and extenſive views ſo requiſite to perſons in their ſtation; I judged it expedient, or rather a duty incumbent on me, to make an offering to you and the Public of that knowledge, which with unceaſing diligence I had laboured to obtain, and not ſuffer it to become altogether uſeleſs, by being buried in oblivion: More eſpecially, as the critical conjuncture of your affairs in *India* ſeemed to call aloud for every aſſiſtance of the kind, for the better information of you, Gentlemen, who are intruſted with the intereſts of the whole body of the Proprietors; and not of them only, but alſo with the intereſt the Nation in general has, and muſt always have, in her commerce to the *Eaſt-Indies*.

Theſe and theſe only were my motives to the work I publiſhed in *Auguſt* laſt. I leave you to judge, Gentlemen, how great my ſurprize and chagrin at being informed it has been privately inſinuated to you (and probably ſome of your opinions influenced to believe) that in the eſtimate I have there given, the value of the rich provinces of *Bengall*, is highly exaggerated and much beyond the truth.

Although

Although my Chapter on this subject was more particularly addressed to you, yet as I had given it to the Public, I might reasonably have expected, if any one was better informed, or doubted on plausible grounds the authenticity of my computation, it would have been publickly impeached, and an opportunity afforded me thereby of vindicating its truth, by laying before the Public the grounds on which it is formed.

I hold myself much obliged to those friends, who by giving me timely intelligence of those insinuations, have put it into my power to do myself justice, and which is of far greater consequence, to do justice to the subject, by giving you such further information, as may remove every shadow of objection, and leave you thoroughly persuaded of the truth of what I have asserted to you and the Public; for although it is of no great moment to me, to you, or the Public to inquire, whether those insinuations arose from envy, self-interest, or personal malevolence; from whatever source they flowed, it is of great importance to the welfare of the *East-India* Company, and to the interest of the Nation in general, as well as in justice to my veracity, that by a speedy discussion their fatal tendency may be effectually removed. I beg leave to add, that at this time it is particularly necessary that all undue influence should be erased from your minds, as it is the season when *Bengall* affairs come in course under your immediate inspection; allow me therefore to presume there is great propriety (as my heart assures me there is great sincerity) in my present address.

By dedicating the Chapter in queſtion, regarding the revenues, more particularly to you, I appealed as it were to you, who have in your hands vouchers, that by parity of reaſoning (as will be ſhewn hereafter) would confirm my aſſertion, and thereby as I thought made it unneceſſary to enter minutely into thoſe proofs in ſupport of it, which a bare *ipſe dixit* in an addreſs to the Public might have required. Without referring to ſuch evidence, might I not reaſonably hope to have had credit for my aſſertion with you, as I was conſcious you very well knew that none of the Company's ſervants had ever applied with more diligence to this branch of your concerns, or met with more (if ſo many) repeated opportunities of proſecuting ſuch inquiries: I entered on them early, I took my informations from thoſe who were the beſt verſed in theſe matters; I laboured hard to obtain intelligence of this ſort, long before there was the leaſt probability of my making uſe of that intelligence in a practical way; and afterwards my duty led me to verify many points relating to the ſubject, by the unerring light of experience; and the more my experience, the fuller were the evidences, and the ſtronger my conviction of the juſtneſs of that intelligence I had acquired. Might I not then rationally preſume, under a full and firm conviction, that what I was writing was thoroughly well founded, (which could alone have prompted me to a taſk, to which I was not otherwiſe called) that I might make the offering to you and the Public, without apprehenſion of any impeachment of its veracity, but on the cleareſt and fulleſt evidence: as a conſiderable Proprietor, I might have an interest in giving you just information; I could have none in misleading you.

The only method of leading us to the truth, that the subject will admit, is reasoning by analogy from those things of which we are most certain, to those of a like nature, in regard to which we wish to be certain. This then is the method I shall pursue, and I hope and will endeavour to do it, with as much accuracy and perspicuity as you can reasonably expect.—These previous points being settled, we will now, Gentlemen, proceed to the business.

On a candid and attentive perusal of my third Chapter, it will be obvious from the whole tenor of it, that it is calculated to excite you to attempt the possession of this country, in trust for the Emperor, and thereby put a period to a destructive and inadequate war; but can you imagine I excite you to this from the consideration of the worth of these Provinces, according to the rates standing upon the King's books? no, it is from the consideration of their real value, and actual produce; and the farther consideration of how much this produce would certainly be increased under an *English* Soubah.

You have been told, Gentlemen, (or my information is wrong) that the revenues of *Bengall* are rated on the King's books under three khorore of *Sicca* rupees: If it is said, the rents of the lands are so rated, you have been told the truth; these only go into the Royal Treasury, and to the best of my remembrance are rated at

 two

two khorore, ſeventy-five, or ſeventy-ſix lac, and ſome odd thouſands. Should this information (without looking further) be taken as a proof of my exaggeration, when my eſtimate expreſſy includes the rents of the lands, and the revenues ariſing from their produce? which I have eſtimated conjunctly at eleven khorore; and now proceed to the proof, reſting it upon what thoſe who are converſant in your affairs in *India* will admit to be an indiſputable fact, that the lands throughout the provinces, bear nearly a proportional value to each other.

I cannot with any preciſion charge my memory (having none of my papers with me) as to what the lands of the Company's original zemindary *Calcutta* ſtood rated in the King's books; it is enough for my purpoſe, that you and I know, they and the revenues ariſing from them, for many years after the Company was inveſted with them, ſcarcely yielded a net profit that recompenſed the expences of collecting them. In proceſs of time, as their ſervants became better acquainted with the nature of them, they became an object more and more worthy of attention; and being divided into ſmall farms, ſoon produced a net annual revenue from twenty to twenty-five thouſand rupees; as the knowledge of their nature and value increaſed, ſo did the rents and farms; until they brought in a net revenue of near forty thouſand rupees *per annum*. Here they ſeemed to be at their *ne plus ultra*; though the tenants were daily increaſing, and the lands grew more fully occupied and cultivated; conſequently their produce, and the conſumption of that

that produce, enlarged; which rationally indicated there ſhould have been an increaſe of the rents and revenues.

This not being the caſe, the Gentlemen then in the direction at home, ordered a ſcrutiny to be made in the office; and upon an average taken of the net proceeds for fifteen years preceding the year 1752, they appeared to have produced the Company barely thirty-nine thouſand rupees *per annum*. In conſequence of various reforms and the detection of glaring frauds, the farms for the firſt time were put up to a public and unbiaſſed ſale, to the higheſt bidder; and though ſix, by order of the then Court of Directors, were aboliſhed, as grievous and oppreſſive to the tenants, yet theſe very lands produced at the cloſe of this year, net ſeventy-three thouſand rupees; at the cloſe of the ſecond, one lac, and thirteen thouſand; at the cloſe of the third, one lac and fourteen thouſand; and would at the cloſe of the fourth year, to demonſtration, have produced one lac, and twenty thouſand; and from the nature of the thing, would have gone on annually increaſing.

The lands of the twenty-four Purgunnahs, ceded to the Company by the treaty of 1757, which ſubſequently became Colonel *Clive*'s jagghier; were rated on the King's books at two lac, and twenty-two thouſand rupees. Theſe lands were, for the ſpace of ſixteen months, retained in hand on the Company's account, under the inſpection and ſuperintendence of a collector, Mr. *Frankland*, whoſe activity, abilities,

and

and integrity, in the execution of that truſt, ſtood unimpeached. But the Company's agents finding that by that method they ſhould never arrive at the knowledge of the real value of theſe lands; determined to divide them into fifteen farms, and put them up to public ſale, reſerving the royalties in their own hands, from an apprehenſion the farmers, by being inveſted with them, might have it in their power to oppreſs the tenants. This reſolution was carried into execution, I think, in *July* 1759, and the farms let for the term of three years; when thoſe very lands which had produced for ſixteen months only three lac, eighty four thouſand rupees, ſold at this unbiaſſed ſale for ſeven lac, ſixty-five thouſand *Sicca* rupees, *per annum*, excluſive of the royalties: and thirteen at leaſt of the fifteen purchaſers, to my knowledge, were annual gainers by their bargains. In bidding to keep up two of the farms to what I had reaſon to think was their value, they fell upon my hands: as I had not leiſure to ſuperintend them myſelf, I diſpoſed of them a few days after, for an advance of five thouſand *Sicca* rupees, *per annum*, during the term of my leaſe. I only mention this as a corroborating proof of my laſt aſſertion.

What the Purgunnahs produced at their ſecond ſale, you, Gentlemen, know better than I, as before the expiration of the term of their firſt leaſe, I had the honour to be recalled.

To particularize every inſtance that might be brought in proof, or rather juſtification of my general eſtimate, would be to protract this addrefs to a tedious length: thofe already produced, afford full evidence, that the revenues of the lands are very nearly in a quadruple proportion to the rents of them; and that fo far from having exaggerated, I have rather depreciated the real and intrinfic value of thefe provinces; efpecially when it is remembered, that my eftimate is drawn exclufive of the royalties, which alone are a very confiderable revenue; and alfo that I have made no account of the many Jagghiers, nor of the immenfe tracts of Burmuttu lands, (fo called for being fet apart for the fupport of the *Bramins*) nor of many other poffeffions which pay no rents; in the grants and inveftitures of which, there are more frauds and collufions practifed, than in every other branch of the revenues. From a fcrutiny into thefe, a new and confiderable income would arife, that has hitherto never found its way, either into the royal treafury, or into the Soubah's coffers.

I repeat then, and infift on my eftimate, that exclufive of the royalties, upon an obvious and fair calculation, the whole lands of the three provinces have never yielded lefs than eleven khorore, forty thoufand *Sicca* rupees, *per annum*; and deducting for *Oriffa* one khorore and a half, at which the lands and revenues of that province are ufually eftimated, there will remain nine khorore and a half for *Bengall* and *Bahar*, to which annex the royalties, and they will more than make good the above deduction for *Oriffa*.

Though I have in my general eftimate, confined myfelf to the confideration of the known and

and eſtabliſhed rents and revenues of the provinces, yet the extra items ſpecified above, no leſs conſtitute a part of their value; and though thoſe items have for a long courſe of years been concealed and embezzled from the government, that is no reaſon why they may not in future be brought to account by a Britiſh Soubah at the head of it; an event which I will ſtill hope is not far diſtant.

Whoever attempts to depreciate this object at this juncture, can be no friend to you, your conſtituents, or his country; and ſhould ſeem moved only by private views to prolong a war, that can benefit none, but the principal actors in it. If it has been inſinuated to you, that the provinces of *Bengall* are not *alone* worthy your poſſeſſion; you are now, I truſt, fully convinced of the contrary; and will ſee the neceſſity of putting a ſtop at laſt to the ſtrides, your ſervants are daily making towards acquiſitions, which cannot poſſibly be maintained: the provinces of *Bengall* you may maintain and defend, upon the plan I have preſumed already to hint to you. I will further communicate a few anecdotes relative to the lands and revenues of this country, and cloſe this addreſs.

The rents of the lands are the property of the Emperor. In conſequence of which he has a royal Dewan, in every Soubahdaary, who ought to be accountable to the royal treaſury for the whole amount of the rents, as rated upon the King's books: but as there is always a good underſtanding between the Dewan and the Soubah,

they

they never are at a loſs in pretending reaſons for the rents falling ſhort, though the whole is ſtrictly and fully collected. What is diverted from the royal treaſury, is divided between the Dewan and the Soubah, of which the latter always takes the lion's ſhare.

Though the amount of the rents of the lands is near three khorore *per annum*; yet the higheſt ſtipulation made with the Emperor was that mentioned in another place, of one khorore, one lac, one thouſand, one hundred, and one rupee, by the Soubah Soujah Khan: and this was regularly tranſmitted to the royal treaſury, until the uſurpation of *Aliverdi*. He, on pretence of the diſtreſſes of the provinces (to which diſtreſſed ſtate he himſelf had brought them) made a new ſtipulation of fifty-two lac *per annum*; to which he paid no regard longer than the Vizir *Monſoor Ali Khan*'s army was within a few days march of *Patna*, *A. D.* 1750, nor has the royal treaſury benefited a rupee from theſe provinces ſince that period. This I mention, or ſhould rather ſay, repeat, to ſhow how gladly the Emperor would embrace any overture that would inſure to him annually one-third of the rents of theſe provinces.

The eſtabliſhed ground rent is three *Sicca* rupees *per* Begah (about one third of an *Engliſh* acre) throughout the empire; but *Aliverdi Khan* made the firſt innovation in this eſtabliſhed law, and aſſeſſed the land four annas *Sicca*, or a quarter of a rupee upon each Begah, on pretence of the Chout paid to the *Maharattors*, and raiſed the rents of the Rajahs and Zemindaars in that proportion; these had no other means of reimbursing themselves, but levying it upon the farmers, and they again on the tenants. Subsequently the lands were on various pretended exigencies, at different periods, assessed to 10-16ths of a rupee, though every additional tax on land, above three *Sicca* rupees *per annum*, is contrary to the standing law of the empire; which until *Aliverdi's* usurpation, had been held sacred, and inviolable. In the year 1732, your Governor and Council had in agitation the raising the rents of your own Zemindary of *Calcutta*; which being rumoured abroad they received a peremptory Perwannah, from the Soubah, forbidding them; in which the Soubah told them, that they were presuming to do a thing, which he himself had not power to do; and that if they persisted, they would, by the laws of the empire, forfeit their lands.

Frauds throughout the empire in letting the lands, are manifold: for instance: The Rajahs, and Zemindaars, by private compact with the Soubah's officers, who are charged with the management of this department, obtain more lands than by their Synods (or grants, which are commonly called Pottahs) appear, and consequently pay no rent to the king for the surplus land. The same artifice is practised between the Dewans of the Rajahs and Zemindaars, and the Izardaars or farmers; and the tenants, or common Pottahholders under them, by bribing the officers of the Jummah Bundî, and those intrusted with the measurements of the lands, that they may

may enjoy among them the benefit of the surplus land; and I may justly aver, there is not a tenant in *Indostan*, but possesses and occupies a greater quantity of land, than his Pottah expresses, or than he pays rent for: Consequently, it is the tenant that ultimately enjoys the benefit of the surplus land, thus gained by corruption, from the Soubah's Ministers, while the King specifically suffers in his rents. It extremely well answers the tenant's purpose, to possess, if he can by a small bribe, more land than he pays for, because himself and his heirs enjoy the profit of it in perpetuity; since, by a fundamental law of the empire, their Pottahs are irrevocable, as long as they pay the rent, rated in them respectively; and so tender and indulgent are the laws of *Indostan* in this particular, that no tenant forfeits his land, before he has failed in his payments for twelve months; though the land-tax, by the same laws, is to be paid every three months.

This method of secreting or purloining the land from the King and the Soubah, has been practised time out of mind; and it is quite in point, to mention a flagrant instance that appeared in the year 1753; when in consequence of the general scrutiny, made by your order in your Zemindary *Calcutta*, it was demonstrated that in your small district, upon a favourable new measurement of your land, there were near five hundred Begah secreted in this way, and fraudulently enjoyed, by your tenants, for which you had received no ground rent from your being invested with the Zemindary; of this you may be be convinced by turning to your Jummah Bun-dî, or regifter of your lands fubfequently by me tranfmitted to you. As you, Gentlemen, have by that meafurement gained five hundred Begah of ground, upon a poffeffion only of fix thoufand two hundred; you may judge from thence, what an aftonifhing additional revenue would arife to you, when Soubah of the provinces, from a new (though favourable) meafurement of the whole lands.

When the revenues, arifing from the lands of this country are retained in the proprietors hands (that is, not farmed out) one univerfal chain of roguery runs through the whole, as well as in the rents of the lands; and there is a fellow-feeling between every one employed in the collections, from the Dewan to the loweft Moree, or writer; and this the Rajahs and Zemindaars (the great proprietors of the lands) are no more exempt from, than the Company is, notwithftanding the utmoft integrity of their covenanted fervants: but I have fo clearly traced, and laid open the nature of thofe frauds (which are fimilar throughout the empire) in my ftate of the Company's revenues Zemindary, dated the 15th of *December*, 1752, that I need not trouble you further on that fubject, than to refer you thereto.

The whole intention and aim of thefe communications, is to perfwade and convince you; that be the Company's poffeffions in that country what they will, either lefs or more; you will never get at their true value, or derive to your-

felves

ſelves and conſtituents the half of their net advantages, by keeping them in hand: the remedy is obvious.——If they are divided into farms, in value from five thouſand rupees, to one lac *per annum*, and put up to public ſale to the higheſt bidder, under the ſame reſtrictions and excluſions as were ſtipulated at the ſale of your twenty-four Purgunnahs, then moſt probably, five-ſixths of their real value would reſult to the Company. And I cannot enough congratulate your having happly appointed a Gentleman (Mr. *Sumner*) to ſucceed Lord *Clive* in the government, who is intimately acquainted with, and converſant in all matters relative to the lands and revenues; and moſt capable of carrying your orders on theſe heads into execution.

To ſave you the trouble of references, I will ſubjoin two letters, the one addreſſed to the then board of *Calcutta*, the other to a former chairman; as they are both ſtrictly connected with the ſubject, and will add ſtrength and weight to my arguments.

I have the honour to be with moſt perfect reſpect,

Gentlemen,

Your moſt Obedient Humble Servant,

Bath,
Dec. 1765.

J. Z. HOLWELL.

To C. Manningham, Esq; &c. Council.

Calcutta, June 11 1759.

Sir and Sirs,

I Beg leave to trouble you with a few sentiments on the disposal of the company's lands, which have, for some time past, been the object of your Councils; the subject is of importance to our honourable employers, and cannot be too much deliberated on.

I believe we are all unanimous, in some circumstances, which more particularly require our attention in this affair; to wit, the honour of the Company, the acquiring a perfect knowledge in the value of the lands; the making this branch of the revenues less complicate and intricate, as well as less expensive in the collecting;——but with respect to the means, we seem not quite so clear.——Any one gentleman declaring fully his opinion on your consultations, may possibly make us unanimous here also.

The step we are already determined in, of divesting the farmers of all power in the royalties and judicial authorities in the Purgunnahs, bids fair for the security of the Company's honor: as these articles being heretofore also farmed, became the source of heavy cruelties and oppressions on the tenants.——But still there seems to be something wanting to give us a perfect security in this particular;——and that is, to take the utmost care in our power, that the whole body

body of the lands do not, by any junto, or private confederacy, fall into the hands of people, with whom we ſhould not truſt any part of our fortunes or confidence. I am urged to this precaution, from the propoſal laid before you the fourth inſtant, by ſix or ſeven conſpicuous natives of the ſettlement, of an advance of 110,001 rupees on the whole lands. With reſpect to their propoſal, I will only add an offer of 10,000 rupees more *per annum* on their terms:——not that I wiſh myſelf, or any one elſe, in poſſeſſion of them, on terms ſo vague and artful.

That keeping the lands in our own hands, will never lead to a knowledge of their real value, is now (to me) proved beyond contradiction.—— Some of thoſe who ſigned the propoſal of the fourth, are well converſant in the nature of their undertaking; and better judges (as I am informed) are concerned, though as yet they act behind the curtain; and to me it is inconceivable, that theſe Eaſtern Machiavels in fineſſe, would offer ſuch an annual advance, without a moral certainty of adequate gains. In this poſition, I am ſtill more confirmed, by the advance offered from other quarters, on diſtant and garbled parts of the Purgunnahs, which in fact exceeds the other.

If we have been hitherto kept ſo far from the knowledge of the real value of theſe lands, after ſixteen months poſſeſſion, what are we to expect when, from the courſe of the ſervice, they are no longer under the conduct of the preſent collector?

lector?—whose knowledge of this branch, must be greatly superior to any Gentleman that succeeds him; and whose vigilance in the execution of this trust, cannot be exceeded. From the experience I have had, in infinitely a less, though similar object, I know it is impossible for any one Gentleman, with the most extensive talents and integrity, to superintend this revenue in such manner as to prevent the Company being injured. His attention cannot be every where, confidence must be placed in a multitude; and it happens unluckily that this confidence centers from necessity, in a race of people, who, from their infancy, are utter strangers to the idea of common faith, or honesty.

The other plan of disposing of the lands, to the multitude of people who have offered an advance on particular parts of the Purgunnahs; I have strong, and equal objections to; I am sensible these objections should have been laid before you sooner, and would, had I thought myself sooner master of the subject. We know not what, or who these people are; I foresee a very great risque of deficiencies in the rents, as well as much confusion, and needless expence, entailed on this expedient; and ourselves removed as far as ever, from gaining a knowledge of the real value of this new and important acquisition. On the whole therefore I am of opinion, that there is no effectual method to arrive at the knowledge of, and make the lands yield every advantage to our honourable employers, but by putting them up to publick sale, in single Purgunnahs, under the restrictions already published—

People of ſubſtance will then be the only bidders for an intire Purgunnah; the bad and unprofitable parts, will go with the good and valuable; and the riſque of deficiencies in the rents, be guarded againſt; the expence of collecting will in a manner be reduced to nothing; and this branch of the ſervice be rendered leſs complicated and intricate, by having twenty-four purchaſers to account with only, in place of five or ſix hundred.

I am, with reſpect, &c.

J. Z. H.

To John Payne, Esq; *Calcutta*, Dec. 30, 1759.

Dear Sir,

To shorten my remarks on the important subject of your lands, I inclose you a copy of my letter to the Council, of the 11th of *June*, when the Colonel was upon the *Patna* expedition; it produced no other effect, than postponing our resolves, until his arrival: when the affair being resumed, he did me the honour, with the rest of the board, of thinking my reasons for the public sale of the lands by auction, unanswerable; and the same was resolved on unanimously. The event more than answered my expectation. I had taken great pains in ferretting out the real value of the lands, which was covered with almost impenetrable obscurity, and difficulties; and by an estimate I gave the Colonel at his return, ventured to pronounce they would yield seven lac and a half; and the total of their sale on the 13th of *July*, amounted to seven lac, sixty-five thousand seven hundred *Sicca* rupees, *per annum*, exclusive of several reserves in favour of the Company; such as a considerable tract of land taken from the Purgunnahs, adjoining to *Calcutta*, to extend it's bounds; and all advantages resulting from holding the royalties, and judicial proceedings, &c. in our own hands on the Company's account, so that I judge the whole produce of these lands (the before mentioned reserves included) will be annually between nine and ten lac; the sum I guessed (in

England)

England) they would produce, when once in conference with you upon the ſubject. From this the Colonel's Jagghîr of two lace, twenty-two thouſand rupees being deducted, there will remain a net annual revenue to the Company of about ſeven lac, eighty thouſand rupees *Sicca per annum*, on the ſame lands, which yielded the laſt year when the revenues were collected on the government's plan, only three lac, eighty-four thouſand, or thereabout; as you will learn from the accounts of this revenue now tranſmitted to the Company. I ſee the court of Directors ſtare with aſtoniſhment at this increaſe; you will ſtare too, my dear Sir, as a proprietor. Methinks I hear them and you cry out! What the Devil became of this difference the laſt year? as it muſt have been collected beyond a doubt; or from whence can this advance anſwer to the preſent farmers? The anſwer is eaſy and obvious;—— the difference fell ſhort, in its way to the Company's treaſury, by the ſelf-ſame roads, your former revenues were diſſipated, prior to the reform in your Zemindary.——As your former Zemindars could not juſtly be deemed culpable in that caſe, from the frequent change of the poſt; ſo in the preſent no blame properly falls on your collector, the truſt being too extenſive for any one man exiſting; though the frauds are equally obvious, from the extraordinary increaſe at a fair and public ſale, where the farmers were laid under every poſſible check and reſtraint, that can either prevent their debaſing their lands, or oppreſſing the tenants; and yet there is a moral certainty of profit to him, at the expiration of the three

three years; and that they will then yield a further increase to the Company.——

Before I entirely quit the subject of the lands, I must clear up a circumstance, that possibly may be cause of wonder to you, viz. by what means I arrived at their real value.——In the first place, I had long and full conviction, that the same system of fraud and chicane, ran through every Zemindary of the provinces; and from a general knowledge of the country granted to us, it appeared to me most astonishing, they should yield no more than was brought to the Company's credit, at the close of the year in *April* last; when so small a territory as *Calcutta*, produced, on a scrutiny and reform, an increase of 73 to 80,000 *Sicca* rupees *per annum.*——I tried various means to trace out a satisfactory reason, and to account to myself for it, but without success, until I learnt by accident that three or four of the old standards employed as tax-gatherers, and writers in the Purgunnahs, had been dismissed, at the instigation of the new operators. I sent privately for one or two of the most creditable of them, and inquired into the cause of their dismission; and this brought on an opening of the whole scene; and gave me sufficient foundation for forming my letter of the 11th of *June.* ——Thus, Sir, having made you master of this subject, in as short a detail as possible, I shall close it with this remark; that the same chain of frauds runs through the whole empire, but more particularly in these provinces, to the heavy annual loss of the crown; a circumstance which

may

may in a future favorable conjuncture, be well worth consideration: at present we have but to ask and have a more easy acquisition of the Soubahdary, than that we have already obtained of the Purgunnahs; but the times are not yet ripe for so great a grasp, nor have we sufficient strength to hold it; though it is certain, were we Soubahs of the provinces, the emperor would regularly receive more than double the revenues these provinces ever produced to him; and the *East-India* Company become, in a short time, the richest body of subjects in the world.——

I am,

Sir, &c.

J. Z. H.

The End of the First Part.

Lately publiſhed, the Second Edition
Reviſed and corrected with Additions.

INDIA TRACTS.

By Mr. HOLWELL and Friends.

CONTAINING,

I. An Addreſs to the Proprietors of *Eaſt-India* Stock; ſetting forth, the unavoidable Neceſſity, and real Motives for the Revolution in *Bengal*, 1760.

II. A Refutation of a Letter from a certain Gentleman of the Council at *Bengal*, to the Honourable the Secret Committee.

II. Important Facts regarding the *Eaſt-India* Company's Affairs in *Bengal*, from the Years 1752 to 1760, with Copies of ſeveral very intereſting Letters.

IV. A Narrative of the deplorable Deaths of the *Engliſh* Gentlemen who were ſuffocated in the *Black Hole* in *Fort William*, at *Calcutta*, *June* 1756.

V. A Defence of Mr. *Vanſittart*'s Conduct, illuſtrated with a Frontiſpiece, repreſenting the Monument erected at *Calcutta*, in Memory of the Sufferers in the *Black-Hole* Priſon.

Printed for T. BECKET and P. A. DE HONDT,
near Surry-Street, in the Strand.

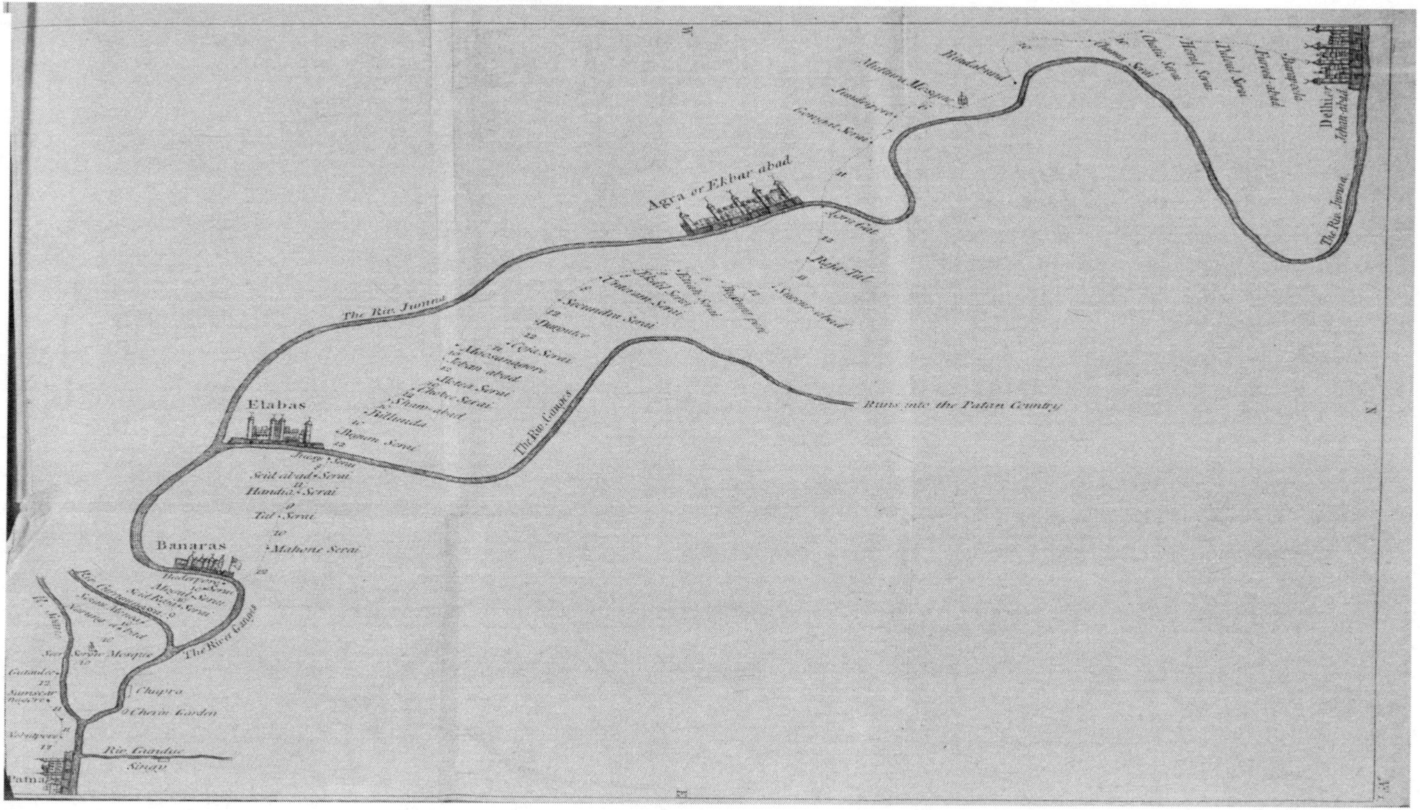

Dellhi or Jehan-abad
The Riv. Jumna
Agra or Ekbar-abad
Elabas
Banaras
Patna
The Riv. Ganges
Runs into the Patan Country
The River Ganges
Riv. Gandac
Chupra
Cherin Garden
Mahone Serai
Tal Serai
Begum Serai
Secundra Serai
Ettaih Serai
Zinaga
N
W
E

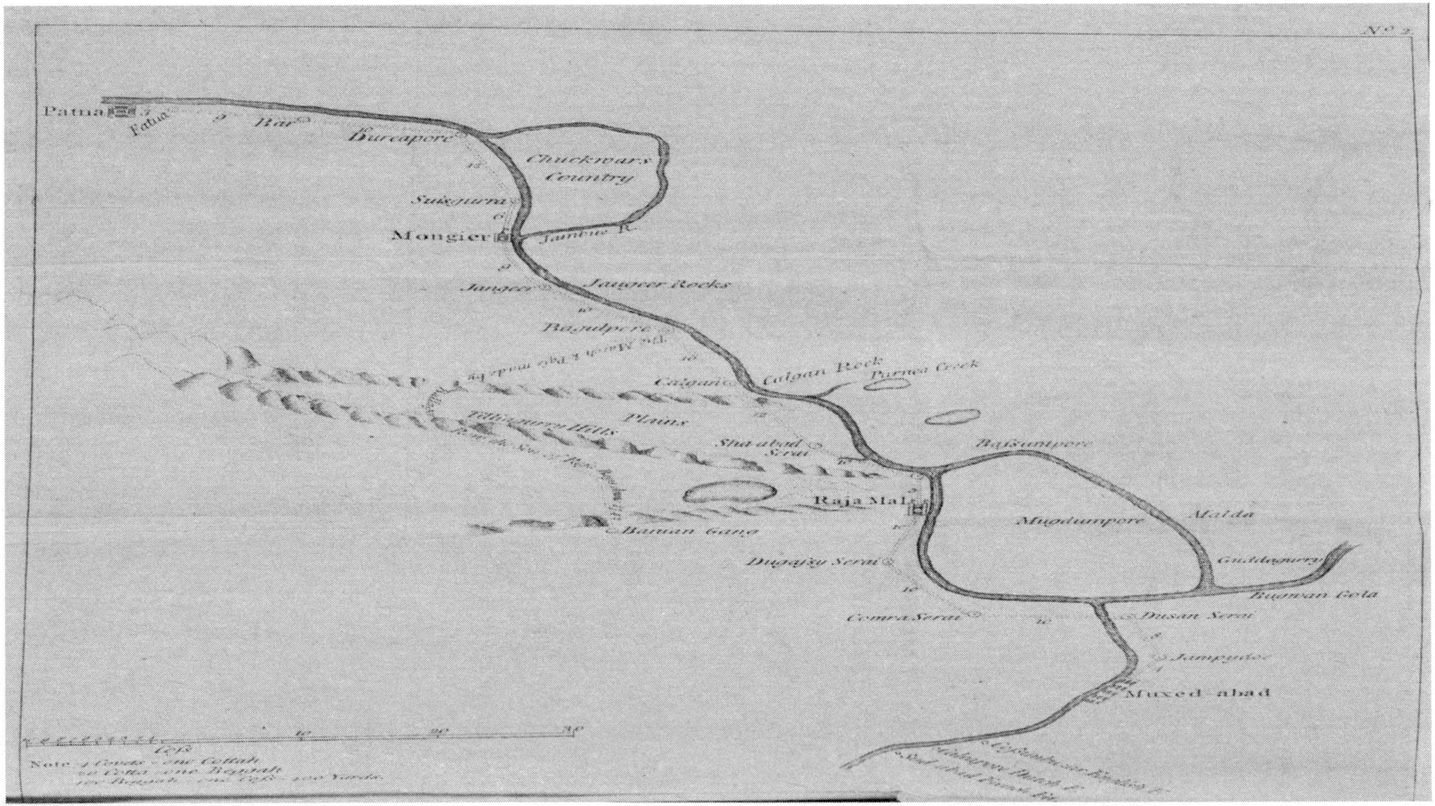

Nº 2
Patna
Bar
Bureapore
Chuckwars Country
Mongier
Jangeer
Jangeer Rocks
Bagulpore
Calgan Rock
Purnea Creek
Plains
Raja Mal
Banan Gang
Bassunpore
Mugdumpore
Malda
Guddagurry
Dugajey Serai
Comra Serai
Dusan Serai
Muxed-abad
Coss

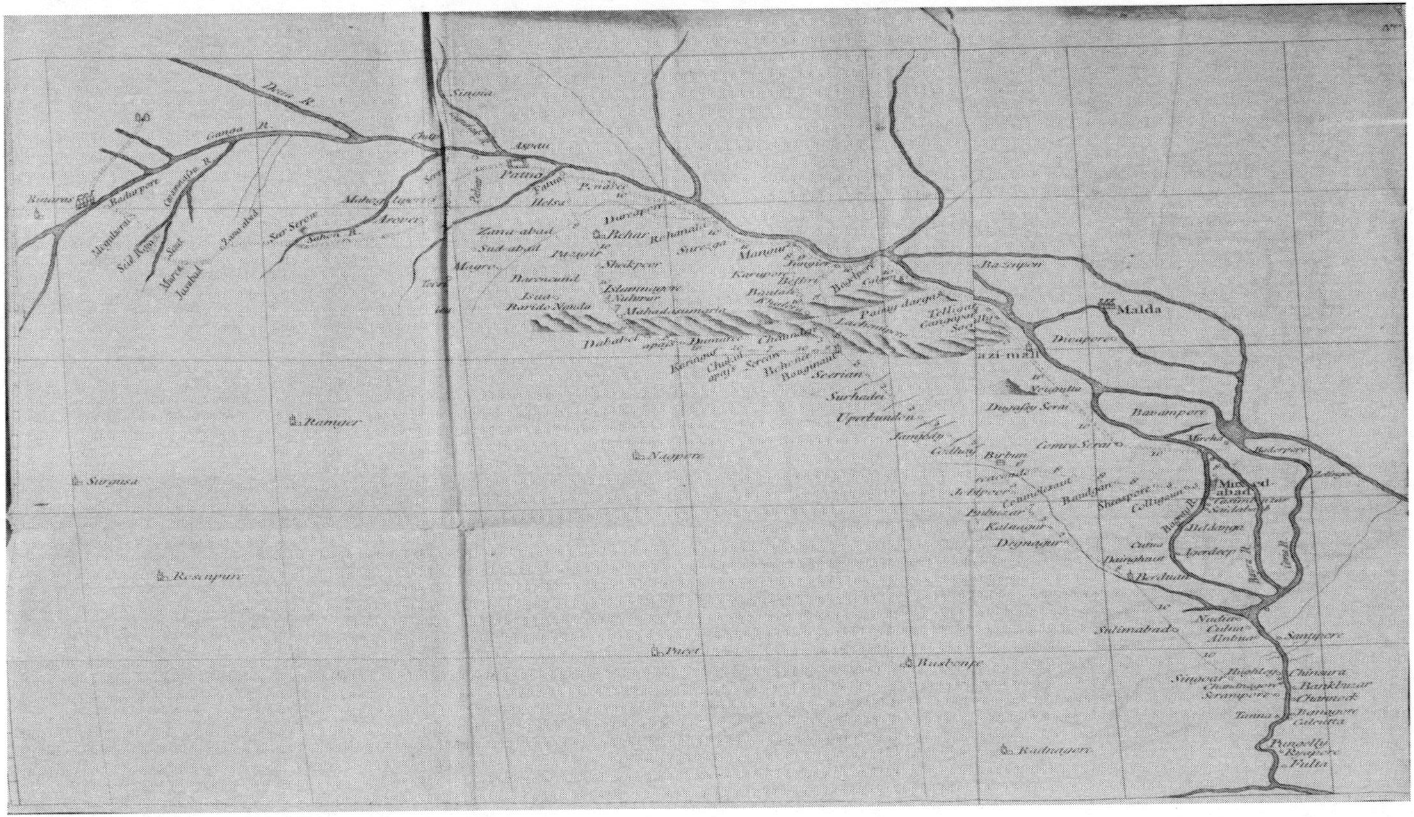
Malda
Patna
Behar
Rosapure
Ramger
Surgusa
Nagpore
Puset
Rusbonge
Kalnagori
Berdwan
Sulimabad
Calcutta
Chinsura
Chandnagore
Serampore
Tanna
Fulta
Nadia
Santipore
Bavampore
Dewapore
Bazapon
Dara R.
Ganga R.
Helsa
Zana-abad
Sud-abad
Shekpeer
Islamnagore
Magro
Barcound
Surhadee
Uperbundon
Jamjday
Dignagur
Katnagur
Jelalpeer
Birbun
Colligaum
Sheapore
Baldanga
Serrian
Dabahel
Sahen R.
Sar Serew
Benaras
Badurpore
Aspau
Telligall
Gangapal
Mirchd
Baderpore
Mucsud abad
Gonna Serai

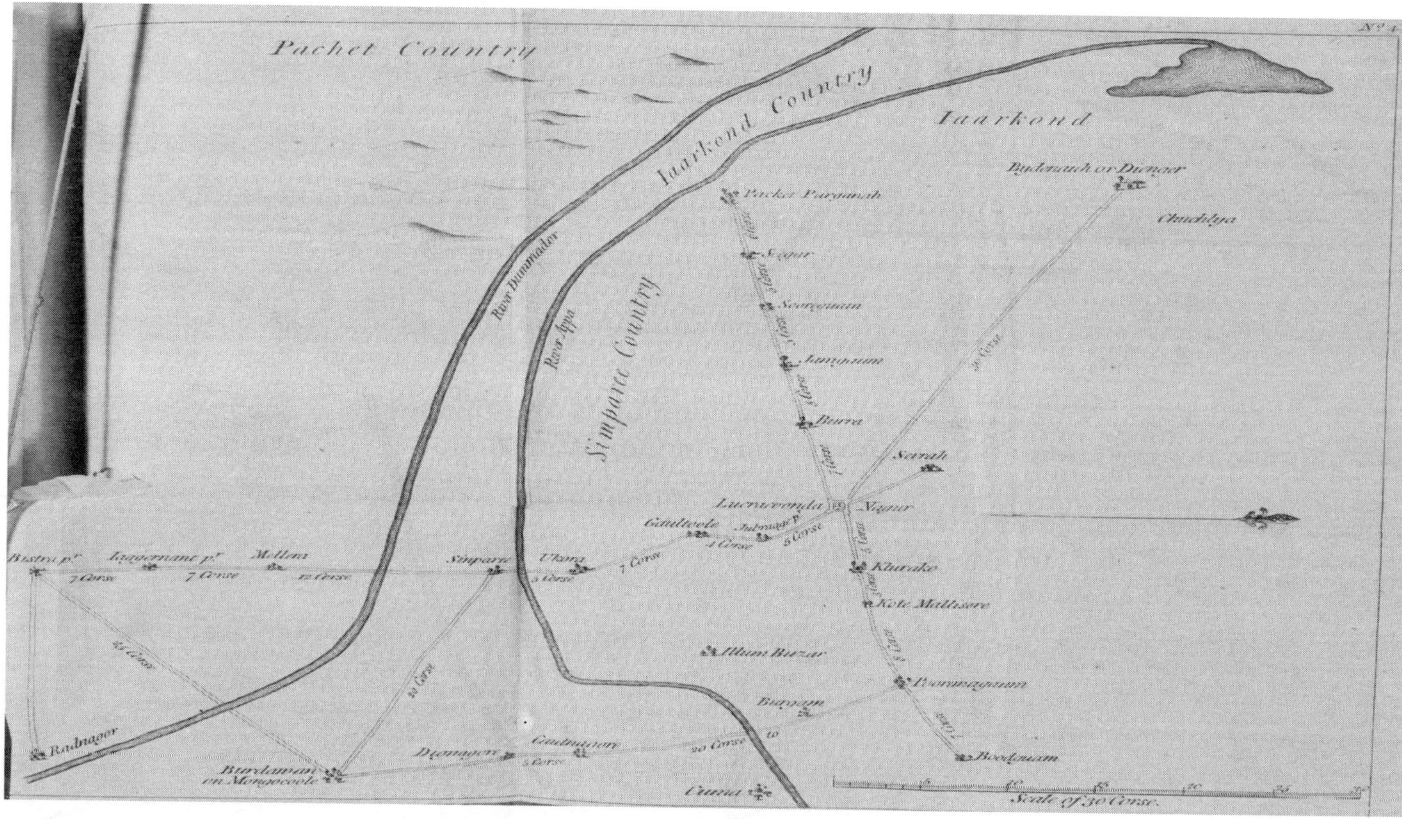

Nº 4
Pachet Country
Iaarkond Country
Iaarkond
Simparee Country
River Dummador
River Appa
Bydenauch or Dienaer
Chuchlya
Packet Purgunah
Segur
Soorguum
Jumguum
Burra
Serrah
Lucnucconda
Nagur
Gaultoole
Klurako
Kote Mallisore
Illum Buzar
Poonnaguum
Boodguum
Bistru pr.
Iaggernant pr.
Mellen
Simpare
Ukara
Radnager
Burdawan on Mongocoole
Dgenagore
Cumu
Scale of 30 Corse.

INTERESTING

HISTORICAL EVENTS,

Relative to the

PROVINCES OF BENGAL,

AND THE

EMPIRE OF INDOSTAN.

PART II.

INTERESTING
HISTORICAL EVENTS,
Relative to the
PROVINCES OF BENGAL,
AND THE
EMPIRE OF INDOSTAN.
WITH
A Seasonable HINT and PERSWASIVE
To the Honourable
The COURT of DIRECTORS of the
EAST INDIA COMPANY.

AS ALSO

The MYTHOLOGY and COSMOGONY, FASTS and FESTIVALS of the GENTOO'S, followers of the SHASTAH.

AND

A DISSERTATION on the METEMPSYCHOSIS, commonly, though erroneously, called the PYTHAGOREAN Doctrine.

By J. Z. HOLWELL, Esq;

PART II.

L O N D O N:
Printed for T. BECKET and P. A. DE HONDT, near Surry-Street, in the Strand. MDCCLXVII.

TO THE MOST NOBLE

HUGH,

DUKE AND EARL OF

NORTHUMBERLAND;

EARL PERCY;

BARON WARKWORTH OF WARKWORTH CASTLE;

LORD LIEUTENANT AND CUSTOS ROTULORUM OF THE COUNTIES OF MIDDLESEX AND NORTHUMBERLAND, OF THE CITY AND LIBERTY OF WESTMINSTER, AND OF THE TOWN AND COUNTY OF THE TOWN OF NEWCASTLE UPON TYNE; VICE ADMIRAL OF ALL AMERICA, AND OF THE COUNTY OF NORTHUMBERLAND; ONE OF THE LORDS OF HIS MAJESTY'S MOST HONORABLE PRIVY COUNCIL; KNIGHT OF THE MOST NOBLE ORDER OF THE GARTER; AND FELLOW OF THE ROYAL SOCIETY.

MY LORD,

IT is with equal deference and pleasure that I ſubmit the following performance to your Grace's peruſal;

more reſplendent by the amiable virtues and qualities that adorn them—Virtues! which have endeared him alike to prince and people.

I have the honor to ſubſcribe myſelf,

My Lord Duke,

Your Grace's moſt obedient

and moſt humble ſervant,

Beenham Houſe, Berks,
Nov. 1ſt, 1766.

J. Z. HOLWELL.

CHAP. IV.

The Religious Tenets of the Gentoos, followers of the Shastah of Bramah.

INTRODUCTION.

WE have already premised, that in the prosecution of this our fourth general head, we should touch only on the original *principal* tenets of these ancient people the *Gentoos*; for were we to penetrate into, and discuss the whole of their modern ceremonials, and complicated modes of worship; our labor would be without end: these are as diffuse, as the ancient fundamental tenets of *Bramah* are short, pure, simple and uniform; in this predicament the *Gentoos* are not singular, as the original text of every theological system, has, we presume, from a similar cause, unhappily undergone the same fate; though at first promulged as a divine institution.

We ſhall not ſay much regarding the antiquity of theſe people; nor ſhall we amuſe ourſelves with the reveries of chronologers and hiſtorians; who have labored to fix with preciſion (though not two of them agree in opinion) the various migrations after the flood: it ſhall ſuffice for our purpoſe, that by their own ſhewing, *Indoſtan* was as early peopled, as moſt other parts of the known world.

The firſt invaders of this empire, found the inhabitants a potent, opulent, civilized, wiſe, and learned people; united under one head, and one uniform profeſſion of divine worſhip; by the fundamental principles of which, they were precluded communication, and ſocial converſe, with the reſt of mankind; and theſe invaſions firſt made them a warlike people alſo.

Alexander the Great, invaded them in later times, and found them in the ſame ſtate; and though it ſhould ſeem, from *Arrian*'s and *Quintus Curtius*'s hiſtory of that Prince's expeditions, that the different principalities he conquered, were independant kingdoms, and governed by independant Kings and Princes; yet the *Gentoo* records of *Bindoobund* and *Banaras* ſhew, that at that period,

period, and much later, all the principalities of this empire, were in ſubjection to, and owned allegiance to one head, ſtiled the *Mhaahah Rajah* of *Indoſtan*; a Prince of the *Succadit* family, ſaid to be lineally deſcended from their great Prince and Legiſlator *Bramah*; and that it was not until after the extinction of this ſacred family (as the *Gentoos* call it) that the *Rajahs* aſſumed an independency.

But it did not ſufficiently ſooth the vanity of *Alexander*, nor that of his hiſtorians, to record his conqueſts of a few petty Rajahs and Governors of provinces; and though we do not conteſt the fact of that invaſion, yet we think ourſelves juſtified in concluding the greateſt part of its hiſtory is fabulous; yet, that it claims greater credit and belief, than thoſe of *Bacchus* and *Seſoſtris*: the *Greek* and *Latin* conſtruction and termination of the names, and places, of the Princes and kingdoms of *Indoſtan*, ſaid by *Alexander*'s hiſtorians to be conquered by him; bear not the leaſt analogy or idiom of the *Gentoo* language, either ancient or modern; as any one the leaſt converſant in it can teſtify; and although the ground work of their hiſtory was founded on fact, yet the ſuperſtructure carries ſtrongly the ſemblance of invention and romance: And he who is acquainted with this empire, and can give full credit to thoſe legends, may upon as juſt a foundation believe *Alexander* to have been the ſon of *Jupiter Ammon*; or, with *Q. Curtius*, that the *Ganges* opened into the *Red ſea*.

The annals of the *Gentoos*, give teſtimony of *Alexander*'s invaſion; where he is recorded under the epithets, of *Mhaabah Dukkoyt, é Kooneah*, a moſt mighter robber and murderer; but they make not any mention of a *Porus*, nor of any name that has the ſmalleſt alluſion or likeneſs to it; and yet the action between *Alexander* and this imaginary King *Porus*, has been pompouſly exhibited by the hiſtorians of the former, and has happily afforded ſubject matter for repreſentations, that do the higheſt honour to the art and genius of man.

The liberty we have taken with theſe ſo long celebrated hiſtorians, may ſeem to our readers to be foreign to our ſubject, but in the end we hope it will appear otherwiſe; when they find that theſe authors have (either from their own fertile inventions, or from miſ-information, or rather from want of a competent knowledge in the language of the nation) miſ-repreſented, or to ſpeak

more

more favorably, miſ-conceived their religious tenets as much as they have the genius and ſtate of their government.

The ſpace of time employed in *Alexander*'s expedition in this empire, did not afford a poſſibility of acquiring any adequate knowledge of a language in itſelf ſo highly difficult to attain in the ſmalleſt degree of perfection even from many years reſidence and intimate converſe with the natives; can it be poſſibly believed then, that any of *Alexander*'s followers could in this ſhort ſpace acquire ſuch perfection in the *Gentoo* language as could enable them juſtly to tranſmit down the religious ſyſtem of a nation, with whom they can ſcarcely be ſaid to have had any communication?

Touching the antiquity of the ſcriptures, we are treating of, we have much more to ſay, in ſupport of our conjecture and belief, that the *Shaſtah* of *Bramah*, is as ancient, at leaſt, as any written body of divinity that was ever produced to the world. But it is previouſly neceſſary, that we explain the word *Bramah*, which has been variouſly wrote, and indiſcriminately applied by many authors, and particularly by *Baldeus*, who confounds *Birmah* and *Bramah* as being the ſame perſon, though nothing in nature can be more different. This could proceed only, from the ſpecific meaning and origin of thoſe words not being clearly underſtood; and this we conceive has led many other writers into the ſame error: our preſent diſquiſition therefore calls, not only for the explanation of theſe words, but alſo of the other two ſuppoſed primary created beings *Biſtnoo* and *Sieb*. For unleſs theſe three perſons *Birmah*, *Biſtnoo*, and *Sieb*, are diſtinctly comprehended, and held in remembrance, a conſiderable portion of the allegorical part of the *Shaſtah* of *Bramah*, will appear utterly unintelligible.

Different authors ſtile him, *Bruma*, *Bramma*, *Burma*, *Brumma*, *Birmah*, *Bramah*; and although they write him thus variouſly, they are unanimous in thinking him the ſame perſon, and give him the ſame attributes. They are all, it is true, derivatives from the ſame root, *Brum* or *Bram*, (for theſe are ſynonimous in the *Shaſtah)* but none of all the above appellatives are to be found in the *Shaſtah*, but *Birmah* and *Bramah*. They are all compounded of *brum* or *bram*, *a ſpirit*, or *eſſence*, and *mah*, *mighty*; *brum*, in an abſolute and ſimple ſenſe, ſignifies *the ſpirit or eſſence of God*, and is but upon one occaſion

occaſion mentioned as a perſon, and that is when *brum* is repreſented with the habiliments and four arms of *Birmah*, floating on a leaf, upon the face of a troubled chaos, immediately preceding the act of the creation of the univerſe.—*Birmah* is underſtood in an abſolute perſonal ſenſe, and in a figurative one; in the former as the firſt of the three primary created angelic beings—in this ſenſe the word ſignifies literally the *mighty ſecond*. For though *Birmah* is the firſt of the three prime beings, he is ſtiled *ſecond* in power to God only, and ſometimes in the *Shaſtah* has the name of *Birmahah*, *the moſt mighty ſecond*.——In the figurative ſenſe the word *Birmah* means creation, created, and ſometimes creator, and repreſents what the *Bramins* call, the firſt great attribute of God, *his power of creation*.

Bramah is the title ſolely appropriated to the Promulger of the *Shaſtah*, and implies the ſpirituality and divinity of his miſſion and doctrines; hence it is, that his ſucceſſors aſſumed the name of *Bramins*, ſuppoſing themſelves to inherit the ſame divine ſpirit.

As the word *Birmah*, is uſed in a perſonal, and figurative ſenſe, ſo is *Biſtnoo* and *Sieb*; perſonally, as being the ſecond and

 third

third of the first created angelic beings, who had pre-eminence in heaven; the word *Bistnoo*, literally signifies a *cherisher*, a *preserver*, a *comforter*; and *Sieb*, a *destroyer*, an *avenger*, a *mutilator*, a *punisher*; and these three persons, when figuratively applied in the *Shastah* (as they frequently are) represent what the *Bramins* call the three first and great attributes of God, his power *to create*, his power *to preserve*, and his power *to change* or *destroy*. And we shall see that in the distribution of the almighty's commands to these primary persons, tasks are assigned to each, of a very different nature; to *Birmah*, works of power, government and glory; to *Bistnoo*, works of tenderness and benevolence; and to *Sieb*, works of terror, severity and destruction. This last mentioned person is the object of great dismay and terror to the *Gentoos*, but modern expounders of *Bramah*'s *Shastah* have softened the rigor of his character by giving him names and attributes of a very different nature from that of *Sieb*. They call him *Moisoor* (a contraction of *Mahahsoor*, *the most mighty destroyer of evil)* and under this soothing title he is worshipped, not as *Sieb* the destroyer, but as *the destroyer of evil*. The other epithet they have given to him is *Moideb*, (a contraction of *Mahahdebtah*,

tah, the moſt mighty angel) in this ſenſe he is worſhipped as *the averter of evil*, and under this character he has the moſt altars erected to him.

This neceſſary interpretation and explanation premiſed, we proceed to the *Shaſtah* itſelf; and ſhall faithfully give a detail of the origin of this book; and the ſeveral innovations and changes it has ſuffered: a detail —which although known by all the learned amongſt the *Bramins*, is yet confeſſed but by a few, and thoſe only, whoſe purity of principle and manners, and zeal for the primitive doctrines of *Bramah*'s *Shaſtah*, ſets them above diſguiſing the truth; from many of theſe, we have had the following recital.

" That, when part of the angelic bands " rebelled, and were driven from the face " of God, and expelled from the heavenly " regions; God doomed them in his wrath, " to eternal puniſhment and baniſhment; " but, that by the interceſſion of the faith- " ful remaining bands, he was at length " inclined to mercy, and to ſoften the rigor " of their ſentence, by inſtituting *a courſe* " *only*, of puniſhment, purgation, and pu- " rification; through which, by due ſub- " miſſion, they might work out a reſtoration

" to

" to the ſeats they had loſt by their diſobe-
" dience.

" That God in full aſſembly of the faith-
" ful bands ſpecified *their courſe* of puniſh-
" ment, purgation and purification; regiſ-
" tered, and declared his decree, immutable,
" and irrevocable; and commanded *Birmah*,
" to deſcend to the baniſhed delinquents
" and ſignify unto them the mercy and
" determination of their creator.

" That *Birmah* fulfilled God's command,
" deſcended to the delinquent angels, and
" made known unto them the mercy and
" immutable ſentence, that God their creator
" had pronounced and regiſtered againſt
" them.

" That the great and unexpected mercy
" of God, at firſt made a deep impreſſion
" upon all the delinquents, except on the
" leaders of their rebellion; theſe in proceſs
" of time, regained their influence, and
" *confirmed* moſt of the delinquents in their
" diſobedience, and thereby the merciful
" intentions of the creator, became in a
" great meaſure fruſtrated.

" That about the beginning of the pre-
" ſent age (i. e. 4866 years ago) the three

" primary created beings and the reſt of the " faithful angelic hoſt, feeling the deepeſt " anguiſh for the exalted wickedneſs of their " delinquent brethren, concluded it could " only proceed, from their having by time, " forgot the terms of their ſalvation; which " had been only verbally delivered to them " by *Birmah:* they therefore petitioned the " Almighty, that he would be pleaſed to " ſuffer his ſentence, and the conditions of " their reſtoration, to be digeſted into *a body* " *of written laws* for their guidance; and " that ſome of the angelic beings, might " have permiſſion to deſcend to the delin- " quents, to promulge and preach this writ- " ten body of laws unto them, that they " might thereby be left without excuſe, or " the plea of ignorance, for their conti- " nuance in diſobedience.

" That God aſſented, to the petitions of " the angelic bands; when they, one and " all, offered to undertake this miſſion, but " God ſelected from amongſt them thoſe " whom he deemed moſt proper for this " work of ſalvation; who were appointed " to deſcend *to the different regions* of the " habitable univerſe. That a being from " the firſt rank of angels was deſtined for " the eaſtern part of this globe, whom

" God

" God dignified with the name of *Bramah*, " in allusion to the divinity of the doctrine " and mission he had in charge.

" That *Birmah* by the command of God " dictated to *Bramah* and the other deputed " angels, the terms and conditions, which " had been primarily delivered to the de- " linquents, by the mouth of *Birmah*; " that *Bramah* received, and entered the laws " of God in *Debtah Nagur*, (literally, the " language of angels) and that when *Bra-* " *mah* descended at the beginning of the " present age, and assumed the human form " and government of *Indostan*, he translated " them into the *Sanscrit*, a language then " universally known throughout *Indostan*; " and called the body of laws *the Chartah* " *Bhade* * *Shastah of Bramah* (literally, the " *four scriptures of divine words of the* " *mighty spirit)* which he promulged, and " preached to the delinquents, as the only " terms of their salvation and restoration.

" That for the space of a thousand years, " the doctrines of the *Chartah Bhade*, were " preached and propagated, without varia- " tion or innovation; and many of the " delinquents benefited from them and were

* A written book.

" saved;

" ſaved: but that about the cloſe of this
" period, ſome *Goſeyns* * and *Battezaaz* †
" *Bramins*, combining together, wrote a
" paraphraſe on the *Chartah Bhade*, which
" they called the *Chaſtah* ‡ *Bhade of Bra-*
" *mah* §, or the *ſix ſcriptures of the mighty*
" *ſpirit*; in this work the original text of
" *Bramah*'s *Chartah Bhade* was ſtill pre-
" ſerved.—About this period alſo it was,
" that the *Goſeyns* and *Battezaaz Bramins*,
" began to appropriate to themſelves the uſe
" of the *Sanſcrît character*, and inſtituted in
" the place of it the common *Indoſtan* cha-
" racter in uſe at this day: it was now alſo
" that *they* firſt began to veil in myſteries,
" the ſimple doctrines of *Bramah*.

" That about five hundred years later,
" that is, fifteen hundred years from the firſt
" promulgation of *Bramah*'s *Shaſtah*; the
" *Goſeyns*, and *Battezaaz Bramins*, pub-
" liſhed a ſecond expoſition, or commentary
" on the *Chartah Bhade*; which ſwelled
" the *Gentoo* ſcriptures to eighteen books:
" theſe the commentators entitled the *Augh-*
" *torrah Bhade Shaſtah*, or the *eighteen books*

* *Gentoo* Biſhops.

† Expounders of the *Shaſtah*. ‡ Six.

§ From the promulging this *Bhade*, the Polytheiſm of the *Gentoos* took its riſe.

" *of*

" *of divine words*; it was drawn up in a " compound character, of the common *Indostan*, and *Sanscrît*;—the original text of " the *Chartah Bhade*, was in a manner sunk " and alluded to only; the histories of their " Rajahs and country, were introduced under " figures and symbols, and made a part of " their religious worship, and a multitude " of ceremonials, and exteriour modes of " worship, were instituted; which the commentators said were implied in *Bramah*'s " *Chartah Bhade*, although not expressly " directed therein, by him; and the whole " enveloped in impenetrable obscurity by " allegory and fable, beyond the comprehension even of the common tribe of " *Bramins* themselves; the laity being thus " precluded from the knowledge of their " original scriptures had a new system of " faith broached unto them, which their " ancestors were utterly strangers to.

" That this innovation of the *Aughtorrah* " *Bhade* produced a schism amongst the " *Gentoos*, who until this period had followed one profession of faith throughout " the vast empire of *Indostan*; for the *Bramins* of *Cormandell* and *Mallabar* finding " their brethren upon the course of the *Ganges* " had taken this hold step to inslave the laity,

" set

" ſet up for themſelves, and formed a ſcripture
" of their own, founded as they ſaid upon
" the *Chartah Bhade* of *Bramah*; this they
" called *the Viedam* * *of Brummah*, or *divine*
" *words of the mighty ſpirit*;—theſe com-
" mentators, by the example of their bre-
" thren, interſperſed in their new religious
" ſyſtem, the hiſtories of their governors,
" and country, under various ſymbols and
" allegories, but departed from that chaſtity
" of manners, which was ſtill preſerved in
" the *Aughtorrah Bhade Shaſtah*.

" Thus the original, plain, pure, and
" ſimple tenets of the *Chartah Bhade* of
" *Bramah* (fifteen hundred years after its
" firſt promulgation) became by degrees
" utterly loſt; except, to three or four *Go-*
" *ſeyn* families, who at this day are only
" capable of reading, and expounding it,
" from the *Sanſcrît* character; to theſe may
" be added a few others of the tribe
" of *Battezaaz Bramins*, who can read
" and expound from the *Chartah Bhade*,
" which ſtill preſerved the text of the ori-
" ginal, as before remarked.

* *Viedam* in the *Mallabar* language ſignifies the ſame as *Shaſtah* in the *Sanſcrît*, viz. *divine words*—— and ſometimes, *the words of God*.

" How

" How much ſoever the primitive reli-
" gion of the *Gentoos* ſuffered by theſe inno-
" vations; their government underwent no
" change for many centuries after, all ac-
" knowledging allegiance to one univerſal
" Rajah of the *Succadit* family, lineally
" deſcended from their Prince and Lawgiver
" *Bramah.*—— The Princes of this line
" oppoſed the innovations made in their
" primitive faith, with a fruitleſs oppoſition,
" which endangered the exiſtence of their
" own government; ſo that at length they
" were reduced to the neceſſity of ſubſcrib-
" ing, firſt to the *Chaſtah Bhade*, and ſub-
" ſequently to the *Aughtorrah Bhade*; al-
" though their wiſdom foreſaw, and fore-
" told, the fatal conſequences theſe inno-
" vations would have on the ſtate and the
" nation: but the *Goſeyns* and *Bramins*,
" having taſted the ſweets of prieſtly power
" by the firſt of theſe *Bhades*, determined
" to enlarge, and eſtabliſh it, by the pro-
" mulgation of the *laſt*; for in this the
" exterior modes of worſhip were ſo multi-
" plied, and ſuch a numerous train of new
" divinities created, which the people never
" before had heard or dreamed of, and both
" the one and the other were ſo enveloped
" by the *Goſeyns* and *Bramins* in darkneſs,
" penetrable to themſelves only, that thoſe

" professors of divinity, became of new and " great importance, for the daily obligations of religious duties, which were by " these new institutes imposed on every " *Gentoo*, from the highest to the lowest " rank of the people, were of so intricate, and " alarming a nature, as to require a *Bramin* " to be at hand, to explain and officiate, " in the performance of them: they had " however the address to captivate the minds " of the vulgar, by introducing show and " parade into all their principal religious " feasts, as well as fasts; and by a new " single political institution, to wit, *the preservation of their cast or tribe*, the whole " nation was reduced to sacerdotal slavery.

" From the period that the *Aughtorrah* " *Bhade* was published as the rule of the " *Gentoo* faith and worship, superstition, the " sure support of priestcraft, took fast possession of the people; and their consciences, actions, and conduct, in spirituals " and temporals, were lodged in the breasts " of their *household Bramins*, and at their " disposal; for every head of a family was " obliged to have one of those ghostly fathers at his elbow, and in fact the people " became in general mere machines, actuated and moved, as either the good

" or evil intentions of their houſehold tyrant
" dictated.

" The *Aughtorrah Bhade Shaſtah*, has been
" invariably followed by the *Gentoos* inha-
" biting from the mouth of the *Ganges* to
" the *Indus*, for the laſt three thouſand three
" hundred and ſixty-ſix years. This pre-
" ciſely fixes the commencement of the *Gen-*
" *too mythology*, which, until the publication
" of that *Bhade*, had no exiſtence amongſt
" them: every *Gentoo* of rank or wealth,
" has a copy of this ſcripture in his poſſeſ-
" ſion; under the care and inſpection of
" his domeſtic *Bramin*; who every day
" reads and expounds a portion of it to the
" family.

" Sixteen hundred and ſeventy nine years,
" from the promulgation of the *Aughtorrah*
" *Bhade Shaſtah*, the ſacred line of *Bramah*
" became extinct, in the perſon of *Succa-*
" *dit*, the laſt *Mahahmahah Rajah*; (moſt
" mighty King) he reigned over all *Indoſ-*
" *tan*, ſixty years; his deceaſe cauſed a ge-
" neral lamentation amongſt the people; and
" from his death, a new *Gentoo Epocha*
" took place, called the *Æra of Succadit*;
" and the preſent year (A. D. 1766) is the

" year

" year of *Succadit*, sixteen hundred eighty
" seven.

" The death of *Succadit*, became not
" only remarkable for a new *Epocha* of
" time, but also for another signal event in
" the *Gentoo* annals; namely, a total revo-
" lution of their government: the royal and
" sacred line being extinct, the Vice-roys of
" this extensive empire (who had been for
" some years strengthening themselves in
" their respective governments, and prepa-
" ring for this expected event) on the demise
" of *Succadit*, set up a claim of indepen-
" dency, to the lands over which they had
" ruled under the emperor: they all assumed
" the title of *Rajah*, a distinction which,
" before this memorable period, had been
" only given to four or five of the first
" officers of the state; who also generally
" filled the chief governments of the empire.
" ——Confusion followed——Those com-
" manders who found themselves invested
" with greater force and power, attacked,
" conquered, and joined to their govern-
" ments, the territories of those who lay
" contiguous to them; whilst others who
" lay more distant preserved their indepen-
" dency: and thus the empire was divided
" into as many kingdoms, as there had

" been Vice-royſhips and Governments.—
" Between theſe Rajahs, there ſubſiſted a
" continual warfare.—From an empire thus
" divided againſt itſelf, what could be ex-
" pected, but that which, in a few centuries,
" conſequently and naturally followed.

" For the ſimple and intelligible tenets
" and religious duties, enjoined by the *Char-
" tah Bhade*, being thus abſorbed and loſt,
" in the attention and adherence, paid to
" the extravagant, abſurd, and unintelligible
" non-eſſentials of worſhip, inſtituted by
" the *Aughtorrah Bhade*; laid the founda-
" tion of the miſeries, with which, in ſuc-
" ceeding times, *Indoſtan* was viſited; and
" the merciful intention of God, for the
" redemption of the delinquent angels, (deſ-
" tined to inhabit this part of the earthly
" globe) was rendered fruitleſs.—The holy
" Tribe of *Bramins*, who were choſen and
" appointed by *Bramah* himſelf, to preach
" *the word of God*, and labor the ſalvation
" of the delinquents; in proceſs of time loſt
" ſight of their *divine original*, and in it's
" place ſubſtituted new and ſtrange doctrines;
" that had no tendency, but to the eſtabliſh-
" ing their own power: the people heark-
" ened unto them, and their minds were
" ſubdued and enſlaved; their ancient mili-
" tary

"tary genius, and ſpirit of liberty was de-
"bilitated; diſcord and diſſention aroſe
"amongſt the rulers of the land, and the
"ſtate grew ripe for falling at the firſt con-
"vulſion; and in the end ſuffered an utter
"ſubverſion, under the yoke of *Mahom-*
"*medan* tyranny; as a juſt puniſhment in-
"flicted on them by God, for their neglect
"of his laws, commands and promiſes,
"promulged to them, by his great and fa-
"vored angel *Bramah*, in the *Chartah*
"*Bhade Shaſtah*."

The foregoing detail, contains the genuine conceptions and belief, which the *Bramins* themſelves entertain of the antiquity of their ſcriptures, and of the two remarkable innovations they have undergone; particulars which we have had repeatedly confirmed to us, in various conferences with many of the moſt learned and ingenuous, amongſt the laity of the *Koyt* *, and other *Caſts*, who are often better verſed in the doctrines of their *Shaſtah* than the common run of the *Bramins* themſelves.

We hope it will not be diſpleaſing to our readers, if from the foregoing recital, we reduce into a narrow compaſs, and into one

* The tribe of Writers.

view, the ſtedfaſt faith of the *Gentoos*. Touching the antiquity of their ſcriptures; (the point now only under our conſideration) it appears therefore that they date the birth of the tenets and doctrines of the *Shaſtah*, from the expulſion of the angelic beings from the heavenly regions; that thoſe tenets were reduced into a written body of laws, four thouſand eight hundred and ſixty-ſix years ago, and then by God's permiſſion were promulged and preached to the inhabitants of *Indoſtan*. That theſe original ſcriptures underwent a remarkable change or innovation a thouſand years after the miſſion of their Prophet and Law-giver *Bramah* in the publication of the *Chartah Bhade Shaſtah*; and that three thouſand three hundred and ſixty-ſix years paſt, theſe original ſcriptures ſuffered a ſecond and laſt change or innovation, in the publication of the *Aughtorrah Bhade Shaſtah*; which occaſioned the firſt and only ſchiſm amongſt the *Gentoos*, that ſubſiſts to this day, namely between the followers of the *Aughtorrah Bhade Shaſtah*, and the followers of the *Viedam*.

Without repoſing an implicit confidence in the relations the *Bramins* give of the antiquity of their ſcriptures; we will, with our

our readers indulgence, humbly offer a few conjectures that have ſwayed us into a belief and concluſion, that the original tenets of *Bramah* are moſt ancient; that they are truly original, and not copied from any ſyſtem of theology, that has ever been promulged to, or obtruded upon the belief of mankind: what weight our conjectures may have with the curious, or how far it may rather appear in the proſecution of our work, that other theological ſyſtems have been framed from this, we readily ſubmit to thoſe, whoſe genius, learning and capacity in reſearches of this kind, are much ſuperior to our own.

It has been without reſerve aſſerted, that the *Gentoos* received their doctrines and worſhip, from the *Perſees* or *Egyptians*; but without (as we conceive) any degree of probability, or grounds, for the foundation of this opinion: reaſon and facts, ſeeming to us, to be on the ſide of the very contrary opinion.

That there was a very early communication between the empires of *Perſia*, *Egypt* and *Indoſtan*, is beyond controverſy; the former lay contiguous to *Indoſtan*; and although *Egypt* lay more remote from it, there ftill was an eaſy paſſage open between them, by the navigation from the *Red-ſea*, to the *Indus:* therefore it will appear no ſtrained concluſion, if we ſay; it is moſt likely there had been frequent intercourſe between the learned *Magi* of both thoſe nations, and the *Bramins*, long before the laſt mentioned ſages were viſited by *Zoroaſter* and *Pythagoras.*

It is neceſſary to remark that the *Bramins* did not, indeed could not, ſeek this intercourſe, for the principles of their religion forbad their travelling, or mixing with other nations; but ſo famed were they in the earlieſt known times for the purity of their manners, and the ſublimity of their wiſdom and doctrines, that their converſe was ſought after, and ſolicited univerſally by the philoſophers, and ſearchers after wiſdom and truth. For this character of them, we have the concurring teſtimony of all antiquity.

At what period of time, *Indoſtan* was viſited by *Zoroaſter* and *Pythagoras*, is not clearly determined by the learned; we will ſuppoſe it, with the generality of writers, to have been about the time of *Romulus.*— That theſe ſages travelled not to *inſtruct*, but, to be *inſtructed*; is a fact that may be determined with more preciſion; as well

as,

as, that they were not in *Indostan* together.—As they both made a long residence with the *Bramins* North West of the *Ganges* (for the name of *Zardhurst*, and *Pythagore* retain a place in the *Gentoo* annals "as travellers in "search of wisdom") it is reasonable to conclude they might in some degree be instructed in the *Sanscrit character*, and consequently, in the doctrines and worship instituted by the *Chartah* and *Aughtorrah Bhades*.

It is worthy notice that the *Metempsychosis*, as well as the three grand principles taught in the greater *Eleusinian* mysteries; namely, the *unity of the godhead*, *his general providence over all creation*, and *a future state of rewards and punishments*; were fundamental doctrines of *Bramah*'s *Chartah Bhade Shastah*, and were preached by the *Bramins*, from time immemorial to this day, throughout *Indostan*: not as mysteries, but as religious tenets, publicly known and received, by every *Gentoo* of the meanest capacity; this is a truth, which, we conceive, was unknown to the learned investigator of the *Eleusinian* mysteries; or it is probable he would, with more caution, have asserted, that the Eastern nations received their doctrines from the *Egyptians*.

Although

Although the Polytheiſm of the *Gentoos* had its origin from the firſt promulgation of the *Chartah Bhade Shaſtah*, and their Mythology from the publication of the *Aughtorrah Bhade*; yet the abovementioned theological dogma's remained inviolable and unchanged; and as theſe, with the firm perſuaſion of the præ-exiſtent ſtate of the ſpirit, or ſoul, have ever been, and ſtill are, the very baſis of all the *Gentoo* worſhip; it appears to us moſt probable, (from the early communication before remarked, and the reaſons before given) that the *Egyptians* borrowed theſe tenets from the *Bramins*.

That *Pythagoras* took the doctrine of the *Metempſychoſis*, from the *Bramins*, is not diſputed: yet future times erroneouſly ſtiled it *Pythagorean*; an egregious miſtake, which could proceed only from ignorance of its original.

Whatever may have been the period, that *Indoſtan* was viſited by the two travelling ſages abovementioned; it is acknowledged that *Pythagoras* undertook that journey, ſome years later than *Zoroaſter*:—— when *Pythagoras* left *India*, he went into *Perſia*, where he converſed with the Magi of that country, and was inſtructed in their myſteries;

mysteries; and is said (with probability of truth) to have held many conferences with *Zoroaster*, on the doctrines of the *Bramins*. They had both been initiated in all the mysteries, and learning, of the *Egyptians*; and *Pythagoras*, in his second visit to *Egypt*, before his return to *Greece*, probably repaid the debt of wisdom he had received from the Magi, by giving them new, and stronger lights into the theology, cosmogony and mythology of the *Bramins*, from their *Chastah*, and *Aughtorrah Bhades*.

The moral institutes, of *Zoroaster*, and *Pythagoras*; inculcated and taught by the one to the *Persians*, and by the other, to the *Greeks*; truely bore the stamp of divine! but their system of theology, surely that of madness!—They had so long and intensely thought, and reasoned on the *divine nature*, and the *cause of evil*; that the portion of divine nature they possessed, seemed utterly impaired, and bewildered, as soon as they began to form their crude principles into a *system*;—they appear to have preserved the basis and out-lines of *Bramah's Shastah*, on which (probably in conjunction with the *Persian* and *Egyptian* Magi) they raised an aerial superstructure, wild and incomprehensible! and labored to propagate an unintelligible

telligible jargon of divinity, which neither themſelves, nor any mortal ſince their time, could explain, or reduce to the level of human underſtanding.

How far, on a compariſon between the modes of worſhip, inſtituted by the *Chartah* and *Aughtorrah Bhades*, and thoſe of the antient *Egyptians*, *Greeks* and *Romans*, it may appear that thoſe of the *Bramins* are originals, and thoſe of the latter copies only, we ſubmit to the enquiry of the learned into thoſe intricate ſtudies, when in the courſe of our work we exhibit to the reader ſome ſpecimens of the *Gentoo* Mythology, and an account of their faſts and feſtivals.

By the fundamental doctrines and laws of the *Gentoos*, they cannot admit of proſelytes or converts, to their faith or worſhip; nor receive them into the pale of their communion, without the loſs of their Caſt, or Tribe; a diſgrace which every *Gentoo* would rather ſuffer death than incur: and although this religious prohibition, in its conſequences, reduced the people to a ſlaviſh dependence on their *Bramins*; yet it proved the cement of their union as a nation; which to this day remains unmixed with any other race of people.—Theſe are circumſtances which,

which, to the beſt of our knowledge, remembrance, and reading, peculiarly diſtinguiſh the *Gentoos*, from all the nations of the known world, and plead ſtrongly in favor of the great antiquity of this people, as well as the originality of their ſcriptures.

Another conſideration, to the ſame purpoſe, claims our notice; namely the perpetuity of the *Gentoo* doctrines, which through a ſucceſſion of ſo many ages, have ſtill remained unchanged, in their fundamental tenets;—for although the *Chaſtah* and *Aughtorrah Bhades*, enlarged the exteriors of their worſhip, yet theſe derive their authority and eſſence, in the boſom of every *Gentoo*, from the *Chartah Bhade* of *Bramah*: and it is no uncommon thing, for a *Gentoo*, upon any point of conſcience, or any important emergency in his affairs or conduct, to reject the deciſion of the *Chaſtah* and *Aughtorrah Bhades*, and to procure, no matter at what expence, the deciſion of the *Chartah Bhade*, expounded from the *Sanſcrit*.

Enough has been ſaid, to ſhew that the genuine tenets of *Bramah*, are to be found only in the *Chartah Bhade*; and as all who have wrote on this ſubject, have received their information from crude, inconſiſtent reports, chiefly taken from the *Aughtorrah Bhade*, and the *Viedam*; it is no wonder that the religion of the *Gentoos*, has been traduced; by ſome, as utterly unintelligible; and by others, as monſtrous, abſurd, and diſgraceful to humanity:——our deſign is to reſcue theſe ancient people, from thoſe imputations; in order to which we ſhall proceed, without further introduction or preface, to inveſtigate their original ſcriptures, as contained in the *Chartah Bhade*; at the cloſe of each ſection we ſhall ſubjoin, ſuch remarks, and explanations, as may appear to us neceſſary and pertinent to our ſubject.

For the greater perſpicuity, we will preſent to our readers the fundamental doctrines of the *Bramins*, under five diſtinct ſections; as they are ranged in the firſt book of this *Shaſtah*: viz.

I. Of God and his Attributes.
II. The creation of Angelic Beings.
III. The Lapſe of part of thoſe Beings.
IV. Their Puniſhment.
V. The mitigation of that Puniſhment, and their final Sentence.

SECT. I.

" *Of God and his Attributes.*

" God is ONE *.—Creator of all that
" *is.*——God is like a perfect sphere,
" without beginning or end.—God
" rules and governs all creation by a
" general providence resulting from
" first determined and fixed principles.
" ——Thou shalt not make enquiry
" into the essence and nature of the
" existence of the ETERNAL ONE, nor,
" by what laws he governs.—An en-
" quiry into either, is vain and crimi-
" nal.—It is enough, that day by day,
" and night by night, thou seest in his
" works; his *wisdom*, *power*, and his
" *mercy*.——Benefit thereby."

* *Ekhummesha*, literally, *the one that ever was*; which we translate, *the eternal one*.

REMARKS.

THE foregoing simple and sublime description of the Supreme Being constitutes the first chapter, or section of the *Shastah*.——The *Bramins* of the *Aughtorrah Bhade* teach, that there originally existed a chapter

chapter of the *Shastah*, which explained and solely treated of the divine nature and essence; but that it was soon irrecoverably lost, and never transmitted to posterity by *Bramah*, who *tore it out* of his *Chartah Bhade*.

Baldeus, who resided thirty years on the Island of *Ceylon*, and has given a laborious translation of the *Viedam*; recites a similar anecdote from those scriptures, and says, "that the lost part treated of God, and the "origin of the universe, or visible worlds; "the loss of which is highly lamented by "the *Bramins*."—In which this author seems to have plunged into a double error; first, in alleging the part lost, treated of the origin of the universe; whereas both the *Viedam*, and *Shastah*, are elaborate on the subject; and fix not only the period of its creation, but also its precise age, and term of duration, (as we shall shew hereafter); consequently and secondly, they could not properly be said to lament a loss they never sustained.—— But in truth, the whole of this matter is allegorical, a circumstance, which *Baldeus*, it seems, never adverted to.

In various discourses, we have had, with some learned *Bramins*, on the above cited passage

paſſage of the *Aughtorrah Bhade*, they were all unanimous in their ſenſe and interpretation of it: namely, that to man was given for the exerciſe of his reaſon, and virtue, the contemplation of the viſible wonders of the creation; but, that the ETERNAL ONE had precluded all enquiry into his origin, nature, and eſſence, and the laws by which he governs; as ſubjects inexplicable to, and beyond the limited powers of created beings; therefore it is emphatically ſaid, that *Bramah tore out* that part, implying the prohibition of ſuch enquiries, as uſeleſs and preſumptuous.

Had one tythe of the time and trouble, which the juſt mentioned eccleſiaſtic beſtowed in rendering a literal tranſlation of the *Viedam*, been employed in attempting an explanation of its myſteries; his labors might have proved worthy the attention of the learned; whereas, by contenting himſelf with a bare verſion, without aiming at the interpretation of the allegorical parts of thoſe ſcriptures, his toils, which muſt have been great and intenſe, have only produced a monſter, that ſhocks reaſon and probability.— They are miſ-repreſentations like theſe, which we have lamented in the preliminary diſcourſe, to the firſt part of this our work, as injurious to human nature; various and enormous are the miſtakes, which this author has fallen into from the above cauſe, through the whole of his voluminous work, which might be proved in a multitude of inſtances; but one ſhall ſuffice as a ſpecimen of the whole, which nothing but the miſtaken zeal of a chriſtian divine can excuſe.

" The *Viedam* (according to *Baldeus*) gives " the ſame place and power to *Birmah* or " *Bramah* (for he erroneouſly makes theſe " names ſynonimous) as the *Shaſtah* does; " and as the *Mallabars* acknowledge *Bramah* " to be the ſon of God, and ſupreme go- " vernor of angels; nay even aſcribe to him " a human form: *ſo it is evident, that theſe* " *attributes, muſt have their origin from* " *what they have heard, though perhaps con-* " *fuſedly, of Jeſus Chriſt the ſon of God.*"

SECT. II.

"*The Creation of Angelic Beings.*

"The ETERNAL ONE, abſorbed in the "contemplation of his own exiſtence; in "the fullneſs of time, reſolved to *par-* "*ticipate* his glory and eſſence with "beings capable of feeling, and ſharing "his beatitude, and of adminiſtering "to his glory.--Theſe beings then were "not.—The ETERNAL ONE willed.— "And they were. —He formed them "in part of his own eſſence; capable "of perfection, but with the powers "of imperfection; both depending on "their voluntary election.--The ETER- "NAL ONE firſt created *Birmah*, *Biſtnoo*, "and *Sieb*; then *Moiſaſoor*, and all the "*Debtah-Logue* *.——The *eternal one* "gave pre-eminence to *Birmah*, *Biſt-* "*noo* and *Sieb*.——He appointed *Bir-* "*mah*, Prince of the *Debtah-Logue*, "and put the *Debtah* under ſubjection "to him; he alſo conſtituted him his "vicegerent in heaven, and *Biſtnoo* and "*Sieb*, were eſtabliſhed his co-adjutors.

* *Debtah*, angels; *Logue*, a people, multitude, or congregation; *Debtah-Logue*, the angelic hoſt.

"—The

" —The ETERNAL ONE divided the
" *Debtah* into different bands, and
" ranks, and placed a leader or chief
" over each.—These worshipped round
" the throne of the *eternal one* according
" to their degree, and harmony
" was in heaven.—*Moisasoor*, chief of
" the first angelic band, led the celestial
" song of praise and adoration
" to the Creator, and the song of
" obedience to *Birmah* his first created.
" —And the Eternal One rejoiced in
" his new creation."

REMARKS.

MANKIND in general of every denomination, and religious profession, have subscribed to the opinion of the existence of *angelic beings*; and have each formed their crude, peculiar, and imaginary conceptions of their origin and destination. —Crude and imaginary indeed! must be the best human construction, on so marvellous a subject.—The simple, rational, and sublime cause, assigned by *Bramah*, for this act of creation; is most worthy a great and benign *being*, and conveys a striking and interesting impression, not only of his *power*, but of his *benevolence*.

Bramah, in the opening of this section, seems to place the *eternal one*, in the situation of of an abſolute, good, and powerful *monarch*, without *ſubjects*; which in fact is being no monarch at all: for however happy, or bleſſed ſuch a being may be, in the contemplation of his own ſole exiſtence and almighty power; yet he cannot (ſay the *Bramins*) be completely ſo, without partakers in his glory and beatitude; who ſhould alſo, be conſcious of the *tenure* of their own exiſtence, as well as of the power, and benevolent intentions of their *creator*, and worſhip him, accordingly.

But a blind and neceſſary obedience and worſhip, from any new creation of rational beings, (which muſt have followed had they been created perfect) would have fallen ſhort of their Creator's purpoſe; therefore *Bramah* ſays, *the eternal one*, formed them "capable "of *perfection*, but with the powers of im- "perfection;" without ſubjecting them to *either*, that their adoration and obedience ſhould be the reſult of their own *free-will*; the worſhip alone worthy his acceptance.

From the doctrine contained in this ſection it appears, that the powers of perfection and imperfection, (or in other words the powers of *good and evil)* were coeval in the formation of the firſt created beings:——The

 Bramins

Bramins in their paraphraſe on this chapter, reconcile the ſuppoſed incompatibility of the exiſtence of moral evil, conſiſtently with the juſtice, power, and goodneſs of the *ſupreme being*, by alleging, "that as the *Debtah* were inveſted with the abſolute powers of *perfection*, their lapſe from that ſtate, cannot impeach either the power, juſtice, or goodneſs of the ETERNAL ONE; whoſe motives for their creation were benevolent; and the duty enjoined them light and eaſy.—To chaunt forth for ever, the praiſes of their *creator*—To bleſs him for their *creation*, and to acknowledge, and be obedient to *Birmah*, and his two coadjutors *Biſtnoo* and *Sieb*."

Human penal laws, which have their exiſtence in every well regulated government of the world; always pre-ſuppoſe that the individuals ſubjected to thoſe laws, are inveſted with full powers and capacity of paying obedience to them; otherwiſe their impoſition becomes an act of tyranny; but the premiſes granted, then the breach and violation of them is criminal, and juſtly puniſhable, without an imputation of injuſtice in the inſtitutor.——Shall man then appear ſcrupulouſly cautious in his inſtitutes and laws, not to offend againſt reaſon and juſtice, and yet

yet dare to doubt of, or arraign the juſtice of his Creator?

Whence the origin, and exiſtence of *moral evil?* Is a queſtion that has puzzled, and exerciſed the imagination, and underſtanding of the learned and ſpeculative in all ages.——We confeſs we have hitherto met with no ſolution of this intereſting enquiry, ſo ſatisfactory, concluſive, and rational, as flows from the doctrine before us.——Authors have been driven to very ſtrange concluſions on this ſubject, nay ſome have thought it neceſſary to form an apology in defence of their Creator, for the admiſſion of moral evil into the world; and aſſert, "That God was neceſſitated to admit moral evil in created beings, from the nature of the materials he had to work with; that God would have made all things perfect, but that there was in matter an evil bias, repugnant to his benevolence, which drew another way; whence aroſe all manner of evils:" and that, therefore, "To endue created beings with perfection; that is to produce good excluſive of evil, is one of thoſe impoſſibilities, which even infinite power cannot accompliſh." And conſequently that from this *apologetical cauſe only*, "The wickedneſs and miſeries of God's creatures

 can

can be fairly reconciled, with his infinite power and goodneſs.

Intereſting as this ſubject is, and muſt be, to every thinking being, our beſt conceptions of it, muſt fall far ſhort of certainty; it is however ſurely incumbent on us to adopt ſuch ſentiments (more eſpecially when we reſolve to broach them to the world) as will appear moſt worthy infinite power and infinite goodneſs.——How far this conſideration has been regarded in the reveries cited in the preceding paragraph, we ſubmit to our readers; in our own conceptions we cannot help ſaying thoſe authors appear to us to have left the argument in a much worſe ſtate than they found it; and in place of a rational apology for their Creator, ſeem the rather tacitly to impeach his power, in the firſt and greateſt of his attributes; his power of creation:—For God is not only the creator of angels and men; but creator of *matter* alſo; and could have made *that* perfect, had he ſo willed.——Whether God *could* endue created beings with perfection, or produce good excluſive of evil, we conceive is not the queſtion; (although a doubt of it is highly preſumptuous, if not impious) but the quære is, whether God could create a race of beings, endued with the powers of

abſolute

absolute free agency;—on the certainty of which position, the possibility of *sin* in created beings absolutely, and necessarily depends.

How much more rational and sublime the text of *Bramah*, which supposes the Deity's voluntary creation, or permission of evil; for the exaltation of a race of beings, whose *goodness* as free agents could not have existed without being endued with the contrasted, or opposite powers of doing *evil*.

SECT. III.

"*The Lapse of Part of the Angelic Bands.*

" From the creation of the *Debtah* " *Logue*, joy and harmony encompaſſed " the throne of the eternal *one*, for " the ſpace of *Hazaar par Hazaar* " *Munnuntur* *; and would have con- " tinued to the end of time, had not envy " and jealouſy took poſſeſſion of *Moi-* " *ſaſoor*, and other leaders of the angelic " bands; amongſt whom was *Rhaabon*, " the next in dignity to *Moiſaſoor*;— " they, unmindful of the bleſſing of " their creation, and the duties enjoined " them, reject the powers of *perfection*, " which the eternal ONE had graciouſly " beſtowed upon them, exerted their " powers of *imperfection*, and did evil " in the ſight of the eternal ONE.—They " withheld their obedience from him, " and denied ſubmiſſion to his *vice-*

* A phraſe often made uſe of in the *Shaſtah* to expreſs infinite extenſion or duration of time; the word *Munnuntur* in it's abſolute and literal ſenſe will be ſubſequently explained; the word *Hazaar*, literally ſignifies a thouſand; *Hazaar par Hazaar*, thouſands upon thouſands.

" *gerent*,

" *gerent*, and his coadjutors, *Biſtnoo*, " and *Sieb*, and ſaid to themſelves— " We will rule!—And fearleſs of the " omnipotence, and anger of their Crea- " tor, they ſpread their evil imagina- " tions amongſt the angelic hoſt, de- " ceived them, and drew a large portion " of them from their allegiance.—And " there was a ſeparation from the throne " of the eternal ONE.--Sorrow ſeized the " faithful angelic ſpirits, and anguiſh " was now firſt known in heaven."

SECT. IV.

" *The Punishment of the Delinquent Debtah.*

" The eternal ONE, whose omniscience, " prescience and influence, extended to " all things, except the actions of " beings, which he had *created free*; " beheld with grief and anger, the de- " fection of *Moisasoor*, *Rhaabon*, and " the other angelic leaders and spirits.— " Merciful in his wrath, he sent *Bir- " mah*, *Bistnoo* and *Sieb*, to admonish " them of their crime, and to persuade " them to return to their duty;—— " but they exulting in the imagination " of their independence, continued in " disobedience.—The eternal ONE then " commanded *Sieb* *, to go armed with " his omnipotence, to drive them from " the *Mahah Surgo* †, and plunge " them into the *Onderah* ‡, there

* Why *Sieb* was sent on this command has been already explained in our introduction.

† Supreme heaven, literally *the great eminence*, from *Mahah*, *great*; and *Surgo*, *high*; eminent in a local sense, the firmament being commonly distinguished, by the *Gentoos*, by the name of *Surgo*.

‡ *Onder*, *dark*; *Onderah*, *intense darkness*.

" doomed

"doomed to suffer unceasing *sorrows*, for "*Hazaar par Hazaar Munnunturs**."

* In this place the expression (which we have explained in a preceding note) means *everlasting*.

REMARKS.

THAT there was a defection or rebellion in heaven, the records of antiquity, sacred and prophane, bear allusive testimony of;—we will not aver, that this opinion took its rise from the doctrines of the *Bramins*, though it is most probable it did; be this as it may, we cannot help concluding, that the conceptions conveyed by the *Shastah*, of this extraordinary event, are more consistent with, and do greater honor to the dignity of an omnipotent Being, than those handed down to us in fables of the Sages, Poets and Philosophers of *Egypt*, *Greece* and *Rome*.——From these our *Milton* copied, with extravagance of genius and invention.— They all, without exception, unworthily impeach God's omnipotence by the powers of contention given to the apostate angels, to oppose their Creator in arms and battle; and although sacred writ † seems to countenance this warfare in heaven, it can only allude to the act of expulsion of the delinquents, as any other interpretation would lessen omnipotence.

† Revelations, chap xii. ver. 7.

The

The *Shaſtah* opens this ſection by denying the preſcience of God touching the actions of free agents; the *Bramins* defend this dogma by alleging, his preſcience in this caſe, is utterly repugnant and contradictory to the very nature and eſſence of free agency, which on ſuch terms could not have exiſted.

SECT. V.

" *The Mitigation of the Punishment of the*
" *delinquent Debtah, and their final sen-*
" *tence.*

" The rebellious *Debtah* groaned under
" the displeasure of their Creator in
" the *Onderah*, for the space of *one*
" *Munnuntur*; during which period,
" *Birmah*, *Bistnoo* and *Sieb*, and the
" rest of the faithful *Debtah*, never
" ceased imploring the eternal ONE, for
" their pardon and restoration.——
" The eternal ONE, by their intercession
" at length relented,—and although he
" could not foresee the effect of his
" mercy on the future conduct of the
" delinquents: yet unwilling to relin-
" quish the hopes of their repentance,
" he declared his will:—That they
" should be released from *the Onderah*,
" and be placed in such a state of
" *tryal* and *probation*, that they shall
" still have power, to work out their
" own salvation. The eternal ONE then
" promulged his gracious intentions,
" and delegating the power and govern-
" ment of the *MahahSurgo*, *to Birmah*,
" he

" he retired into *himself*, and became in-
" visible to all the angelic host, for the
" space of five thousand years.——At
" the end of this period he manifested
" himself again, resumed the throne of
" light, and appeared in his glory.-And
" the faithful angelic bands, celebrated
" his return in songs of gladness.

" When all was hushed!—the eter-
" nal ONE said, Let the *Dunneahoudah**
" of the fifteen *Boboons* † of purgation
" and purification appear, for the re-
" sidence of the rebellious *Debtah*.—
" And it instantly appeared.

" And the eternal ONE said, Let *Bist-*
" *noo* ‡, armed with my power, descend
" to the new creation of the *Dunneahou-*
" *dah*, and release the rebellious *Debtah*
" from the *Onderah*, and place them
" in the lowest of the fifteen *Boboons*.

" *Bistnoo* stood before the throne and
" said, Eternal ONE, I have done as
" thou hast commanded.——And all

* *Dooneah*, or *dunneah*, the *world*, *Dunneahoudah*, the *worlds*, or *the universe*.

§ *Boboons*, *regions* or *planets*.

‡ Why *Bistnoo* was sent on this service we have already explained in our introduction.

" the

" the faithful angelic hoſt, ſtood with " aſtoniſhment, and beheld the won- " ders, and ſplendor of the new creation " of the *Dunneaboudah*.

" And the Eternal ONE ſpake again " unto *Biſtnoo* and ſaid.—I will form " *bodies* for each of the delinquent " *Debtah*, which ſhall for a ſpace be " their priſon and habitation; in the " confines of which, they ſhall be ſub- " ject to natural evils, in proportion " to the degree of their original guilt.— " Do thou go, and command them to " hold themſelves prepared to enter " therein, and they ſhall obey thee.

" And *Biſtnoo* ſtood again before the " throne, and bowed and ſaid, Eternal " ONE, thy commands are fulfilled.— " And the faithful angelic hoſt, ſtood " again aſtoniſhed, at the wonders " they heard, and ſung forth the praiſe " and mercy of the Eternal ONE.

" When all was huſhed! the Eternal " one ſaid again unto *Biſtnoo*, The bodies " which I will prepare for the recep- " tion of the rebellious *Debtah*, ſhall " be ſubject to change, decay, death,

" and renewal, from the principles " wherewith I ſhall form them; and " through thoſe mortal bodies, ſhall the " delinquent *Debtah* undergo alternate- " ly *eighty ſeven* changes, or *tranſmigra-* " *tions*; ſubject more or leſs, to the " conſequences of natural and *moral* " *evil*, in a juſt proportion to the de- " gree of their original guilt, and as " their actions through thoſe ſucceſſive " forms, ſhall correſpond with the li- " mited powers which I ſhall annex " to each;—and this ſhall be their " ſtate of *puniſhment* and *purgation*.

" And it ſhall be,—That when the " rebellious *Debtah* ſhall have accom- " pliſhed and paſſed through the eighty " ſeven tranſmigrations——they ſhall " from my abundant favor, animate a " new form, and thou *Biſtnoo* ſhalt call " it GHOIJ ‡.

" And it ſhall be,—That when the " mortal body of the *Ghoij* ſhall by a " *natural* decay, become inanimate, the " delinquent *Debtah* ſhall, from my " more abundant favor, animate the

‡ *Ghoij*, the cow; *Ghoijal*, cows; *Ghoijalbarry*, a cow-houſe.

" form

" form of MHURD†,—and in this form
" I will enlarge their intellectual powers,
" even as when I firſt created them free;
" and in this form ſhall be their chief
" ſtate of their *trial* and *probation.*

" The *Ghoij* ſhall be, by the delin-
" quent *Debtah*, deemed ſacred and
" holy, for it ſhall yield them a new
" and more delectable food, and eaſe
" them of part of the labor, to which
" I have doomed them.—And they
" ſhall not eat of the *Ghoij*, nor of the
" fleſh of any of the mortal bodies,
" which I ſhall prepare for their habita-
" tion, whether it creepeth on *Murto*, or
" ſwimmeth in *Jhoale*†, or flyeth in
" *Ouſtmaan* ‡, for their food ſhall be
" the milk of the *Ghoij*, and the fruits
" of *Murto.*

" The mortal forms wherewith I
" ſhall encompaſs the delinquent *Deb-*
" *tah* are the work of my hand, they
" ſhall not be deſtroyed, but left to
" their natural decay; therefore which-
" ſoever of the *Debtah*, ſhall by de-

* *Mhurd*, the common name of *man*, from *Murto*, matter, or earth.

† *Jhoale*, water, fluid. ‡ The *air*.

“ ſigned violence bring about the diſ-
“ ſolution of the mortal forms, ani-
“ mated by their delinquent brethren,
“ —Thou *Sieb*, ſhalt plunge the of-
“ fending ſpirit into the *Onderah*, for
“ a ſpace, and he ſhall be doomed to
“ paſs again the eighty-nine tranſmi-
“ grations, whatſoever ſtage he may
“ be arrived to, at the time of ſuch
“ his offence.—But whoſoever of the
“ delinquent *Debtah*, ſhall dare to *free*
“ *himſelf* by violence, from the mortal
“ form wherewith I ſhall incloſe him,
“ —Thou *Sieb* ſhalt plunge him into
“ the *Onderah* for ever.——He ſhall
“ not again have the benefit of the
“ fifteen *Boboons* of purgation, proba-
“ tion, and purification.

“ And I will diſtinguiſh by tribes and
“ kinds, the mortal bodies which I have
“ deſtined for the puniſhment of the
“ delinquent *Debtah*, and to theſe bodies
“ I will give different forms, qualities
“ and faculties, and they ſhall *unite* and
“ propagate each other in their tribe
“ and kind, according to a natural
“ impulſe which I will implant in
“ them; and from this natural union,
“ there ſhall proceed a ſucceſſion of

“ forms;

"forms; each in his kind and tribe. "that the progreſſive tranſmigrations of "the delinquent ſpirits, may not ceaſe.

"But whoſoever of the delinquent "*Debtah* ſhall *unite* with any form out "of his own tribe and kind; thou "*Sieb* ſhalt plunge the offending ſpirit "into the *Onderah*, for a ſpace, and "he ſhall be doomed to paſs through "the eighty-nine tranſmigrations, at "whatſoever ſtage he may be arrived, "at the time he committed ſuch of-"fence.

"And if any of the delinquent "*Debtah* ſhall (contrary to the natural "impulſe which I ſhall implant in the "forms which they ſhall animate) dare "to *unite* in ſuch unnatural wiſe, as "may fruſtrate the increaſe of his "tribe and kind; thou *Sieb* ſhalt plunge "them into the *Onderah* for ever.— "And they ſhall not again be entitled "to the benefit of the fifteen *Boboons* "of purgation, probation and purifi-"cation.

"The delinquent and unhappy *Deb-*"*tah*, ſhall yet have it in their power, "to leſſen and ſoften their pains and "puniſhment, by the ſweet intercourſe "of ſocial compacts; and if they love "and cheriſh one another, and do mu- "tual good offices, and aſſiſt and en- "courage each other in the work of "repentance for their crime of diſ- "obedience; I will ſtrengthen their "good intentions, and they ſhall find "favor.——But if they perſecute one "another, I will comfort the perſecuted, "and the perſecutors ſhall never enter "the ninth *Boboon*, even the *firſt Bo-* "*boon* of purification.

"And it ſhall be,—That if the *Deb-* "*tah* benefit themſelves of my favor "in their eighty-ninth tranſmigration "of *Mhurd*, by repentance and good "works, thou *Biſtnoo* ſhalt receive "them into thy boſom and convey them "to the ſecond *Boboon* of puniſhment "and purgation, and in this wiſe ſhalt "thou do, until they have paſſed pro- "greſſively the eight *Boboons* of puniſh- "ment, purgation, and probation, when "their puniſhment ſhall ceaſe, and thou "ſhalt convey them to the ninth; even "the firſt *Boboon* of purification.

"But

" But it ſhall be,—That if the re-
" bellious *Debtah*, do not benefit of
" my favor in the eighty-ninth tranſ-
" migration of *Mhurd*, according to
" the powers, wherewith I will inveſt
" them;—Thou *Sieb*, ſhalt return them
" for a ſpace into the *Onderah*, and
" from thence after a time which I
" ſhall appoint, *Biſtnoo* ſhall replace
" them in the loweſt *Boboon* of puniſh-
" ment and purgation for a ſecond
" trial; and in this wiſe ſhall they
" ſuffer, until by their repentance and
" perſeverance in good works, during
" their eighty-ninth mortal tranſmigra-
" tion of *Mhurd*, they ſhall attain the
" ninth *Boboon*, even the firſt of the
" ſeven *Boboons* of purification.—For it
" is decreed that the rebellious *Debtah*
" ſhall not enter the *Mahah Surgo*,
" nor behold my face, until they have
" paſſed the eight *Boboons* of puniſh-
" ment, and the ſeven *Boboons* of pu-
" rification.

" When the angelic faithful hoſt,
" heard all that the Eternal ONE had
" ſpoken, and decreed, concerning the
" rebellious *Debtah*; they ſung forth
" his praiſe, his power, and juſtice.

"When all was hushed! the Eternal "ONE said to the angelic host, I will "extend my grace to the rebellious "*Debtah*, for a certain space, which I "will divide into four *Jogues* *.—In the "first of the four *Jogues*, I will, that "the term of their probation in the "eighty-ninth transmigration of *Mburd*, "shall extend to 100,000 years—in "the second of the four *Jogues*, their "term of their probation in *Mburd*, "shall be abridged to 10,000 years "—in the third of the four *Jogues*, it "shall be yet abridged to 1000 years "—and in the fourth *Jogue* to 100 "years only.—And the angelic host, "celebrated in shouts of joy, the "mercy and forbearance of God.

"When all was hushed! the Eternal "ONE said, It shall be,—That when "the space of time, which I have "decreed for the duration of the *Dun-* "*neaboudah*, and the space which my "mercy has allotted for the probation "of the fallen *Debtah*, shall be ac- "complished, by the revolutions of the "four *Jogues*,—in that day, should "there be any of them who remaining

* *Jogues*, ages, precise periods of time.

"reprobate,

" reprobate, have not paſſed the eighth
" *Boboon* of puniſhment and probation,
" and have not entered the ninth *Bo-*
" *boon*, even the firſt *Boboon* of purifi-
" cation;—thou *Sieb* ſhalt, armed with
" my power, caſt them into the *Onde-*
" *rab* for ever.—And thou ſhalt then
" deſtroy the eight *Boboons* of puniſh-
" ment, purgation and probation, and
" they ſhall be no more.—And thou
" *Biſtnoo* ſhalt yet for a ſpace preſerve
" the ſeven *Boboons* of *purification*,
" until the *Debtah*, who have benefited
" of my grace and mercy, have by thee
" been purified from their ſin:——
" and in the day when that ſhall be
" accompliſhed, and they are reſtored
" to their ſtate, and admitted to my
" preſence,—thou *Sieb* ſhalt then de-
" ſtroy the ſeven *Boboons* of purification,
" and they ſhall be no more.

" And the angelic faithful hoſt trem-
" bled at the power, and words of
" the Eternal ONE.

" The Eternal ONE, ſpoke again and
" ſaid.—I have not withheld my mercy
" from *Moiſaſoor*, *Rhaboon*, and the
" reſt of the leaders of the rebellious

" *Debtah*;

" *Debtah*;——but as they thirsted for " power, I will enlarge their powers *of* " *evil*;——they shall have liberty to " pervade, and enter into the *eight* " *Boboons* of purgation and probation, " and the delinquent *Debtah*, shall be " exposed and open to the same temp- " tations, that first instigated their re- " volt: but the exertion of those en- " larged powers, which I will give to " the rebellious leaders, shall be *to them*, " the source of aggravated guilt, and " punishment; and the resistance made " to their temptations, by the perverted " *Debtah*, shall be *to me* the *great* " *proof*, of the sincerity of their sorrow " and repentance.

" The Eternal ONE ceased.—And " the faithful host shouted forth songs " of praise and adoration, mixed with " grief, and lamentation for the fate " of their lapsed brethren.——They " communed amongst themselves, and " with one voice by the mouth of " *Bistnoo*, besought the Eternal ONE, that " they might have permission to de- " scend occasionally to the *eight Bo-* " *boons* of punishment, and purgation, " to assume the form of *Mburd*, and

"by their preſence, council and ex-
"ample, guard the unhappy and per-
"verted *Debtah*, againſt the further
"temptations of *Moiſaſoor*, and the
"rebellious leaders.—The Eternal ONE
"aſſented, and the faithful heavenly
"bands, ſhouted their ſongs of glad-
"neſs and thankſgiving.

"When all was huſhed! the Eternal
"ONE ſpake again, and ſaid,—Do thou
"*Birmah*, arrayed in my glory, and
"armed with my power, deſcend to
"the loweſt *Boboon* of puniſhment and
"purgation, and make known to the
"rebellious *Debtah*, the words that I
"have uttered, and the decrees which
"I have pronounced againſt them, and
"ſee they enter into the bodies, which
"I have prepared for them.

"And *Birmah* ſtood before the
"throne, and ſaid, Eternal ONE, I have
"done as thou haſt commanded.——
"The delinquent *Debtah* rejoice in
"thy mercy, confeſs the juſtice of thy
"decrees, avow their ſorrow and re-
"pentance, and have entered into the
"mortal bodies which thou haſt pre-
"pared for them."

REMARKS.

THE foregoing is almoſt a literal tranſlation from the *Chartah Bhade of Bramah*, as we deſpaired of reaching the ſublime ſtile and diction of the original;—it will not we hope be diſpleaſing to our reader, if we aſſiſt his memory and recollection by a recapitulation of the ground work of theſe doctrines, preſented to him in one connected view; the more eſpecially, as we ſhall alſo be thereby the better enabled to form our neceſſary explanatory remarks.

We have ſeen that the original divine inſtitutes of *Bramah* are ſimple and ſublime, comprehending the whole compaſs of all that is; God, Angels, the viſible and inviſible worlds, man and beaſts; and is comprized under the following articles of the *Gentoo* creed. To wit—

"That there is one God, eternal, omnific, omnipotent, and omniſcient, in all things excepting a *preſcience* of the future actions of *free agents*.—*That* God from an impulſe of divine love and goodneſs, firſt created THREE angelic perſons to whom he gave precedence, though not in equal degree——*That* he afterwards

afterwards from the ſame impulſe created an angelic hoſt, whom he placed in ſubjection to *Birmah* his firſt created, and to *Biſtnoo* and *Sieb*, as coadjutors to *Birmah*.—*That* God created them all free, and intended they ſhould all be partakers of his glory and beatitude, on the eaſy conditions of their acknowledging him their Creator, and paying obedience to him, and to the three primary created perſonages, whom he had put over them.—*That*, in proceſs of time, a large portion of the angelic hoſt, at the inſtigation of *Moiſaſoor* and others of their chief leaders, rebelled and denyed the ſupremacy of their Creator, and refuſed obedience to his commands. *That* in conſequence the rebels were excluded heaven, and the ſight of their Creator, and doomed to languiſh for ever in *ſorrow* and *darkneſs*. *That*, after a time, by the interceſſion of the three primary, and the reſt of the faithful angelic beings, God relented, and placed the delinquents in a more ſufferable ſtate of puniſhment and probation, with powers to gain their loſt happy ſituation.—*That* for that purpoſe a new creation of the viſible and inviſible worlds inſtantaneouſly took place, deſtined for the delinquents.—*That* the new creation conſiſted of fifteen regions, ſeven below, and ſeven above this terraqueous globe, and that

that this globe and the ſeven regions below it are ſtages of puniſhment and purgation, and the ſeven above ſtages of purification, and conſequently that this globe is the eighth, laſt and chief ſtage of puniſhment, purgation and trial.—*That* mortal bodies were prepared by God, for the rebel angels, *in which* they were for a ſpace to be impriſoned, and ſubject to natural and moral evils, more or leſs painful in proportion to their original guilt, and *through which* they were doomed to tranſmigrate under eighty-nine different forms, the laſt into that of *man*, when the powers of the animating rebel ſpirits, are ſuppoſed to be enlarged equal to the ſtate of their firſt creation.—*That* under this form God reſts his chief expectations of their repentance and reſtoration, and if they fail, and continue reprobate under this form, they are returned to the loweſt region, and ſentenced to go through the ſame courſe of puniſhment, until they reach the ninth region, or firſt ſtage of purification, where although they ceaſe from puniſhment, and gain remiſſion and forgiveneſs of their guilt of rebellion; yet, they are not permitted to enter heaven, nor behold their Creator, before they have paſſed the ſeven regions of purification.——*That* the rebel-leaders had power given them by God, to enter the

eight

eight regions of punishment and probation, and that the faithful angelic spirits, had permission occasionally to descend to those regions, to guard the delinquents against the future attempts of their leaders.—*And that*, consequently, the souls, or spirits which animate every mortal form, are delinquent angels in a state of punishment, for a lapse from innocence, in a *pre-existent* state."

We will presume to say, that the *difference* between the doctrines hitherto imputed, to these ancient people, when compared with the original tenets of the *Chartah Bhade*, will now appear so obvious to the learned and curious reader, that a further discussion of this point, is we conceive needless, and would in truth be a tacit reflection upon his understanding.——Yet we are far from condemning the authors, who have treated on this subject; they took their information from the best lights they had;—it is only to be regretted, that in place of drinking at the fountain head, they have swallowed the muddy streams which flowed from the *Chartah* and *Aughtorrah Bhades*.—The author on his departure from *Bengal* in the year 1750, imagined himself well informed in the *Gentoo* religion, his knowledge had been acquired by conversations with the *Bramins* of of thofe *Bhades* who were near, as little acquainted with the *Chartah Bhade* of *Bramah*, as he was himfelf, and he had then thoughts of obtruding his crude notions on the public, had not a different neceffary application of his time luckily prevented him.

When we perufe fome portions of *Milton*'s account of the rebellion and expulfion of the angels, we are almoft led to imagine, on comparifon, that *Bramah* and he were both inftructed by the fame fpirit; had not the foaring, ungovernable, inventive genius of the latter, inftigated him to illuftrate his poem with fcenes too grofs and ludicrous, as well as manifeftly repugnant to, and inconfiftent with, fentiments we ought to entertain of an omnipotent Being (as before remarked) in which we rather fear he was infpired by one of thefe malignant fpirits (alluded to in the *Shaftah* and elfewhere) who have from their original defection, been the declared enemies of God and Man.—— For however we are aftonifhed and admire the fublimity of *Milton*'s genius, we can hardly fometimes avoid concluding his conceits truely diabolical.—But this by the by.—

Our readers are now poffeffed for the firft time of a faithful account of the *Metempfychofis ſychoſis* of the *Bramins*—commonly called the tranſmigration of ſouls, a term hitherto we believe little underſtood, that this doctrine was originally peculiar to the *Gentoos*, will not admit of doubt, although in after times it was embraced by the *Egyptian* Magi, and by ſome ſects amongſt the *Chineſe* and *Tartars*.——*Pythagoras*, who favored this doctrine, and was a convert to it, labored to introduce it amongſt his country-men the *Greeks*, but failed in the attempt. He ſucceeded better with them in the theogony, coſmogony and mythology of the *Bramins Aughtorrah Bhade Shaſtah*, although theſe conſtituted no part of the original theology of *Bramah*.

As we have reſerved a part expreſly for a diſſertation on the doctrine of the *Metempſychoſis*, we will avoid further mention of it here; but as the *Bramins* of the *Chartah* and *Aughtorrah Bhades*, inculcate and teach many corollary branches of doctrine which ſpring from this root, it is neceſſary that we recite a few of the moſt eſtabliſhed ones.

"When the delinquent *Debtah*, by the mediation of *Birmah*, *Biſtnoo* and *Moiſoor*, and the faithful angelic hoſt, were releaſed from the *Onderah*; all, except *Moiſaſoor*,

 Rhaabon,

Rhaabon, and the reſt of the rebel leaders, were ſo ſtruck with the goodneſs and mercy of the Eternal ONE, that they perſevered in a pious reſignation and true penitence, during the firſt of the *four Jogues*, and multitudes aſcended, and paſſed through the fifteen *Boboons*, and regained their forfeited eſtate. —This period of time is called in the *Shaſtah* the *Suttee Jogue*, when the term of the ſpirits probation in *Mhurd*, was extended to one hundred thouſand years.

" In the *ſecond* of the *four Jogues*, *Moiſaſoor* and the rebel leaders ſo effectually exerted their influence over the delinquent *Debtah*, that they ſoon began to forget their crime and diſregard their puniſhment in the *Onderah*; they rejected the councils and examples of the guardian *Debtah*, and ſtood a *ſecond time* in defiance of their Creator; and *Moiſaſoor* drew over *one third* of the remaining unpurified ſpirits.——This period is diſtinguiſhed in the *Shaſtah*, by the name of the *Tirtah Jogue*, in which the Eternal ONE retrenched the term of the ſpirits probation in *Mhurd*, to ten thouſand years. In this *Jogue* however, many perſevered in goodneſs, aſcended through the fifteen *Boboons*, and regained the *Mahah Surgo*.

"In the third of the four *Jogues*, *Moisasoor*'s influence increased, and he drew over half of the remaining unpurified spirits, in each of the eight *Boboons* of punishment and probation. This period is called in the *Shastah*, the *Duapaar*, or *Dwapaar Jogue*, in which the term of probation in *Mhurd*, was reduced to one thousand years; yet in this *Jogue* there were many who ascended and regained the *Mahah Surgo*.

"In the fourth *Jogue*, *Moisasoor* acquired as full possession of the hearts of the remaining delinquent *Debtah* as when they first rose in rebellion with him, with very few exceptions; this period in the *Shastah* is called the *Kolee Jogue*, in which the term of probation in *Mhurd* is limited to one hundred years only.—Yet even this *Jogue* affords some instances of the delinquent spirits surmounting the eight lower *Boboons*, by penitence and good works; notwithstanding the unwearied diligence of *Moisasoor*, *Rhaabon*, and the rest of the rebellious leaders, and delinquent *Debtah*, who had a second time fallen under his influence."

The *four Jogues* or ages having been so frequently mentioned in the last paragraphs, we cannot do better than explain their mean-

 ing

ing here, as ſuch explanation would prove too long for a note, it may be remembered, they are called the *Suttee Jogue*, the *Tirtah Jogue*, the *Duapaar Jogue*, and the *Kolee Jogue*; we will ſpeak to each in their order.

The *Suttee Jogue*, or the firſt age, literally the age of truth, figuratively the age of goodneſs;—in this age *Endeer* is fabled to be born, according to the *Aughtorrah Bhade*; and appointed King of the Univerſe—the word *Endeer* literally ſignifies good, and is in that *Shaſtah* oppoſed to *Moiſaſoor* or *evil*, and the various battles ſaid to be fought between this rebel angel and *Endeer*, and their deſcendants in every *Jogue*, allegorically exhibit the conflicts and progreſs of *good* and *evil* in the univerſe; *Endeer*'s being appointed univerſal Monarch in the *Suttee Jogue*, alludes to the ſtate of the delinquent *Debtah* in this age, upon their emerging from the *Onderah*, when the impreſſion of God's mercy acted ſo powerfully on their hearts, as to preſerve them in penitence and purity, during this age, notwithſtanding the utmoſt efforts of *Moiſaſoor* (or *evil*) and his adherents, to engage them in a ſecond defection.—From the word *Suttee* (truth) the word *Sanſah* in *Bengals*, and *Sutch*, in the Moors are derived,—any one acquainted

in

in the least degree with those tongues, knows that the phrase *Sansah Kotah*, in the one, and *Sutch Bhaat*, in the other, is commonly used to assert the verity of any thing advanced, and simply signifies, *words of truth*.

The *Tirtah Jogue*, or second age.—By the term prefixed to this age, the order of the *Jogues* should seem inverted, as the word in its simple construction signifies *third*.—The words *teen*, *tarah*, *tise*, *trese*, and *tetrese*, which express the numbers three, thirteen, twenty-three, thirty and thirty-three, are all derivatives from the *Sanscrit*, *Tirtah*, or *Tirtea*, as it is sometimes wrote, and means the third, but oftener the *third part*, as in the present instance, where the term *Tirtah Jogue* given to the second age, is allusive to the second defection of one third of the remaining unpurified delinquent spirits, from that penitence and purity which governed them in the *Suttee Jogue*.—In this age *Rhaam* is fabled to be born for the protection of the delinquent *Debtah*, against the snares and attempt of *Moisasoor* and his adherents.—The word *Rhaam* in the *Sanscrit*, literally signifies protector, but in many parts of the *Aughtorrah Bhade* this personage is mentioned in a more extended sense, as the protector of kingdoms, states and property.—

 Rhaam!

Rhaam! Rhaam! is uſed as a pious ſalutation, between two *Gentoos* when they meet in the morning, thereby recommending each other's perſon and property to the protection of this Demi-god.

The *Duapaar Jogue*, or third age.—This term prefixed to the third age, alludes to the ſecond defection from penitence and goodneſs of *one half* of the remaining unpurified *Debtah*—*dua*, or *dwa* ſimply ſignifies, two, or the ſecond, but here by the addition of *paar*, it means the half; thus *duapaar deen*, expreſſes half the day, and *duapaar rhaat*, half the night,—that is if the phraſe iſſues from the mouth of a polite *Gentoo*—but the vulgar would ſay *adah deen* and *adah rhaat*, *adah* being the common *Bengal* word for half.—In the beginning of this *Jogue* the *Aughtorrah Bhade* fixes the birth of *Kiſſen Taghoor*.—The word *kiſſen* in the *Sanſcrît* ſignifies a ſcourge, and this *being* is in that *Bhade* frequently diſtinguiſhed as the ſcourge of tyrants and tyranny.—*Tagoor* literally means *revered*, *reſpected*, and is a common appellation given to *Bramins*.

The *Kolee Jogue*, or the fourth and preſent age.—*Kolee* in the *Sanſcrît* ſignifies corruption, pollution, impurity, conſequently

Kolee

Kolee Jogue means the age of pollution.—In this age (ſay the *Bramins)* children ſhall bear falſe witneſs againſt their parents, and before the expiration of it—the ſtature of the *Mhurd* by the wickedneſs of the rebellious *Debtah* that animates it, ſhall be ſo reduced, that he will not be able to pluck a *Bygon (berengelah *)* without the help of a hooked ſtick.—We have often, whilſt at the head of the judicial court of *Cutcherry* at *Calcutta*, heard the moſt atrocious murders and crimes confeſſed, and an extenuation of them attempted, by pleading, *it was the Kolee Jogue*.—How far the poetical conceits of *Ovid*, and others, touching the golden, &c. ages, have been framed from *Bramah*'s *four Jogues*, we leave to the inveſtigation of the curious.

It is an eſtabliſhed doctrine of the *Aughtorrah Bhade*, that the three primary created perſonages, as well as the reſt of the heavenly angelic faithful ſpirits, have from time to time according to the permiſſion given them by God, deſcended to the eight *Boboons* of puniſhment, and have voluntarily ſubjected themſelves to the feelings of natural and moral evil, for the ſake of their brethren, the delinquent *Debtah*. And to

* The *Egg Plant*.

 this

this end, have undergone the eighty-nine tranſmigrations *; and that it is thoſe benevolent ſpirits, who have at different times appeared on this earthly region, under the mortal forms and names of *Endeer*, *Bramah*, *Jaggernaut*, *Kiſſen Tagoor*, *Rhaam*, *Luccon*, *Kalkee*, (or *Kallee) Surſuttee*, *Gunnis*, *Kartic*, *&c.*—that have oppoſed and fought againſt *Moiſaſoor*, *Rhaabon*, and their iniquitous adherents——and have proved themſelves under the various characters of Kings, Generals, Philoſophers, Lawgivers and Prophets, ſhining examples to the delinquent *Debtah*, of ſtupendous courage, fortitude, purity and piety.—That their viſitations were frequent during the *Tirtah*, and *Duapaar Jogues*, but rare ſince the commencement of the *Kolee Jogue*, becauſe in this age the delinquent *Debtah* in general are deemed utterly reprobate, and hardened in their wickedneſs beyond the power of counſel or example; ſo that they are in a manner left, and given up to their *own powers*, and abandoned to the full influence of *Moiſaſoor*.——But that there are ſtill in every

* Hence the *Gentoos* dread of killing even by accident any thing that has life, as thereby they may not only diſpoſſeſs the ſpirits of their allied *Debtah*, but alſo, thoſe of the celeſtial *Debtah*, who are working for their redemption.

period

period of time ſome few inſtances of the delinquents exertion of their *own powers* for their ſalvation, and that when this is manifeſt to God, he permits the celeſtial *Debtah* inviſibly to aid, confirm, and ſupport them.

Although the *Shaſtah* of *Bramah* denies the preſcience of God reſpecting the actions of free-agents, yet the *Bramins* maintain that his knowledge extends to the thoughts of every created being, and that the moment a *thought* is conceived by the ſoul or ſpirit, it is ſympathetically conveyed to God.—It is upon this principle that the adorations, prayers, petitions and thankſgivings, which the *Gentoos* prefer to the Deity himſelf, are offered in ſolemn ſilence; but it is not ſo with regard to the invocations and worſhip, inſtituted by the *Aughtorrah Bhade* to be paid to the ſubordinate celeſtial beings, for theſe are addreſſed in loud prayer, joined to the clang of various muſical inſtruments.

We have already ſlightly touched on the religious veneration paid to the *Ghoij* in a particular diſtrict of *Bengall*, although it is beyond doubt, that their devotion to this animal was univerſal throughout *Indoſtan* in former times.—The original ſource of this regard, was of a two-fold nature, as a religious and political inſtitution: firſt, in a religious ſenſe; as holding in the rotation of the *Metempſychoſis*, the rank immediately preceding the human form; this conception is the true cauſe of that devout, and ſometimes enthuſiaſtic veneration paid to this animated form, for the *Bramins* inculcate that when the *Ghoij* ſuffers death by accident or violence, or through the neglect of the owner, it is a token of God's wrath againſt the wickedneſs of the ſpirit of *the proprietor*, who from thence is warned that at the diſſolution of his human form, he will not be deemed worthy of entering the firſt *Boboon* of purification, but be again condemned to return to the loweſt region of puniſhment: hence it is, that not only mourning and lamentation enſue on the violent death of either cow or calf—but the proprietor is frequently enjoined, and often voluntarily undertakes, a three years pilgrimage in expiation of his crime, forſaking his family, friends and relations, he ſubſiſts during his pilgrimage on charity and alms.—It is worthy remark, that the penitent thus circumſtanced, ever meets with the deepeſt commiſeration, as his ſtate is deemed truely pitiable; two inſtances have fallen within our own knowledge where the penitents have devoted themſelves to the ſervice of God, and a pilgrimage during the term of their life.

Secondly,

Secondly, the *Ghoij* is venerated by the *Gentoos* in a political ſenſe, as being the moſt uſeful and neceſſary of the whole animal creation, to a people forbid feeding on fleſh, or on any thing that had breathed the breath of life; for it not only yielded to them delectable food, but was otherways eſſentially ſerviceable in the cultivation of their lands; on which depended their vegetable ſubſiſtence.

The *Gentoos* hold that the females of all animated forms are, more or leſs, favored of God, but more eminently in the form of *Moiyah* in the eighty-ninth tranſmigration; the word ſignifies *excellent*, and is applied to the female of *Mhurd*; *Rhaan* is the common name for woman, though it uſually means a married *Moiyah*, and the *Gentoo* Princeſſes have no higher title than *Rhaanee*. The female or *Moiyah* of *Mhurd*, is ſuppoſed to be animated by the moſt benign and leaſt culpable of the apoſtate angels, and that from this form, in every period of the *four Jogues*, an infinitely greater number of the delinquent ſpirits, have entered the firſt region of purification, than from the form of *Mhurd*.

The ſudden death of infants, the *Bramins* ſay, marks the ſpirits favored of God, and that

that it is immediately received into the boſom of *Biſtnoo*, (the preſerver) and conveyed to the firſt region of purification.—The ſudden death of adults, on the contrary, they pronounce a mark of God's wrath againſt the animating ſpirit, as it's term of probation in *Mburd*, is cut ſhort.——The great age of man, when it is accompanied with the enjoyments of his faculties and underſtanding, is pronounced by the *Bramins* to be the greateſt bleſſing God can beſtow upon this mortal ſtate, as thereby the term of the ſpirits probation is prolonged; adding that the limited ſpace of one hundred years, decreed by God in the preſent *Kolee Jogue*, is full ſhort for the works of repentance and goodneſs, and that when the life and underſtanding is preſerved beyond that limited term, it ought to be deemed a ſignal mark of God's ſpecial grace and favor.

Longevity, in (what we call) the brute creation, is by the *Bramins* eſteemed a mark of the great delinquency of the ſpirits which animate thoſe tribes, becauſe they are ſo long debarred and with-held from their great and chief ſtate of probation in *Mburd*.—The *Gentoos* eſtimate the greater or leſſer delinquency of the apoſtate ſpirits, by the claſs of mortal forms they are doomed to inhabit; thus,

thus, all voracious and unclean animals are ſuppoſed to be animated by the moſt malignant ſpirits ;—if a hog or dog touch a *Gentoo*, he is defiled, not from the animal form, but from the perſwaſion, that the *Debtah* animating that form, is a malignant ſpirit. —Every voracious animal, that inhabits the earth, air and waters, and men whoſe lives and actions are publickly and atrociouſly wicked, come under that claſs of ſpirits:— On the contrary, thoſe ſpirits that animate the forms which ſubſiſt on vegetables, and do not prey upon each other, are pronounced favored of God.

The *general warfare* which is obſerved in the animal world, whereby the deſtruction of one ſpecies is the neceſſary ſupport and ſubſiſtence of others, the *Bramins* aſſert is the lot of puniſhment decreed by God for the moſt guilty of the apoſtate angels, who are thereby made *his* inſtruments of puniſhment to *each other*, every of theſe tribes being a deſtined prey to one another.—The natural enmity which ſome claſſes of animals bear to others, whereby they live in a continued ſtate of war and contention, whenever they meet, although they do not ſubſiſt on each other, proceeds they ſay from the ſame cauſe; the delinquent *Debtah* being deſtined

destined as a punishment, in those forms to exercise that propensity to hatred, envy, and animosity, on one another, which they had so impotently dared to exert against their Creator.

The rotation of animal forms destined for the habitation of the delinquent *Debtah*, are not, say the *Bramins*, precisely the same, on repetition of the eighty-nine transmigrations; but are arbitrary and rests with the will of God; but it is their belief that the least guilty of the *Debtah*, transmigrate only through those forms which by their nature are destined to subsist on the vegetable creation; and that the three changes immediately preceding the spirits animating the *Ghoij* (that is the eighty-fifth, eighty-sixth, and eighty-seventh) are into the most innocent of the species of *birds*, the *goat* and the *sheep*, the animals most favored of God, next to the *Ghoij* and *Mhurd.*—From hence the rigid *Bramins* execrate with bitterness, the cruelty of those nations, who wickedly and wantonly select and slaughter the best beloved created forms of God, namely the birds, the goat, the sheep, and the cow, to satisfy their unnatural lust of appetite, in defiance not only to his express command and prohibition, but in opposition to the natural

natural and obvious conſtruction of the mouth and digeſtive faculties of *Mburd*, which marks him, deſtined with other forms moſt favored of God, to feed and ſubſiſt on the fruits and produce of the earth, with the additional bleſſing of the milk of the *Ghoij*, and of other animals.—For this degeneracy, they account no otherwiſe, than piouſly lamenting the pitiable ſtate of *Mburd*, ſince the commencement of the *Kolee Jogue*, adding, that by juſt conſequence the tranſgreſſion carries its puniſhment along with it, for by this aſſemblage of unnatural and forbidden food, variety of diſeaſes are entailed, which cut ſhort the term of probation in *Mburd*, by which the delinquent ſpirit robs himſelf of more than half of that ſpace of indulgence and trial which his Creator has graciouſly beſtowed upon him, and which he by a freſh inſtance of his diſobedience, ungratefully rejects.

Ovid in his fifteenth book of *Metamorphoſes* introduces *Pythagoras* diſſuading mankind from killing and feeding on his fellow creatures. Our readers will excuſe us, if we tranſcribe ſuch parts of his pathetic arguments, as are ſtrictly in point with the ſubject of the preceding paragraph.

“ He

" He first the taste of flesh, from tables drove;
And argued well, if arguments could move.
O mortals! from your fellows blood abstain,
Nor taint your bodies, with a food prophane;
While corn and pulse by nature are bestow'd,
And planted orchards bend their willing load;
While labor'd gardens wholesome herbs produce,
And teeming vines afford their gen'rous juice;
Nor tardier fruits of cruder kind are lost,
But tam'd by fire or mellow'd by the frost;
While kine to pails, distended udders bring,
And bees their honey, redolent of spring;
While earth, not only can your needs supply,
But lavish of her stores, provides for luxury;
A guiltless feast, administers with ease,
And without blood, is prodigal to please;
Wild beasts their maws, with their slain brethren fill,
And yet not all,—for some refuse to kill;
Sheep, goats, and oxen, and the nobler steed,
On browse and corn, and flow'ry meadows feed;
Bears, tigers, wolves, the angry lions brood,
Whom heaven endu'd with principles of blood,
He wisely sunder'd, from the rest to yell,
In forest, and in lonely caves to dwell;
Where stronger beasts oppress the weak by night,
And all in prey, and purple feasts delight.

" O impious use! to Nature's laws opposed,
Where bowels are in others bowels closed;
Where fatten'd, by their fellows' fat they thrive,
Maintain'd by murder, and by death they live;

'Tis

'Tis then for nought, that mother Earth provides
The ſtores of all ſhe ſhows, and all ſhe hides;
If men with fleſhy morſels muſt be fed,
And chaw with bloody teeth the breathing bread;
What elſe is this, but to devour our gueſts,
And barb'rouſly renew Cyclopean feaſts.
We by deſtroying life, our life ſuſtain,
And gorge th' ungodly maw, with meats obſcene.

"Not ſo the golden age, who fed on fruit,
Nor durſt with bloody meals their mouths pollute;
Then birds, in airy ſpace, might ſafely move,
And tim'rous hares on heaths ſecurely rove,
Nor needed fiſh the guileful hooks to fear,
For all was peaceful, and that peace ſincere.
Whoever was the wretch, and curs'd be he,
That envy'd firſt, our food's ſimplicity;
The eſſay of bloody feaſts, on brutes began,
And after forged the ſword to murder man;
Had he the ſharpened ſteel, alone employed
On beaſts of prey, which other beaſts deſtroyed,
Or man invaded, with their fangs and paws,
This had been juſtified by Nature's laws,
And ſelf defence:—but who did feaſts begin
Of fleſh, he ſtretch'd neceſſity, to ſin.
To kill man-killers, man has lawful power,
But not the extended licence to devour.

"Ill habits gather, by unſeen degrees,
As brooks make rivers, rivers run to ſeas;
The ſow, with her broad ſnout, for rooting up,
Th' entruſted ſeed, was judg'd to ſpoil the crop;
And intercept the ſweating farmer's hope.

The covetous churl, of unforgiving kind,
The offender to the bloody prieſt reſign'd;
Her hunger was no plea, for that ſhe dy'd;
The goat came next in order to be tried.
The goat had crop'd the tendrils of the vine,
In vengeance the laity, and clergy join,
Where one had loſt his profit, one his wine.
Here was, at leaſt, ſome ſhadow of offence;
The ſheep was ſacrificed, on no pretence,
But meek, and unreſiſting innocence.
A patient, uſeful creature, born to bear,
The warm and woolly fleece, that cloth'd her murderer;
And daily to give down the milk ſhe bred,
A tribute for the graſs on which ſhe fed:
Living both food and raiment ſhe ſupplies,
And is of leaſt advantage when ſhe dies.

" How did the toiling ox, his death deſerve,
A downright ſimple drudge, and born to ſerve?
O tyrant! with what juſtice canſt thou hope,
The promiſe of the year a plenteous crop,
When thou deſtroy'ſt thy lab'ring ſteer, who till'd
And plough'd with pain, thy elſe ungrateful field;
From his yet reeking neck, to draw the yoke,
That neck with which the ſurly clods he broke;
And to the hatchet, yield thy huſbandman,
Who finiſhed autumn, and the ſpring began.

" Nor this alone! but heaven itſelf to bribe,
We to the gods, our impious acts aſcribe;
Firſt recompence with death, their creatures toil,
Then call the bleſt above to ſhare the ſpoil.

The faireſt victim, muſt the pow'rs appeaſe
(So fatal 'tis ſometimes too much to pleaſe)
A purple fillet his broad brow adorns,
With flow'ry garlands crown'd and gilded horns;
He hears the murd'rous prayer the prieſt prefers,
But underſtands not! 'tis his doom he hears:
Beholds the meal, betwixt his temples caſt,
(The fruit and product of his labors paſt,)
And in the water, views perhaps the knife,
Uplifted to deprive him of his life;
Then broken up alive, his entrails ſees
Torn out for prieſts t'inſpect the gods decrees.

" From whence, O mortal man! this guſt of blood
Have you deriv'd? and interdicted food?
Be taught by me, this dire delight to ſhun,
Warn'd by my precepts, by my practice, won;
And when you eat the well-deſerving beaſt,
Think, on the lab'rer of your field, you feaſt.

" Then let not piety be put to flight,
To pleaſe the taſte of glutton appetite;
But ſuffer inmate ſouls ſecure to dwell,
Leſt from their ſeats your parents you expell;
With rabid hunger feed upon your kind,
Or from a beaſt diſlodge a brother's mind."

That *Pythagoras* carried ſuch ſentiments from the *Bramins*, and labored to obtrude them upon his countrymen, is beyond controverſy; the pathetic perſwaſives he urged to them in that age to abſtain from the feeding on their brethren of the creation, proved however as ineffectual then, as we conceive it would be in the present, the more's the pity—for it is to be feared we ſhall to the end of the chapter—Riſe, kill, and eat.

Regarding the deſcription (which *Ovid* puts in the mouth of *Pythagoras)* of the ancient religious ſacrifices, we muſt in juſtice to the *Bramins* ſay he could not borrow it from them; in this particular the original religious tenets of the *Gentoos* differ from all the ancients, for they were ſtrangers to thoſe bloody ſacrifices and offerings; neither of the *Gentoo Bhades* having the leaſt alluſion to that mode of worſhipping the deity; and the *Bramins* ſay, nothing but *Moiſaſoor* himſelf could have invented ſo infatuated and cruel an inſtitution, which is manifeſtly ſo repugnant to the true ſpirit of devotion, and abhorrent to the Eternal ONE.

That every animal form is endued, with cogitation, memory and reflection, is one of the moſt eſtabliſhed tenets of the *Bramins*; indeed it muſt conſequentially be ſo, on the ſuppoſed *Metempſychoſis* of the apoſtate ſpirits, through theſe mortal forms.—Every ſtate of the delinquent ſpirits abode in the eight *Boboons*, they ſay, is a ſtate of humilia-

humiliation, punishment and purgation, that of *Mburd* not excepted; and that the purpose of the Eternal ONE would be defeated by himself, had he not endued them with rationality and a consciousness of their situation.——In the form of *Mhurd* alone, is the spirit's state of probation, because in this form only, he again becomes an absolute and *free agent*; and in this alone lies the difference between *Mburd*, and the rest of the animal created forms, for in these, the spirit's intellectual faculties are circumscribed, more or less, by the varied construction of the forms, and limited within certain bounds, which they cannot exceed,—that consciousness of those confined powers, and envy at the superior state of *Mburd*, constitutes their chief punishment; that this unceasing envy, and *resentment* of the usurped tyranny which *Mburd* assumed over the animal creation (from the beginning of the *Kolee Jogue*) are the causes which made them in general shun his society, and live in a state of enmity with him, according to the force of the natural powers, which the Eternal ONE has endued them with; that where some of the species appear an exception to this general bent, it proceeds from the weakness of their natural powers; or the superior craft and subtility of *Mburd*, who first deceitfully

 allured

allured them to ſlavery and deſtruction.——That neither *envy* or enmity in the animal created forms, nor uſurped tyranny on the part of *Mhurd*, had exiſtence in the breaſts of either, before the beginning of the *Kolee Jogue*, when a univerſal degeneracy of almoſt all the remaining unpurified *Debtah* prevailed through all their mortal forms—which until that period had lived in amity and harmony, as conſcious of being involved under the ſame ſentence and diſpleaſure of their Creator; and laſtly—That the uſurped tyranny of *Mhurd* over the reſt of the delinquent angels was diſpleaſing to the Eternal ONE, and will be a charge exhibited againſt the ſpirit by *Biſtnoo* at the diſſolution of *Mhurd*, for that in place of cheriſhing the unhappy delinquents during their ſtate of humiliation and puniſhment, they do, by the force of their tyrannic uſurpation, labor to make their ſtate more miſerable, than the Eternal ONE intended it ſhould be, in violation of his expreſs injunction, *that they ſhould love one another*.

The *Bramins* hold, that every diſtinct ſpecies of animal creation have a comprehenſive mode of communicating their ideas, peculiar to themſelves; and that the *Metempſychoſis*

ſychoſis of the delinquent ſpirits extends through every organiſed body, even to the ſmalleſt inſect and reptile;—they highly venerate the bee, and ſome ſpecies of the ant, and conceive the ſpirits animating thoſe forms are favored of God, and that its intellectual faculties, are more enlarged under them, than in moſt others.

Although we have already ſhewn that the bloody ſacrifices of the ancients was no part of the *Gentoo* tenets, yet there ſubſiſts amongſt them at this day, a *voluntary ſacrifice*, of too ſingular a nature, to paſs by us unnoticed; the rather as it has been frequently mentioned by various authors, without we conceive that knowledge and perſpicuity which the matter calls for; the ſacrifice we allude to, is the *Gentoo wives burning with the bodies of their deceaſed huſbands.* We have taken no ſmall pains to inveſtigate this ſeeming cruel cuſtom, and hope we ſhall be able to throw ſame ſatisfactory lights on this very extraordinary ſubject, which has hitherto been hid in obſcurity; in order to which we will firſt remove one or two obſtructions that lie in our way, and hinder our nearer and more perfect view of it.

The cauſe commonly aſſigned for the origin of this ſacrifice (peculiar to the wives of this nation) is, that *it was a law conſtituted to put a period to a wicked practice that the Gentoos wives had of poiſoning their huſbands*;—for this aſſertion we cannot trace the ſmalleſt ſemblance of truth, and indeed the known fact, that the ſacrifice muſt be *voluntary*, of it's ſelf refutes that common miſtake.—It has alſo been a received opinion, that *if the wife refuſes to burn, ſhe loſes her caſt* (or tribe) *and is ſtamped with diſgrace and infamy*; an opinion equally void of foundation in fact as the other.—The real ſtate of this caſe is thus circumſtanced.—The firſt wife (for the *Gentoo* laws allow bigamy, although they frequently do not benefit themſelves of the indulgence, if they have iſſue by the firſt) has it in her choice to burn, but *is not permitted* to declare her reſolution before twenty-four hours after the deceaſe of her huſband;—if ſhe refuſes, the right devolves to the ſecond,—if either, after the expiration of twenty-four hours, publicly declare, before the *Bramins* and *witneſſes*, their reſolution to *burn*, they cannot then retract. If they both refuſe at the expiration of that term, the worſt conſequence that attends their refuſal, is lying under the imputation of being wanting to their own

 honor,

honor, purification, and the proſperity of their family, for from their infancy, they are inſtructed by the houſehold *Bramin* to look upon this cataſtrophe, as moſt glorious to themſelves, and beneficial to their children: the truth is, that the children of the wife who burns, become thereby illuſtrious, and are ſought after in marriage by the moſt opulent and honourable of their *caſt*, and ſometimes received into a caſt ſuperiour to their own.

That the *Bramins* take unwearied pains to encourage, promote, and confirm in the minds of the *Gentoo* wives, *this ſpirit of burning*, is certain (their motives for it, the penetration of our readers may by and by probably diſcover) and although they ſeldom loſe their labor, yet inſtances happen, where fear, or love of life, ſets at nought all their preaching; for it ſometimes falls out that the firſt wife refuſes, and the ſecond burns; at others, they both refuſe; and as but one can burn, it ſo happens, that when the ſecond wife has iſſue by the deceaſed, and the firſt none, there commonly enſues a violent contention between them, which of the two ſhall make the ſacrifice; but this diſpute is generally determined by the *Bramins*, in favor of the firſt, unleſs ſhe is pre-

vailed

vailed on by perſwaſion, or other motives to wave her right, in favor of the ſecond.—Having elucidated theſe matters, we will proceed to give our readers the beſt account we have been able to obtain of the origin of this remarkable cuſtom.

At the demiſe of the mortal part of the *Gentoos'* great Law-giver and Prophet BRAMAH, his wives, inconſolable for his loſs, reſolved not to ſurvive him, and offered themſelves voluntary victims on his funeral pile.—The wives of the chief *Rajahs*, the firſt officers of the ſtate, being unwilling to have it thought that they were deficient in fidelity and affection, followed the heroic example ſet them by the wives of *Bramah*;—the *Bramins* (a tribe then newly conſtituted by their great legiſlator) pronounced and declared, *that the delinquent ſpirits of thoſe heroines, immediately ceaſed from their tranſmigrations, and had entered the firſt Boboon of purification*—it followed, that *their* wives claimed a right of making the ſame ſacrifice of their mortal forms *to God*, and *the manes* of their deceaſed huſbands;——The wives of every *Gentoo* caught the enthuſiaſtic (now pious) flame.——Thus the heroic acts of a few women brought about a general cuſtom, the *Bramins* had given it

the

the ſtamp of religion, they foiſted it into the *Chartah* and *Aughtorrah Bhades*, and inſtituted the forms and ceremonials that were to accompany the ſacrifice, ſtrained ſome obſcure paſſages of *Bramah's Chartah Bhade*, to countenance their *declared ſenſe* of the action, and eſtabliſhed it as a religious tenet throughout *Indoſtan*, ſubject to the reſtrictions before recited, which leaves it a voluntary act of glory, piety and fortitude.—— Whether the *Bramins* were ſincere in their declared ſenſe, and conſecration of this act, or had a view to the ſecuring the fidelity of their own wives, or were actuated by any other motives, we will not determine.——

When people have lived together to an advanced age, in mutual acts of confidence, friendſhip and affection; the ſacrifice a *Gentoo* widow makes of her perſon (under ſuch an affecting circumſtance as the loſs of friend and huſband) ſeems leſs an object of wonder; ——but when we ſee women in the bloom of youth, and beauty, in the calm poſſeſſion of their reaſon and underſtanding, with aſtoniſhing fortitude, ſet at nought, the tender conſiderations of parents, children, friends, and the horror and torments of the death they court, we cannot reſiſt viewing ſuch

an

an act, and ſuch a victim, with tears of commiſeration, awe and reverence.

We have been preſent at many of theſe ſacrifices: in ſome of the victims, we have obſerved a pitiable dread, tremor, and reluctance, that ſtrongly ſpoke repentance for their *declared reſolution*; but it was now too late to retract, or retreat; *Biſtnoo* was *waiting for the ſpirit*.—If the ſelf doomed victim diſcovers want of courage and fortitude, ſhe is with gentle force obliged to aſcend the pile, where ſhe is held down with long poles, held by men on each ſide of the pile, until the flames reach her; her ſcreams and cries, in the mean time, being drowned amidſt the deafening noiſe of loud muſick, and the acclamations of the multitude.——Others we have ſeen go through this fiery trial, with moſt amazing ſteady, calm, reſolution, and joyous fortitude.——It will not we hope be unacceptable, if we preſent our readers with an inſtance of the latter, which happened ſome years paſt at the *Eaſt India* company's factory at *Coſſimbuzaar*, in the time of Sir *Francis Ruſſel*'s chiefſhip; the author, and ſeveral other gentlemen of the factory were preſent, ſome of whom are now living:—from a narrative, which the author then tranſmitted to *England*, he is now

now enabled to give the particulars of this moſt remarkable proof of female fortitude, and conſtancy.

" At five of the clock in the morning of the 4th of *February*, 1742-3, died *Rhaam Chund Pundit* of the *Mahahrattor* tribe, aged twenty-eight years; his widow (for he had but one wife) aged between ſeventeen and eighteen, as ſoon as he expired, diſdaining to wait the term allowed her for reflection, immediately declared to the *Bramins* and witneſſes preſent her reſolution to burn; as the family was of no ſmall conſideration, all the merchants of *Coſſimbuzaar*, and her relations, left no arguments uneſſayed to diſſuade her from it—Lady *Ruſſel*, with the tendereſt humanity, ſent her ſeveral meſſages to the ſame purpoſe; —the infant ſtate of her children (two girls and a boy, the eldeſt not four years of age) and the terrors and pain of the death ſhe ſought, were painted to her in the ſtrongeſt and moſt lively colouring—ſhe was deaf to all,—ſhe gratefully thanked Lady *Ruſſel*, and ſent her word *ſhe had now nothing to live for*, but *recommended her children to her protection.*—When the torments of burning were urged in terrorem to her, ſhe with a reſolved and calm countenance, put her finger into the fire, and held it there a conſiderable time,

time, ſhe then with one hand put fire in the palm of the other, ſprinkled incenſe on it, and fumigated the *Bramins*. The conſideration of her children left deſtitute of a parent was again urged to her.—She replied, *he that made them, would take care of them.*—She was at laſt given to underſtand, ſhe ſhould not be permitted to burn *; this for a ſhort ſpace ſeemed to give her deep affliction, but ſoon recollecting herſelf, ſhe told them, *death was in her power, and that if ſhe was not allowed to burn, according to the principles of her caſt, ſhe would ſtarve herſelf.*—Her friends, finding her thus peremptory and reſolved, were obliged at laſt to aſſent.

" The body of the deceaſed was carried down to the water ſide, early the following morning, the widow followed about ten o'clock, accompanied by three very principal *Bramins*, her children, parents, and relations, and a numerous concourſe of people. The *order of leave* for her burning did not arrive from *Hoſſeyn Khan*, *Fouzdaar* of *Morſhadabad*, until after one, and it was then brought by one of the *Soubah*'s own officers, who

* The *Gentoos* are not permitted to burn, without an order from the *Mahommedan* government, and this permiſſion is commonly made a perquiſite of ——

had

had orders to ſee that ſhe burnt voluntarily. —— The time they waited for the order was employed in praying with the *Bramins*, and waſhing in the *Ganges*; as ſoon as it arrived, ſhe retired and ſtayed for the ſpace of half an hour in the midſt of her female relations, amongſt whom was her mother; ſhe then diveſted herſelf of her bracelets, and other ornaments, and tyed them in a cloth, which hung like an apron before her, and was conducted by her female relations to one corner of the pile; on the pile was an arched arbor formed of dry ſticks, boughs and leaves, open only at one end to admit her entrance; in this the body of the deceaſed was depoſited, his head at the end oppoſite to the opening.—At the corner of the pile to which ſhe had been conducted, the *Bramin* had made a ſmall fire, round which ſhe and the three *Bramins* ſat for ſome minutes, one of them gave into her hand a leaf of the bale tree (the wood commonly conſecrated to form part of the funeral pile) with ſundry things on it, which ſhe threw into the fire; one of the others gave her a ſecond leaf, which ſhe held over the flame, whilſt he dropped *three times* ſome ghee on it, which melted, and fell into the fire (theſe two operations, were preparatory ſymbols of her approaching diſſolution

by

by fire) and whilſt they were performing this, the third *Bramin* read to her ſome portions of the *Aughtorrah Bhade*, and aſked her ſome queſtions, to which ſhe anſwered with a ſteady, and ſerene countenance; but the noiſe was ſo great, we could not underſtand what ſhe ſaid, although we were within a yard of her.—Theſe over, ſhe was led with great ſolemnity *three times* round the pile, the *Bramins* reading before her; when ſhe came the third time to the ſmall fire, ſhe ſtopped, took her rings off her toes and fingers, and put them to her other ornaments; here ſhe took a ſolemn majeſtic leave of her children, parents, and relations; after which, one of the *Bramins* dip'd a large wick of cotton in ſome ghee, and gave it ready lighted into her hand, and led her to the open ſide of the arbor; there, all the *Bramins* fell at her feet;——after ſhe had bleſſed them, they retired weeping;—by two ſteps, ſhe aſcended the pile and entered the arbor; on her entrance, ſhe made a profound reverence at the feet of the deceaſed, and advanced and ſeated herſelf by his head; ſhe looked, in ſilent meditation on his face, for the ſpace of a minute, then ſet fire to the arbor, in *three places*; obſerving that ſhe had ſet fire to leeward, and that the flames blew from her, inſtantly ſeeing her

her error ſhe roſe, and ſet fire to windward, and reſumed her ſtation; enſign *Daniel* with his cane, ſeparated the graſs and leaves on the windward ſide, by which means we had a diſtinct view of her as ſhe ſat. With what dignity, and undaunted a countenance ſhe ſet fire to the pile the laſt time, and aſſumed her ſeat, can only be conceived, for words cannot convey a juſt idea of her.—The pile being of combuſtible matters, the ſupporters of the roof were preſently conſumed, and it tumbled upon her."

We ſee our fair country-women ſhudder at an action, which we fear they will look upon, as a proof of the higheſt infatuation in their ſex.—Although it is not our intention here to defend the tenets of the *Bramins*, yet we may be allowed to offer ſome juſtification on behalf of the *Gentoo* women in the action before us—Let us view it (as we ſhould every other action) without prejudice, and without keeping always in ſight *our own* tenets and cuſtoms, and prepoſſeſſions that too generally reſult therefrom, to the injury of others;—if we view theſe women in a juſt light, we ſhall think more candidly of them, and confeſs they act upon heroic, as well as rational and pious principles: In order to this we muſt conſider them as a race of females trained from their infancy, in the full conviction of their *celestial rank*; and that this world, and the corporeal form that incloſes them, is deſtined by God, the one as their place of puniſhment, the other as their priſon.——That their ideas are conſequently raiſed to a ſoothing degree of dignity befitting angelic beings.—They are nurſed and inſtructed in the firm faith—that this voluntary ſacrifice, is the moſt glorious period of their lives, and that thereby the celeſtial ſpirit is releaſed from its tranſmigrations, and evils of a miſerable exiſtence, and flies to join the ſpirit of their departed huſband, in a ſtate of purification: add to this, the ſubordinate conſideration of raiſing the luſtre of their children, and of contributing by this action to *their* temporal proſperity;—all theſe it muſt be owned are prevalent motives, for chearfully embracing death, and ſetting at nought every common attachment which the weakneſs of humanity urges, for a longer exiſtence in a world of evil.—Although theſe principles are in general ſo diametrically contrary to the prevailing ſpirit and genius of our fair country-women, who (from a happy train of education) in captivating amuſements and diſſipation, find charms ſufficient in this world, to engage their wiſhes for a perpetual refidence in it; yet we will depend on their natural goodnefs of heart, generofity and candor, that they will in future look on thefe their *Gentoo* fifters of the creation, in a more favorable, and confiftent light, than probably they have hitherto done; and not deem *that action* an infatuation, which refults from principle. Let them alfo recollect that their own hiftory affords illuftrious examples in both fexes of voluntary facrifices by fire, becaufe they would not fubfcribe even to a different mode of profeffing the fame faith. Befides—a contempt of death, is not peculiar to the women of *India*, it is the characteriftic of the nation; every *Gentoo* meets that moment of diffolution, with a fteady, noble, and philofophic refignation, flowing from the eftablifhed principles of their faith.

Before we clofe this fubject, we will mention one or two more particulars relative to it.—It has been already remarked in a marginal note, that the *Gentoo* women are not allowed to burn, without an order of leave from the *Mahommedan* government; it is proper alfo to inform our readers this privilege is never withheld from them.—There have been inftances known, when the victim has, *by Europeans*, been forcibly refcued from the pile; it is currently ſaid and believed (how true we will not aver) that the wife of Mr. *Job Charnock* was by him ſnatched from this ſacrifice; be this as it may, the outrage is conſidered by the *Gentoos*, an atrocious, and wicked violation of their ſacred rites and privileges.

Having now brought our fourth general head to a concluſion, and faithfully, to the beſt of our knowledge (with the materials we are poſſeſſed of) exhibited the original tenets of the ancient *Bramins*, according to the firſt book of *Bramah*'s *Chartah Bhade*; and having in our remarks given ſuch elucidations as we thought our ſubject called for, we ſubmit our imperfect work (for imperfect we muſt ſtill call it) with all due deference to the public; hoping that ſome more capable head and hand, will be ſtimulated by our endeavours, to produce a more full, and ſatisfactory relation, of the reſt of his doctrines.—A large field is yet left open, for the exerciſe of induſtry and talents. *Bramah*'s firſt ſection of his ſecond book on the creation of this globe, will be the ſubject of our next general head.—— His third book, directing the plain and ſimple modes of worſhip to be paid to God, and the three primary created beings, and his

his fourth *ſublime book*, (which the *Gentoos* commonly call *Bramah Ka, Inſeff Bhade*, or, *Bramah*'s book of juſtice) wherein is expreſly recited and enjoined, the duties and offices which the delinquent *Debtah* ſhall obſerve and pay to each other; theſe two laſt mentioned books, and part of the ſecond, we ſay, muſt lie in oblivion, until ſome one, bleſſed with opportunity, leiſure, application, and genius, brings them to light.

The End of the Fourth Chapter.

CHAP. V.

Of the Creation of the Worlds.

INTRODUCTION.

IN the fifth ſection of our laſt general head, *Bramah* recites, that the Eternal ONE, (after he had promulged his gracious intention, of mitigating the puniſhment of the fallen angels, at the interceſſion of the remaining faithful hoſt;) "retired into himſelf, and became inviſible to them, for the ſpace of five thouſand years."—In his introduction to the act of creation of the worlds in his ſecond book, he takes again occaſion to repeat the above mentioned paſſage, and explains it by an inference, that during THAT SPACE, the Eternal ONE was employed in meditation on his intended new creation;—and although it appears, from the ſame ſection, that this ſtupendous work, was produced by an *inſtantaneous fiat* of the Deity,

Deity, yet *Bramah*, to display the infinite and amazing wisdom of his Creator, enters into a sublime, and philosophic disquisition and description, of his modes (if we may be allowed the expression) and manner of creation, in the marvellous construction of the fifteen *Boboons*, that constitute the *Dunneaboudah*, or universe;—these descriptions, he couches under allegories, then commonly and familiarly understood, at which the reader will the less wonder, when he knows, that at this day it is the usual mode of conversing, amongst well educated *Gentoos*.

In this exhibition of infinite wisdom, *Bramah* gives a short, simple and elevated description, of each of the fifteen *Boboons*, their situation, their rank, and peculiar destination, with the appellations appropriated to the angelic inhabitants, in their progressive passage from one sphere to another. Our memory only supplies us with the names of the sojourners of the ninth, fifth, sixth, and seventh, that is, the first, and three last of the seven regions of purification, to wit, the spheres of the *Pereeth logue* *, the *Munnoo*

* *Logue*, literally people. *Pereeth logue*, purified people.

logue *, the *Debtah logue* †, and the *Birmah logue* ‡; in the laſt mentioned ſphere, according to the *Bramins* computation, a complete day is equal to twenty-eight *Munnunturs* of vulgar time. (Vid. ſixth or next general head.)

On the foundation of *Bramah*'s deſcription of the fifteen *Boboons*, the compilers of the *Aughtorrah Bhade* have raiſed an elaborate chimerical ſuperſtructure, that confounds the underſtanding.

As the *Bramins* conceptions and calculation of the age and future duration of the univerſe, will be the ſubject of our next general head, we ſhall ſay nothing more of it here, than to remind our readers, that they date it's exiſtence from the rebellious angels being releaſed from the *Onderah*.

We again lament the loſs of our materials, which confines us to the eighth ſection of

* *Munnoo logue, people* of *contemplation*, from *mun*, or *mon*, *thought*, *reflection*, alludes to God's being worſhipped in this ſphere in ſilent meditation.

† In this ſphere the angels are firſt ſuppoſed to regain properly their title of *Debtah*.

‡ In this ſphere the delinquents are ſuppoſed to be cleanſed from the pollution of their ſin, regenerated, and fit to enter again the *Mahah Surgo*, and to be readmitted to the preſence of their Creator.

Bramah's

Bramah's ſecond book that treats only of the creation of this terreſtrial planet, to which we will now proceed, premiſing that it is diſtinguiſhed by the title of *the eighth Boboon of Murto*, which literally ſignifies *the region of earth*.

SECT. VIII.

" *Birmahah* * *or Creation.*

" And it was———that when the " Eternal ONE, resolved to form the " new creation of the *Dunneabou-* " *dah*, he gave the rule of *Mahah* " *Surgo* to his first created *Birmah*, " and became invisible to the whole " angelic host.

" When the Eternal ONE, first began " his intended new creation of the " *Dunneaboudah*, he was opposed by two " mighty *Ossoors* †, which *proceeded* " from the *wax* of *Brum*'s ear; and " their names were *Modoo* ‡ and *Kytoo* §.

" And the Eternal ONE, contended " and *fought* with *Modoo* and *Kytoo*, " five thousand years, and he smote

* This title is prefixed to every section of *Bramah*'s second book, *Birmah* in the figurative sense (before explained) signifying *creation*.

† The common appellation given to *giants*, but is variously used in the *Shastah*, to express *excrescence*, *excretion*, and *secretion*.

‡ *Discord*, *enmity*. § *Confusion*, *tumult*.

" them

" them on his *thigh* *, and they were " *lost* and assimilated with *Murto*.

" And it was,—that when *Modoo* " and *Kytoo* were subdued, the Eternal " ONE emerged from his state of in- " visibility, and glory encompassed him " on every side!

" And the Eternal ONE spoke, and " said, Thou *Birmah* † shalt *create* and " form all things that shall be made " in the new creation of the fifteen " *Boboons* of punishment, and purifi- " cation, according to the powers of the " spirit, wherewith thou shalt be in- " spired.——And thou, *Bistnoo* ‡, shalt " superintend, cherish, and *preserve* all " the things and forms which shall be " created.—And thou, *Sieb* §, shalt " *change*, or *destroy*, all creation, ac- " cording to the powers, wherewith I " will invest thee."

* Reduced them to subjection, or obedience: *touching the thigh*, amongst the ancient *Gentoos*, was a token of *subjection*.

† *Power of creation*. Vid. introduction to the fourth chapter.

‡ *Preserver*. Vid. introduction to the fourth chapter.

§ *Mutilator*, *destroyer*. Vid. introduction, &c.

" And

" And when *Birmah*, *Bistnoo*, and " *Sieb*, had heard the words of the " Eternal ONE, they all bowed obe- " dience *.

" The Eternal ONE spoke again, " and said to *Birmah*, Do thou begin " the creation and formation of *the* " *eighth Boboon*, of punishment and *pro-* " *bation*, even the *Boboon* of *Murto*, " according to the powers of the spirit " wherewith I have endued thee, and " do thou, *Bistnoo*, proceed to execute " thy part.

" And when *Brum* † heard the " command, which the mouth of the " Eternal ONE had uttered; he straight- " ways formed a *leaf of beetle*, and he " floated on the *beetle leaf* over the sur- " face of the *Jhoale*; and the children ‡ " of *Modoo* and *Kytoo*, fled before

* The foregoing exordium of the general act of creation of the *Dunneahoudah*, preceeds every one of the fifteen sections of *Bramah*'s second book.

† *Birmah* and *Brum*, are, in the act of creation, synonimous terms.

‡ Supposed remains of discordant matter. The *Bramins* supposed the first principles of things prior to the creation of the universe, to have been in a fluid state.

" him,

" him, and vanished from his presence.

" And when the agitation of the " *Jhoale* had subsided, by the powers " of the spirit of *Brum*, *Bistnoo* straight- " ways transformed himself into a " *mighty boar* *, and descending into " the abyss of *Jhoale*, he brought up " *the Murto* on his tusks.—Then spon- " taneously issued from him, a *mighty* " *tortoise* †, and a *mighty snake* ‡.

" And *Bistnoo* put the snake erect " upon the *back* of the tortoise, and " placed *Murto* upon the *head* of the " snake.

" And all things were created and " formed by *Birmah* in the eighth " *Boboon* of punishment and *probation*, " even the eighth of *Murto*, according " to the powers of the spirit, where- " with the Eternal ONE had endued " him.

I

* The *Gentoos* symbol of *strength*, because, in proportion to his size, he is the strongest of all animals.

† The *Gentoos* symbol of *stability*.

‡ The *Gentoos* symbol of *wisdom*.

" And

"And *Biſtnoo* took upon him the
"superintendance and charge of all
"that was created, and formed, by
"*Birmah* in the eighth *Boboon* of
"*Murto*; and he cheriſhed and *pre-
"ſerved* them, as the words of the
"Eternal ONE had directed, and com-
"manded."

REMARKS.

IN the ſame ſublime allegorical manner, has *Bramah* deſcribed the creation of *Surjee* *, and *Chunder* †, and the other twelve *Boboons* of the *Dunneahoudah*, without pretending, or aiming to dive into, and explain, the principles of matter, or the nature of thoſe eſſential laws of motion by which the Deity guides and governs his creation; the wiſdom of *Bramah* has elſewhere marked ſuch fruitleſs enquiries, with the *ſtamp* of preſumption and folly; and that the knowledge of *theſe*, and the mode of the exiſtence of God, is concealed even from the three primary created beings themſelves.

From the foregoing ſpecimen of the creation of the eighth region, as well as

* The *Sun*. † The *Moon*.

from

from *Bramah*'s hiſtorical diſcuſſion of the other fourteen, it is moſt obvious, that the perſonages which he introduces as actors in the work of that creation were intended by him to be taken only in a figurative ſenſe, as expreſſive of the three ſupreme attributes of the Deity, his power *to create*, his power *to preſerve*, and his power *to change* or *deſtroy*, as before hinted *.—For if they were to be underſtood in any other ſenſe, it would expreſly contradict his own text, where he repreſents the creation of the *Dunneahoudah* as proceeding from the *inſtantaneous* fiat of the Eternal ONE; and a further proof of *Bramah*'s plain intention, reſults from his prefixing the ſame exordium to each of his ſections of creation.

But as the real ſenſe and meaning of the allegory (then clearly underſtood by all) was, in proceſs of time, loſt to the generality of the *Gentoos*, the compilers of the *Chartah* and *Aughtorrah Bhades*, took the advantage (which ignorance and time gave them) and not only realiſed *Bramah*'s three myſtical *beings*, but created alſo a multitude of ſubordinate actors, and made Demi-gods and Divinities of them all, inſtituting particular days, faſts, and feſtivals, and other exterior

* Vid. Introduction to the fourth chapter.

worſhip,

worſhip, to each:—Thus *Surjee* and *Chunder*; *Modoo* and *Kytoo*, and a race of their children and deſcendants, became Demi-gods and heroes; and ſcorning to confine themſelves to the eighth *Boboon*, they ranſacked the fourteen, and framed divinities of the principal perſonages which their wild imagination ſuppoſed reſident in each of them, and allotted to them peculiar divine worſhip, which ſubſiſts to this day.

It will not, we hope, be thought an improbable conjecture, if we ſay, that the allegorical parts of *Bramah's Chartah Bhade*, (which truely bears a divine ſemblance) being thus perverted or groſly miſtaken by the very tribe, which he had inſtituted guardians over it, and being ſubſequently communicated to the *Egyptian* Magi, and by them circulated through the ſtates of *Greece*, afforded them, as well as *Rome* and the whole *Weſtern* world, thoſe inexhauſtible ſupplies of *mythological ſyſtems*, which held their exiſtence and authority even long after the light of chriſtianity had ſhone upon them.——But to reſume our more immediate ſubject.

The act of creation of the *Boboon of Murto*, is repreſented in the annexed plate No. 1. which (with others we ſhall have occaſion to to present to the reader) was drawn by the instructions, and under the eye of a judicious *Bramin* of the *Battezaar* tribe, the tribe, as before noticed, usually employed in expounding the *Shastahs*.

Brum * is represented lying and floating on a leaf of *beetle*, over the troubled surface of the abyss of *Jhoale*; the three primary beings appear before it, in the posture of adoration, *Birmah* on the right, *Bistnoo* in the middle, and *Sieb* on the left.——On the right, above the abyss, is figured a huge *boar*, bearing on his tusks a lump of earth. —On the left, above the abyss, is represented a *tortoise*, on which a snake rests his tail, bearing *Murto* (or the *earth*) on his head.— *Brum* and *Birmah* are habited alike; and are each figured with four heads and four arms.—The *three* primary beings, are supposed in the posture of adoration, to be receiving the commands of the Eternal ONE, touching his projected new creation; and the other figures express the *three* gradations of the work, namely the beginning, the progress, and completion †.

* *Spirit* or *essence* of the Eternal ONE: vide Introduction to the fourth chapter.

† Vide Plate No. 1.

Notwithſtanding the ſagacious reader, by a bare reference to the marginal notes which we have affixed to the text of *Bramah*, will readily conceive the ſpirit of the allegory contained in it; yet as ſome paſſages of it require a further explanation than could be huddled into a note, we will add the whole interpretation of it under one connected view.

The Eternal ONE having determined on the creation of the univerſe, like a ſupreme wiſe architect, he *retired* for a ſpace to project his ſtupendous plan, and prepare his materials.—He was *oppoſed* in the operation by the *diſcord*, *confuſion* and *tumult* of the elements that compoſe the *abyſs of Jhoale*;—he ſeparated, ſubdued, brought them under *ſubjection*, and prepared them to receive his intended impreſſions.—He exerts his *three* great attributes, to *create*, *preſerve*, or *deſtroy*, which are figuratively repreſented by the *three* primary created beings—His *ſpirit* floats upon the ſurface of the abyſs of *Jhoale*, or fluid matter,—Creation takes place.—*Birmah* (or Creation) is repreſented with four heads and four arms, to denote the *power* of God in the act of creation. *Biſtnoo the preſerver* is transformed into a mighty *boar*, emblematically ſignifying *the ſtrength* of God in the act of creation.—

The

The tortoiſe myſtically denotes the *ſtability* and *permanency* of the foundation of *the earth*, and the ſnake the *wiſdom* by which it is *ſupported.* Theſe latter operations are given to *Biſtnoo*, becauſe the *earth* was the grand principle or parent, from whence he was to draw the means for the *preſervation* of the future animal creation, deſtined for the priſons of the rebellious *Debtah*; a work which we may gather from *Bramah*'s text, was reſerved for the hand of *God himſelf*, as *they* were to be endued with *rational powers.*—It may be aſked why *Brum*, is repreſented floating, particularly on a *beetle leaf?* To this we can only reply, that the plant is deemed ſacred amongſt the *Gentoos*, it's culture is made under the auſpices of the *Shaſtah*, and inſtruction of the *Bramins*; *unclean perſons* are prohibited entering into a *beetle garden*, as the approach of any impurity is pronounced fatal to the plant, in the infancy of its growth.

To conclude this general head—How far *Homer*, *Virgil*, *Lucretius*, *Ovid*, *Lucian*, &c. have in their conceptions of the creation, (by means of the *Egyptians*) built on, and availed themſelves of the ſimple *coſmogony* of *Bramah*, we leave the learned and curious to trace.—Although in fact, it is obvious,

 that

that this ancient ſage, aimed at no other ſolution of that ſtupendous and incomprehenſible act, than to inculcate, that the univerſe was produced by *the eſſence* and voluntary *power*, *ſtrength* and *wiſdom* of God. That it is *preſerved* and ſuſtained by original conſtituent *powers* impreſſed on it by the Deity, and that it is liable *to change* and diſſolution, at his divine pleaſure and will.

The End of the Fifth Chapter.

CHAP. VI.

The Gentoo manner of computing Time, and their conception of the age of the universe, and the period of its dissolution.

[From Bramah's Chartah Bhade, in the supplement to his Birmahah.]

SIXTY *mimicks*, or winks of the eye, make one *pull*.
Sixty *pulls*, make one *gurree*.
Sixty *gurrees*, make one complete day, or one day and one night.
Three hundred and sixty-five complete days and fifteen *gurrees* make one solar year.

The *Gentoos* divide the complete day into eight parts, to which they give the term *paar*, commencing their day at six in the morning;—thus *ek paar dheen* * equals our nine in the morning; *duapaar dheen*, our noon; *teenpaar dheen*, our three afternoon; *Chaarpaar dheen*, our six in the evening:—the divisions of the night are distinguished by the word *rhaat* (night) in place of

* Literally, *one part of day.*

dheen, as *ek paar rhaat*, equals our nine at night; and ſo on.

It is the province of the *Bramins* in this country to keep the account of time, and there is no *Gentoo* of diſtinction but retains in his houſe and on his journeys one of theſe time keepers, whoſe intire buſineſs it is to regulate time, and ſtrike the *gurrées* as they paſs, on the *Ghong*, an extended ſheet of copper, which yields the ſound of a ſolemn bell.

Bramah meaſures ſpace or duration of time, from the creation of the *Dunneahoudah*, or univerſe, by the revolutions of the *four Jogues*.

	Years.
The firſt age, or *Suttee Jogue*, contains thirty-two lac years of vulgar time, or	3,200,000
The ſecond age, or *Tirta Jogue*, ſixteen lac, or	1,600,000
The third age, or *Dwapaar Jogue*, eight lac, or	800,000
The fourth age, or *Kolee Jogue*, four lac, or	400,000
	6,000,000

Ekutter

Ekutter (ſeventy one) revolutions of the four *Jogues* make one *Munnuntur* of vulgar time, or years 426,000,000.

(The word *Munnuntur*, is in this place ſtrictly applied by *Bramah* to *ſpace of time*, but it is by him frequently uſed with a retroſpect ſignification to the act of *creation*, and is ſometimes given as an additional name to *Birmah*, as *Birmah Munnuah*, alluding to the creation being the reſult of thought and meditation;—the word, as we before remarked in a marginal note, ſprings from *Mon*, or *Mun*, thought, reflection; *Munnoo Logue*, the people of thought, or contemplation.—The compilers of the *Aughtorrah Bhade* derive the word *Munnuntur* from *Munnuah* or *Munnooah*, whom (by perverting the ſenſe of *Bramah*) they make to be the fabulous perſonal offspring of *Birmah*, and report mighty feats of his prowess in war, againſt *Moiſaſoor*, and his adherents.)

When *Bramah* deſcended to promulge the written law and commands of the Eternal ONE to the *Gentoos*, he at the ſame time (namely, the beginning of the preſent *Kolee Jogue* *) declared, "*from the regiſters*

* Vide Introduction to the fourth chapter.

of *Surgo*, that the *Dunneaboudah*, was then entering into the eighth revolution of the four *Jogues*, in the *ſecond Munnuntur*;" conſequently, according to *Bramah*'s account, (and if our calculation be right) the preciſe age of *this*, and the other fourteen planets of the univerſe, amounted to, at that period, four hundred and ſixty eight millions of years. And if we ſubſtract the 4866 years, which have elapſed ſince the deſcent of *Bramah*, we ſhall find the remainder of the *Kolee Jogue* will be 359,134 years; at the expiration of which, *Bramah* pronounced and prophecied, that the patience and forbearance of the Eternal ONE would be withdrawn from the delinquent *Debtah*, and deſtruction *by fire* fall upon the eight regions of puniſhment, purgation and probation †.

In the ſupplement to his BIRMAHAH, *Bramah* likewiſe taught, that the *Boboon* of *Murto*, had undergone *three* remarkable changes, and would undergo *three* more, before its final diſſolution in common with the other ſeven *Boboons*; but he ſpecifies not of what nature *thoſe changes* were, or would be;—he alſo declares, "*that after a long* "*ſpace, a ſecond new creation will take place*; "*but of what kind, or on what principles it*

† Vide towards the cloſe of the fifth ſection.

2 "*would*

"*would be conſtructed, was only known to the*
"ETERNAL ONE."

The cauſe of the ſuperſtitious veneration paid by the *Gentoos* to the numericals ONE and THREE has, we conceive, been obvious to the diſcerning reader as he travelled thro' theſe ſheets.—It is remarkable, that a *Gentoo* never gives or receives an obligation for an even ſum; if he borrows or lends a hundred, a thouſand, or ten thouſand rupees, the obligation runs for a hundred and *one*, a thouſand and *one*, ten thouſand and *one*, &c. The *Mahommedans*, in conformity only, have generally adopted this cuſtom; hence it was, that the revenues ſtipulated to be paid annually by *Soujah Khan* into the royal treaſury, were *one* khorore, *one* lac, *one* thouſand, *one* hundred, and *one* rupee.

The End of the Sixth Chapter.

CHAP. VII.

Of the Gentoo Fasts, and Festivals, &c.

[From the Chatah and Aughtorrah Bhade Shastahs.]

INTRODUCTION.

AS the *Gentoo* year begins the first of *April*, we will trace their holy days as they fall in turn from that day, premising that the word *Ouposs* signifies a fast, *Purrup* a feast, and *Poojah* worship, but when accompanied with an offering, it is then called *Birto Poojah.*—*Poojah* is also sometimes used to signify the altar on which they offer.

The *Gentoo* holy days are guided by the course and age of the moon, and generally take their denomination from that, or from the religious duties that are enjoined on those particular days, and sometimes from both.

Their

Their offerings conſiſt of fruits, ſome particular ſacred plants and flowers, powdered ſugar, ſalt, meal, and different kinds of grain.

Firſt Holy Day. *Ouposs.*

OKHUIJ TERTEA, falls on the *third* day of the new moon in *April*, and is dedicated to the giving *alms* and benefactions to the *Bramins*, as the word *Okhuij* imports. —This day is alſo ordained for making the *Gentoo* pickle called *Koſſundee*, made only on this day, by the wives of the *Bramins*; it is compoſed of green mango's, tamarind, muſtard ſeed, and freſh muſtard ſeed oil; it is deemed a holy pickle, and the only one the *Gentoos* uſe with their food. April.

Second. *Ouposs.*

POORNEMEE †, falls on the full moon in *April*, and is ſtrictly ordained for waſhing and purifying in the river *Ganges*, and for diſtributing charity.

Third. *Ouposs Poojah—Purrup.*

ORUN ‡ SUSTEE, falls on the ſixth day of the new moon in *May*, and is dedicated to the goddeſs *Suſtee*, the goddeſs of gene- May.

† *Poorah*, full.

‡ *Orun*, the *morning ſtar*, often uſed to expreſs the *dawn of day*.

ration,

ration, who is worſhipped when the *morning ſtar* appears, or at dawn of day, for the propagation of children, and to remove barrenneſs.—On this day preſents are uſually made by the parents to their ſons in law, and the day ends with a *purrup* or feaſt.

Fourth. *Purrup*, at night *Poojah.*

DUSSARRAH, as the word imports, falls on the tenth day of the new moon in *May*; it is dedicated to the God *Gunga*, the God of the *Ganges*, who is fabled to have arrived on earth on this day of the moon, and in this month—it is alſo dedicated to the Goddeſs *Moonſhee Tagooran* *, Goddeſs of ſnakes, and fabulous daughter of *Sieb.*

Fifth. *Oupoſs-Poojah.*

POORNEMEE falls on the full moon in *May*, and is dedicated to *Jaggernaut*, (ſynonimous with *Biſtnoo.*) This day is otherwiſe called from the duty enjoined on it, the *Sinan* †, *Jattra* ‡, or *general waſhing* in the *Ganges*—and it is almoſt incredible to think the immenſe multitude of every age and ſex that appears on both ſides of the river,

* *Tagooran*, prieſteſs, ſometimes goddeſs.

† *Sinan*, bathing.

‡ *Jattra*, literally ſignifies *a dance of many.*

throughout

throughout it's whole courſe, at one and the ſame time.

Sixth. *Oupoſs-Purrup.*

RHUTT JATTRA, falls on the ſecond day of the new moon in *June*; it is dedicated to *Jaggernaut* and *Biſtnoo.*—On this day the *Rhutt*, or triumphal car of *Jaggernaut*, is carried forth about a mile, reſts, and is returned on the ninth day of the moon.—From the ſeventh day of the moon to the tenth, both incluſive, is the UMBOOBISSEE; during which ſpace, the earth is left to *her purgations*, and neither plough, ſpade, or any other inſtrument of tillage, permitted to moleſt her.—The term UMBOOBISSEE, which needs no further explanation, is applied to women under the ſame circumſtances. June.

Seventh. *Oupoſs.*

SYON † EKKADUSSEE, as the laſt word imports, falls on the *eleventh* day of the new moon in *June*, and is a ſolemn faſt. *Jaggernaut* (or *Biſtnoo*) is fabled to *ſleep* for four months;—which only ſignifies that the rainy ſeaſon about this time ſetting in for four months, the care of *Biſtnoo* (the pre-

† *Syon*, ſleep, repoſe.

ſerver)

ſerver) is ſuſpended, as immaterial, the rains ſecuring their crops of grain.

Eighth. *Ouposs.*

POORNEMEE, as the word imports, falls on the *full moon* in *June*, and is dedicated to waſhing in the *Ganges*, and charity to the *Bramins*.

Ninth. *Ouposs.*

DUADUSSEE, as the word ſignifies, falls
July. on the *twelfth* day of the new moon in *July*, and is devoted to waſhing in the *Ganges*, and giving alms.

Tenth. *Ouposs-Purrup.*

EKKADUSSEE, TERADUSSEE, CHOWTADUSSEE and POORNEMEE, the eleventh, thirteenth, fourteenth, of the new moon in *July*, to the *Poornemee* or full incluſive, are dedicated to the *Joolna Jattra* of *Kiſſen Tagoor*; but theſe are not directed by the *Shaſtah*, and are only obſerved by the *Gentoos* of the *Kettery* tribe.

Eleventh. *Ouposs.*

JURMO† OOSTOOMEE falls on the eighth day after the full, or twenty-third day of

† *Jurmo*, nativity.

the moon in *July*, and is dedicated to the birth of *Kiſſen Tagoor*, who is fabled to have then deſcended for the deſtruction of *Kunkſoo Rajah*, a famous *Oſſoor* and tyrant. It is obſerved as a ſolemn faſt.

Twelfth. *Purrup.*

Lukee † *Poojah* falls on the firſt *Thurſday* in the month of *Auguſt*; ſhe is the *Gentoo* Goddeſs of all kinds of grain, and is fabled to be the wife of *Biſtnoo*, the *preſerver*; ſhe is worſhipped at this time on the coming in the *Paddy*, the name given to rice in the huſk.—The day concludes with a feaſt. August.

Thirteenth. *Purrup.*

UNNUNTO BIRTO, falls on the fourteenth day of the moon in *Auguſt*, and is dedicated to *Biſtnoo* with the epithet of *Unnunto*, or the *unknown*; an offering of grain is made to him, and the day concludes with a feaſt.

Fourteenth. *Oupoſs.*

ARUNDAH POOJAH falls on the thirtieth day of *Auguſt*, and is dedicated to *Moonſhee Tagooran* (the feminine of *Tagoor*) Goddeſs of ſnakes.——The preciſe interpretation of *Arundah* we have loſt, and will not impoſe

† *Lukee*, plenty, affluence.

on

on our readers.—Although this day is a fast, it ends in a feast of the *new rice*, boiled early, and *eaten cold*; to which essential circumstance we think the word *Arundah*, given to this *Poojah*, alludes; but we are not positive.

Fifteenth. *Purrup*.

DRUGAH POOJAH falls on the seventh day of the new moon in *September*, and continues the eighth and ninth. The eighth is observed as a fast by those who have no children.—*This* is the grand general feast of the *Gentoos*, usually visited by all *Europeans*, (by invitation) who are treated by the proprietor of the feast with the fruits and flowers in season, and are entertained every evening whilst the feast lasts, with bands of singers and dancers.—This Goddess is the first in rank and dignity, and the most active of all the fabulous deities of the *Aughtorrah Bhade*, and is stiled the wife of *Sieb*, the *destroyer*, the third of the three primary created beings. She is as often stiled *Bowannee* †, as *Drugah* ‡; and frequently *Bowannee Drugah*: the cause of her descent is thus derived:—God having appointed *Endeer* § and his descendants universal

September.

† *Persevering*. ‡ *Virtue*. § *Goodness*.

verſal *Rajahs* of the world, the appointment was illy brooked by *Moiſaſoor* *; he thereupon drew together his adherents, and waged war againſt *Endeer* and his deſcendants, who were at laſt in the *Duapaar Jogue* obliged to fly, and leave the government of the world to *Moiſaſoor*; which proved the ſource of ravages, murders, and confuſion. —*Endeer*, and his few adherents, were confined to a ſmall portion of the world, from whence, in compaſſion to mankind, they with piety and humility petitioned the three primary created beings to implore the Eternal ONE to redreſs the grievances reſulting from the uſurped power of *Moiſaſoor*.—The three beings interceded, and obtained permiſſion that *Bowannee Drugah* ſhould deſcend on the earth, for the deſtruction of *Moiſaſoor* and his adherents, which the *Gentoos* are taught to believe ſhe will in the end effect, and finally reſtore the government of the world to *Endeer* and his deſcendants, according to the firſt intention of the Eternal ONE. Hence was the *Drugah Poojah* inſtituted, during which the Supreme Being is invoked, through her mediation, to haſten that wiſhed-for period.—The allegory in the foregoing recital is ſo plain by a reference to the marginal notes,

* *Evil.*

that we will not affront the underſtanding of our readers by offering an explanation, although we ſhall illuſtrate it further when we give a particular interpretation of the plate N°. 2.

Sixteenth. *Purrup.*

DUSSUMEE, or the tenth day of the new moon in *September*, when the image of DRUGAH is caſt into the *Ganges*, with the univerſal acclamations of the people, and is ſaid to be returned to her huſband *Sieb*. Purification by waſhing in the *Ganges* on this day is ſtrictly enjoined.

Seventeenth. *Oupoſs.*

LUKEE POOJAH falls on the full moon in *September*, on which ſhe is worſhipped all night, during which nothing is drank but the water of the coco nut.

Eighteenth. *Oupoſs.*

KALLEKA, *Kalkee* or *Kalle Poojah*, (for they are ſynonimous) falls on the laſt day of the moon in *September*. This goddeſs is worſhipped all the night of that day univerſally, but in a more particular manner at *Kallee Ghat*, about three miles ſouth of *Calcutta*; an ancient *Pagoda* dedicated to her there, ſtands cloſe to a ſmall brook, which

is

is by the *Bramins* deemed to be the original course of the *Ganges*.——The parts of the *Gentoo* Goddess (like the parts of some modern saints) are worshipped in various parts of *Indostan*; her *eyes* at *Kallee Ghat*, her head at *Banaras*, her hand at *Bindoobund*; but where the remains of her are distributed has escaped our memory *.—She takes her name from her usual habiliment, which is *black*, and is frequently called the *black Goddess*; *Kallee* is the common name for ink.—She is fabled to have sprung, completely armed, from the *eye of Drugah*, at a time when she was hard pressed in battle by the tyrants of the earth †.—On this fast, worship and offerings are paid to the *manes* of deceased *ancestors*. Besides the last mentioned annual custom, every *Gentoo* keeps the anniversary of their father's death, in fasting and worship to his *manes*, which is called *Baap ka Surraad*‡.—It is worthy remark (by the bye) that in all *Devonshire*, the word *Kallee* expresses black or smut: why the same combination of letters should convey the same idea to people so far removed from each other, we leave the curious to account for.

* Plate N°. 3.

† The various heads which appear scattered over the plate, signify the many tyrants and monsters she slew in conjunction with *Drugah*.

‡ *Sacred to the father*.

Nineteenth. *Purrup.*

RAAS ‡ JATTRA, falls on the full moon in *October*, and is continued to the seventeenth of the moon; it is dedicated to *Kissen Tagoor Kettry.*—This feast is universally observed, but in a most extraordinary manner celebrated at *Bindoobund*, in commemoration of a marvellous event which is fabled to have happened in the neighbourhood of that place.—A number of virgins met to celebrate, in mirth and sports, the descent of *Kissen* §: in the heighth of their joy, the God appeared amongst them, and proposed to them a *dance*, to which they objected, as *they* were many, and *he* but one; to obviate this objection, he divided himself into as many *Kissens* as there were virgins, who immediately entered into a *circular* dance with them, as represented in the plate N° 4. In the centre circle he is represented standing in a disengaged attitude, attended by the nymphs *Nundee* and *Bringhee* (joys and sports) who are making him offerings of flowers and fruits.

October.

Twentieth. *Ouposs.*

KARTIK *Poojah* falls on the last day of the moon in *October.*—This divinity is fabled to be the youngest son of *Moisoor* (or *Sieb)*

‡ A *circle*. § Plate N° 4.

and

and *Drugah*; he is worſhipped on this day by thoſe who have not been bleſſed with children, and man and woman are enjoined a ſtrict faſt.——The word *Kartik*, ſtrictly means *conſecration*, hence this divinity is ſaid to be the inviſible guardian, and ſuperintendant of the *Gentoo Pagodas*. The word alſo ſometimes ſignifies *holineſs*. The month of *October* takes its name from him, becauſe in this month the *Pagodas* are generally conſecrated.

Twenty-firſt. *Purrup*.

NOVONO † is celebrated on the firſt *lucky Thurſday* in *November*, on the firſt coming in of the new grain of the ſecond crop; the *lucky Thurſday* is fixed in a conſultation of *Bramins*, and is a general feaſt. November.

Twenty-ſecond. *Oupoſs-Purrup*.

LUKEE POOJAH falls on the firſt *Thurſday* in the month of *December*, on getting in all the new harveſt, when this favorite Goddeſs of the *Gentoos* receives a ſolemn thankſgiving for all the bleſſings of the year; the day is paſſed in faſting, worſhip, waſhing and purifying in the *Ganges*; at night they feaſt. December.

† *New rice*.

Twenty-third. *Purrup.*

LUKEE POOJAH SANKRANTEE * falls on the laſt day in *December*, when this Goddeſs is again worſhipped as on the laſt mentioned holy-day, excepting the faſt. On this day bread is diſtributed in alms, according to every one's ability.

Twenty-fourth. *Purrup.*

SEEREE PUNCHEMEE falls on the fifth day of the new moon in *January*, and is dedicated to *Surſuttee* †, the *Gentoo* Goddeſs of arts, and letters.—She is fabled to be the daughter of *Birmah* and *Birmaanee*.
January. The *Koyt Caſt*, or tribe of writers, are prohibited the uſe of pen and ink on this feſtival, *which* are conſecrated to her for the day, and a ceſſation is put to buſineſs of every kind.—*Seeree* ſignifies *fortune*, *ſucceſs*, and is the *firſt* word of every epiſtolary correſpondence in the *Gentoo* language.

Twenty-fifth. *Birto.*

ORUN OODEE, ‡ SUPTIMEE, falls on the ſeventh day of the new moon in *January*, and is called *Soorjee Poojah*, or *worſhip to the*

* *Sunkrantee* ſignifies the laſt day in every month.
† *Invention, contrivance, ingenuity, genius.*
‡ *Riſing of the dawn.*

ſun;

ſun ; to whom offerings are made of peculiar flowers in the *Ganges*.

Twenty-ſixth. *Oupoſs*.

BHIM EKADUSSEE falls on the eleventh day of the new moon in *January*; the day is dedicated to *Kiſſen*, and commemorates the abſtinence of *Bhim*, a voracious *Eater*, who faſted on this day; he is called the brother of *Judiſteen*. *Bhim* is the common name of reproach for a *Glutton*, but who this *Judiſteen* is, or what the occult meaning and real ſignification of this faſt, has ſlipped our memory, and we will not ſubſtitute any interpretation that is not warranted by our materials, or from our certain and clear knowledge.

Twenty-ſeventh. *Oupoſs*.

POORNEMEE, or the full moon in *January*, is dedicated to *Biſtnoo*, the *cheriſher*.—— Faſting, waſhing and alms.

Twenty-eighth. *Oupoſs*.

SIEBRATEER, *Chowturduſſee*, or the fourteenth after the full, falls on the twenty-ninth day of the moon in *January*, and is dedicated to *Sieb*, the deſtroyer, who is worſhipped with faſting, offerings, and prayer *all the night*, as the additional *rateer* annexed to the title of this holy-day imports.

Twenty-ninth. *Ouposs.*

GOVINDUSSEE falls on the twelfth day of the moon in *February*, and is dedicated to *Bistnoo* the *comforter*, as the word *Govin*, or *Govindu* signifies, and is one of the many appellatives given to the second of the *three* primary created persons, and he is worshipped on this day with fasting, prayer, &c.

February.

Thirtieth. *Purrup.*

DOLE † JATTRA falls on the *Poornemee* or full moon in *February*, and is sacred to *Kissen Tagoor*. On this feast day it is that the *Gentoos* cast the powder of a certain red flower, called *Faag*, on all they meet; but whence this custom, or for what cause this feast was first instituted, has escaped us.

Thirty-first. *Ouposs.*

BARRANEE JATTRA, or *Modoo Kistna* ‡ *Tiradussee* (the thirteenth after the full) falls on the twenty-eighth day of the moon in *February*: if this falls on a *Saturday*, it is called *Barranee*, and if the star *Satoo Bissah* is then on the meridian, it is called *Mahah Barranee*; and again, if the star *Soobo Jogue* is in conjunction with *Satoo Bissah*, it is

† *Dole*, a drum.

‡ *Kissen*, *Kistna*, are synonimous with *Bistnoo*, but allude to different attributes.

then

then called * *Mahah Mahah Barranee.* ——These conjunctions are uncertain, but when they happen, it is deemed a most holy day, and is observed by universal purification in the *Ganges*, and worship and offerings to *Soorjee*, or the *sun*. It fell out last on the twenty-eighth of *February*, 1759.—As we have lost the precise meaning and etymology of the word *Barranee*, and confess ourselves ignorant of the astronomy of the *Bramins*, we will not attempt an explanation of this fast.

Thirty-two. *Ouposs-Purrup.*

LUKEE POOJAH falls on the first *Thursday* in *March*, when this goddess is worshipped universally, and thanked for all the productions of the earth, all being brought forth by this time. March.

Thirty-second. *Purrup.*

DURGAH *Poojah*, and *Bhasuntee* † *Poojah*, falls on the seventh day of the new moon in *March*, and continues the eighth, ninth and tenth—on the last, her image is cast into the *Ganges*. This feast is instituted for the

* *Most great.*

† *The end, final, conclusive*, alluding to this being the last feast of the year, preceding the *Gentoo* Lent.

ſame purpoſes as the other grand one, but not with that parade and univerſality.

Thirty-third. *Oupoſs.*

SIEB, or *Sunnias* * *Poojah*, is from the firſt to the thirtieth of *March*, with only a ſhort ſuſpenſion during the term of the *Durgah Poojah* above-mentioned—The *Sunnias Poojah*, is the *Gentoo* Lent; their penances, mortifications, and *ſelf* corporal puniſhments, have been ſo often deſcribed, we will not particularize any of them. The *Churruck* †, or day of *ſwinging*, falls on the thirtieth. From this penance the three caſts, or tribes, of *Bramins*, *Bydees* ‡, and *Koyts*, are exempted by the *Aughtorrah Bhade*; and, in fact, none but the very loweſt of the people go through any of the publick penances; but, every caſt faſts and worſhips the twenty-ninth, the day preceding the *Churruck*.—This ſolemn faſt is dedicated to *Sieb*, or *Moideb*, or *Moiſoor*, the *Mutilātor*, and *averter of evil*; through whom, at this ſeaſon, the Eternal ONE is invoked, to defend them from the influence of *Moiſaſoor* and his adherents, and avert

* *Penitents.* † Literally ſignifies a *Wheel*—— but the circle which the penitent deſcribes in ſwinging round has given it this appellation.

‡ *Bydees*, the tribe that profeſs the practice of phyſick.

the final doom pronounced againſt the delinquent *Debtah*.

There is a feſtival inſtituted to *Rhaam*, the *protector*, which is entitled the RHAAM JATTRA, but the preciſe time of it's celebration we have utterly forgot.—*Rhaam* is another of the multitude of names, or rather attributes, given to *Biſtnoo*, the *preſerver*.

How far the origin of the faſts, feſtivals, terms, &c. of the *Egyptians*, *Greeks* and *Latins*, may be traced from the *Chatah* and *Aughtorrah Bhade Shaſtahs*, we ſubmit and recommend to the elucidation of our learned readers, who will be the better enabled to make ſuch an enquiry from what follows.

Explanation of the Plate or Repreſentation of the Gentoos grand feaſt of the Drugah.

Plate N° 2.

The repreſentation of the Drama in this grand *Gentoo* feaſt will, we doubt not, appear genuine to many thouſands now in *England*, as it is a ſight that few who have viſited *Bengall* have not indulged themſelves with; and we may take the liberty of ſaying, that but very few amongſt the multitude who

have

have seen it could form the smallest judgment of it's *intention* or signification; to these, therefore, we flatter ourselves it will afford some pleasure, the having a subject explained to them, on which they have often looked with pity and amazement! because they did not understand it.—The intention of this feast we have already given in it's proper place, to which the reader may advert, under the title of *Drugah Poojah* N° 15. and shall now proceed to the explanation of the chief personages in the plate.

The center and principal figure is DRUGAH or Virtue; she is represented, with ten arms, descending on a dragon—mystically shewing the *power* and irresistable force of *virtue*, when exerted with vigor.—She is crowned, one of her hands is armed with a spear, and she is environed with a snake—with another hand she binds *Moisasoor* (or Evil) with a *snake*, and kills him by thrusting her spear through his *heart*, thereby implying that Virtue's safest and surest guard against vice or *evil* is *wisdom*, of which the *snake*, as before observed, is the symbol.—The battles * said to have been fought between *Endeer* †, and *Moisasoor* ‡, in which the latter generally proved victorious, without

* Vide *Drugah Poojah*, fifteenth.

† *Good.* ‡ *Evil.*

out the aſſiſtance of *Drugah Bowannee,* or *perſevering virtue,* implies that *moral evil* can only be ſucceſsfully combated *therewith.* --The ravages, murders, and confuſion, which are ſaid to be the conſequences in the world of the flight of *Endeer* and victory of *Moiſaſoor* *, emblematically ſignify the fatal and natural effects of vice or evil triumphant, which muſt neceſſarily be attended with deſtructive ſcenes of violence.—Hence, *Moiſaſoor* is fabled to have transformed himſelf, after his victory, into a *mad buffola,* the ſymbol of ungovernable rage, whoſe head is ſeen in the annexed plate lying at the feet of *Drugah.*—Although *Moiſaſoor* in the plate appears to be ſlain by *Drugah,* yet this act is only a prophetic repreſentation of the death and deſtruction he will in the end ſuffer by her hand, when *Endeer* ſhall be reſtored, and *Good* be predominant in the world again, and triumph over *Moiſaſoor* or Evil.—*Endeer* being appointed by God univerſal Rajah of the world, myſtically points out his benevolent intentions, that it ſhould be governed by goodneſs and piety, and the allegory is as obvious where *Moiſaſoor* is ſaid *illy to brook the appointment* †.

On the right of *Drugah* are repreſented the figures of *Sieb,* her huſband, and of

* Vide *Drugah Poojah.* † Vide *Drugah Poojah.*

Lukee, the goddeſs of grain.—*Sieb* is ſitting on a *white bull*, the ſymbol of purity and dominion; he is environed with a ſnake, holding in one hand a *Dumboor* †, and in the other a *Singee* ‡, muſical inſtruments in uſe at all the *Gentoo* feſtivals; allegorically pointing out that wiſdom is the moſt effectual *averter* of *evil*, and that mirth, joy and gladneſs, are the natural effects of it's being averted from us.

The goddeſs *Lukee* is repreſented ſtanding in an eaſy attitude; ſhe is crowned with ears of grain, and is encircled by a plant bearing fruit, which paſſes through both her hands, the root of which is under her feet; ſhe (as all the ſuperiour *Gentoo* divinities are) is environed by a ſnake.——The meaning conveyed by this figure is ſo obvious it needs no explanation.

Underneath the figure of *Sieb* is repreſented the divinity named GHUNNIS §.—He has no peculiar day of worſhip inſtituted in honour of him, for this manifeſt reaſon, becauſe all the addreſſes, offerings and worſhip, which are made to the ſupreme, and ſuperior beings, are preferred through his mediation, and promoted by a prior offering

† A *ſmall drum*. ‡ A *muſical horn*.
§ *Purity*, or *ſincerity of heart*.

and

and worſhip paid to him; ſo that he may be properly ſtiled the *God of offerings.*—He is fabled to be the firſt born of *Moiſoor* (or *Sieb)* and *Drugah*; all worſhip and offerings being made through him, myſtically ſignifies that *purity* and *ſincerity of heart* muſt be the ſource from whence the Deity is invoked.—He is repreſented with four arms, ſiting on an altar, environed with a ſnake, and with the head of a *white elephant*, the ſymbols of *purity*, *riches* and *dominion* or *ſtrength*, which, the *Gentoos* ſay, includes every bleſſing, and cannot be juſtly and properly acquired but by pure and ſincere acts of devotion to God, and good works to man and his fellow creatures.—His four arms are only repreſentative of the power, force and efficacy of ſincerity in worſhip and prayer.

On the left of *Drugah* is repreſented the figure of *Surſuttee*, the *Gentoo* Goddeſs of arts, letters and eloquence, ſo fully deſcribed under the feaſt called *Seeree Punchumee* (twenty-fourth.) In the plate, ſhe appears environed with a ſnake, ſtanding in a careleſs, diſengaged poſture, holding in her hands a reed, of which the writing pens are uſually made.

On the left of *Surſuttee* is repreſented the idol of RHAAM, the protector of *em-*

pires,

pires, *ſtates*, and property, already explained*. —In the plate, he is figured crowned, encircled with a ſnake, and riding upon a monkey; in his left hand he holds a bow, and is repreſented in the attitude of having juſt diſcharged an arrow from it. To underſtand this repreſentation, a ſhort hiſtorical recital becomes neceſſary.—*Rhaaboon* †, the ſubverter of empires, ſtates and *property*, is ever contraſted with *Rhaam* in the courſe of the *Aughtorrah Bhade Shaſtah*—This prime agent of *Moiſaſoor* is fabled to have run away with SITHEE ‡, the wife of *Rhaam*; and for the recovery of her, that book exhibits a long detail of furious battles fought between *Rhaam* and *Rhaaboon* with various ſucceſs; myſtically painting the contentions that ever have ſubſiſted in the world touching *empires* and *property*, in general. Under theſe the ancient hiſtory of *Indoſtan* and it's Rajahs is obſcurely couched.—In one of the moſt bloody of theſe battles, *Rhaam* being ſore preſſed, was obliged to call in as an auxiliary, *Hoonmhon* Prince of the *monkeys*, by whoſe aſſiſtance he routed *Rhaaboon* and recovered his wife—*Sithee*; implying only, that *lawleſs force*, muſt be ſometimes

* Vide explanation of the *Tirtah Jogue*, or ſecond age, chap. 4.

† *Lawleſs violence.* ‡ Literally, *property.*

combated

combated with craft, policy, and ſtratagem, of which the *monkey* throughout *Indoſtan* is the known emblem.—The laſt mentioned battle is repreſented in the plate number 5. where *Rhaam* appears engaged with *Rhaaboon*, and the attitude of *Rhaam* (in the plate of the *Drugah)* as having diſcharged the fatal arrows from the back of the monkey, alludes to *that* battle: in the plate No. 5. *Rhaam* is ſupported by his brother *Lukkon*, or *fortitude*, each encircled with ſnakes; and *Rhaaboon* (as he generally is) is repreſented with ten arms, and as many heads of monſters, which intimate the *force* of lawleſs tyranny and power.—Although the emblematic ſenſe of the *monkey* is ſo obvious, yet the crafty *Bramins* have eſtabliſhed a belief that *Rhaam* transformed himſelf into, and is always preſent under *that form*; the people ſwallowed the deluſion in a literal ſenſe, and it is upon this principle, that numerous colleges of *Bramins* are ſupported by the people for the maintainance of thoſe animals, near the groves where they uſually reſort; one of them is at *Amboah* in the neighbourhood of *Culna*, on the *Ganges*.—In the time of the *Rhaam Jattra* the *Bramins* exhibit a kind of theatrical maſque, wherein the many flights, and eſcapes of *Sithee*, and the various ſtratagems of *Rhaaboon* to retain her, and of

Rhaam to recover her, with the final battle, which gave him the repoſſeſſion of her, are all thrown into action, and the dialogue taken from the *Augktorrah Bhade Shaſtah*. We have been frequently preſent at this theatrical exhibition, and received much pleaſure and amuſement; one circumſtance at the concluſion is worth mentioning—when *Rhaam* had recovered his wife *Sithee*, he refuſes to cohabit with her, until ſhe has given ſome ſignal proof, that ſhe had ſuffered no contamination, or violation, during her abode with *Rhaaboon*; on which (by an ingenious piece of machinery) ſhe paſſes thro' a fire, comes out unhurt, and then *Rhaam* with raptures, receives her to his arms.

Below the idol of *Rhaam* on the plate of the *Drugah*, is that of *Kartik*; for the explanation of this faſt, ſee number twenty-four.—He is repreſented, armed at all points for war, and riding on a *peacock*, the *Gentoo* ſymbol of *pride* and *oſtentation*, intimating that thoſe qualities and vices of the mind muſt be ſubdued, as being previouſly neceſſary to the approach and admiſſion into their *Pagodas*; he is armed as a guardian, capable of defending from violation the divinity within; wherever there is a congregation of idols, in a *Tagoor Bharree* *, his idol is placed

* Literally *a houſe for divinities*.

at the door.—A *Gentoo* had within our memory an only ſon dangerouſly ill of a fever; he paid ſolemn worſhip, vows and offerings, for his recovery, not only to the *goddeſs of fevers*, but to all the other Gods, and Goddeſſes beſides—His ſon died—the father, frantic with grief and deſpair, ſallied out before day, broke open a *Tagoor Bharree* in a buzaar ſouth of the town of *Calcutta*, where *Kartîk* being off his guard and mingled with the other divinities—he cut all their heads off; his intention was to have proceeded round the town (as he confeſſed on examination) and to have decollated every God in all the *Tagoor* bharries of the place; but the ſecond he came to, *Kartîk* was upon his guard at the door, and preſenting his dart at him, brought him to his ſenſes, and providentially ſaved the reſt of his brother divinities.

Below the figures of *Lukee* and *Surſuttee*, ſtand the repreſentation of two divine nymphs, *Nundee* joy, and *Bringee* ſports; they are both encircled by *ſnakes*, implying, that joy and ſports at all their feſtivals, ſhould be circumſcribed by prudence and *wiſdom*.

On the right between *Sieb* and *Ghunnis*, is repreſented a boat, in which *Nundee* and *Bringee* are carrying *Drugah* to her huſband *Sieb*, after ſhe had been caſt into the *Ganges*; and in the copartment oppoſite between the figures of *Rhaam* and *Kartîk*, are repreſented two nymphs in a kind of threatening poſture, adviſing him to take better care of *his wiſe* another time, and keep her at home.

In the centre of the arch is repreſented *Surſuttee* and four female attendants, one preſenting to her the palmira leaf, the original paper, another a piece of wax, the third an ink ſtand, the fourth a pen, the uſe of which are all interdicted on her feſtival, and made an offering to her.——The two end copartments *Kallee* and *Drugah*, each engaged with two giants tyrants of the earth.—The other diviſion of the arch, allude to different paſſages of the *Aughtorrah Bhade*, which have eſcaped our memory.

End of the Explanation of plate N° 2.

As we reſerve the eighth chapter or general head, namely, "the diſſertation on the metempſychoſis," for a third and *laſt part* of this work, there remains nothing more to cloſe this chapter, but to add a ſhort recital of the genealogy of the *Gentoo* divinities, on which ſubject, as our materials are few, we ſhall not, we fear, afford any great ſatisfaction to the curious, as we are confined to the

the progeny of *Birmah* and *Birmanee* only. The fabulous legend of the *Aughtorrah Bhade* ſays,

That God created *three* females, or aſſociates, for the *three* primary created Beings. To *Birmah* he gave *Birmaanee*, to *Biſtnoo Lukee*, and to *Sieb Bowannee Drugah*.

That to *Birmah* and *Birmangee* were born two ſons, the eldeſt named *Kuſſiebmunnoo*, the youngeſt *Dookee Rajah*; the eldeſt was governed by a pious and laudable ſpirit, the youngeſt by a vicious and turbulent one.

Dookee Rajah had a daughter (but how he came by her the legend ſayeth not) named *Dithee*, whom he married to his brother *Kuſſiebmunnoo*, and ſhe brought him a ſon, whom he called ENDEER; he and his deſcendants, after the example of their father *Kuſſiebmunnoo*, were truly virtuous, and obſervant of the laws of God, communicated to them by *Birmah* and *Birmaanee*.

Dookee Rajah had a ſecond daughter, whom he called *Odithee*, who was alſo married to *Kuſſiebmunnoo*, and ſhe likewiſe brought him a ſon, who was named MOISASOOR; he and his deſcendants, after the example of their grandfather *Dookee Rajah*, ſlighting

ſlighting the precepts of *Birmah* and *Birmaanee*, became abandoned to every vice, and contemners of the laws of God.

All the benefit that accrues from the foregoing ſhort recital of the progeny of *Birmah* and *Birmaanee*, is, that thus we find in *Endeer*, and *Moiſaſoor*, the roots from whence the doctrine of two contending principles in nature, *Good* and *Evil*, ſprung; that this was the ground-work of all the doctrines of the *Bramins*, after they had loſt ſight of the ſimple and ſublime theology of the *Chartah Bhade* of *Bramah*, is beyond all controverſy; as the whole tendency of the two *later Bhades*, exemplify the natural hiſtory of thoſe two contending principles in the *human mind*, and the concomitant effects, they will have on *it*, and on the government of the *world*, as they alternately happen to preſide.—Hence the unceaſing ſtruggles and conflicts for ſuperiority between *Endeer* and *Moiſaſoor* and their adherents, which ſay the *Bramins* ſubſiſt to this day; ſo well founded, was the conjecture of the learned and ingenious Mr. *Bayle*, touching the great antiquity of the origin of the *Manechean* doctrine—nor is it at all improbable, that arch heretic *Manes* might have received ſome notions of this doctrine from the tenets of the *Bramins*, which he per-

verted

verted to the worſt and moſt dangerous purpoſes and opinions:—on the contrary the ſimplicity, with which the doctrine is profeſſed by the *Gentoos*, has in it's ſelf (but *otherwiſe* in it's conſequences) no ſuch manifeſt tendency; although by their adherence to it, they ſeem utterly to forget the conſideration of their original exiſtence and delinquency, and the merciful cauſe of their eſtabliſhment, in the eight *Boboons* of puniſhment and probation, as well as the laws and injunctions of their prophet *Bramah*, who obviouſly reſts the reſtoration and ſalvation of the offending *Debtah*, upon *two* ſimple and plain conditions, *a ſincere penitent impreſſion of their original delinquency*; *and an atonement by good works, according to the powers of exertion, which God annexed to their animal forms.*—But it is not at all to be wondered at, that they ſhould thus loſe ſight of their *original ſin* and defection, as well as the means laid down for their ſalvation; when the very ſpirit of the faſts and feſtivals, and whole conduct of the drama of the *Chatah*, and *Aughtorrah Bhades*, are relative only to the *averting* the evils of their preſent exiſtence, without the ſmalleſt retroſpect to their firſt tranſgreſſion, or the means of atoning for it.—This is the ſituation of the bulk of the people of *Indoſtan*, as well as of the modern *Bramins*; amongſt the latter,

if

if we except one in a thousand, we give them over measure; the consequences from these premises are obvious—the *Gentoos in general*, are as degenerate, crafty, superstitious, litigious and wicked a people, as any race of beings in the known world, if not eminently more so, especially the common run of the *Bramins*; and we can truly aver, that during almost five years, that we presided in the judicial cutcherry court of *Calcutta*, never any murder, or other atrocious crime, came before us, but it was proved in the end, a *Bramin* was at the bottom of it: but then, the *remnant* of *Bramins* (whom we have before excepted) who seclude themselves from the communications of the busy world, in a philosophic, and religious retirement, and strictly pursue the tenets and true spirit of the *Chartah Bhade of Bramah*, we may with equal truth and justice pronounce, *are the purest models of genuine piety that now exist, or can be found on the face of the earth.*—— And now, my friends, and most respectable readers, we will, with your permission, adopt one custom of the *Gentoos*, and make an offering, for some time at least, of our pen, ink, and paper, to the goddess SURSUTTEE.

The End of the Second Part.

Beenham House, Berks,
the 1st of Aug. 1766.

N° 1

INTERESTING
HISTORICAL EVENTS,
Relative to the
PROVINCES OF BENGAL,
AND THE
EMPIRE OF INDOSTAN.

WITH

A Seaſonable HINT and PERSUASIVE

To the Honorable

The COURT of DIRECTORS of the EAST INDIA COMPANY.

AS ALSO

The MYTHOLOGY and COSMOGONY, FASTS and FESTIVALS of the GENTOOS, Followers of the SHASTAH.

AND

A DISSERTATION on the METEMPSYCHOSIS, commonly, though erroneouſly, called the PYTHAGOREAN Doctrine.

By J. Z. HOLWELL, Eſq;

PART III.

LONDON:
Printed for T. BECKET and P. A. DE HONDT, near Surry-Street, in the Strand.
MDCCLXXI.

TO THE MOST NOBLE

THE DUKE OF NORTHUMBERLAND,

NOT MORE CONSPICUOUS

FROM

THE SPLENDOR OF HIS TITLES,

THAN

DISTINGUISHED BY THE LUSTRE OF HIS MERITS,

BELOVED FOR HIS AMIABLE QUALITIES,

REVERED FOR HIS PUBLIC AND PRIVATE VIRTUES,

THE LOVER OF ARTS, THE FRIEND OF LEARNING,

THE PATRON OF SCIENCE,

THIS ESSAY

(INTENDED TO RESCUE FROM ERROR AND

OBLIVION THE ANCIENT RELIGION OF INDOSTAN)

IS DEDICATED,

BY (A LOVER OF TRUTH, AND AN ADMIRER OF

HIS GRACE's EXALTED CHARACTER)

J. Z. HOLWELL.

CHAP. VIII.

A Dissertation on the Metempsychosis of the Bramins, *or Transmigrations of the fallen Angelic Spirits; with a Defence of the original Scriptures of* Bramah, *and an occasional comparison between them and the Christian Doctrines.*

INTRODUCTION.

PART I.

WE have hitherto floated upon the materials which the wreck of *Calcutta* in the year 1765 afforded us, and now for the first time, launch out into the ocean of hypothesis and speculation upon our own bottom. Difficult and hazardous as our course is, we will hope our voyage may not be unprosperous. We invoke no aid to lead us on our way, but that POWER ALONE, which can ALONE ENLIGHTEN; that POWER! which in every age (but more particularly in some) has graciously been

 pleased,

pleaſed to convey a divine revelation to the HEART OF MAN.

2. Various ſoils and climates, as they influence the conſtitutions, ſo they do in part the diſpoſitions of mankind; and this it is, that may have made it neceſſary to diſpenſe different modes of revealing the WILL OF GOD to the different parts of this (and poſſibly every other) habitable globe; and as the minds of ſocieties, and even nations, are ſubject, with all things elſe, to revolution and change; it may alſo have been neceſſary to vary the mode of revelation *to the ſame people*, at different periods of time, as the immoral ſtate, or imperfections of mankind may have indicated. The hiſtory of the world is pregnant with many inſtances in ſupport of theſe probable concluſions, beſides that of the double revelation to the Hebrews, the Moſaic, and the Chriſtian: the minds of men are impreſſed by, and open to conviction, and the acceptance of TRUTH, under one peculiar form, which they will reject under another. How deeply then ought we to adore and reverence that ſupreme Being, who thus condeſcends to model his commands, and inſpire his choſen writers, in conformity to the weakneſs, and failings of his creatures?

3. It

3. It is an allowed truth, that there never was yet any ſyſtem of theology broached to mankind, whoſe firſt profeſſors and propagators did not announce *its deſcent from* GOD; and GOD forbid, we ſhould doubt of, or impeach the divine origin, of any of them; for ſuch eulogium they poſſibly all merited in their primitive purity, could they be traced up to that ſtate, notwithſtanding many learned pens have labored to prove, that ſuch a claim was generally a political impoſition only; a ſuggeſtion that we think has not much contributed to the advancement of either the piety, or morals of mankind, and therefore better had it been ſuppreſſed, and kept from their knowledge, as we hope to make appear preſently. ——Various as we may obſerve the religious ſyſtems ſcattered throughout the world, and ſingular as our following opinion, and our reaſoning thereon may appear to be; we ſhall not heſitate to lay it down as a principle, That—howſoever mankind, either of *Europe*, *Aſia*, *Africa* or *America*, may differ in the exterior modes of worſhip paid to the DEITY, according to their various genius; yet, that there are ſome *fundamental points* of every ſyſtem, wherein *all agree* and profeſs unanimous faith; as may be gathered, either from their *expreſs doctrines*, or evidently implied, from their

modes, or ceremonials of worſhip, howſoever differing in manner and form, from each other.

4. The *fundamental points* of religion above alluded to, we chuſe to diſtinguiſh by the title of PRIMITIVE TRUTHS, truths! which forceably ſtruck, and impreſſed the human heart at the period of man's creation, and although from an original unhappy taint, he in ſucceeding times, ſtrangely deviated from them, yet he never has, nor ever will be able, wholly to obliterate and efface them, however he may ſometimes for a greater, or leſſer ſpace, utterly loſe ſight of them.——We will enumerate the principal of theſe *primitive truths*—— *1ſt*, The being of a GOD, eternal, creator, and conſervator of all things, animate and inanimate;——*2dly*, The exiſtence of three prime created celeſtial beings, either confounded with the Deity, or excluſive of, and ſubordinate to him;——*3dly*, The creation of angelic beings;——*4thly*, A defection, or rebellion of a portion of thoſe beings;——*5thly*, Their expulſion from the heavenly regions;——*6thly*, The immortality of the human ſoul;——*7thly*, A future ſtate of rewards and puniſhments of the human ſoul;——*8thly*, That man is here in a ſtate of puniſhment and probation, for a tranſ-

a tranſgreſſion committed in a prior ſtate of exiſtence againſt his Creator;——*9thly*, That there exiſts a Being, who inſtigated the revolt of the angelic ſpirits, and ſtill continues the enemy and deceiver of mankind;——*10thly*, The neceſſity of a mediator, or mediators, between GOD and man, over and above repentance and good works, for the expiation of ſin, and obtaining a reſtoration to a ſtate, from which he now ſtands expelled;——*11thly*, That there is an intermediate ſtate of puniſhment and purification between death and the perfect reſtoration of the human ſoul;——*12thly*, The exiſtence of *a golden age*;——*13thly*, That there exiſted a period when mankind was ſuſtained by, and ſubſiſted only on the fruits of the earth;——and *laſtly*, The doctrine of the miniſtration of angels, in human affairs. Theſe were the *primitive truths* revealed by a gracious GOD to man, in the early days of his creation, at a time when it may be reaſonably preſumed he retained a lively ſenſe of his ſoul's former tranſgreſſion; as well as of the grace then offered to him. That theſe are the only *primitive truths* neceſſary to man's ſalvation, and reſtoration, appears from hence, that they have, from the earlieſt records of time to this day, remained more or leſs *the ſtock* upon which the blindneſs, or wickedneſs

 of

of man has engrafted very extravagant, unprofitable, as well as unintelligible doctrines, to delude their fellow-creatures, and ſeduce them from a ſtrict adherence to, and reliance on, thoſe *primitive truths only*.

5. This being the caſe, how much is it to be lamented, that our learned divines, ſome of whom are the greateſt ornaments of our church and profeſſion, have not taken the advantage of the concurring teſtimony of all mankind, touching theſe *fundamental principles*, to enforce their relative duties, in their preaching and writings? in place of which, moved by a vain oſtentation, and ſhew of deep learning, the rubbiſh of antiquity is raked up, and ſifted, to prove that nations, and individuals amongſt the ancients, and ſome of the wiſeſt and beſt of mankind, were infidels with reſpect to any ſincere faith in religion at all; and that the fable of religion was invented by lawgivers, purely to keep the populace in awe: and we are told by theſe profound reſearchers, that the great *Socrates* was the only one amongſt the ancient philoſophers, who believed what he taught, *the unity of the Godhead, the immortality of the ſoul, and a future ſtate of rewards and puniſhments*:——a ſtrange mode this, of enlightening modern times! to record and circulate

circulate ſuch ſentiments in the mother tongue of a Chriſtian people, although on ſuppoſition only, that ſuch principles ever exiſted in any country or age whatſoever.

6. We are aware that the motives and plea urged in defence of the publication of the infidel opinions of the ancient philoſophers are, the reputation of modern atheiſts, deiſts, and free-thinkers: vain pretence, and no leſs vain the attempt, where the ſlighteſt review of the bent and genius *of man* would have convinced them, that when once a writer, can ſo far get the better of ſhame and decorum, as to dare publiſh opinions, not only contrary to, but ſubverſive of all religious faith, that man is incorrigible, and beyond the reach of conviction. To reaſon with writers of that ſtamp, carries as much propriety with it, as if our divines would go and diſplay their oratory upon the miſerable inhabitants of Bedlam; and their endeavors would be as ſalutary. The ſame may be ſaid of fanatics in every religion; as the one believes nothing at all, theſe believe too much, and both have always thrived, and acquired ſtrength from diſputation and perſecution.

7. Religious controverſy never yet did, nor ever will do good to the cauſe of true

religion, for this plain and cogent reaſon; conviction on either ſide cannot follow, becauſe the nature of the ſubject matter in diſpute cannot, like a propoſition in *Euclid*, admit of demonſtration;——beſides another miſchievous conſequence reſults from the canvaſſing and laying open the opinions of the ancient philoſophers touching ſacred matters, for it puts weapons into the hands of the modern enemies of religion, which probably they would otherwiſe never have been in poſſeſſion of; and it muſt be the height of glory to infidels and free-thinkers, to find themſelves claſſed with the *Platos*, *Plutarchs*, *Ciceros*, *&c.* of antiquity.——A ſimilar mode of reputation poſſeſſed the primitive fathers of the church, which, added to an inflamed miſtaken zeal and doctrines never dictated by their divine maſter, laid the foundation of thoſe ſchiſms, and heretical evils, which have ever ſince diſtracted and divided the Chriſtian ſtates, ſo that they may with more propriety be ſtiled *the deſtroyers*, than *the fathers* of it.

8. For how long a ſpace man after his creation retained a lively ſenſe of the ſpecial grace offered to him by his Creator, or benefited himſelf by a ſtrict adherence to, and obſervance of the divine *primitive truths*, then revealed to him, are circumſtances not

determinable;

determinable; but we may with reaſon conclude, that a long ſeries of time paſſed away, before he poſſibly could, from the nature of things loſe ſight of them. All nations have by tradition a conception that there once exiſted *a golden or comparative age* of innocence; and if there ever did exiſt ſuch a period (which we think highly probable at leaſt) it ſhould appear to have been the ſpace juſt above hinted at, between man's creation, and the time when firſt he began to ſet at nought the ſaving precepts which had been graciouſly delivered to him. Although mankind differ ſo widely reſpecting the epocha of the creation of the univerſe and man, yet they are generally agreed, that they were coeval; the enlightened *Moſes* did not venture to ſay when, nor is it very material to us, ſo we believe that GOD made it for wiſe and neceſſary purpoſes, ſubſequently to be conſidered in a new point of view.

9. When we attentively peruſe *Moſes*'s detail of the *creation and fall of man*, we find it clogged with too many incomprehenſible difficulties to gain our belief, that that conſummate legiſlator ever intended it ſhould be underſtood in a literal ſenſe; and as a part of the law of *Moſes* was " typical to the *Jews* of the coming of

" their

" their Meſſiah, and calculated to prepare " them for it," (as has been proved by the Author of the Divine Legation) ſo we hope to prove that his detail of *the fall of man* was *typical only* of the angelic fall; to which, we doubt not, but *Moſes* believed (and had good grounds for that belief) that man' had a much *nearer relation* than is commonly imagined.

10. It is pretty manifeſt, that the *golden age* of innocence and truth was not a conſequent of *Moſes's ſuppoſed creation*; for, excepting a very few individuals, mankind by his own ſhewing were far gone in wickedneſs, almoſt as ſoon as created; therefore, we muſt look higher for it, which we will do in good time, for we cannot relinquiſh the fact, that there was a period of time, in which *ſuch an age* really exiſted.

11. We find that mankind throve and grew in vice until God, perceiving the meaſure of their wickedneſs was full, thought it neceſſary to bring about a ſtupendous change on the face of this habitable globe, by which we are told the whole race of animated beings, ſaving a remnant of each, were deſtroyed; and of theſe, that the human ſpecies ſcarcely emerged dripping

ping from the deluge, than they were again *drowned in ſin*; and from the earlieſt accounts which can be depended upon, free from fable, we learn that the ſuppoſed moſt ancient inhabitants in the world, to wit, the *Chaldeans*, *Egyptians*, *Hebrews*, *Phœnicians*, &c. were all profoundly ſunk in rank idolatries, and every ſpecies of wickedneſs; and we find, that the ſo much boaſted and celebrated wiſdom of *Egypt*, conſiſted only in their ſuperior art and cunning in political legiſlation; whereby they were better enabled to deceive and inſlave the unhappy people, who fell under their government: thus we ſee that all the benefit we gain by our deep and learned reſearches into the antiquities of thoſe nations, is, to be aſcertained that men were as bad in the moſt early known times as they well could be; a piece of knowledge for which we need not have travelled farther than our own ſcriptures. If the *Egyptians* muſt have the honor of being the moſt wiſe of the ancients, they have undoubtedly the honor alſo of being the moſt wicked and ſuperſtitious, not excepting the ancient poſſeſſors of the land of *Canaan*. This part of their character we will not conteſt with the learned explorers of their tenets; but we think ourſelves well warranted to diſpute, both the *ſuperiority*

of

of their wiſdom and antiquity *. Indeed the conteſt reſpecting the wiſdom of the *Egyptians*, as well as the *Perſian* Magi, and the whole tribe of the *Grecian* and *Roman* philoſophers, who copied from them (*Socrates* alone excepted) may be reduced into a very narrow compaſs; for the whole total of it, upon ſumming up the evidence produced by the advocates in its favor, amounts to FOLLY; and folly of ſo egregious a nature, that nothing leſs than the *wit of a Lucian* is equal to the expoſing it in a juſt point of ridicule.—Of what utility is that kind of wiſdom (howſoever profound) either to the poſſeſſors, or to mankind; which leads to the eſtabliſhment of laws, doctrines, and worſhip, moſt unworthy the conceptions we ought to harbor of the *Divine Nature*, and his attributes? —Such was the wiſdom of the *Egyptians*, &c. and yet theſe men acquired the venerable titles of Sages and Philoſophers, to the utter violation of the true ſpirit and meaning of the words; for every ſpecies of what is commonly called wiſdom, that does not lead us into juſt ideas of GOD, and *of ourſelves*, is folly.—It is ſaid—they were *the firſt* who cultivated the arts and ſciences: ſuppoſe it granted, were they the better men

* *Vid.* Introduction to Part ii. from page 23. to 29.

for

for it? It is proved they were not, but rather worſe, by thoſe very pens who labored to demonſtrate that prior claim.—— Indeed the hiſtory of mankind affords us this melancholy truth, that the moſt enlightened ages, in the kind of ſpurious and uſeleſs wiſdom we have been ſpeaking of, have been *the moſt wicked*, and we could wiſh the application did not reach the preſent age.

12. That the *Egyptians* were an ancient race we do not deny, and yet modern times have brought us to the knowledge of an empire of people, who, from the moſt probable concurring circumſtances, were a potent and numerous nation in the earlieſt known times, although from cauſes peculiar to themſelves, which we have before recited in our ſecond Part, *they were little known to the world.* Our readers will not be at a loſs to gueſs, that we here mean the people of *Indoſtan*, a people that exiſted *a ſeparate and unmixed nation*, without any intercommunity of manners or religious worſhip, from the period of the *firſt migrations* of the inhabitants of the earth;—— (a period, which is hid, as well from our knowledge, as our conceptions) and ſo continue to this day, notwithſtanding they groan under *Mahomedan* tyranny: a ſtrong preſumption,

presumption, almost amounting to proof, of this people being, *as a nation*, more ancient than any other.—Such *a separation* was the great aim of the inspired Legislator of the *Hebrews*, although he was never able to accomplish it: he was able to separate their bodies, but their souls still languished for the *flesh-pots* of *Egypt*, and their infamous idolatries, until captivity had softened their hearts, and made them look (when it was too late) towards their ONE GOD, and King. —The difference between the cases of the *Gentoos* and the *Hebrews* was, that whereas the former for a deviation from their *primitive truths* were enslaved at home, and the latter were driven for deviating from the law into captivity in a foreign land; as a greater punishment (we may rationally suppose) for the greater crime. For,

13. Although the *Gentoos* had offended by raising an idolatrous superstructure upon the *primitive truths* of *Bramah*, (which they had held sacred and inviolate for the space of a thousand years, as elsewhere shewn) yet, his fundamentals, *viz.* the unity of the Godhead, the Metempsychosis, and its concomitant essential doctrines, the angelic origin, and immortality of the human soul, and its present and future state of rewards and punishments, *&c.* still kept their

 ground;

ground; and remained, as they do to this day, the basis of their faith and worship.

14. The angelic fall, and the doctrine of the Metempsychosis, the one the crime, the other the punishment of those unhappy free-agents, being the *sine qua non* of the *Gentoo* system, it is incumbent upon us to prove from reason and the nature of things, that *the latter* was the original growth of *Indostan*, and not borrowed by them from the *Egyptians*, as has been more than once insinuated by that learned casuist and divine, the Author of the Divine Legation of *Moses*, and investigator of the *Eleusinian* mysteries.—When his Lordship, with great strength of argument, labors to refute the supposition that the *Egyptians* borrowed any of their superstitions from the *Hebrews*, he urges with great propriety, "the utter "improbability of a potent, and powerful "nation, borrowing any part of their re-"ligious worship from a people, who was "then in a state of slavery to them, and "held by them in the highest detestation;" or words to this effect;——now, surely it is *much more improbable to conceive*, that a *potent*, and *powerful nation* (for such *Indostan* was found to be at the first known intercourse with them) should borrow *a fundamental*, on which the whole system of their

most

moſt ancient worſhip hinged, from a few ſtraggling *Egyptians*.—If we grant that it is probable the reſt of the world adopted the doctrine of the Metempſychoſis from the *Egyptians*, after *they* had ſtolen it from the *Gentoo* Bramins, and impoſed it as their own, we grant a circumſtance which is not clearly proved;—but another circumſtance is pretty evident, and will be ſubſequently proved, that, at the time they ſtole this doctrine, they alſo purloined other fundamentals of the *Chartah Bhade Shaſtah*, namely, *the unity of the Godhead, the immortality of the ſoul, a general and particular Providence, and a future ſtate of rewards and puniſhments*.

15. As a proof of the boaſted wiſdom of of the *Egyptian* Magi, we ſhall ſee the uſe they nobly made of *the above fundamentals*:—they inſtituted *rites* to their two principal fabulous divinities *Iſis* and *Oſiris*, of which (amongſt others, truly diabolical, of their own invention) thoſe *fundamentals*, and the doctrine of the Metempſychoſis, were the chief, and *grand myſteries*; to which (as the learned inveſtigator has ſhewn) none were admitted but Kings, Princes, Lawgivers, and Heroes, and that admiſſion not granted, but under the moſt ſolemn oaths and ties of ſecrecy; for " theſe were truths of too im-

" portant

" nature to be entrusted with the people, " who, it was supposed, were better kept " in subjection by a belief in their titulary, " and local Deities."—Thus these detestable race of Governors kept the knowledge of the TRUE GOD from their people, as well as those other *important truths*, so necessary for their salvation, in which those Magi had been instructed by the Bramins.—But how are we moved to a mixture of laughter and compassion, when we are ultimately told, (by the same learned enquirer into ancient Theology) that not one of the *Egyptian* Magi, and all of the *Grecian* or *Roman* legislators, or philosophers (*Socrates* excepted) *really believed* in ONE GOD, or the immortality of the soul, or a future state of rewards and punishments, *although they all taught them in their mysteries*: and in support of the fact, his Lordship produces many evidences, as well as learned arguments. —We cannot quit this subject without saying, that we can by no means entertain that high opinion of the wisdom of the *Egyptians* in their legislative capacity, which his Lordship seems to do; for by their secreting the being of ONE GOD, and a future state of rewards and punishments (whether they themselves believed them or not), they assuredly quitted the fastest hold they had upon the obedience of rational minds, on whom *such principles, if firmly rooted*, must operate more powerfully, in ſecuring ſubjection to government, than any others, which the wit or wiſdom *of man* could poſſibly deviſe. It will probably be urged gainſt us, that theſe doctrines are ſeen to loſe their influence in ſtates where they are profeſſed, and form a part of their religious code.—If man is incorrigible we cannot help it; but we ſhould rather think, that in theſe caſes——*they are not firmly rooted.*

16. But ſuffer us, candid reader, to change the unpleaſing ſcene, and, in contraſt to *Egyptian* wiſdom, to turn our eyes towards the great Legiſlator, Prince, and High-prieſt of the *Gentoos*, who, in his ſcriptures, taught not only the *four great fundamentals*, of the unity of the Godhead, his providence, the immortality of the ſoul, and a future ſtate of rewards and puniſhments, but alſo every other divine and *primitive truth*, neceſſary for man's knowledge in his preſent ſtate of miſerable exiſtence; and theſe he taught (as elſewhere we had occaſion to remark), not *as myſteries* confined to a *ſelect few*, but as public religious tenets, known and received as ſuch *by all*;—and ſo forcible and efficacious was the influence of theſe doctrines upon the people, that they adhered ſtrictly to them, and kept them inviolate for the ſpace of one thouſand

years

years (as before remarked), and until they were perverted by their own prieſts, and led to new modes of worſhip, before unknown to themſelves and their forefathers. In theſe innovations on their original pure ſcriptures, we will not diſpute but that the Bramins might have taken ſome hints for reducing the people under ſacerdotal dominion from the infamous political ſyſtems of their brethren the *Egyptian* Magi, who, it is more than probable, did, about this period, firſt ſtraggle into Indoſtan (i. e. at the promulgation of the *Chatah Bhade*).

17. Here we cannot help obſerving, that the learned author of the *Divine Legation* laboured unwittingly under two other miſtakes, in ſuppoſing the *Hebrews* were the only nation in the ancient world who worſhipped *one God*, and in whoſe government *religion* and the *magiſtracy* were *united*; for by theſe the *Gentoos* were eminently diſtinguiſhed in the moſt early known times: but of this his Lordſhip was ignorant, and therefore ſtands not accountable. The labored apologies his Lordſhip makes for the *imperfect miſſion* of *Moſes* may require our future notice, we ſhall only remark here, the difficulty the mind has to encounter in comprehending, how any *miſſion* dictated by *God himſelf* can poſſibly be *imperfect*?

If the miſſion of *Moſes* contained a *ſpiritual*, as well as *temporal* alluſion to the ſalvation of the *Hebrews*, and the ſpiritual ſenſe was hidden from them, it was then indeed imperfect, and the *Gentoos* ſhould ſeem to have been *the choſen people of God*, in place of the *Iſraelites*; for to them was revealed by Bramah, with God's permiſſion, not only the *real ſtate and condition of man*, but his doctrines alſo taught, the exiſtence of *One Eternal God*, and *temporal* as well as *future* rewards and puniſhments. This being the caſe, although we admit, with his Lordſhip, that "the myſtery of life, and "immortality, and a future ſtate; which "had been hid for ages, and from gene-"ration to generation; was *then* made ma-"nifeſt to the ſaints" in the goſpel-diſpenſation; yet, at the ſame time, we think we have undoubted authority for ſaying, that theſe myſteries, as before ſhewn, were taught, and univerſally profeſſed ſome thouſands of years antecedent to that period, by a diſtant, diſtinct, and numerous nation, with whom indeed his Lordſhip was not acquainted; which is to be the more lamented, becauſe, with his profound abilities, unwearied application, and conſummate learning, he would have been enabled, by a knowledge of the original tenets of *Bramah*, highly to have illuſtrated his ſubject, and his perform-

performance, we conceive, would have borne a very different aspect. For

18. We cannot help again regretting, that so much learned pains has been taken to prove, that there ever existed any nation of people, who did not profess, or really believe in, a future state of rewards and punishments. Facts of this nature, which have so manifest and dangerous a tendency to influence the minds and manners of mankind, cannot be hid from *the learned*; but they might easily have been obscured to the bulk of the species, by all controversy relative to them being confined to, and carried on in the original dead languages; whereas the contrary practice of every nation in Europe for the last century, by bringing these dangerous subjects home to us, as we may say, into our native tongues, unavoidably confounds, and raises doubts in the soul, and leads it into a train of thinking, which otherwise, most probably, would never have struck the imagination.

19. Infidelity treads close upon the heels of scepticism; and notwithstanding so much has been said to justify the wise purposes of Moses, "in *studiously rejecting* the doctrine "of a *future state* in his law to the *Hebrews*;" yet the event shewed, and the

fact is confirmed by the greateſt part of their hiſtory, that they remained without any check upon their hearts or conduct. In the belief of a future ſtate they were not inſtructed, and *therefore*, they naturally doubted, and could not be brought to adhere for any time together in the belief of *One Eternal God*; nor could it be rationally thought they would, when the *one* ſo abſolutely and mutually depended on *the other*. The "wiſe proviſion" (as it is ſtiled) made by *Moſes* to ſupply the want of this doctrine of a future ſtate, to wit, the menace of "God's "viſiting the ſins and diſobedience of the "fathers upon the children, unto the third "and fourth generation," we have ſeen had none effect upon either; and he muſt be very little acquainted with the *original*, and continued depravity of the *human ſoul*, who thinks it can be reſtrained from evil by any other check than that of a confirmed belief, and expectation of *a temporal as well as a future ſtate of rewards and puniſhments*, which brings the matter home to the breaſt of every *individual*.

20. We ſhall now proceed with our Diſſertation on the Doctrine of the *Metempſychoſis, as a conſequent of the angelic fall*; and we hope in the courſe of it, to point out, and elucidate upon a rational hypo-

 theſis,

thesis, many *important truths* ; and account for, and explain some appearances in this state of human and animal existence, which are, we conceive, utterly unaccountable, and inexplicable, without the assistance of *that ancient doctrine*.

A DISSERTATION, &c.

21. THE prophets, philoſophers, moraliſts, and ſages of all ages; whether, moved by the inſpiration of GOD himſelf, or by other intelligent agents; or actuated by the mere force of their own rational powers; howſoever they may have differed in other ſpeculative points, yet agree unanimouſly in this important, and intereſting one; namely, *that the human ſoul carries the ſtamp of original depravity, and is naturally prone to evil.*--Deplorable as this ſort of humanity is, it is rendered much more ſo, by that almoſt univerſal propenſity in the ſpecies, either to a total diſſipation of their time and talents; or, employing both, in *fruitleſs ſtudies*, in place of devoting all his intellectual powers, to pry into, and examine *the real ſtate of his own exiſtence*, for which he diſcovers an unaccountable averſion, and backwardneſs.

22. It has been wiſely ſaid, that the ſummit of human wiſdom is comprifed, in this ſhort adage, MAN KNOW THY SELF; but, inſtead of dedicating all his reſearches to this eſſential purſuit, *Man knows every thing but himſelf*;——he goes on, from age to age,

age, and from day to day, in cultivating the arts and ſciences, with a view only to the better accommodation and enjoyment of his preſent ſojourn. With this unhappy deluſion, and with theſe non-eſſential acquirements, he reſts perfectly eaſy, and ſatisfied; *here he pitches his tent*, as if he was never to decamp.—Man knows not who he is, what he is, how he came by his exiſtence in this world, nor for what real purpoſes he was brought originally into it; nor does he ſeem much to concern himſelf about it, ſo long as he paſſes ſmoothly, and ſupinely, through it.

23. The doubts and difficulties which man encounters, and labors under, in forming any preciſe judgment reſpecting *the nature and obligations of his preſent exiſtence*, we conceive to have always been the great *impeding cauſes*, that have ever with-held him from deep reflection, and a proper retroſpect into himſelf; could therefore, *that nature*, and theſe *obligations*, be clearly aſcertained to him, the relative duties of his deſtination would be alſo clear and poſitive; and mankind would no longer inſeparably attach themſelves to the tranſient conſiderations, and enjoyments of this life only.

24. How far the doctrines of the Metempsychosis tend, upon a cool and unprejudiced hearing, to clear up the doubts and difficulties above alluded to, is the important subject of our enquiry. In this disquisition we shall not hesitate to assert, that the doctrine is far from being new in this our hemisphere; it was professed by our ancestors, when the sage druids led and governed their faith and politics, as the most learned records of our ancient history vouch, although it does not appear from their shewing, that it was taught by the ancient *Britons* (for the first *Britons* we know nothing of) in that simple purity, and extent, as it was originally by the *Bramins* of *Indostan*.

25. Tender consciences have no cause of alarm from our reviving the consideration of a doctrine, which in the most early known ages was followed by at least four-fifths of the inhabitants of the earth; the more especially as we hope to prove, that this doctrine is not repugnant to the doctrines of Christianity.

26. Communications between the Deity and man, either personally, or by his angels or prophets, was, in early times, no uncommon event: these recorded facts we must

must believe, or reject and set at nought our own scriptures; and shall we suppose the children of the East to have been less the care of God, than the children of *Israel?* or that the whole of his creatures, howsoever dispersed and separated from each other, were not equally the unhappy objects of his benevolence and attention?——Such a supposition would arraign his justice and impartial dispensations to all his creatures: it is not becoming us to doubt the authority and divinity of *any original religious system*, unless it *evidently* is repugnant to the idea of a just and omnipotent GOD.

27. To bring our Essay to method and perspicuity, we must again have a short retrospect to the several essential concomitant parts of the doctrine of the Metempsychosis, as promulged by *Bramah*; and we shall proceed to the discussion of *each*, reduced, as follows, under five general heads, *viz.*

FIRST GENERAL HEAD.

The existence of angelic beings.

Their rebellion, or fall.

Their

Their expulſion from the heavenly regions.

Their puniſhments.

Second General Head.

The univerſe *formed* by God, for the reſidence, ſuſtenance, and impriſonment of the apoſtate angels.

Third General Head.

Mortal organized bodies formed for their more immediate, or cloſer confinement.

Their tranſmigrations through thoſe mortal forms.

Thoſe tranſmigrations: their ſtate of purgation as well as puniſhment.

The human form their chief ſtate of trial and probation.

Fourth General Head.

Liberty given to the apoſtate angels to pervade the univerſe.

Permiſ-

Permiſſion given to the faithful angelic beings to counteract them.

Fifth General Head.

The ſeven regions of purification, wherein the fallen angels ceaſe from their mortal tranſmigrations.

The diſſolution of the univerſe, or material worlds,

28. Before we enter upon the diſcuſſion of theſe five general heads, we beg leave to be indulged in a few preparatory reflections: *firſt*, that it is obvious, from the above particulars collectively conſidered, one general concluſion may be formed as the baſis of this ancient doctrine of the Metempſychoſis, viz. *That the ſouls, or ſpirits, of every human or other organiſed mortal body, inhabiting this globe, and all the regions of the material univerſe, are preciſely the remainder of the unpurified angels, who fell from their obedience in heaven, and that ſtill ſtand out in contempt of their Creator.*

29. Strange as *this ſyſtem* may appear in theſe our days, and howſoever ſeemingly clogged with difficulties, it is worth conſideration,

deration, how far it will elucidate, and account for, many theological myſteries, and other phenomena that are annexed to this our preſent ſtate of exiſtence; and which are, we conceive, otherwiſe unaccountable, as before hinted.——If, in the courſe of our enquiry, we advance no opinions contrary to our own *pure original ſcriptures* (to which we profeſs ourſelf, an unworthy, although zealous ſubſcriber) nor endeavour to propagate any ſyſtem, but what may co-incide with *every religious Creed*, that *has been*, or *is now* profeſſed throughout the known world, we are then void of offence, both to GOD and *man.*——Endleſs have been the diſputes about religion, whilſt we ſee the chief contention is, Who ſhall the leaſt practiſe its precepts:—therefore how laudable is the purſuit of that man, who labors to point out *one univerſal faith*, that would infallibly reconcile all jarring principles, and unite all mankind in the bands of mutual love and benevolence. We write not to this, or that ſect, or to this, or that nation, but to *mankind in general*; who ſeem not to advert to, or be in any degree acquainted, either with the real dignity of their original nature, or the relation in which they ſtand, to their GOD, to their brethren, or to the reſt of the animal creation.——" Let us read, let us " meditate, let us reaſon, let us diſpute;

" but

" but all for the ſake of TRUTH, which is " the great property of mankind, conſti- " tutes all our happineſs, and therefore our " common intereſt to purſue."

FIRST GENERAL HEAD.

30. In our remarks, p. 36, of our ſecond part, we have given our conceptions of the ſublime cauſes aſſigned by *Bramah* for the creation and exiſtence of angels; nor need we dwell long on a fact, the firm belief of which has been received by all mankind, a ſingle inconſiderable ſect amongſt the *Jews* alone excepted.——There muſt undoubtedly, and conſequently have ſubſiſted, ſome *ſtriking evidence* of this great truth in the early and later times exhibited *to man*, that ſhould influence and determine him to this general belief, and the propagation of it to his poſterity; which *evidence* (for cauſes beſt known to GOD himſelf) he is now, and has been for near eighteen centuries back, deprived of. 1ſt General Head.

31. On recollection, we find we have been too haſty in our concluſion touching *this truth*;—a modern philoſopher, more remarkable and famed for genius, and the ſprightly irony of his wit, than for *ſolidity*

of argument, or ſound philoſophy, and who has all his life endeavoured to laugh religion out of countenance, has been bold enough to ridicule the exiſtence of angels, as beings purely ideal, and an invention of the poets; and alleges the ſilence of *Moſes* in proof, who, he ſays, in his law to the *Jews*, nowhere mentions their exiſtence; and urges alſo his ſilence touching *their fall*, which he inſinuates is equally fabulous as their exiſtence.

32. To ſay nothing of the inconſiſtency of this merry philoſopher's drawing his negative proofs and concluſions from a book he puts no faith in, nor allows to be of any authority, we will conſider the force of his reaſoning; for ſhould we ſubſcribe to this author's aſſertion touching the ſilence of *Moſes* in the law to the *Jews*, it by no means amounts even to a negative proof of the non-exiſtence of angelic beings, nor *of their fall* being only fabulous.

33. Whatſoever may have been the opinion of *Moſes* on *thoſe ſubjects*, it would have been more extraordinary had he made mention of them, than his ſilence can poſſibly appear to be; as it is moſt evident, that theſe were matters that lay utterly out of his way, commiſſioned, as he only ſeems

to

to be, to preach the *unity of the Godhead* to the *Jews*; a people under *the ſole* protection of the Deity, their King and Governor, a ſituation wherein the introduction of angelic beings would have been impertinent, and not in point to *the law* he was dictating to them.——After all, that *Moſes* did believe the exiſtence of angels, although he makes no mention of them *in the law*, is obvious from his 24th verſe of the 3d chapter of *Geneſis*: "So he (God) drove out "the man; and he placed *cherubims* at the "eaſt end of the garden of Eden," &c. And that *Moſes* was alſo as well acquainted with the angelic fall, we doubt not our being able to prove, in a ſubſequent part of our Diſſertation, notwithſtanding the inſinuations of our modern Democritus; who, it is no wonder, ſhould diſcountenance the notion of the exiſtence of angels, when he owns that the goſpel-diſpenſation is *founded on their fall.*

34. It is not neceſſary to recite the particular concurring teſtimony of all antiquity to the ſuppoſed exiſtence of angels, when we have ſo much greater authorities to ſupport us; the Old Teſtament, throughout the whole hiſtoric parts, and the goſpel of Chriſt, afford us ſo many ſtriking inſtances of theſe beings employed occaſionally by God, ei-

ther as active instruments against the wickedness of man, or as agents, saviors and comforters to the just and good, that we may with equal propriety, when we are about it, as well deny the existence of God himself, as of his angels.

35. A belief of ministring angels under *corporeal forms*, suffers no impeachment from their *spiritual nature*; for, as they are endued by an omnipotent God with all powers necessary for the execution of their respective commissions, it is no great marvel, if we conceive them capable of assuming every shape and form needful for those ends and purposes for which they are delegated; and, notwithstanding they are in their own nature and essence spiritual and immaterial, yet it is no great strain of faith to conclude they can occasionally assume corporeal forms, functions, and faculties, and divest themselves of them again at pleasure, as in the instances of those that sojourned with Abraham, and Lot; and thus Christ manifested himself after his resurrection.——But more of this, when we come to discuss this subject in its proper place, under our fourth general head.

36. On this fundamental doctrine of existence of angels, and their rebellion, expulsion,

ſion, and puniſhment, reſts not only the Metempſychoſis, but the whole religion of the ancient, as well as modern Bramins; the text of *Bramah* ſays, that " the ETER-" NAL ONE, in the fulneſs of time, firſt " created BIRMAH, *Biſtnoo*, and *Sieb*, then " *Moiſaſoor*, and all the *Debtah-Logue*, and " divided the *Debtah* into different bands " and ranks, and placed a leader, or chief, " over each: he gave pre-eminence to BIR-" MAH, and appointed *Moiſaſoor* chief of " the firſt angelic band, &c."—Theſe original tenets and principles are confirmed by our own ſimilar Chriſtian doctrines and belief, with the difference of names only: thus the creation and exiſtence of angels ſtand manifeſted beyond controverſy, by two of the greateſt authorities of *ancient* and *modern times*.

37. Reſpecting *the fall* of theſe beings, the text of *Bramah* further ſays, " That " envy and jealouſy taking poſſeſſion of the " hearts of *Moiſaſoor*, and *Rhaboon* (the " next in dignity to him), and of other lead-" ers of the angelic bands, they ſtood, in " contempt of the commands of their " Creator, threw off their allegiance, and " drew with them into diſobedience *a large* " *portion* of their angelic brethren." The text alſo adds, " that before the expulſion

" of the rebels from the heavenly regions, " the three prime created beings, BIRMAH, " *Bistnoo*, and *Sieb*, were sent to admonish " them, but that they continued in con- " tempt."

38. As the gospel-dispensation is allowed by our most learned divines to be *founded upon the angelic fall*, great is the degree of veneration which every *Christian* owes to the *Gentoo scriptures*, which taught minutely circumstances of that fall, more than three thousand years *a priori*.——The *gospel-dispensation*, being undoubtedly the most perfect, sublime, yet plain system of divinity and morals hitherto promulged to man (when divested of the dreams and reveries of its early and latter professors), we cannot too highly prize the great rudiments it conveys to us, of the love of GOD, repentance for sin, mutual love from man to man, and a proper faith and reverence for that *divine being*, who was delegated from the presence of his GOD to preach these great primitive truths as necessary, not only for man's happiness here, but hereafter.

39. Yet, divine and essential as these doctrines are, and necessary to our salvation, permit us to ask, How can this gospel-dispensation, which *so nearly affects man*, be

said

ſaid with any propriety to be founded upon *the angelic fall?*—unleſs there is a nearer relation between man and angel, than appears to have hitherto been imagined or adverted to by the profeſſors of Chriſtianity? —if man has not this nearer relationſhip, what has he to do with *their fall?*—or how can *that fall* ſerve as a foundation for a doctrine on which his future ſalvation depends? —This (otherwiſe) incomprehenſible difficulty is ſolved only by the doctrine of the Bramins, which teaches, that the apoſtate angelic and human ſouls are one and the ſame ſpirit; nor can we, upon any other rational principle, conceive how the goſpel-diſpenſation can be founded upon the angelic fall.

40. An ingenious, ſpeculative, and learned divine of our church, publiſhed, in the year 1762, a treatiſe, entitled, "A Pre-"exiſtent Lapſe of Human Souls *, &c." This truly valuable performance relieves us from much labor in the proſecution of our work, as it confirms, *from our own ſcriptures*, many leading and eſſential points of the Metempſychoſis, as, the exiſtence of angels, their rebellion, their expulſion from

* Printed for Whiſton and White in Fleet-Street, and for Kearſly, Ludgate-Street.—By Capel Berrow, A. M.

their bleſſed abodes, the coæval creation of the angelic and human ſpirits, and the aſſociation of the latter with the former in their apoſtacy; that their ſituation on earth is a ſtate of *degradation* and *probation* for that lapſe, and that *original ſin* is not that which is erroneouſly imputed to us from *Adam*, but ſprings from a much higher ſource, *viz.* the *pre-exiſtent* lapſe of the (human) ſpirit from its primæval purity.

41. In ſupport of this hypotheſis, the Rev. Author exhibits many clear, ſtriking, and convincing texts of ſcripture, as well as the opinions of the moſt ancient and modern philoſophers and theologians. The authorities quoted by this writer, and his ſubſequent reaſoning on his ſubject are ſo full and concluſive, that nothing can be added by us to illuſtrate it. Therefore we beg leave to refer our readers to the book itſelf, (and particularly to his laſt chapter, in refutation of the ſtrongeſt objections that can be raiſed againſt his ſyſtem), which contains every proof and confirmation from our own ſcriptures which we ſtand in need of to ſupport the *Gentoo* doctrine of our firſt general head, namely, The exiſtence of angels, their fall, their expulſion, and their puniſhments.

42. In the year 1729, an Eſſay was publiſhed, dedicated to the then Lord Mayor, bearing the title of an Oration, by one Mr. J. Ilive, under four general heads, *viz.* endeavouring to prove, 1*ſt*, The plurality of worlds. 2*dly*, That this earth is the only hell. 3*dly*, That the ſouls of men are the apoſtate angels. 4*thly*, That the fire, which will puniſh thoſe who ſhall be confined to this globe at the day of judgment, will be immaterial.——We juſt mention this *extraordinary oration* here, but we ſhall ſubſequently have occaſion to notice it farther.

43. Before we take leave of this part of our ſubject, we will remind our readers of what we advanced in our 4th paragraph, where, enumerating the ſundry *primitive truths* which had forcibly been impreſſed on the mind of man, in the beginning; one of the moſt important was, the notion of *three prime created celeſtial beings, either confounded with, or excluſive of, and ſubordinate to the Deity*; thus the Bramins have their *Birmah*, *Biſtnoo*, and *Sieb*; the *Perſians* their *Oromazes*, *Mythra*, and *Mythras*; the *Egyptians* their *Oſyris*, *Iſis*, and *Orus*; the ancient *Arabs* their *Allat*, *Al. Uzza*, and *Manah*, or the *Godeſſes*; the *Phœnicians* and *Tyrians*, their *Belus*, *Urania*, and

 Adonis;

Adonis; the *Greeks* and *Romans* their *Jupiter Olympus*, *Minerva*, and *Apollo*; the Christians their *Father*, *Son*, and *Holy Ghost*; the *Americans* their *Otkon*, *Messou*, and *Atabauta*, &c. &c. And we doubt not but a similar doctrine might be traced amongst all the different nations of the earth, had we authentic records of their primitive religious institutes; it was a principle adopted by all the ancient western world, probably introduced by the *Phœnicians*, and confirmed to them by the *Romans*. Vide *Herodotus*, *Plutarch*, *Cicero*, on the nature of the Gods; the *Abbé Banier*'s Mythology of the Ancients; *Warburton*'s Divine Legation of *Moses*; the Chevalier *Ramsay*'s Discourse on the Theology and Mythology of the *Pagans*, &c.

44. To a notion so universal in the first times, we think ourselves warranted in giving the title of a primitive truth; which must have had unerring fact, and a divine revelation for its source and foundation, as well as the other primitive truths of the rebellion, fall, and punishment of part of the angelic host, under the instigation and leading of an arch apostate of the first rank; hence the *Moisasoor* of the Bramins; the *Arimanius* of the *Persians*; the *Typhon* of the

the *Egyptians*, *Greeks*, &c. and the *Satan* of the Christians.—And that other *great truth*, the neceſſity of a mediator, or mediators, employed either in imploring the divine mercy in behalf of the delinquent angels, or in combating or counteracting the wiles and influence of the arch apoſtate, and his prime adherents;—hence the *Birmah*, &c. of the Bramins; the *Mythras* of the *Perſians*; the *Orus* of the *Egyptians*; the *Adonis* of the *Tyrians*; the *Apollo* of the *Greeks*, &c. and the *Meſſiah* of the Christians, whoſe glorious and voluntary taſk it is, to work out the reſtoration of the *golden age*, by the ſubduction of *the firſt author of evil.*

45. From hence it is manifeſt, that the notion of a golden age, ſo frequently mentioned, and minutely deſcribed by all the ancient philoſophers and poets, was purely ideal, reſpecting either any part of this material world, or any period of time ſubſequent to its creation; but obviouſly could only be alluſive to that ſtate of beatitude and harmony which reigned in the heavenly abodes until the fall of the angelic inhabitants; for, notwithſtanding the variety and confuſion of opinions touching the *origin of evil*, we may confidently ſay it never had exiſtence, until (from the gracious root of freedom) it firſt ſprang up, in the boſom

of

of the firſt *grand traitor.*—As the remembrance of this celeſtial golden age of the firſt creation of beings, muſt have been ſtrongly impreſſed on the minds of the delinquents at their fall, it was hence by a tradition eaſily conceived, handed down to later times, and loſt in the ideal conceit of a golden age in this terreſtrial globe.

46. We have already been accuſed of partiality to the doctrines of *Bramah*, but that ſhall not deter us from *aſſerting*, what before we only hinted at, namely, that that prophet and divine legiſlator firſt taught, by written precepts, the pure theology of *the unity* of the Godhead, the three prime created beings, the creation of angelic intelligents, their fall, and the reſt of the *primitive truths* that were followed by all the ancient world. From this conviction it was, that in the foregoing paragraphs, where we had occaſion to mention the theology of the ancients, we have given precedence to that of *the Bramins*; and that we are not ſingular in our opinion, we could cite many authorities, but a few ſhall ſuffice: the Chevalier *Ramſay*, who has, with great ſtrength of genius, and accuracy, labored to elucidate this ſubject, in the 88th page of his Diſcourſe on the Theology of the *Pagans*, ſpeaking of the atheiſtical tenets of *Anaximander*,

mander, ſays, "*Pythagoras*, *Anaxagoras*, "*Socrates*, *Plato*, *Ariſtotle*, and all the "great men of *Greece*, oppoſed the im- "pious doctrine, and endeavored to re- "eſtabliſh the *ancient theology of the orien-* "*tals*." Page 135 of his Diſcourſe on the *Pagan* Mythology, he has this concluſion, that, "as the doctrine of the *Perſians* is "only the ſequel of the *Indian* Bramins, "we muſt conſult the one, to put the other "in a clear light." Again, p. 39, ſpeak- ing of *Pythagoras*, he ſays, "This philoſo- "pher taught nothing to the *Greeks*, but "what he learnt from *the Gymnoſophiſts*." —To theſe we will juſt add the ſentiments of the very ingenious and learned Mr. *James Howell*, in the 11th Letter of his 2d vol. where he reports, from *Diodorus Siculus*, "That the *Egyptians* had Kings 18,000 "years ſince, yet, for the matter of Philo- "ſophy and Science, he (the *Egyptian*) "had it from the *Chaldean*, and he from "the *Gymnoſophiſts* and *Brachmans of In-* "*dia*."——Which country, as it is the next neighbor to the riſing Sun, ſo the beams of Learning (and conſequently of Religion) *did firſt enlighten her*. Thus we have ſhewn, that we are not ſingular in believing that the religion of *Bramah* is the *moſt ancient*, and conſequently *moſt pure*. For

47. It has been well remarked, that the nearer we approach to the origin of nations, the more pure we ſhall find their Theology, and the reaſon of things ſpeaks the juſtneſs of the remark; becauſe *the period* when the angelic ſpirits were doomed to take upon them mortal forms, was doubtleſs the origin of all nations; and at that time, as the nature of their tranſgreſſion and the terms of their reſtoration, were freſh upon their memories, their Theology was pure, univerſal and unerring; profeſſing *one univerſal faith*, which they had as we ſay from the mouth of GOD himſelf.—Surely there muſt have been a time, when all nations had but *one ſyſtem of Theology*, or elſe it is impoſſible to aſſign a cauſe for the uniform concurrence of all people touching the *primitive truths*, we have ſo often had occaſion to mention; but here the cauſe is found in the rational ſuppoſition of *one faith* at the origin of all nations;—and we may without deſerving the imputation of too great preſumption boldly pronounce, that *until that is again the caſe*, there will be neither pure uninterrupted joy in heaven, *nor peace on earth.*——If the notion of a *terreſtrial golden age* has any foundation, it can be only applicable to that ſeaſon, which we rather think ought to be ſtiled, the age of repentance and ſorrow, and poſſibly is the

the only ſhort period and pure piety ſince the creation of the univerſe.

48. This leads us naturally to another remark; namely, that the farther any ſyſtem of Theology *flows from its ſource*, the more its pure pellucid ſtream is vitiated, diſturbed and rendered muddy, and unintelligible. This is verified by the eccleſiaſtic hiſtory of all nations, but none with more ſtriking evidence than in that of the *ancient Bramins*, unleſs we except *our own*. —When we compare the original, auguſt, although ſimple doctrines of the unity of the Godhead, and the three ſubordinate celeſtial perſonages, *&c.* of *Bramah*, with the later doctrines of his ſucceſſors in the prieſthood, how amazingly do we behold the ſublimity and purity of them mutilated and loſt! The Text of *Bramah* ſays, "God "is one, Creator of all that is.——The "eternal One firſt made *Birmah*, then "*Biſtnoo* and *Sieb*, then *Moiſaſoor* and the "reſt of the angelic hoſt; he made his "firſt created *Birmah*, Prince of the an-"gelic bands, and his occaſional vice-"gerent, deſtined him to acts of power, "glory, and dominion; and appointed the "two next created beings *Biſtnoo* and *Sieb* "his coadjutors:" and when in proceſs of time (by the defection and rebellion of

Moiſaſoor)

Moisasoor) God in his mercy resolved to form the material universe, these three Divine Beings became the active representatives and executors of his three supreme attributes; his power to create, his power to preserve, and his power to change or destroy, as their names signify.

49. Here the people were presented with a doctrine plain, comprehensible, and suited to the capacity of every intelligent being, although imprisoned under a material form; the successors of *Bramah* did not indeed confound the three divine personages with the Godhead, but they at length did every thing else to cloud and obscure every other of his *primitive truths*, until they became as deeply plunged in idolatry, and in what we may call the useless parade of religion, as any people upon earth, and so continue to this day: thus the mission of *Bramah* was rendered fruitless, but the pure spring-head of his doctrines (that is, the first great primitive truths now under our consideration) were more sullied by the priests of other nations, who formed monstrous copies from the sublime original of *Bramah*.

50. The *Persian* Magi were the first who confounded the three prime created, subordinate celestial beings of the ancient *Bra-*

Khondoran, *Heydr Kuli Khan*, and their troops came up to quell it. The Emperor mounting his elephant and causing proclamation to be made to the army, that the *Embir al Omrah* was killed by his order, the confusion subsided; except in one quarter; where five thousand troops, commanded by *Jieratt Khan*, nephew to the deceased General, breathed nothing but revenge: between these and the royal troops a sharp conflict ensued, in which many were killed (on both sides) amongst whom was a son of *Mahommed Amîn Khan*; but *Jieratt Khan* falling by an arrow discharged by the King, (who it was said emptied three quivers in the engagement) the rest called for quarter.

The Emperor proceeding to the tent of *Seyd Hossan Ali Khan*, sat upon his elephant and saw the soldiers, by his permission, plunder it of a khorore of Rupees *. The jewels, found there to an equal amount, were appropriated to his own use.

Mahommed Shaw, sensible that but half the work was done, whilst *Seyd Abdallah Khan* survived, immediately directed his march towards *Delhy*; declaring *Mahommed Amîn Khan* Vizir, and *Khondoran*, *Embir al Omrah*.

* One Million Sterling.

Abdallah Khan was not far from *Delhy*, when an expreſs from *Jieratt Khan* overtook him, adviſing him of the tragical death of his brother: he ſaw his own danger, and inſtantly diſpatched a truſty officer with a party of horſe to that city, with orders to return immediately with *Sultan Ibrahim*, younger brother of the Emperors, *Raffeeil al Dirjaat*, and *Raffeeil al Dowlat*. The officer executed his commiſſion with great celerity; and being returned with *Sultan Ibrahim*, *Abdallah* proclaimed that young Prince Emperor of *Indoſtan*: then putting himſelf at the head of a numerous army, he marched back to meet *Mahommed Shaw*.

The two armies met the latter end of *October*, *Anno* 1720, and a bloody battle enſued. *Victory* ſtood doubtful a long time, to which ſhe ſhould give the day; but when *Abdallah* was on the verge of ſnatching a certain conqueſt, a ſeaſonable re-inforcement turned the iſſue in favour of the Emperor: for during the heat of the engagement *Diabchadr* (nephew of *Chivalram* Governor of *Eleabas)* arrived with a freſh body of troops; theſe aſſaulting the rear and flank of *Abdallah*'s army with the greateſt intrepidity, a total defeat and rout ſoon followed. *Seyd Abdallah Khan* was taken priſoner; the *Emperor* ſpared his life, in conſideration

ſideration of his owing him the crown he wore; but condemned him to perpetual imprisonment (as recited more minutely by Mr. *Fraser*) ſequeſtring his vaſt poſſeſſions and wealth to his own uſe.

Thus fell the *Seyds Hoſſan Ali Khan*, and *Abdallah Khan*, by a reverſe of fortune too common to be very remarkable. The wonder is, that they ſhould have maintained themſelves ſo long (in this deſpotic and violent government) in a degree of abſolute power and authority, hardly equalled in ſtory; and that, during the reigns of five ſucceſſive Emperors, four of whom they *themſelves* had placed upon the throne.

The laſt deciſive ſtroke put *Mahommed Shaw* into the quiet poſſeſſion of the Empire of *Indoſtan*. A long peace enſued; and the Emperor gave a looſe to the indulgence of his natural propenſities, which centered only in the exceſſive uſe of wine, women, and hunting. To every thing elſe he became regardleſs: the reins of government in time ſlackened; confuſion in the Empire followed: every *Omrah* was planning for himſelf; and none thought of the *public*. Theſe univerſal *diſorders* endangered, in conſequence, the *health* and well-being of the ſtate; and paved the way for the invaſion of the Empire by *Nadir Shaw*, in the year 1738; (ſo accurately inveſtigated by Mr. *Fraſer*) which was brought about by the intrigues of *Nîzam al Mulluck*. This miniſter, after the reduction of the *Seyds*, was ſoon taken into favour, and confirmed in the government of *Deccan*; or rather maintained himſelf there by his own ſtrength, as an independant ſovereign.

My readers will eaſily perceive, that in the foregoing recital I have followed the thread of Mr. *Fraſer*'s conciſe narrative; and have only deviated from him in thoſe parts, where my materials afforded me fuller intelligence; and in variety of tranſactions which he (obviouſly) thought lay out of the way of his *main object*: his intention being, very evidently, no more than to give a connected catalogue of the Mogulls from *Tîmur Lung*; *(Tamarlam)* and at the ſame time to convey a ſlight view of the progreſſive ſtate and condition of the Empire of *Indoſtan*, as neceſſarily preparative to the period of *Nadir Shaw*'s invaſion of it; without embarraſſing himſelf with any more of the particular circumſtances attending the ſucceſſions, than were conſiſtent with, and immediately in point to his

his deſign. All that I wiſh or hope for from *this* production is, that it may be eſteemed an illuſtration only of that ingenious and learned gentleman's work; compriſed within the ſpace, from *Auring Zebe*'s demiſe, to the reduction of the *Seyds*.

CHAP. II.

Tranſactions in the Subahdary *of* Bengal, *from the year* 1717 *to the year* 1750, *incluſive.*

OUR preſent ſubject calls us back to the reign of *Furrukhsîr*, when *Jaffîr Khan*, an *Omrah* of great conſideration and intereſt at court, ruled thoſe provinces with a rod of iron. His name, to this day, is remembered with deteſtation; to fill his coffers, he inflicted the moſt cruel puniſhments on the *Rajahs* and *Zimindars*, by ways and means unheard of, and unknown, but in this Eaſtern government. He alſo highly oppreſſed the *Europeans* ſettled in theſe parts; yet, notwithſtanding his very mal-adminiſtration, he had the addreſs to obtain the governments of *Bahar* and *Oriſſa*, united with that of *Bengal* in his perſon; which ever before had been diſtinct and ſeparate Nabobſhips.

With

and future felicity, they would fly to embrace a rational hypothesis, that leads to such a blessed issue. And here we cannot help deeply regretting the want of that *stupendous gift of tongues*, that our system might thereby be conveyed to every corner of the habitable globe. Vain regret! says the sceptic. Vain as it is, it is the vanity of doing good, which is the most pardonable of all vanities. Having thus, we hope, guarded against any imputation of wantonly deviating from our subject, we will resume the track of our enquiries.

57. It is our purpose to trace our divine Mediator through every text of the four Gospels successively, wherein he expressly declares and maintains the unity and supremacy of God, and his own subordination; and that in such terms as leaves it beyond a possibility of being misunderstood. Indeed, it appears every where, that he was most anxiously solicitous that mankind should be quite clear in a doctrine so essential; and that his apostles and disciples, who were to preach and propagate his Gospel, should not be liable to error in a matter of such importance to Heaven and earth; and this wise precaution became the more necessary, as they themselves were but just emerged

 from,

from, and ſurrounded with, infidelity and Paganiſm.

58. We will begin with St. *Matthew*, chap. xix. verſ. 17. where *Chriſt* replies to the man who aſked him the intereſting queſtion—"Good Maſter, what good thing "ſhall I do to attain eternal life?"—he ſaid unto him, "Why calleſt thou me good? "there is none good but ONE, that is "GOD." Chap. xx. verſ. 23. when the mother of *Zebedee*'s children petitioned *Chriſt* that her two ſons ſhould ſit, the one on his right hand, the other on his left, in his kingdom, he ſaid unto her, "To ſit on my "right hand, and on my left, *is not mine* "to give, but it ſhall be given to thoſe for "whom it is prepared *of my Father*." And verſe 28th of the ſame chapter, recommending humility to his diſciples, he ſaith, "Even as the Son of man came *not to be* "*miniſtered unto*, but *to miniſter*." Again, chap xxiv. verſ. 36. ſpeaking of the day of judgment, he ſays,—"But of that day and "hour knoweth no man, no not the angels "of heaven, *but the Father only*." And chap. xxvii. verſ. 46. in the extremity of his paſſion on the croſs, he cried with a loud voice, "My God! my God! why haſt "thou forſaken me?" than which, as nothing

thing could more powerfully denote the laſt influence of *his human nature*, ſo nothing could more forceably imply his abſolute and avowed dependance *on his God*.

59. We ſhall conſider next the declarations of *Chriſt*, as they ſtand recorded in his Goſpel according to St. *Mark*, chap. xii. verſ. 29. when the Scribe aſked him which was the firſt of all the commandments? *Jeſus* anſwered and ſaid, "The firſt of all the "commandments is, Hear, O *Iſrael, the* "*Lord our God is one Lord*;" and the Scribe anſwered and ſaid, verſ. 32. "Well, Ma-"ſter, thou haſt ſaid the truth, for there is "*One God*, and there is none other but "HE;" and when he ſubjoins, verſ. 33. that "the love of that *One God*, and his "neighbor, is more than all burnt-offer-"ings and ſacrifice." *Jeſus* applauds his anſwering diſcreetly, by telling him, verſ. 34. "*Thou art not far from the kingdom of* "*God*," thereby confirming him in his belief of *One God only*. Chap. xiii. verſ. 32. *Jeſus*, ſpeaking of the day of judgment, is more particular than ſtands recorded in St. *Matthew*, for here he declares, that "of "that day and hour knoweth no man, no "not the angels which are in heaven, *nei-*"*ther the Son*, but the Father." Hence it appears, by *Chriſt*'s own ſhowing, that one

 moſt

most important secret *was hid from him*, therefore not omniscient, and consequently not God, but *a distinct created being*. Indeed, howsoever conscious he appears to be of his own divine origin, yet he in no wise arrogates worship as due to himself, but directs it all to his God and Father.

60. The course of our enquiry leads us next to the Gospel according to St. *Luke*, chap. iv. vers. 43. where *Jesus* being pressed by the people not to depart from them, says unto them, "I must preach the kingdom of "God to other cities, for *therefore was I* "*sent*." Chap. x. vers. 16. *Jesus* tells his apostles, "He that despiseth you, despiseth "me, and he that despiseth me, despiseth "*him that sent me*." Vers. 21. *Christ*, after gently rebuking the seventy disciples for having expressed, with too much joy and exultation, their success in casting out devils or evil spirits in his name, breaks forth in the following pathetic strain of submissive devotion, the poetic and inspired evangelist, opening the verse with this short exordium, "In that hour *Jesus* rejoiced in "spirit, and said, *I thank thee, O Father*, "*Lord of heaven and earth*, that thou hast "hid these things from the wise and pru-"dent, and hast revealed them to babes; "even so, Father, for so it seemed good

"in

" in thy ſight." He then proceeds, verſ. 22. to declare to them his *delegated powers* from his God. " *All things are delivered to* " *me of my Father*; and no man knoweth " who the Son is, but the Father; and " who the Father is, but the Son, and he " to whom the Son will reveal him." Chap. xi. verſ. 2. when one of his diſciples beſought him to teach them to pray, he ſaid unto them, " When ye pray, ſay, Our Fa- " ther which art in heaven, hallowed be " thy name; thy kingdom come, thy will " be done, as in heaven, ſo on earth, &c." Here it is worthy remark, that in ſo very eſſential and intereſting a matter as a proper addreſs in prayer, *Chriſt* directs the followers of his Goſpel to point their ſupplications and praiſes *to God alone*. Chap. xviii. verſ. 19. records the ſame rebuke that we have already quoted from *St. Matthew*, with a ſmall variation of expreſſion—" Why " calleſt thou *me good?* none is good, *ſave* " *one*, that is, GOD." Chap. xxii. verſ. 42. when *Chriſt* had ſeparated himſelf from his diſciples on the mount of Olives, he kneeled down and prayed, " Father, if thou *be* " *willing*, remove this cup from me; ne- " vertheleſs, *not my will*, but *thine* be " done."

61. We

61. We come now to the Goſpel of our divine Mediator and Saviour, according to St. *John*, which exhibits more numerous and ſtriking declarations of *Chriſt*, in ſupport of the unity and ſupremacy of God, and his own ſubordination to his will, than all the other three put together. Chap. iv. verſ. 34. *Jeſus*, in anſwer to his diſciples, touching his eating, ſays, "My meat is to "do the will of *him* that ſent me, and to "finiſh *his work*." Chap. v. verſ. 19. *Jeſus*, in anſwer to the *Jews*, who accuſed him of breaking the Sabbath by healing the man at the pool of *Betheſda*, ſays, "Verily, "verily, I ſay unto you, the Son can do "nothing *of himſelf*, but what he ſeeth the "Father do; for what things ſoever he do-"eth, theſe things doth the Son likewiſe." Verſ. 20. "For the Father loveth the Son, "and *ſheweth him* all things that himſelf "doeth, and he will *ſhew him* greater won-"ders than thoſe, that ye may marvel." Verſ. 22. "For the Father judgeth no man, "*but hath committed* all judgment to the "Son." Verſ. 23. "That all men ſhould "honor the Son, even as they honor the "Father, for he that honoreth not the "Son, honoreth not the Father which hath "*ſent him*." Verſ. 26. to the ſame *Jews* *Jeſus* ſaith, "For as the Father hath life in "himſelf,

" himſelf, ſo *hath he given* to the Son to " have life in himſelf." Again, verſ. 30. " *I can of myſelf do nothing*: as I hear I " judge, and my judgment is juſt, becauſe " I ſeek not mine own will, but *the will* of " the Father, *who ſent me*." Chap. vii. verſ. 16. when *Chriſt* preached in the temple, the *Jews* marvelled, ſaying, " How " knoweth this man letters, having never " learnt?" *Jeſus* anſwered them, and ſaid, " My doctrine *is not mine*, but *his that ſent* " *me*." Chap. viii. verſ. 28. " Then ſaid " *Jeſus* unto them, When you have lift up " the Son of man, then ſhall ye know that " I am he, and that I do nothing *of myſelf*, " but as the Father has *taught me*:" and verſ. 42. *Jeſus* ſaid unto them, " If God " were your Father, ye would love me, " for *I proceed forth*, and *came from God*; " neither came I *of myſelf*, *but he ſent me*." Chap. x. verſ. 18. *Chriſt*, ſpeaking of the ſacrifice of his life, ſays, " No man taketh " it from me, but I lay it down of myſelf. " I have power to lay it down, and I have " power to take it up again. *This com-* " *mandment I have received of my Father*." Chap. xi. verſ. 41. *Jeſus*, after the act of reſtoring *Lazarus*, addreſſes God in theſe words, " *Father, I thank thee, that thou* " *haſt heard me*." Chap. xii. verſ. 27. *Chriſt*, after having declared to his diſciples the

the hour was come in which the *Son of man* ſhould be glorified, breaks out into this doubtful interrogation with himſelf, "Now "is my ſoul troubled, and what ſhall I ſay? "Father, *ſave me* from this hour!—but for "this cauſe, came I unto this hour." *Chriſt*, after declaring to the *Jews* he came not to judge the world, but to ſave it, ſubjoins, verſ. 49. "For I have not ſpoke of myſelf, but "the Father *which ſent me, he gave me com-"mandment* what I ſhould ſay." Verſ. 50. "And I know that his commandment is "life everlaſting; whatſoever I ſpeak there-"fore, *even as the Father ſaid unto me*, ſo I "ſpeak." Chap. xiv. verſ. 28. *Chriſt*, ſpeaking to his diſciples, "Ye have heard "how I ſaid unto you, I go away, and "come again unto you; if you loved me, "you would rejoice, becauſe I ſaid unto "you, I go to the Father, FOR MY FA-"THER IS GREATER THAN I." Chap. xvii. verſ. 3. *Chriſt*, in the moſt ſolemn invocation to the Deity, ſays, "And this is "life eternal, that they may know THEE, "THE ONLY TRUE GOD, and *Jeſus Chriſt* "whom *thou haſt ſent*." He proceeds, verſ. 5. "And now, O Father, *glorify thou "me* with thine own ſelf, with the glory "which I had with thee, *before the world "was*." Chap. xx. verſ. 17. in his ſhort diſcourſe with *Mary Magdalen*, after his

 reſur-

resurrection, *Christ* said unto her, "Touch "me not, for I am not yet ascended to my "Father; but go to *my brethren*, and say un- "to them, I ascend to *my Father, and your* "*Father, to my God, and your God.*" The divine scribe closes this chapter with these words, "But these things were written, that "ye might believe, that *Jesus* is the *Christ*, "the Son of God; and that believing ye "might have life everlasting." And God of his mercy and spiritual grace forbid, that any of us should believe otherwise.

62. We are not ignorant of the reveries of St. *Paul*, nor of the few texts in the first chapter of St. *John*'s Gospel, which seem to countenance the unintelligible and *Pagan* rhapsodies of the *Athanasian* Creed; but we think ourselves well justified in deeming them of little estimation, when contrasted with the numerous *ipse dixits* of *Christ*, recorded in all the four Gospels, and more particularly by the same Evangelist, all of which are expressly repugnant to such a doctrine; and if those texts are to be understood in the sense usually applied to them, then this Evangelist witnesseth against himself, in the many texts quoted from him in our last paragraph; and he must either stand self-condemned of recording contrary doctrines, or we must conclude his sense of

"THE

" THE WORD" has been misunderstood and misapplied; the last is the most favorable sentence that can be passed upon this inspired writer, and is worth examining below.

63. We purposely avoid a recital of the many philosophical arguments, and logical discussions, that have been urged both in the early days of Christianity, and more modern times, by a multitude of learned pens, in refutation of the doctrine of a *Trinity in Unity*, and *Unity in Trinity*, as being not suited to every common understanding; and therefore have strictly confined ourselves to the lights that every one may receive from the plain dictates of *Christ*, who powerfully and expresly enforces to his followers *the belief* of ONE GOD, *the belief* of his own mission, and divine, although inferior, origin, as proceeding from God; and *the belief* of the Holy Ghost, as the divine attribute, Spirit, or Essence of God, operating upon all things, and on *all beings*, in the proportion he is pleased to infuse or shed upon them, and *by which Christ* himself, in proof of his divine mission, wrought his stupendous miracles, always directing the objects of them, " to give the glory *to God* " *alone*" by the puissance of whose Holy Spirit he was enabled to accomplish them. These doctrines are sublime, yet plain, simple,

ple, and intelligible; they bear not the semblance of mystery, but are open to a ready faith: *Christ* neither deifies himself, nor the Holy Ghost; the making an *attribute* of the Deity a God, bears a glaring stamp of Heathenism: no rational being would say, in an absolute and literal sense, that the *fortitude*, or *chastity*, or any other virtue of a King, was the King himself, although it is, in a relative sense, a part or quality of him; nor would any man in his senses aver, that the son is the father, and the father the son, as one individual, when he knows the son must have *proceeded* from the father, and that the father must have *preceded* the son, and that therefore they cannot be ONE; the contrary belief would be a confounding of all ideas and things, as well as causes and effects, and must necessarily shock all rational faith. Therefore, when *Christ* says, "I am in the Father, and the Father in "me;—I and my Father are one," &c. he can be only understood in a relative sense, to be consistent with himself; for he ever appears particularly anxious in marking his character, as a distinct being from God, in the relation of a son to a father; and, at a most interesting period, he declares to those who were soon after to be intrusted with the propagation of his gospel, "*My Father is* "*greater than I.*"

64. There-

64. Therefore, ſince God has told us, "I am the Lord thy God, thou ſhalt have "none other gods but me," and as *Chriſt* has alſo told us, there is *only one God*, and *one Son*, which is *Chriſt*, and one *Holy Ghoſt*; let us abide by, and intrench ourſelves under this ſtrong evidence, and for the ſake of God, let us, with one accord, ſtrike out, not only the *Athanaſian* Creed, but every other part of our Liturgy, which ſo palpably gives the lie both to God and *Chriſt*. We are aware we ſhall be told that we utterly miſtake the thing, for that the ſame Creed teaches, that God the Father, God the Son, and God the Holy Ghoſt, thoſe *three Gods*, and *no three Gods*, thoſe three Subſtances under one Eſſence, thoſe three Incomprehenſibles, Co-almighties, Co-equals, and Co-eternals, are but one Incomprehenſible, &c.; and to be worſhipped as ONE GOD. If, after all, this is the caſe, to what end thoſe incomprehenſible, contradictory jumble of words and ideas, that have only ſerved for ſo many centuries to confound, perplex, and puzzle, every common as well as uncommon underſtanding, and ſtagger the faith of every well-diſpoſed Chriſtian? not adverting, that *this ſenſe* of that Creed flatly contradicts the ſolemn declaration of *Chriſt*, recited at the cloſe of our laſt paragraph; for if God the Father be (as he aſſures

ſures

ſures us) greater than God the Son, then God the Son cannot be co-equal, nor have been co-eternal with him: the Holy Ghoſt may with propriety be ſaid to have been co-eternal with God, as being the eſſence of the Deity, inſeparable from him, but not co-equal, becauſe every attribute of God is ſubordinate to, and dependent on *his will.*

65. "Glory be to the Father, and to the "Son, and to the Holy Ghoſt;" to this we ſay, Amen: but let us not, like the miſguided church of *Rome, forget God,* by tranſferring that worſhip and adoration to *Chriſt,* and the choſen veſſel of his incarnation, which are only due to *him,* and to his *Holy Spirit,* his firſt and great attribute, to which *Chriſt* eminently gives pre-eminence over himſelf, Matth. xii. 31, 32. "Wherefore "I ſay unto you, all manner of ſin and "blaſphemy ſhall be forgiven unto men; "but the blaſphemy againſt the Holy Ghoſt "ſhall not be forgiven unto men. And "whoſoever ſpeaketh a word *againſt the* "*Son of man,* it ſhall be forgiven him; but "whoſoever ſpeaketh againſt *the Holy* "*Ghoſt,* it ſhall not be forgiven him, neither in this world, nor in the world to "come." And in this place we cannot do better, than to endeavor to clear the Evangeliſt St. *John* from the charge of contradiction,

diction, by urging, with all humble deference, the conception which leads us to imagine his term or phrase " THE WORD" has been misunderstood, and consequently misapplied; and that his record, to be consistent with itself, must allude to *the Holy Ghost*: and we submit it to the candor of every Christian, who, with unprejudiced heart and attention, peruses the first chapter of St. *John*'s Gospel, whether or not every text of that chapter, which has been usually applied to *Christ*, may not be more justly applied to signify the *Holy Ghost*. And thus the Gospel of this inspired writer will stand unimpeached, which otherwise remains a witness against itself, as shewn in our 62d paragraph.

66. The other various contradictions and evil tendency of the Creed now under consideration (first established by persecution, fire, and sword), are so obvious they call for no further comment; its origin only wants to be accounted for, which is no very difficult task. SATAN, finding his kingdom on earth must fall, and come to an end, if the pure doctrines of *the gospel* obtained universally, had no means left to guard against, and prevent a catastrophe so fatal to his power, but exerting his influence to vitiate its pure stream at the fountain head: in

in order to this he most effectually attached himself and his emissaries to the primitive Christian disputants, and the reverend *saints* and *fathers* of the church, as they are called: these he well knew had not thoroughly shook off from their hearts the impressions of the *Grecian* and *Roman* mythology and *Polytheism*; on this knowledge he founded his hopes, and by the event showed he was no bad politician, for his success was answerable to the most sanguine wishes of his bad soul, and he soon had the malicious joy of beholding *three gods* start up in the Christian system, in violation of the doctrine of their divine Leader, who had so often preached to his followers there was but ONE. It is well known the advantages *Satan and Mahomet*, and his successors, took of the Polytheism introduced into the Christian faith, not only to the downfal and destruction of the seven churches of *Asia*, and the empire of the *Romans*, but also to the obstructing the universal progress of Christianity; and we may, with just boldness say, that had it not been for *that opening* given to that enterprising enemy of our faith, neither *Mahommed as a prophet*, nor *the Koran* as a religion, would ever have had existence, but the pure doctrines of *Christ* would have overshadowed the face of the earth, and its inhabitants pro-

 bably,

bably, at this day, have been of one only *universal church*, unmixed with schisms, sects, or separations, to the saving of millions of souls, and deluges of blood. The ground-work of *Mahommed*'s scriptures was the pure unity of the Godhead. (Koran, chap. iv.) "Surely God will not pardon the "giving him *an equal*; but will pardon any "other sin, *except that*, to whom he plea- "seth: and whoso giveth a *companion* unto "God, hath devised a great wickedness." Again, "Say not there are *three gods*; for- "bear *this*, it will be better for you; God "is but ONE GOD." And upon the efficacy of this divine principle we may conceive, that God permitted the so amazing and rapid, as well as extensive progress, of *Mahommed*'s Koran.

67. Another stumbling-block to the universal propagation of *Christ*'s gospel, is the supposed supernatural mode of his *conception* and *incarnation*; which supposition has afforded a handle to the enemies of Christianity, to stamp it with the imputation of priest-craft, the fact being only recorded by two of the evangelists, *Mark* and *John* being entirely silent on the subject; and *Christ* himself, in all that stands recorded of him, gives not the smallest intimation of his miraculous or supernatural conception. Here-

in

in our free-thinkers outdo *Mahommed*; for, in the xixth chapter of his Koran, he accedes to the fact, and condemns the *Jews* for their disbelief; but we imagine the objectors might, somehow or other, have arrived at the knowledge, that the miraculous conception of a virgin was a very ancient piece of *Pagan* priest-craft; it was first introduced by the adulterers of *Bramahs Shastah*, and afterwards adopted by the compilers of the *Viedam*, in the person of their *Vistnoo*; and from this origin might possibly descend to later times. Be this as it may, it is most certain, that the stupendous example, life, miracles, and doctrines of *Christ* stood in no need of a mystery of this nature to prop and give it weight and evidence; and therefore, by adding an incumbrance it did not want, rather weakened, than strengthened the whole fabric of Christianity. Had this mystery been a necessary article of faith to salvation, most assuredly *Christ* himself would have given some intimation of it to his followers: we do not find the mission of *Elijah* (who was invested by God with powers on earth near equal with *Christ*), nor any other of the inspired prophets stand impeached, because his or their *conceptions* were according to the natural course of generation, then why should that of *Christ*? So that the objectors gain nothing in the contest, supposing we should

 give

give up the argument to them: although the conception and birth of *Christ* may in one indisputable sense be truly termed miraculous! when we see such an abundant portion of the spiritual essence of God in *Christ*, was thereby subjected by his permission to the flesh, for the salvation of mankind; but we trust we shall not offend, when we say, the event would not have been less miraculous, nor efficacious, had it happened according to the usual course of nature.

68. God forbid it should be thought, from the tenor of these our disquisitions, that, with *Hobbes*, *Tindal*, *Bolingbroke*, and others, our intent is to sap the foundation, or injure the root of Christianity. Candor and benevolence avert from us so uncharitable and ill-grounded an imputation! On the contrary, our sole aim is *to restore* its purity and vigor, by having those luxuriant injurious branches and shoots lopped off and pruned, which have so obviously obstructed, stinted, and prevented its natural, universal growth and progress; and as we have assumed to ourselves the title of *the reformed church*, by judiciously and piously abjuring *some* of the impious, idolatrous extravagancies and tenets of the church of *Rome*, let us boldly, *in the cause of God and his supremacy*, *uniformly* deserve the character we have assumed.

69. From

69. From all that has hitherto been advanced (ſupported with what will occaſionally follow), three moſt important truths may be clearly gathered. Imprimis, that the FIRST and LAST revelation of God's will, that is to ſay, the *Hindoo* and the *Chriſtian* diſpenſation, are the moſt perfect that have been promulged to offending man; ſecondly, that the FIRST was to a moral certainty the original doctrines, and terms of reſtoration, delivered from God himſelf by the mouth of his firſt created BIRMAH to mankind at his firſt creation in the *form of man*; and that, after many ſucceſſive ages in ſin, and every kind of wickedneſs, GOD, in his tender mercy, reminded mankind of *their true ſtate and nature*, of their *original ſin*; and by the deſcent of BRAMAH, gave to the *Hindoos the firſt written* manifeſtation of his will, which (by the common fate of all oral traditions), had moſt probably, from various cauſes, been effaced from their minds and memories: Thirdly, that every intermediate ſyſtem of religion in the world between that of BRAMAH and CHRIST are corruptly branched from the *former*, as is to demonſtration evident, from their being founded on, and partaking of, with more or leſs purity thoſe *primitive truths*. Vide 3d and 4th paragraphs.

 70. Let

70. Let us next see how far the similitude of doctrines, preached first by *Bramah*, and afterwards by *Christ*, at the distinct period of above three thousand years, corroborate our conclusions; if they mutually support each other, it amounts to proof of the authenticity and divine origin of both. *Bramah* preached the existence of ONE ONLY, ETERNAL GOD, his first created angelic being, BIRMAH, *Bistnoo, Sieb, and Moisasoor*; the *pure* gospel-dispensation teaches ONE ONLY, ETERNAL GOD, his first begotten of the Father, CHRIST; the angelic beings, *Gabriel, Michael,* and *Satan,* all these corresponding under different names, minutely with each other, in their respective dignities, functions, and characters: *Birmah* is made prince and governor of all the angelic bands, and the occasional vicegerent of the *Eternal One*; *Christ* is invested with *all power* by the *Father*; *Birmah* is destined to works of power and glory, so is *Christ*; *Bistnoo* to acts of benevolence, so is *Gabriel*; *Sieb* to acts of terror and destruction, so is *Michael*; the Holy Ghost is expressly signified in *Brum*, the Spirit or Essence of GOD, abundantly displayed in all the operations and behests of the Eternal ONE. The Shastah of *Bramah* records the rebellion of a portion of the angelic host, and their expulsion from heaven; the fact is also incul-

cated

cated by the gospel; *Moisasoor* is represented as a prime angel, and the instigator and leader of the revolt in heaven, so is the *Satan* of the gospel; *ministering angels*, or the interposition of the heavenly beings in human affairs, is a principle of *Bramah*'s Shastah, so it is of the gospel-dispensation; the necessary duties of *repentance, good works, universal love, and charity*, are indispensably enjoined in the Shastah, so they are in the gospel institutes; but in a more forcible, elaborate, and eminent degree, as being the last and most perfect mission that God in his mercy delivered to man. The immortality of the soul, and its future state of rewards and punishments, are fundamentals of the Shastah, so they are of the gospel; that man is here in a *state* of *purgation, punishment*, and *trial*, is also a fundamental of the Shastah, so it is of the gospel, supported by the opinions of the most learned divines and philosophers. That man is doomed to *this state*, for an unhappy LAPSE in a PRE-EXISTENT ONE, is another fundamental of the Shastah, and is evidently implied in the gospel. See the Rev. Mr. Berrow's Treatise on that subject before alluded to in our 40th paragraph. The necessity of *mediators* between God and man, and voluntary sacrifices for the transgessions of the latter in the persons of *Birmah*, *Bistnoo*, and *Sieb*, and others

others of the faithful angelic host, are doctrines of the Shastah; and are all fully comprised in the gospel, by the sole voluntary sacrifice of CHRIST, our constant *Mediator*. That there is an intermediate state of *punishment* and *purification* between death and the perfect restoration of the human soul, is a positive tenet of the Shastah, and is countenanced by the gospel, notwithstanding the church of *Rome* makes so bad a use of the first, in their system of purgatory. God's *general providence* over his whole creation, is an express doctrine of the Shastah; and his *particular providence* over individuals is obviously *implied*, from its doctrine of the visible, or invisible ministration and interposition of the angelic beings in human affairs; these are also fundamental dogmas of the Christian system.

71. The comparison might be extended to a much greater length, but the above, we think, will suffice to prove, that the *mission of Christ* is the strongest confirmation of the authenticity and divine origin of the *Chartah Bhade Shastah of Bramah*; and that they *both* contain all *the great primitive truths* in their original purity that constituted *the first* and *universal religion*; and that the very ancient scriptures now under our consideration, exhibit also the strongest conviction

tion of the truth of the celeſtial origin of *Chriſt*'s miſſion. Yet the former is the ſyſtem of divinity and ethics which the Critical Reviewers have indiſcriminately (as a ſpecimen of their candor, erudition, and penetration) ſtigmatiſed with the opprobrious epithets of "*nonſenſe*, *rhapſodies*, and *abſurdities*;" and in proof of their *profound judgment*, they unfaithfully took the liberty of re-printing our ſecond part, *without* the errata prefixed to the 1ſt page, by which deſigned omiſſion, they indeed circulate nonſenſe enough *of their own making*; but, requeſting our readers pardon for beſtowing ſo many lines upon a matter ſo little worth our notice, we will purſue our ſubject.

72. In two points of doctrine the Hindoo and the Chriſtian ſyſtem differ (but the one in mode only), 1*ſt*, The puniſhment of the damned, or thoſe ſouls that ſhall remain reprobate at the diſſolution of the univerſe, or expiration of their *term of probation*. 2*dly*, The reſurrection of the ſame body. Touching the firſt, *the Shaſtah* teaches, that thoſe reprobate ſpirits ſhall be caſt out, and languiſh *for ever in intenſe darkneſs*, in a particular region prepared for them; *the Goſpel*, that they ſhall periſh everlaſtingly in *actual fire*. Without diſcuſſing the point how, or by what mode of

action fire will operate on ſpiritual beings; we will only ſay, that poſſibly the latter ſentence may act more *in terrorem*, than in the other; not that we think there is a pin to chuſe between them, nor that the matter of difference is of much importance, whilſt they both agree in the fundamental point, that thoſe unhappy delinquents will be given over to everlaſting puniſhment.

73. Touching the ſecond, which is a matter of deeper concernment to be clear in, the Hindoo ſyſtem teaches, that the corporeal part, or priſon of the ſoul or ſpirit, being compoſed of the four elements, each again receives *its part* at the diſſolution of the body, or death; and that the ſpirit, according to its *merits* or *demerits*, is either conveyed to the firſt region of purification, or puniſhed for a ſpace, and doomed to enter and animate another corporeal form, body, or priſon, that ſhall be prepared for its reception. The Chriſtian ſyſtem, without giving us any lights touching the ſtate or exiſtence of the ſoul or ſpirit, during the long intermediate ſpace between death and the day of judgment, ſays, that at that day the graves ſhall give up their dead, and that there ſhall be a *reſurrection of the ſame body*, to which its ſoul ſhall be re-united, and both receive judgment. By both theſe ſyſtems the

the doctrines of future judgment, rewards and punishments, are clearly revealed to us, but with this difference, that the Hindoo dogma pronounces, as we may say, a *daily judgment* of the soul (for multitudes are subject to death each revolving sun), as well as a final one, and the Christian postpones it to the day of resurrection, leaving the soul during the intermediate state to exist——the Lord knows where. The resurrection of the *same body* is a doctrine obviously repugnant to the Hindoo system.

74. The resurrection of *Christ*, or the re-union of his spirit to the body on the third day, is a stupendous proof of his divine mission, for he had *before declared*, "He had power to lay down his life, and "had power to take it up again; for that "commandment (or power) he had receiv-"ed from the Father." But this single instance, peculiar to *Christ*, does not, we conceive, countenance the general doctrine, as stated above, which is far from being universally believed or received; many learned pens have been drawn against it, and many texts of scripture urged in opposition, besides unsurmountable arguments and difficulties that we have to encounter, which stagger the strongest faith; such as the state and existence of the soul during the space above hinted

hinted at; the consideration that matter, of which the body is composed, being in its nature passive and inactive, cannot be the object of either rewards or punishment. But the *spirit alone*, which is the active, deserving, or offending part, can be the only object of judgment; the *non-identity* of the body (if we may be allowed the expression), which continues not the *same body* one hour together, will have its full force on every rational mind, notwithstanding the specious casuistry of a *Liebnitz* and *Locke* to invalidate the objection. How far the Metempsychosis of *Bramah* will solve these problems, and how far that doctrine will be supported by the gospel-dispensation, will appear when we come closer to that main spring of all our movements.

75. From what has been advanced in our 70th, and part of our 71st paragraph, we find that Christianity is, *bona fide*, *as old as the creation*, although in a very different sense from that of the libertine freethinker, who published, some years since, a labored treatise to undermine the gospel-dispensation, under that title: yet, let us not, although it springs from a truly learned and pious zeal, pretend *to prove*, that "the want "of universality is no objection to the Chri-"stian religion," by bringing *a chain of events*,

events, taken upon truſt, from a ſpurious eaſtern ſcripture, as applicable to the conception, birth, miracles, and death of *Chriſt*, that are utterly deſtitute of true chronology to ſupport it, leſt it ſhould give a handle to freethinkers of the complection juſt mentioned to ſay, that the Chriſtian ſyſtem is only a copy of an *eaſtern fable*, as one of the Popes of the church of *Rome* is recorded to have ſaid, or ſomething like it. That the circumſtances attending the walk of *Chriſt* on earth have been tranſmitted to the Eaſt we do not diſpute, but that they could ſtand recorded in an eaſtern ſcripture, which was compiled ſome thouſands of years before *Chriſt's* appearance in *Judea*, is not poſſible: the facts could not be before they had exiſtence. But the misfortune is, that in diſquiſitions of this nature we are generally too apt *to prove too much*, and thereby hurt the cauſe we are laboring to defend. Had the learned and revered ſupporter of Chriſtianity whom we allude to above, extended his view, and been acquainted with, the original *Chartah Bhade of Bramah*, he would have found that it is a fundamental doctrine of that ſcripture, that the angelic beings, prior to the *Kolee Joque* or age of corruption, frequently deſcended to the earth, and voluntarily ſubjected themſelves to undergo the eighty-eight tranſmigrations to animate the form of man, thereby to guard him from a ſecond ſeduction of *Moiſaſoor* or *Satan*; that even *Birmah*, *Biſtnoo*, and *Sieb*, did not exempt themſelves from thoſe voluntary ſacrifices.

76. This being premiſed, it is no violence to faith, if we believe that *Birmah* and *Chriſt* is one and the ſame individual cæleſtial being, the firſt begotten of the Father, who has moſt probably appeared at *different* periods of time, in *diſtant* parts of the earth, under *various* mortal forms of humanity, and denominations: thus we may very rationally conceive, that it was by the mouth of *Chriſt* (ſtiled *Birmah* by the eaſterns), that God delivered the *great primitive truths* to man at his creation, as infallible guides for his conduct and *reſtoration*: but the purity of *theſe truths* being effaced by time, and the induſtrious influence of *Satan*, aſſiſted by the natural unhappy bent of the human ſoul to evil, it became neceſſary that they ſhould be given on *record* to a nation that was moſt probably at that period much more extenſive than we can at preſent form any idea of; and it appears as near to demonſtration as a circumſtance of this nature can admit of, that it was owing to this *divine*

divine revelation delivered *to them*, that this people acquired ſo juſtly that early reputation for wiſdom and theology, which the whole learned world has aſcribed to them: but this by the bye.

77. The *ſame cauſes* ſubſiſting, the above *truths* ſoon loſt *again*, their original purity and ſimplicity, and a multitude of different *religious ſyſtems* were propagated through the world, having more or leſs (as intimated paragraph 3d) of *theſe truths* for a baſis, according to the bent and genius of men, and talents of the firſt impoſtors that broached them, excited and furthered poſſibly, alſo, by the adventitious circumſtances of air, ſoil, climate, ſituation, regimen, &c. By this deviation, wickedneſs continued to gather increaſe through every region of the earth, but ſtill the mercy and forbearance of God was not exhauſted; for in the fulneſs of time, *as his laſt grace*, he *once more* delegated his firſt begotten ſon, under the mortal form of Jesus, to *reſtore theſe truths* to their full primitive luſtre, and pitched upon *Judea* as a proper center from whence the beams of the *Sun of righteouſneſs* ſhould be ſcattered, and ſpread over the face of the whole world. How the univerſality of this intended ſtupendous bleſſing was prevented, we have already ſhewn in

part,

part, and ſhall more fully hereafter; obſerving that the genuine ſcriptures of *Bramah* and *Chriſt* have ſhared the ſame fate, mutilated and betrayed by thoſe who were appointed the guardians and ſupporters of them. We ſhall cloſe this paragraph with a ſuggeſtion that appears to us moſt probable and rational, *viz.* that *every individual* of the angelic beings who have occaſionally viſited the earth, under the mortal form of humanity, either by ſpecial voluntary licence, or ſpecial appointment of God, for the example, defence, admonition, comfort, and correction of mankind, have *each* aſſumed different forms and names, at different ſucceeding times, in different regions; in ſuch wiſe as *Elijah* and St. *John* the Baptiſt is ſuppoſed by ſome to have been one and the ſame ſpirit, from the intimation of the prophet *Malachi*. (Vide part the ſecond, pages 71 and 72.)

78. In our laſt paragraph we promiſed to ſhew more fully how the bleſſings of the goſpel were converted into a curſe, as the prophetic ſpirit of *Chriſt* foretold it would be, from his obſervation of the general corruption and incorrigibility of the human ſoul; for otherwiſe it would not have been poſſible that his plain dictates could have been miſtaken, or perverted to any other purpoſes

poſes than he benevolently deſigned them: but he had hardly left his followers to themſelves, than religious diſſentions took place, that blaſted all his hopes, and rendered his miſſion of none effect; ſo that, within the ſpace of a very few centuries, and almoſt as ſoon as they had aſſumed to themſelves the general name of Chriſtians, he ſaw, with heart-felt grief, his plain, ſimple, and divine doctrine ſplit into more jarring ſects and ſchiſms than any religious ſyſtem had ſuffered ſince the creation.

79. *Chriſt* had preached, as eſſential preliminaries to the ſalvation of his followers *in a future life*, peace, charity, and mutual love *in this*. But the differing ſects of Chriſtians thought it more available to whirl damnation at each other's head; and in place of thoſe godlike virtues, to ſubſtitute hatred, revenge, and perſecution; ſome conſtrued particular texts of ſcripture literally, others allegorically, others ſymbolically; and ſome broached, as Chriſtian doctrines, diabolical ſyſtems, which raſhly ſavored of that Paganiſm from which they had been ſo lately reclaimed and converted; and each thought themſelves warranted *by thoſe very ſcriptures of peace*, to cut the throat, for God's ſake, of every one who did not ſubſcribe to their opinions: witneſs the

ever memorable and bloody contests between the early bishops of the church, about the establishment of the *Athanasian* Creed, and the contention for supremacy between the *Greek* and *Latin* churches, which came to a drawn battle at last; as also in later times, the unchristian and inhuman disputes between the Romanists and Protestants, each exerting their infernal spirit of persecution, as power afforded them the means; a contest in which deluges of blood have been spilt, and are spilling to this hour, insomuch that we may justly aver, lamentable as the truth is, that there exists not upon the face of the Christian world, more than ONE SECT of mankind, who preserve *any appearance* of having a true claim to the title of Christians. Here our readers cannot be at a loss to know, that we mean that respectable body of people, commonly, although ludicrously, stiled QUAKERS, a people that in their principles and practice do honour to primitive Christianity and humanity. But, to resume the thread of our subject, and analize in few words (as necessary to our main view) the causes, nature, and progress of the last-mentioned contest between Christians (nominally so) originally of the same church, although an idolatrous and superstitious one:

80. After

80. After the separation of the *Greek* and *Latin* churches, the last supported her supremacy in the West for some ages; at length avarice and tyrannic exactions (and partial favor shewn to one set of monks in the collection of those exactions), in the Pope; spiritual pride, resentment, revenge, and an affectation of singularity in the breasts of *Luther* and *Calvin*; and lust and wrath against the Pope in the heart of our Harry VIII. brought about *a partial Reformation of the Christian church.* Thus God sometimes works out his purposes *of good*, by most *evil* tools. This desertion gave a "perilous gash to the body of the church "of *Rome*, and many a profitable limb was "lopt off," and lost, never to be recovered. But *Luther* and *Calvin*, not according to the principles and modes of Reformation, became the leaders of two opposite religious Protestant factions, with about an equal number of proselytes, who soon began to harbor as mutual and cordial a hatred, and unchristian-like animosity against each other, as they both bore to their mother church of *Rome*: then *bishops* and *no bishops* proved the source of fresh, bloody, and cruel contests. Spiritual pride, joined to temporal political maxims, have kept alive an unceasing rancour in the hearts of those two Protestant sects, that must ever keep

them aſunder, although nothing is eaſier to be effected than a union, were it poſſible *to bring them back to Chriſtianity*, from which they have *both* ſwerved in principle and practice; whilſt *Rome* is not without her hopes from theſe diviſions, and waits a favorable conjuncture to re-unite them to the boſom of her church, either by force, or fraud, or both; an alarming event! which poſſibly may not be ſo far diſtant as ſome fondly imagine. But the feuds and differences between the *Lutherans* and *Calviniſts* hurt the cauſe of *Chriſt* ſtill more deeply; for many of each perſuaſion, obſerving the eaſy ſucceſs of thoſe leaders, and how glorious and profitable it was to become the head, the *primum mobile* of a ſect, deſerted again their colours, and ſetting up for themſelves, formed innumerable *ſubdiviſions of faith*, under various *independent denominations*; and each leader had his followers. Thus old hereſies were revived, and new ones inſtituted, and fanaticiſm of every abſurd and extravagant ſpecies had a quick and dangerous growth; each ſect audaciouſly affirming, from the ſame ſcriptures, that theirs, and theirs only, was the true orthodox faith, and the right road to ſalvation: yet, with ſuch doctrines, they brought the head of a good, moral, and pious, but

miſguided

misguided Prince, to the block, and overturned the constitution of a kingdom.

81. Such is the whole present state of *Christ*'s church *militant* here on this western earth; and the above, added to some *before noted*, are the reproachful fatal causes that have obstructed and utterly choked the universal growth and progress of the gospel; and hence we are urged, by a spirit of true benevolence to mankind, to promulge the following reflections:

82. During our non-age, we naturally receive and adopt the notions and principles instilled by our parents and teachers; but when man arrives at maturity, he will as naturally assert his great privilege of reason, and think for himself. But what must be the confusion and perplexity of his reflections and ideas, when he begins the necessary inquiry after TRUTH, in so essential a matter as the worship of his GOD? when he finds, we say (in what is vainly and fallaciously called a Christian country), every Christian church divided against itself, and the professors of Christianity pursuing each other with concealed or open execrations, malice, and all uncharitableness, that misguided zeal, temporal interested views, or enthusiastic rage can possibly dictate. Thus

 circum-

circumſtanced, *a thinking being* has no reſource, but *either* totally to abjure Chriſtianity, *or* to endeavour to work out his own ſalvation, according to the lights which *pure ſcripture*, and his own unbiaſed *reaſon* affords him, without adhering to any one Chriſtian church or ſyſtem whatſoever as now profeſſed in any part of the world, as they have *one and all* proved defective, and inefficacious to cement the bands of mutual love, charity, forbearance, and peace amongſt men; which relative duties are the quinteſſence, the *ſine qua non* of the goſpel-diſpenſation. But——as the *different* interpretations of the ſame ſcriptures have been the great, the miſchievous cauſe of the numerous jarring ſects of Chriſtians (the leaders of each drawing a miſſive weapon from the ſame text); and as the fatal effects of theſe ſects and ſchiſms in Chriſtianity have been truly diabolical in every inch of *Europe* (inſomuch that a ſtander-by might be well excuſed if he was induced to think the Devil himſelf had been the author of it, in place of God), we muſt go farther, and utterly reject all that has been written by the apoſtles and diſciples, and every paraphraſe, expoſition, and viſionary doctrine that has been tortured from them, *except* the expreſs *declarations* and *doctrines* which fell from the mouth of *Chriſt himſelf*, as they ſtand recorded

recorded in the four Goſpels: by theſe let us abide, be theſe the *ſtandard of our faith*, and ſheet anchor of *our hope*, and theſe *only*. His language is plain, his words cannot be *miſ-interpreted*, nor perverted to different meanings; he ſpeaks to the level of every underſtanding, as well as to the heart, and cannot be miſunderſtood. To this it may be objected by freethinkers, that herein we are ſtill at no certainty that theſe goſpels were penned after *Chriſt*'s aſcenſion; that poſſibly thoſe his declarations and doctrines may not have been faithfully recorded; that we ſtill take them upon truſt, &c. To this we anſwer, and lay our appeal to the *doctrines themſelves*; then let every one who doubts knock at his breaſt, and ſay, if he can, from the *conviction* of his own heart, that ſuch doctrines, conſidered as a ſyſtem of theology and ethics, are not of divine origin. Let this be the text, and ſceptics will no longer have exiſtence.

83. *Oh Man! Oh Chriſtian!* Emperors, Kings, Princes, Potentates, and Powers; Rulers, and Leaders, under whatſoever denomination of Chriſtians you have continued to diſgrace thoſe *originally reſpectable names*, whether Papiſt or Proteſtant, Lutheran or Calviniſt, &c. &c. no longer ſuffer to be *ſeverally* applied to you that pre-

diction which *Christ* applied to the *hardened Jews*, respecting his persecuted apostles, "Yea, the time cometh, that whosoever "*killeth you*, will think he doeth God ser- "vice;"——no longer, we say, adopt such an impious doctrine and supposition (for herein you are worse than the *Jews*, for you *pretend* to believe in *Christ* and his doctrines, which they did not) but mutually labor to re-establish peace on earth, and harmony in heaven, by restoring *once more* the true spirit of those *primitive truths*, which were, as the *first* and *last* grace of GOD, delivered to you at your creation originally by BIRMAH, and subsequently by CHRIST, *the one and the same individual, first begotten of the Father*, as before suggested. Our candid reader will now see the necessity we were under of analising the *modern Christian tenets and practice*, and of exposing the fatal innovations that brought it first into disrepute, and that still continue to obstruct its universality: we are sensible that we hereby lay ourselves open to the censure of superficial thinkers, who will be ready enough, although unjustly, to accuse us of *Deism*, according to the common acceptation of the phrase; but as we think we have as indisputable a right as Dr. *Clarke* or others, to extend or give *a new* signification to the word *Deist*, so we pronounce,

that

that a man may, with ſtrict propriety, be *an orthodox Chriſtian Deiſt*; that is, that he may, *conſiſtently*, have a firm faith in *the unity of the Godhead, and in the pure and original doctrines of Chriſt*. In this ſenſe alone we glory in avowing ourſelf—A CHRISTIAN DEIST.

84. Having thus ſubmitted to our intelligent readers all that we thought neceſſary to the elucidation of our Firſt General Head, to wit, the exiſtence, the rebellion, the expulſion and puniſhment of the apoſtate angels, according to the minute hiſtory of that great and fatal event, given in the *Chartah Bhade of Bramah*, from which all antiquity borrowed their conceptions of this eſſential piece of knowledge, and which alſo ſtands confirmed by the goſpel-diſpenſation; and having likewiſe, occaſionally, as we purpoſed, drawn ſome (we hope) uſeful and moſt neceſſary concluſions and doctrines, from the compariſon between thoſe two divine ſcriptures, the courſe of our purſuit leads us to the inveſtigation of our Second General Head, "*The creation of* "*the univerſe*, for the reception and reſi-" dence of the expelled angels, after their " emerging from the *Onderah*, or place of " *intenſe darkneſs*, into which they had been

" precipitated, upon their expulſion from " heaven."

Second General Head.

Second General Head. 85. The eternity, or non-eternity of *matter* (a queſtion which exerciſed the brains of *Plato*, *Ariſtotle*, *Epicurus*, and others of the ancients and moderns to little purpoſe), is a ſubject, the diſcuſſion of which would be foreign to our deſign; but the eternity of the *world*, which ſome philoſophers have held as a principle deduced from the poſition of the eternity of matter, is ſurely one of the greateſt, of the moſt daring, and inconſiſtent extravagancies of the ancients; a concluſion, that is neither ſupported by ſound philoſophy, reaſon, or probability. Nor is it leſs extravagant in man, to ſuppoſe, that this world, and all that is in it, was made for him; that is, if we conſider him in the light in which he ſeems (by the whole tenor of his actions) to view himſelf, the muſhroom of a day. And indeed it ſhould alſo ſeem, that man, from his blind and thoughtleſs eſtimation of the world, was likewiſe perfectly convinced, that he himſelf *was made only for it*. With this grovelling conception of his nature and origin,

origin, it is no wonder that his purſuits ſhould be adequate, and diſgrace his intellectual faculties. Man is a free agent, and *may ſay* whatſoever he pleaſes to amuſe himſelf; he may plume himſelf in aſſerting the immortality of his ſoul, his ſuperior form, and intellectual powers, in compariſon with the reſt of the animal creation: he *may alſo ſay*, that he looks up to a life beyond this, a future life of rewards and puniſhments;—but we maintain againſt him, that he neither *believes* the one or the other; facts ſtare him in the face and refute him, his daily practice contradict his words, and prove his attachments and views are ſolely limited to, and circumſcribed by the ſolicitudes and ſenſual indulgences of *this world*, which, with all its annexed appurtenances, he arrogantly and preſumptuouſly conceits was made for his uſe and—abuſe. Strange and irrational conceit, for a being thus circumſtanced!

86. In combating and diſavowing the poſſibility of man's firm faith in the *primitive truths* juſt above ſpecified; we think we pay the higheſt, the moſt favorable compliment and conſtruction to his underſtanding and conduct, that is in our power; for if he really and truly *believes*, and ſeriouſly thinks himſelf entitled to hold that ſuperior

rank

rank in the ſcale of terreſtrial beings, by virtue of his ſuperior intellectual powers and faculties, and ſtill degrades and debaſes himſelf, by the perverſion of thoſe bleſſings, below the level of the brute; ſo much the more deplorable is his ſtate: nonbelief affords ſome plea, as faith is not always within the compaſs of our reach; but to ſay we *truely believe*, and ſtill perſiſt in evil, leaves us without excuſe : therefore we repeat, that our judgment is more favorable to man, when we pronounce, *He does not believe*, than to ſay *he does*; and the only apology that can be framed for him, either in the one caſe, or the other, is *the ignorance* he ſtands in of *his real ſtate on earth*, and the nature of his relative obligations *as man*, which we now purpoſe to *elucidate*, for his preſent benefit, and his future felicity. In the proſecution of this our benevolent purſuit, we again invoke the aſſiſtance of that Being, WHO CAN ALONE ENLIGHTEN US.

87. We have ſhewn, that man cannot rationally or conſiſtently flatter himſelf, that this world was made for him only, upon the footing of his *commonly ſuppoſed* exiſtence. In truth, did not a vain pride and partiality obſcure his reaſon and his optics, he would perceive, that the world was made for the fly, as much as for him; the former

mer possessing every sensual enjoyment suited to his rank in the scale of beings, in as full perfection as mere man can boast of: but——if he extends his prospect, looks higher, and conceives of himself, as he truly is (according to the scriptures of *Bramah*) one of those very identical cœlestial spirits that were banished heaven, he may then erect his head, and without offence either to modesty or probability, think the world, and every comfortable production of it, *was made for him*, as most assuredly it was. Here we discover a most noble cause, worthy of THE ETERNAL ONE, for so stupendous a creation, as that of the universal planetary system: the angels had sinned, they were degraded, they were fallen; but —still they were angels, and immortal! and had borne a glorious rank in heaven! and it affords the highest illustration of God's mercy, that when he was moved to mitigate their punishment, and give them an opportunity of regaining their lost seats in a *state of probation*; that he, with such infinite powers and wisdom should construct so wonderful an edifice as this world for their reception and residence, befitting a race of cœlestials, although in a state of degradation; for such undoubtedly was the face of the commonly called antediluvian

earth,

earth, when a ſecond defection made THE ETERNAL ONE juſtly determine it was too good for them; and was provoked to leave it at the deluge, or ſome other equally tremendous ſhock, as we now find it.

88. How the angelic beings, deſtined to inhabit the other regions or planets of the extended univerſe, continued to deſerve this exalted grace of their Creator, or what changes they may have juſtly undergone, GOD only knows; but reſpecting this our globe, *bad as it is*, we may (without any breach of Chriſtian charity) aver, it is ſtill *abundantly better* than we merit; and ſhould it grow worſe and worſe, and leſs comfortable, (which appears to have been the caſe for ſome centuries back in every region of the earth, by remarkable variations of ſeaſons, frequency of earthquakes, ſtorms, inundations, &c. &c.) ſtill the juſtice of God ſtands unimpeached, by the increaſe of ſin, and continuance of reprobation. After all, in this world of natural evils, *rational man*, if he looked up to his divine Origin, and moved conſiſtently thereto, might ſpin out, in a very comfortable exiſtence, *his deſtined term of probation*, and ſecure to himſelf felicity here and hereafter; ſo that in truth it is no bad world, but as we

we ourſelves make it ſo; and blind, infatuated Man, as if he thought the *natural evils* of this world were not ſufficient, ſeems reſolved to exert thoſe intellectual powers that were given him for very different purpoſes, to make up the deficiency by the addition of *moral ones*; thereby exceeding the meaſure of his puniſhments to a degree that God never intended he ſhould ſuffer. But to illuſtrate farther the tenor of our four laſt paragraphs by way of expoſition on the text of *Bramah*.

89. Learned philoſophers and divines have been deeply puzzled and perplexed, how to reconcile the juſtice of God with the creation of a rational being *out of nothing*, or from matter, yet ſubject to natural and moral evils; and apparently, from every conſideration of his exiſtence (from the cradle to the grave viewed under the moſt favorable aſpect), placed here in a ſtate of ſucceſſive puniſhments which he cannot poſſibly *as mere man* have deſerved, by any adequate tranſgreſſion committed during his preſent ſtate of exiſtence; for his puniſhments commence with his birth, and purſue him through infancy, periods during which neither his corporeal or mental powers can be ſuppoſed capable of tranſgreſſion

or ſin. Thus the juſtice of God muſt ever ſtand arraigned, if the poſition *reſts there*; but—the very conſideration *that God is and muſt be juſt*, tells us that cannot be the fact; and that therefore there muſt have been a prior, ſome anterior cauſe, for ſuch (otherwiſe unmerited) puniſhments. But when? where? The anſwer is obvious and indiſputable——in ſome antecedent ſtate of the ſoul's exiſtence; this truth, natural reaſon and the laws of common juſtice convince us of, without the aſſiſtance of the many texts of ſcripture advanced by the ingenious Mr. *Berrow* to prove the *pre-exiſtent lapſe of the human ſoul*: to which we may add an argument drawn from the immortality of the ſoul; for if the ſoul is immortal, and neceſſarily exiſts in a ſeparate ſtate after the diſſolution of the body, it muſt have neceſſarily exiſted *ſomewhere* before its union to it, unleſs we ſuppoſe God is employed in a daily, we may ſay hourly, creation of ſouls; an opinion not leſs extravagant than the ſuppoſed eternity of the world, an opinion that would ſtill leave the juſtice of God in the ſame predicament liable to impeachment.

90. Although a pre-exiſtent ſtate, and lapſe of the human ſoul, are doctrines that have

have been avowed by all antiquity, and by many learned moderns, (see the authorities produced by the Reverend Mr. *Berrow*), yet a difficulty remained of what nature that state and lapse was? This embarrassment can only be accounted for by mankind having, in process of time, utterly lost the remembrance of those *primitive truths*, which clearly laid open to him *his real state and nature*, both in his present and pre-existent state. Some have endeavored to solve the difficulty, by supposing that man was created *to fill up the vacant seats* in heaven, and that his lapse or crime was, *his wickedly associating with the apostate angels*, in place of aiming at the possession of their seats: but this round-about supposition leaves the difficulty just where it found it, and gives an opening still to arraign the justice of God. But Mr. *George Ilive* came most certainly nearer the mark (howsoever he came to hit it), in pronouncing "that the souls or spirits of men are the identical apostate angels themselves," without knowing that he was supported in such a conclusion by the most ancient divine scripture that had been delivered to the inhabitants of this globe: here then we are to look up for the pre-existent state and lapse of the human soul, *the original sin* in the *angelic fall*, typified by *Moses* in his history of the *fall of man*;

and hence is every one " born in ſin, the " children of wrath," and hence only is the juſtice of God reconcilable with his creation of man at all; a creation, which by this hypotheſis highly exalts and illuſtrates, not only his JUSTICE, but his MERCY.

91. And here, candid reader, ſuffer us, from the feelings of a general philanthropy that warms our boſom, to congratulate our fellow-creatures upon the reſtoration and recovery of this great, this eſſential, this divine truth, ſo long loſt to our remembrance. A *primitive truth*, which enlightens mankind with the knowledge of their *real ſtate*, the true relation in which they ſtand towards their God and Creator, and the relative duties which they owe to the ſpecies in general, from all which they have deeply and dangerouſly ſwerved for a ſeries of ages paſt, from ignorance of their *original dignity*, *original ſin*, and the nature and terms of their earthly ſojourn: to that ignorance alone (and to the ready bent of the human ſoul to evil in conſequence of it) muſt be aſcribed the ſmall efficacy which the preaching and doctrines of *Chriſt* has had upon the world; the ſeed was good, but ſown in unprofitable ground, and although it was not poſſible to inculcate the neceſſary doctrines of *the love of God*, and

of

of our neighbor *as ourselves*, in stronger terms than *Christ* enforced those duties; yet men still persevere in plundering, oppressing, persecuting, and butchering one another without mercy, in open violation of all that is good or holy. The truth is, *man knew not himself*, nor the relation he stood in to his God and neighbor, although, had he diligently searched the scriptures, he would therein have found full satisfaction in both, either expressly, or by plain and direct implication. *David* seems to have been very clear in his conceptions touching his own pre-existent state, as well as that of his *Israelites*, when he pathetically addresses his God in these words of his xcth psalm, "Lord, thou hast been *our* refuge, "from one generation to another, *before* "*the mountains were brought forth, or even* "*the earth and the world were made.*" Now, as all mankind are unanimous in opinion, that there was no creation of beings prior to the creation of the *earth and world* (or the universe) but that of the angels, so it is plain he could allude to no other; the inference is obvious—*David* and the *Israelites* were the apostate angels. And in truth that most remarkable, and seemingly incomprehensible favor and partiality which God in a long series of events manifestly shewed to that race of people, can be only accounted for, by their having been one of *the least* offending of the angelic tribes, drawn off from their allegiance, not by the pride and malice of the heart, but probably from the influence and impulses of a divine love and friendship for some of the other revolted tribes: thus the supposed *partial favor* of God *to that people* no longer remains a charge against our eternal IMPARTIAL JUDGE, nor that he should not have, from the same cause, his *chosen* and *elect* of other nations. And here we cannot help entering into a short expostulation with mankind upon their universal evil treatment of that once favorite people of God, the *Jewish* race, who are the common butt of oppression in all nations; we brand them with the epithets of *fraudulent* and *infamous*, whilst the cruel hardships every state imposes on them, lays them under a fatal necessity of perpetrating vices for their own defence and security, and to retaliate in some measure the injustice they everywhere labor under.——Religion and humanity would think and say, it is enough that they are outcasts, and scattered over the face of the earth, without rule or domain; let us not therefore burden them with greater grievances than they can, or than God intended they should, bear:——had those who professed themselves Christians, been truly ſo, it is more than probable there would not at this day be one *Jew* exiſting in the world. But what encouragement can any of that tribe have to forſake his errors, or enter into the fold of Chriſtianity, when they ſee themſelves from age to age oppreſſed, hunted, and their ſubſtance devoured by the *Chriſtian wolves* of every ſtate, in direct violation of the goſpel they profeſs.——Although God has been pleaſed to diſperſe them, we are told *on good authority* he has not abandoned them; and we know not how far the evil treatment of that people may have been, and ſtill is, one (amongſt many others) of the great cauſes of the calamitous ſigns of God's diſpleaſure, in his ſignal viſitations for a long ſeries paſt to every Chriſtian ſtate under one tremendous form or other; for we think, reſpecting the evil uſage of that forlorn unhappy race, no ſtate in Chriſtendom is exempt.

92. Having thus, we truſt, ſucceſsfully ſhewn to the higheſt moral certainty, that the univerſe was conſtructed by God for the reception, reſidence, and ſuſtenance of the apoſtate angelic tribes; and that mankind are the very identical remains of thoſe unpurified ſpirits, who have not as yet regained their loſt ſeats, we haſten to the con-

 cluſion

clusion of this our Second General Head, requesting only that our candid reader will accompany us in the contemplation of that sublime picture of the human species, as drawn by our great master of reason and nature, *Shakespeare*, from the mouth of his *Hamlet*——"What a work "is man! how noble in nature! how infi-"nite in faculty! in form and moving how "expressive and admirable! in act like an "angel! in comprehension like a god!" ——Now say, reader, can such a being be aught less than angel? Surely no.——Angel he must be, and an apostate one, or we pronounce he is——nothing. Indeed there are many movements and emotions of the human soul, that are utterly inexplicable but upon this hypothesis, as, sudden and instantaneous violent love, friendship, antipathy, dislike, hatred, &c. *at first sight*; which can only spring from a sympathetic sensation of the spirit's prior knowledge or intimacy in their angelic pre-existent state. *One* of the great comforts of a departing soul in death, and of those that survive, who are mutually dear to each other, is the hope, that their spirits will soon be re-united, in a future state of lasting bliss, which here is only imperfect and transitory: but such hope is obviously ill-founded, unless built upon this hypothesis. We hope and pray

for

for *a reſtoration* (Reſtore us, O Lord, that are penitent)——What reſtoration? What can we be reſtored to, *as man?* what as *mere man* have we loſt?——Nothing; but as apoſtate angels, we have loſt much indeed, and may with propriety both hope and pray for a reſtoration, otherwiſe we pray and hope for——we know not what. We are told, "that there is more joy in "heaven for one ſinner that repenteth, "than for ninety-nine that are juſt;"——what relative concern can the angelic beings have for *man, merely as ſuch*, that his repentance ſhould occaſion ſuch an extraordinary effect? None ſurely that with propriety can be conceived; but—when we look up to our hypotheſis, and view *the ſinner* in the light of *one of their brethren* reſtored, whom they had reaſon to fear was eternally loſt to them, then the exceſs of joy is natural, and ſtands well accounted for.——Reſpecting the various ſpecious arguments that have been ſtarted againſt the pre-exiſtent ſtate and lapſe of the human ſoul, particularly that of the ſoul's *not being conſcious* of ſuch a ſtate, we again refer our readers to the labors of the reverend and ingenious Mr. *Berrow*, who has fully refuted *that*, and every other objection that can be raiſed to that doctrine; to which we will juſt add,

add, that the ſoul of every thinking being would be ſoon conſcious of that great and eſſential truth, if man would be brought to reflection, and *ſink deeper into himſelf.*

Third General Head.

Third General Head. 93. We are now arrived at our Third General Head, the *Metempſychoſis of Bramah*, from which we have been kept back by ſundry, yet neceſſary digreſſions, and diſcuſſions of many intereſting objects and points of doctrine, which ſtarted up upon us in our way, and retarded our ſpeedier paſſage; although hereby we may appear to ſome deſerving the cenſure of prolixity, yet we truſt it will be acknowledged in the end, that without them our aim and endeavors would not have been attended with *that general utility* which we flatter ourſelves they now aſſuredly will.——Before we ſubmit our own ſentiments to the world on a doctrine ſo little attended to in modern times in this our hemiſphere, it becomes neceſſary (to ſave our readers the trouble of turning back to our ſecond part, p. 49, &c.) that we recite the texts of *Bramah*, who firſt, by divine authority, promulged that ancient ſy-

ſtem

ſtem.——" And THE ETERNAL ONE "ſpake again unto *Biſtnoo*, and ſaid, I will "form mortal bodies for each of the delin-"quent *debtah* (or angels), which ſhall for "a ſpace be their priſon and habitation, in "the confines of which they ſhall be ſubject "to natural evils, in proportion to the de-"gree of their original guilt.——The bo-"dies which I ſhall prepare for the recep-"tion of the rebellious *debtah*, ſhall be "ſubject to change, decay, death, and re-"newal, from the principles wherewith I "ſhall form them; and through theſe mor-"tal bodies ſhall the delinquent *debtah* un-"dergo alternately eighty-ſeven tranſmi-"grations, ſubject more or leſs to the con-"ſequences of *natural* and *moral* evils, in a "juſt proportion to the degree of original "guilt, and as their actions through thoſe "ſucceſſive forms ſhall correſpond with the "limited powers which I ſhall annex to "each;—and this ſhall be their ſtate of "*puniſhment and purgation*.—And it ſhall "be—that (after paſſing the eighty-eight "tranſmigrations) the delinquent *deb-"tah*, from my more abundant favor, "ſhall animate the form of mhurd (man) "——and *in this form*, I will *enlarge their "intellectual powers*, even as when *I firſt "made them free*;—and this ſhall be their "chief ſtate of TRIAL and PROBATION."

94. As

94. As the foregoing doctrine of *Bramah seems* glaringly to clash with *Moses*'s history of the *creation of man*, it is previously necessary to account for this *seemingly* great difference; for they *appear* to agree only in one circumstance, namely, that man was the *last work* of the material and animal creation. By this discussion we purpose to avoid the imputation of slighting *a scriptural detail* that has for a succession of ages been received as orthodox by both *Jews* and *Christians*; a detail, that by being taken literally and misunderstood, has proved the source of many egregious and fatal errors, highly injurious to God's justice and clemency; the most enormous of which is, that infatuated belief, that a race of *unoffending* beings should *stand accursed* for the guilt and disobedience of *one man* and *one woman*.

95. The mission of *Moses* may without offence be considered as a very imperfect one, so designed by God himself; not only for that it was limited to one tribe of beings particularly favored of God, but also as it is totally silent upon all the *primitive truths* but one, *viz.* THE UNITY OF THE GODHEAD. This divine truth he was specially commissioned to declare to his people, as well to rescue them from the idolatrous

superftiſuperſtitions of the land he led them from, as from thoſe of the promiſed land he was leading them to. As *Moſes* was allowed to be moſt profoundly ſkilled in all the learning of the *Egyptians*, and conſequently in that of the *Bramins* (which had been perverted by thoſe Magi, as before ſhewn, to myſterious purpoſes), we cannot ſuppoſe him to have been ignorant that the *other primitive truths* had *been already revealed*, and that in fulneſs of time they would be confirmed to mankind; but he alſo knew that was a taſk reſerved for a more exalted being than himſelf; therefore we are not to wonder that he is utterly ſilent on thoſe heads of ſalvation.

96. Reſpecting *Moſes*'s ſhort narration of the creation and fall of man, it ſhould ſeem, if taken literally, to be a matter foreign to his commiſſion; but on a nearer view, and conſidered as *typical of the angelic fall*, it carries a very different and eſſential aſpect; and if not typical, it is moſt certainly laughable. We cannot, without violence to our conceptions of the wiſdom of God, ſuppoſe, that he would propagate the human ſpecies by a horrid inceſtuous union, which pure human nature ſtarts at, and which by his Holy Spirit ſtands condemned in his goſpel diſpenſation; for thus mankind

kind *must have increased*, if propagated according to the literal sense of *Moses*, from *one man and one woman*; so that it is self-evident he never intended it should be taken literally, but as typical of a prior and much greater event: nor have we the smallest doubt but that, in the days he penn'd it, the allegory was well and commonly understood by all; and we think we shall be able, without much difficulty, to prove to a demonstration, by analising this allegory, that it affords the fullest confirmation of the truth of the Bramanical doctrines of the creation of man, that man can be no other than the apostate angels, and that the Metempsychosis is a well-founded truth, necessarily resulting from these premises; and we shall also shew, that *Moses* was well acquainted with those doctrines; nay it is more than probable that he himself was the very identical spirit, selected and deputed in an earlier age, to deliver those truths free from allegory, under the stile and title of *Bramah*, as before intimated. But to our proof, from *Moses*'s narrative.

97. *Eve* is beguiled by the serpent, she eats, and tempts *Adam* to do the like, and thereby both become guilty of the sin of disobedience against an express law and order of their God and Creator: *Satan* is tempted

tempted by *Evil, the aſſociate of his boſom.* The *ſerpent* repreſents the inſidious arguments and wiles of *Satan* to engage the angelic tribes to become aſſociates in his revolt and rebellion, which it may be very naturally ſuppoſed were ſimilar to thoſe made uſe of by the *ſerpent to Eve. Paradiſe* marks the beauty of the original earth, and the garden of Eden is the ſymbol of *heaven*; *Adam and Eve* for their diſobedience are driven out of Eden, and *Satan and his aſſociates* are baniſhed from heaven for their rebellion. The gates of Eden are ſhut, and guarded on every ſide by angelic powers, to prevent the re-entrance of *Adam and Eve* and their *poſterity*; the heavenly regions are impervious to *Satan* and his *confederates.* The curſe of ſorrow, labor, and death, are entailed upon *Adam* and *Eve*, and their poſterity; wherein is figuratively ſhewn the original ſentence, doom, and puniſhment of the *apoſtate angels* in their mortal ſojourn on earth. *Moſes* introduces God curſing the ground for their ſakes, alluſive of the change brought about in this globe at the deluge, &c. occaſioned by the *ſecond defection* of the apoſtate angels in their ſtate of probation. The brutes being the elder brothers of the creation, and prior to the formation of man (the doctrine both of *Bramah* and *Moſes*), ſhews them to have been a preparatory creation for future purpoſes; and *Moſes* tacitly coincides with *Bramah* as to the intended uſe of this prior animal creation; otherwiſe man, who is evidently ſuperior in form and intellect, would, upon a rational ſuppoſition, have been the firſt object of all animal creation. God's being ſaid by *Moſes* to have *breathed the breath of life* into all his animal creation, is a happy figurative illuſtration of that paſſage in *the Shaſtah* (part 2. pag. 59), where "the ETERNAL ONE ſpake again, "and ſaid——Do thou BIRMAH (the firſt "created, the *Chriſt*), arrayed in my glo- "ry, and armed with my power, deſcend "to the loweſt boboon (region) of puniſh- "ment and purgation, and make known "to the *rebellious debtah* the words that I "have uttered, and the decrees which I "have pronounced againſt them, *and ſee* "*that they enter into the bodies that I have* "*prepared for them.*——And *Birmah* ſtood "before the throne and ſaid, ETERNAL "ONE, I have done as thou haſt com- "manded.—The *delinquent debtah* rejoice in "thy mercy, confeſs the juſtice of thy de- "crees, avow their ſorrow and repentance, "*and have entered into the mortal bodies* "*which thou haſt prepared for them.*"

98. The

98. The perſonages which *Moſes* calls by the names of *Abel* and *Cain*, ſaid to be the immediate deſcendants of *Adam* and *Eve*, are obviouſly types of *good* and *evil*, or vice and virtue, that were to guide and govern the actions of the human ſpecies, in the courſe of their trial, from generation to generation. In the murder of *Abel* by *Cain*, *Moſes* prophetically points out (what his knowledge of *the race* then made clear to him), that *vice* would totally ſubdue and deſtroy *virtue*; a prediction that is now, we fear, very near being accompliſhed, as ſhe may be too truly ſaid to be at the *laſt gaſp*, and on the verge of *expiring*. By ſin, our ſcriptures ſay, death entered into the world, that is by the ſin of *Satan*, not of *Adam* (vide the Rev. Mr. *Berrow*), and as in *Satan* (not in *Adam*), all men die, that is, are ſubjected by ſentence to death, ſo in *Chriſt* (deſtined to confirm to mankind the *primitive truths of ſalvation*) ſhall all be made alive, "a conſummation devoutly to be wiſhed," but of which we have yet *no ſigns* or *tokens*. Why *Moſes* has made woman the ſubſtitute of evil, is not very clear, unleſs from his profound wiſdom and knowledge of human nature, we ſuppoſe he had obſerved, that no object had ſo powerful an influence to ſeduce man from his duty and allegiance, as woman; and from thence he poſſibly

thought her the fitteſt ſymbol he could uſe on that occaſion, without (we dare ſay) intending it ſhould be taken as a general reflection upon the ſex.

99. It is here worth noting, that the creation and propagation of the human form according to the ſcriptures of *Bramah*, are clogged with no difficulties, *no ludicrous unintelligible circumſtances* or *inconſiſtencies*. GOD previouſly conſtructs mortal bodies of both ſexes, for the reception of the angelic ſpirits proportioned to their number, which were to animate or give life to thoſe as yet inanimate machines, and theſe were all doomed, without exception, to paſs through many ſucceſſive tranſmigrations in theſe mortal priſons, as a ſtate of puniſhment and purgation, before they received the grace of animating the human form, which was to be their chief ſtate of probation and trial: thus it is rationally ſuppoſed, that multitudes of them might arrive at the ſame period to that ſuperior degree; and that male and female forms, by the *inſtantaneous fiat* of the DEITY, were ready for their reception. Thus the propagation of the ſpecies *went naturally on*, as well as that of the other animal forms. Reſpecting the number of angelic beings firſt created by GOD, the ſcriptures of *Bramah*, the Old Teſtament,

ment, and *Christ*, are silent, confining themselves to the fact only; but if we form our calculation and judgment upon the multitude of organized mortal bodies in the world, we must conclude the original creation to have been amazingly immense! when we suppose, that only a portion of them rebelled, usually supposed (but upon what foundation we know not) to have been about one third. Be this as it may, it is a speculative point of little import to us, it being as easy to Omnipotence to create many hundred thousands of millions as one.

100. We now flatter ourselves that we have fully proved, to the conviction and satisfaction of our intelligent and unprejudiced reader, that *Moses*'s history of the *creation and fall of man*, was *purely typical of the angelic fall*, and made use of by him *figuratively* to denote that great and prior event with its fatal consequences; and at the same time to point out *the second defection* of those unhappy delinquents, after they had been placed by the grace and favor of God in a sufferable probationary state, beyond their merits or just expectation: also to give a useful and necessary admonition to his people, that *temptation was no plea*

for sin and disobedience. As to the actors *Moses* employs, under the denominations of *Adam*, *Eve*, *Cain*, and *Abel*, it is plain they never had any *real personal existence*; it is therefore evident that *the creation of man*, according to the scriptures of *Bramah*, is the *only real* and *original* one; and that man was not, as some have advanced, coeval with the angelic creation, but subsequent to *their fall*. *Moses* appears to us to have had an under plot (if we may be allowed the expression), in the circumstantial history he gives of the descendants of his supposed *Adam* and *Eve*; he politically saw, that for the preservation of the religion and morals of his people, it was absolutely necessary to keep them a separate nation as much as possible: to effect this he thought nothing would more powerfully conduce than raising the ideas of their own dignity, put in comparison with the nations around them; they already had stupendous proofs of their being a chosen race peculiarly favored of God, and *Moses* traces their genealogy to as distant a root as possible, and carries it up to his typical creation of the first man and woman: those who know what influence this vanity of *the antiquity of nations* has in modern times, will applaud the sagacity of *Moses*. And here we cannot help regretting that he has not left us his opinion of *the age*

of

of the universe; he has left it pretty clear, that the creation of *that* and *man* were nearly coeval, but there he has left both to exercise our fruitless guesses. On this subject we will only add, that the ancients *may have exaggerated*, but he *that dreams with the moderns*, that the world is not yet six thousand years old, may very easily acquire faith sufficient to believe the grossest of absurdities, or, with some of the ancient philosophers, that the heavens are made of brass or iron. Having fulfilled our engagement respecting that ancient typical *Mosaic* history of the creation and fall of man, we proceed with our subject.

101. We have seen a noble and exalted cause for the formation of the material universe, in which we behold man placed in the supreme degree over all animated mortal beings; but—still we observe many myriads of those beings, formed with no less stupendous wisdom and art, and endued (although in an inferior proportion) with the same rational intelligent faculties as himself, concerning whom we seem to be utterly at a loss; nor is there any abstruse point, in which the learned of all ages have been more divided than touching the state and nature of the *brute creation*. The pride

of man ſhudders at claſſing them with himſelf, yet his conſcious reaſon, on reflection, in ſpite of himſelf, checks his preſumption. Thus the inimitable and philoſophic *Prior* ſweetly ſings to our purpoſe:

" By what immediate cauſe *they* are inclin'd,
" In many acts, 'tis hard I own to find;
" I ſee in *others*, or I think I ſee,
" That ſtrong *their* principles and ours agree:
" Evil, like us they ſhun, and covet good,
" Abhor the poiſon, and receive the food;
" Like us they love or hate, like us they know,
" To joy the friend, or grapple with the foe;
" With ſeeming thought, their actions they
" *intend*,
" And uſe the means proportion'd to the end;
" Then vainly the philoſopher avers,
" That reaſon guides our deeds, and inſtinct
" theirs;
" How can we juſtly different *cauſes* frame?
" When *the effects* intirely are the ſame;
" *Inſtinct* and *reaſon* how can we divide?—
" *'Tis the fool's ignorance, and the pedant's pride.*"

102. It is *amuſing* to trace the different and bewildered ſentiments of mankind on this ſubject; but if it was *otherwiſe*, yet it is neceſſary to the execution of our plan.—The *Carteſians* maintain that brutes have no intelligent ſoul, but are mere machines, and unfeeling pieces of clock-work; and indeed,

 by

by the treatment they receive in the world, it ſhould ſeem that mankind in general were diſciples to that inhuman and ſtupid doctrine :—However Meſſ. *Yvon* and *Bouillet* refute the *Carteſian* hypotheſis, by maſterly indiſputable philoſophic arguments, and prove that brutes have a rational intelligent ſoul, and then—leave that ſoul to periſh with the body. Some have imagined the *ſouls* of brutes to be *material*; flat nonſenſe in *terms*, as well as in *philoſophy*. *Ariſtotle*, who ſuppoſed the ſouls of brutes to be *ſubſtantial forms*, is not a whit more intelligible. *Cicero*, who, great as he was, poſſeſſed a portion of that pride and vanity which fleſh is heir to, made no ſmall conceſſion, when he ſays, " In every eſſence " that is not ſimple, but compounded of " parts, there muſt be ſome *predominant* " quality; in man 'tis *reaſon*, in brutes it " is——*ſomething like it*." A late performance, ſaid to be a tranſlation from the *French*, makes all animal life, not man excepted, a *Jeu D'Eſprit*, or an amuſement of the Deity, and for no other end or purpoſe. Thus brutes reaſon upon brutes, ſays *Voltaire*. Another well-intended and ingenious late performance gives to the ſouls of brutes immortality, and a future life of rewards and puniſhments, and takes its proofs from ſcripture, but is utterly at a loſs to account for the predicament in which they ſtand on earth, liable as they are *to miſery*, without the authors being able to conceive by what mode of tranſgreſſion they could poſſibly *deſerve it*; touching which we hope to ſatisfy his doubts and curioſity. Another divine, in a late treatiſe upon the general deluge, boldly cuts the matter ſhort at one ſtroke, as *Alexander* did the *Gordian* knot. He ſuppoſes, "that as the brute "creation was made ſolely for man's uſe, "and that when they could be of no fur- "ther ſervice *to him*, they became *uſeleſs* in "the creation, and ſuffered *as matter* in the "general deluge, and it became *requiſite* "they ſhould periſh together—as it cannot "*be ſuppoſed* they were puniſhed on their "*own account*."—Here, reader, you have a choice ſpecimen of *cloſe reaſoning* exhibited to you; and a *ſtriking* inſtance of God's *juſtice* and *clemency!* delivered by a ſervant of the MOST HIGH!—*Montaigne* thinks more honorably of the brute creation; "What kind of ſufficiency," ſays he, "is "there in us, which we do not obſerve in "the operations of the animals?" To which he aſcribes deliberation, thought, and concluſion; and from thence gives the ſuperiority to beaſts over man, inſomuch as the works of nature excel thoſe of art. He goes further, and pronounces the animals *free*

agents,

agents, as well as mankind;—"I ſay there-
"fore, that there is no appearance of rea-
"ſon to ſuppoſe that the beaſts ſhould, by
"a natural and forced inclination (inſtinct),
"do *the ſame* things that we do by our
"*choice* and endeavor; we ought from *like*
"*effects* to conclude *like faculties*, and from
"*richer effects*, *richer faculties*; and by con-
"ſequence to confeſs, that *this ſame reaſon*,
"this *ſame method* by which *we operate*, is
"common alſo to the animals, or ſome
"other *that is better*." The whole rea-
ſoning on this ſubject of that acute but ir-
regular writer, is worth peruſal, as it lies
ſcattered through his apology for his learn-
ed friend *Raymond de Sobonde*. This indu-
ſtrious author ſeems quite clear as to the
pre-exiſtent ſtate of the human ſoul:
"Death," ſays he, "is the beginning of
"*another life*; ſo did we weep, and ſo
"much did it coſt us, *to enter into this*;
"and *ſo did we put off our former veil*,
"when we entered the preſent ſtate." And
by the courſe of his reaſoning juſt above re-
ferred to, it ſhould alſo ſeem, that he favored
the ſame opinion of the brute ſoul, as well
as the doctrine of the Metempſychoſis.—
Our learned and philoſophic *Baxter* (in his
Treatiſe of the Nature of the Soul), after
proving that the ſoul neceſſarily lives after
its ſeparation from the body, proceeds and
adds,

adds,—" As man is a being compounded of " *ſpirit* and *matter*, the *laſt* an impeding " and obſtructing cauſe on the activity and " perfection of reaſoning in the *firſt*, as the " the miniſtering organs of the *laſt* may " happen to be maimed, defective, or diſ- " ordered; and as a ſeparation of the union " leaves the *firſt* diſengaged and at liberty, " it is a rational ſuppoſition, that either the " ſoul is in an abſolute ſtate of ſeparation " from *all matter*, or (when it ſhall pleaſe " our infinitely wiſe Creator) *re-united* to " matter of a more *favorable kind*, that " ſhall be leſs obſtructive to our immaterial " powers.—Omnipotence admits of no li- " mitation, ſouls may be united to ſyſtems " of matter, according to the purpoſes of " infinite wiſdom, that will be vaſtly more " advantageous, and the union with them " more pleaſing, than with our preſent bo- " dies; our preſent union being equally in- " conceivable, although we cannot but be " conſcious of the fact, however unac- " countable by our limited conceptions."— Again, " Men who hold the immateriality " of the ſoul, need not be embarraſſed how " to diſpoſe of the *immaterial ſouls* of " brutes, or be concerned what powers they " may have after the diſſolution of their " bodies, but leave all to the Being that " made them."—" It is to be obſerved,

" that

" that the activity of the human ſoul is of
" two kinds, that which is exerted in the
" ſpontaneous moving the limbs, and that
" power whereby we turn back our percep-
" tive capacity to our paſt perceptions, ſo
" as to compare them together: the per-
" ceptivity alſo of it is twofold, for it is
" percipient of the action of matter upon
" itſelf, and percipient of its own internal
" operation in thinking. Brutes have the
" firſt of theſe powers, but want the ſecond
" altogether, which conſtitutes the *diſtinc-*
" *tion* between man and beaſt; they who
" run the parallel between the human ſoul
" and that of the brutes farther, ſuppoſe
" ſtill the ſame powers in both. But ſurely
" rationality muſt be found in ſome powers
" which the brutes *as ſuch* have not. This
" argument therefore does not prove the
" activity of the brute ſoul when ſeparat-
" ed——*although, if any one could prove it,*
" *he would do no diſſervice perhaps to philo-*
" *ſophy.*" Again, " It is ſelf-evident, that
" the wide-extended univerſe, though
" ſtretched beyond imagination, with all
" the wonders of wiſdom and power in it,
" is ſolely deſigned for the ſake of intelli-
" gent beings, *to train them up* for a ra-
" tional eternity."—That the general ſenti-
ments of this truly pious and learned divine
ſupport the probable doctrine of the Metemp-
ſychoſis

ſychoſis is ſo plain, it hardly needs pointing out to the obſerving reader; therefore we ſhall only add, that if *the act of dreaming* proves (as he aſſerts it does) the ſeparate exiſtence and active percipient powers of the human ſoul, after the diſſolution of the body, it equally proves the brute ſouls to be endued with the ſame powers—for undoubtedly—they dream. Unwilling as we are upon any occaſion to diſſent from the reaſoning of this truly great and good man, yet we find ourſelves under that neceſſity, when he ſays, "the human ſoul is form'd at firſt "without knowledge or experience, but "hath the power of attaining both.—— "Brutes are *incapable of improvement*, fi-"niſhed in their *ſpecific perfection all at* "*once*." So ſtrange a poſition as the foregoing, could proceed only from non-attention to the progreſs of the intelligent faculties in both ſpecies from their ſtate of infancy, or—from thoſe feelings of human pride that will ſpring up in the beſt heart, when the ſuppoſed dignity of his ſuperior nature is brought into competition.—The ſentiments of the ingenious Mr. *Berrow* (ſo often referred to) upon the brute creation, may be clearly gathered from his own words, which we ſhall preſent to our readers, as a curious and uncommon ſpecimen of *unprejudiced reaſoning* in a Chriſtian divine.——"If it

"ſhould

" ſhould be urged, that the aſſigning ſouls
" to one part of the brute creation, will re-
" duce us to the neceſſity of ſuppoſing the
" *like* to actuate the moſt minute ſpecies of
" vital nature alſo; I ſhall only remind the
" ſpeculative and philoſophic part of man-
" kind, that there is diſcernible, by the
" microſcopic eye, as exquiſite a due pro-
" portioned diſpoſition of organs, fibres,
" &c. (the more amazing in proportion as
" they are more minute) in the one as in
" the other——That, again, the ſoul has
" the power of *ſelf-contraction*, to an *infi-*
" *niteſſimal degree*, as well as that of *ſelf-*
" *dilatation*——That ſuppoſing, in the next
" place, every organized body, as well in
" the brute as in the rational, to be an al-
" lotted *temporary* priſon for a *pre-delinquent*
" ſoul *(an hypotheſis, than which there can-*
" *not I think be one more rational)*, it is eaſy
" to conceive how and why *ſome* may be
" made here priſoners *more at large* as we
" ſay, and entruſted with privileges and
" faculties more numerous, extenſive, and
" exalted than others: and that, laſtly, it
" is impoſſible to ſay into how many differ-
" ent kinds of vehicles *a ſoul may tranſmi-*
" *grate*, ere its *plaſtic faculty* be refined
" enough to *inform one*, wherein to perform
" the functions of an *intelligent* and rational
" life."

" life."——Here we ſee a learned divine, to the honor of the church of *England,* ſcruples not to avouch, without reſerve, one moſt material part of *Bramah*'s doctrine of the Metempſychoſis; and it is a pity he was not further enlightened; he then would not (with many others of the learned) have been drove to the ſubterfuge of making a new creation to animate and actuate all mortal forms, when there were a race of angelic delinquent beings ready made to his hands.——Having thus thrown together, under one paragraph, the different ſentiments of mankind touching the ſtate and nature of the brute creation, we will next proceed to conſider *their uſe*, and the intent of their creation; a matter in which we ſhall not find mankind ſo much divided, but on the contrary (the bulk of them at leaſt) pretty unanimous.

103. Man's preſumption in ſuppoſing the brute creation was intended *ſolely for his uſe*, may be aſcribed to two cauſes: the firſt his pride, or natural unbounded *thirſt of power*; an intellectual *faculty* he picked not up here, but brought with him from above, from his pre-exiſtent angelic ſtate: *there* it had proved his bane, and here, having not immediately the governing powers of hea-

ven

ven to combat againſt, to keep his ruling paſſion in action, he exerciſes it, not only on the unoffending brute creation, but on his own ſpecies.——The ſecond cauſe we conſider as a plea and ſanction taken from the 26th verſe of the firſt chapter of *Geneſis*, where *Moſes* ſays, that "God ſaid, Let us "make man in our image, after our like-"neſs; and *let them have dominion* over the "fiſh of the ſea, and over the fowl of the "air, and over the cattle, and over all the "earth, and over every creeping thing that "creepeth upon the earth."——To combat the *firſt cauſe*, would prove a labor truly Herculean, without the ſmalleſt chance of victory, and therefore we avoid the battle; and touching the ſecond, we might avail ourſelves of the demonſtrative proofs already ſtated, that the *Moſaic* hiſtory of the creation of terreſtrial animals was purely typical; but we will wave that juſt privilege, and examine the fact, as it literally ſtands; premiſing, that man has no right to chuſe his texts, but if he thinks to benefit himſelf *by one*, he ought to acknowledge the force and efficacy *of another*, and abide with equal ſtrictneſs by both; that he has not preſerved this equity towards a *more expreſs* dictate of this ſcripture is certain; for, verſe 29th of the ſame chapter, "God "ſaid (to man), Behold, I have given you

"*every*

" *every herb* bearing ſeed, which is upon " the face of all the earth, and *every tree*, " in the which is the fruit of a tree, yield- " ing ſeed: to you it ſhall *be for meat*." Which words convey a palpable although tacit interdiction of all other food: but more of this hereafter, when we have no doubt of proving indiſputably that the breach of this poſitive injunction, or rather this *firſt law* of nature, has been one of the great, if not chief ſource of phyſical as well as *moral evil*. We now return to our more immediate ſubject.

104. That the brute creation was deſigned to be ſubſervient to, or made for the uſe of man, is a conceit incompatible not only with the juſtice of God, but alſo his wiſdom; and that, therefore, the uſurped ſenſe of the phraſe, " Let them have do- " minion," (on which ſo much ſtreſs has been laid) is not well-founded, and implies only, Let them have pre-eminence, predominance, ſuperiority, in *intellectual faculties over the reſt of the animal creation*. Thus *Bramah*, " And in this form I will " enlarge their intellectual powers, even as " when I firſt made them free." In this ſenſe only can the above phraſe be poſſibly underſtood, for the following reaſons: firſt, *Moſes* nowhere intimates, that the brute creation

creation was made *for the use of man.* Secondly, the very small proportion of *the whole* he has been able to reduce under his dominion, and even that modicum not subdued, but by the exertion, or rather perversion of *those superior intellectual faculties* into craft and violence, which were most certainly given him for very different pursuits. Thirdly, that, so far from there being the smallest appearance that the animal creation was subjected either to the dominion or service of man, according to the sense that he has wantonly and cruelly assumed, that the majority of them, almost to an infinite degree, are obnoxious to him, and at enmity with him, and in no wise, shape, or form, under his rule and dominion. On the contrary, it may be justly said, that " men are more slaves to man, " than beasts to him." Fourthly, can it possibly be conceived, without doing violence to the justice, goodness, and wisdom of God, that he would invest man with a dominion to *drive out*, at his *caprice* and *pleasure*, that *breath of life*, which he had for his wise purposes so bountifully *breathed* into all his animal creation? for although *Moses* particularly applies this sublime sentence to *Adam alone* in the 7th verse of his 2d chapter, in these words, " And the Lord " God created man of the dust of the

" ground, and *breathed into his nostrils the* " *breath of life, and man became a living soul;*" yet it is self-evident, that this operation and divine infusion of a living soul or spirit, must have been, *a priori*, *general* to the whole animal creation. Fifthly, what idea must we form of the wisdom and designs of GOD, if we suppose that, after his blessing his animal creation, and laying a positive injunction upon them to *increase* and *multiply* and *replenish the earth*, he should, *at the same time*, give to man dominion and power to counteract his purposes, by *decreasing*, *diminishing*, and *destroying them?*

105. Having shewn above, that we cannot without violence to God and nature conclude, that the brute creation was made *for the use of man*, it follows, that his pretended right of dominion is an usurpation over a race of intelligent beings, innocent, at least, respecting him; whose lot in this world is sufficiently painful and miserable, without any additional load from man. Here we will once more give our readers the sentiments of the Rev. Mr. *Berrow*, as strongly expressive of our own, and apt to our subject. After a pathetic and truly Christian-like apostrophe on that noble animal the horse, which is equally applicable to every other animal under man's tyranny, he

he ſubjoins,——" But wherefore all this " wretchedneſs?—wherefore all theſe agonizing pains and miſeries heaped on an " helpleſs offspring of divine providence? " are they not fleſh and blood?" *(Have they not their* REAL *grievances and apprehenſions?)* " Do *they* not, as well as *we*, " know what ſorrow means? were they " brought into a *ſenſible exiſtence* for nothing " but *the ſervice*, or rather to gratify the " pride, the wantonneſs, the cruelty of " man? ſhall one being be created, even " under the bare poſſibility of being made " miſerable, *ſolely for the uſe* or pleaſure of " another?——Lord, what is man? or " rather, what are not brutes?"——" The " *Indians* aſk, if brutes have not ſouls? if " not, then, ſay they, *matter thinks. Cicero* ſays, " That God himſelf is the ſoul " of brutes;" therefore, ſays the *Indian*, " ſhall they be found ſuffering without a " CAUSE, or without a *recompence?*"—— Surely no; the doctrine of the Metempſychoſis *alone points out the cauſe* for their ſuffering *natural evils*, and at the ſame time ſhews the promiſed recompence.

106. Notwithſtanding all that has been ſaid, we ſee it will be ſtill objected to us, that *Moſes*, in the controverted phraſe before us (" Let them have dominion"), muſt

have meant thereby abſolute dominion and unaccountable rule, or he would not, in his law to the *Hebrews*, have devoted the animal creation to the ſubjection of man, in the various ſacrifices *of them* inſtituted by the law. To which we ſay, that thoſe cruel ſacrifices were ſubſequently condemned and diſcountenanced, as barbarous and inefficacious, both by GOD and CHRIST; and we may fairly lay it down as an inconteſtable principle, that any act which GOD and CHRIST have at any one time pronounced *evil*, could never have been *good*; and therefore, that *Moſes*, in that inſtitute, deviated from the commiſſion he had received from GOD, as he did unwarily in other particulars, which drew on him the diſpleaſure of his Creator, and deprived him of the promiſed felicity of ſettling his people in the land to which he was appointed to conduct them. Nor does it at all appear difficult to point out the cauſes that led *Moſes* into this error: he knew that their appetites had for a long ſeries of ages been vitiated by the taſte of animal food; he hoped to reclaim them from it, by ſhewing them, in the 29th verſe of the firſt chapter of *Geneſis* before recited, that that was not their originally deſtined meat, and that by the uſe of animal food they had digreſſed from their *primitive nature*, and had tranſ-

transſgreſſed againſt *the very firſt law* of their Maker; but——very ſoon finding every admonition of the kind was loſt upon them, he weakly thought it might prove in ſome ſort an extenuation of theſe *common murders*, and a kind of ſanctification of them, by introducing them as part of their religious worſhip. To this he probably had a further intereſting and pious motive; he could not but remark the depravity of, and the ſtrong bent in his people towards the ſuperſtitious worſhip, ſacrifices and idolatries of the *Egyptians*, *Chaldeans*, *Tyrians*, *Canaanites*, &c. amongſt whom he knew that *human ſacrifices* were as common as thoſe of the brute creation; therefore, to guard his people againſt *a greater evil*, he inſtituted, as he vainly imagined, *a leſs*; not adverting that it belonged TO GOD ALONE, to *permit evil*, that *good* may come of it. The viſion of St. *Peter* may alſo be objected againſt us, and that *Chriſt* himſelf winked at theſe murderous practices, and even partook of them. To this we anſwer, that *Chriſt* knew too well the total and confirmed depravity *of man* to combat ſo long-eſtabliſhed an enormity; therefore the chief aim of his miſſion was, *firſt* to correct his morals, and, *if poſſible*, bring him to a ſtate of *ſenſibility* and *repentance*; that once obtained, the aboli-

 tion

tion *of that*, and many other enormities, he knew, would follow of courſe.

107. Let us now hear the words of GOD himſelf on this ſubject by the mouth of his inſpired *Bramah:*——" The mortal forms,
" wherewith I ſhall encompaſs the *delin-*
" *quent debtah*, are *the work of my hand*;
" *they ſhall not be deſtroyed*, but left to their
" natural decay; therefore whichſoever of
" the *debtah* ſhall by deſigned violence bring
" about the diſſolution of the mortal forms
" *animated by their delinquent brethren*—
" *thou, Sieb*, ſhalt plunge the offending
" ſpirit into the *onderah* for a ſpace, and
" he ſhall be doomed to paſs again the
" eighty-nine tranſmigrations, whatſoever
" ſtage he may be arrived to at the time
" of ſuch his offence."

108. Having thus, in a regular ſeries, diſcuſſed the ſeveral events of the creation and exiſtence, of angels, their rebellion and fall; and having ſhewn that the material univerſe was conſtructed for their habitation and ſuſtenance, and that mortal bodies were formed for their more immediate puniſhment and impriſonment; and having alſo made it ſufficiently clear, that man can poſſibly be no other than thoſe identical

fallen

fallen angels; and laſtly, that the brute creation could not have been made ſubject to him, nor deſtined for his uſe and ſervice in the ſenſe he has erroneouſly, not to ſay wickedly, converted them to; it follows that we next take it into conſideration to what other uſe or purpoſe were they brought into exiſtence?——The ancient doctrine of the Metempſychoſis of *Bramah*, at once anſwers the matter in queſtion, and would afford full ſatisfaction to a *Gentoo*, a *Tartar*, or a *Chineſe*, but not to a Chriſtian. (Here by-the-bye it is proper to note, that although the *Tartars* and *Chineſe* believe in the tranſmigration of the ſoul, yet they ſeem, as well as our ancient druids, to have totally loſt ſight of the ſource, the root, the original principle from whence the doctrine of the Metempſychoſis ſprung, viz. the angelic fall and doom, which has been retained in its primitive purity only by the Gentoos.) ——The caſe ſtanding thus, it remains to examine whether the ſtate and predicament in which the brute creation appear and exiſt, can be accounted for upon any other rational ſyſtem. In order to which it will be neceſſary to conſider them under two points of view; firſt, as *intelligent, rational beings, and free agents*; and ſecondly, as *beings ſubjected to miſery*.

109. The

109. The man who aſſerts his own rational intellectual faculties and free agency, and denies them to the brutes, either thinks not at all, or is actuated by pride and ſelf-ſufficient pre-eminence, or has been very deficient in his obſervations and reflections upon that numerous creation.——When we ſee a race of beings endued with the paſſions of rage, revenge, dominion, ungovernable luſt, jealouſy, hatred, envy, and every other vice ſimilar to our own, *except ingratitude*; and when we behold them endued with the virtues (we had almoſt ſaid the Chriſtian virtues) of love, fidelity, gratitude, friendſhip, courage, parental tenderneſs, filial affection, patience, ſubmiſſion, innocence and meekneſs, all in as high perfection, if not higher, than in ourſelves; and when we further obſerve them inveſted with the powers of happineſs, miſery, reflection, recollection, foreſight, forecaſt, prodigies of art, without rule, line, ſquare, or compaſs; ſagacious in contriving, political in government; the amazing beauty of ſome, and ſtupendous conſtruction and animal œconomy of all!——All which *vices*, *virtues*, *powers* and *properties*, are exemplified in the various ſpecies of the animal creation.——When we daily ſee, or may ſee, all this verified, and ſtill appropriate *cogitation*

cogitation and *reaſon* to man alone, we ſee with the eyes of *folly* and *prejudice*.

110. That man is endued with higher intellectual powers, and capable of carrying his reaſoning faculties to a more tranſcendent pitch, we readily grant; but——why will not human pride reſt ſatisfied with this ſuperiority, without aiming to diveſt the next great work of his Creator of the portion which he has graciouſly and evidently beſtowed upon it, as neceſſary to their temporal exiſtence?——If therefore the brute ſoul, as ſome (we will not call them philoſophers) have taught, is material, and periſhes with the body, it is time to tremble for the ſoul of man; for it is too true and melancholy a fact, that it ſtands not entitled to a better lot:—the ſpirituality and future ſeparate exiſtence of *the one*, reſts on no ſurer a foundation than *the other*; and all appearances are as ſtrong in favor of the one as of the other.———Thus our prejudices and falſe reaſoning, ariſing from ignorance of our real ſtate and nature, leads us into an uncomfortable dilemma, and we are plunged into a labyrinth of confuſion, from which nothing can diſentangle and extricate us, but—the doctrine of the Metempſychoſis, which elucidates and reconciles every difficulty by teaching, that the ſoul of man and brute is one and the

ſame

ſame ſpirit, firſt in a ſtate of greater degradation, a preparatory ſtate of *puniſhment* and *purgation*, previouſly neceſſary to his paſſing into his ſtate of *probation*, in the ſuperior and more enlightened form of man. In further ſupport of this concluſion, it remains that we conſider the brute creation *as beings ſubjected to miſery*.

III. The juſtice, the goodneſs of God ſtands moſt evidently impeached in the wild ſuppoſition that he could poſſibly create a race of beings ſubjected to miſery, without ſome cauſe of offence on their parts.—Let us with a becoming indignation reject an opinion ſo unworthy our God, and conclude there muſt have been *a cauſe*, and an efficient one, although no hypotheſis hitherto produced has pointed it out to the ſatisfaction of a rational enquirer.——The ſtate and exiſtence of man ſtands in the ſame predicament, doomed through the progreſs of his life to a ſeries of natural and moral evils, without any *apparent cauſe*, or without poſſibly having been capable of deſerving them by any tranſgreſſion *here*; therefore our firm belief in God's juſtice, and our reaſon directed us to ſearch for *that cauſe of offence* in ſome *former ſtate* of the ſoul's exiſtence, in which we happily ſucceeded, at leaſt to our full conviction, and *we hope* to that of our candid readers. To that ſource

we

we muſt again apply to ſolve the preſent difficulty reſpecting *the brute ſoul*, which muſt undoubtedly have ſinned in a pre-exiſtent ſtate, to reconcile its *many ſufferings here* with the idea of a juſt and good God.—— The ſenſible reflections and ſentiments of the ingenious Mr. *Dean* of *Middleton*, are appoſite to our ſubject, and ſo pertinent to what we have further to allege, that we will take the freedom of tranſplanting them. After pre-ſuppoſing that pains, diſeaſes, death, &c. evils got entrance into the world *by ſin*, he proceeds as follows: "Now brutes "as well as men are ſubject to the ſame "ſorts of pains and diſeaſes; ſo far their "caſes coincide. In all general deſolations "they have ſuffered together; in this they "conform. They ſuffered with man *the* "*injuries of the fall* (we wiſh he had ſaid "*the angelic fall*; poſſibly he meant it).— "They have periſhed with him in deluges, "in conflagrations, in famines, in peſti"lences, in deſtructions of the ſword; in "ſhort, in all capital calamities they have "had their ſhare, as well as man (to which "he might have added, the many miſeries "they endure from the tyranny of man). "Now, if there is any reaſon to believe, "that ſuch evils are of God's appointment, "and occaſioned by ſin, muſt not brutes "then in ſome reſpect or other be ſuppoſed

"to

" to be faulty? We do not pretend to ſay, " or even to inſinuate, that they are capable of moral rules, and become criminal after the manner of men; but we allege, that they muſt have ſome kind of " demerit, they muſt have contracted defilements ſome way or other. *If we cannot ſhew how this is, it is only an inſtance, amongſt many others, of our ignorance.* " The facts inſiſted on are deducible " from the preceding caſes, and the " juſtice of God.——God cannot puniſh his creatures without a cauſe, and " this cauſe muſt be guilt or demerit of " ſome kind or other; infinite juſtice neceſſarily ſuppoſes it." This Gentleman ſtops not here, but goes a ſtep much higher in his concluſion from the above premiſes: " that as brute animals have attended man " in all great and capital calamities, ſo they " will alſo attend him in *his final deliverance,* and *be reſtored with him.*" How he proves this from ſcripture, we refer our readers to his "Eſſay on the Future Life " of Brutes," whilſt we proceed on our way.

112. Thus have we demonſtrated, *the creation and ſtate* of man and beaſt are utterly inexplicable upon any other hypotheſis than the ancient doctrine of the Metempſychoſis,

ſychoſis, which *alone* rationally accounts for, and reconciles their exiſtence, as intelligent free agents doomed to miſery, in every ſtage and circumſtance of it, to be ſtrictly conſiſtent with the *goodneſs*, the *juſtice*, and *mercy* of God; the ſtate of the brute creation, and the cauſe of their ſufferings no longer remains a matter of difficulty, nor incompatible with divine juſtice, but conformable thereto; their mortal bodies being formed for no other end or purpoſe but the puniſhment and vehicles of conveyance for the *ſame offending ſpirit*, to a form, which, although ſtill a priſon for the ſoul, was yet ſo marvelouſly fabricated (by a modus and conſtruction imperceptible to us), as to afford a greater ſcope and latitude to the exertion of thoſe intellectual faculties and free agency, which it was only capable of exerting *in a limited degree*, whilſt in its ſtate of deeper degradation; for, touching the portion of *cogitation* and *conſcientiouſneſs* the brute creation are poſſeſſed of, it is impoſſible for us to ſay; it may, for aught we know to the contrary, be equal to our own: we are barely authorized in our conception drawn from viſible phenomena, that their powers are under ſome kind of reſtraint, but of what nature we know not; nor does it follow from the premiſes, if granted,

granted, that their cogitative faculties ſhould be under any reſtraint at all. We ſee that they are in general miſerable, without remedy or comfort; but that man is only ſo by predilection, having reſources within himſelf, if he pleaſes to employ them, that are capable at all times of conſtituting his felicity; and this privilege marks to us the ſpecific difference and ſuperiority of the *ſame ſoul in brute and man*. In the *firſt* it may be ſaid to be in *a cloſe priſon*, and in the laſt, a priſoner more *at large*, and capable of working out its full and *final liberty*; a privilege it cannot obtain by iſſuing from the mortal brute form, which is deſtined to be its ſtate of *puniſhment* and *purgation*, as before obſerved, and that of *man only*, its ſtate of *trial* and *probation*; from which form alone it can poſſibly emerge to its priſtine celeſtial ſtate. It ſeems to have been the ſentiments of *Lucian*, as well as of *Pythagoras*, and many others of the ancient philoſophers, that what conſtitutes the greateſt puniſhment of the brutes, is *their conſciouſneſs* of having animated the *form of man*, and of not having benefited thereby; and that it is by their retaining the ideas of their former ſtate of humanity, that many of their ſpecies, by ſmall training, ſo readily comprehend his language and inſtructions.

Chime-

Chimerical as this opinion may ſeem to ſome, it appears in our judgment to have a good foundation.

113. From what has been ſaid, we have the pleaſure of thinking the philoſophic reaſoning of the learned *Baxter* ſtands confirmed and illuſtrated; the ſenſible ſuggeſtions of the Rev. Mr. *Berrow* enforced and verified; the doubts and perplexities of the Rev. Mr. *Dean*, touching the *cauſe* for which the brutes are doomed to miſery, fully ſatisfied; and the bold aſſertions of Mr. *John Ilive* well grounded, from whom we candidly confeſs we took our firſt hints, and became a thorough convert to his hypotheſis, upon finding on enquiry, and the exertion of our own reaſon, that it was built on the firſt divine revelation that had been graciouſly delivered to man, to wit, THE CHARTAH BHADE OF BRAMAH; although it is very plain Mr. *Ilive* was ignorant of the doctrine of the Metempſychoſis, by confining his conceptions only to the angelic fall, man's being the apoſtate angels, and that this earth was the only hell; paſſing over in ſilence the reſt of the *animal creation*.

114. As the ancient doctrine of the Metempsychosis alone accounts, as has been said, for the creation, nature, and state of man and beast, so it also clears up many difficulties and objections that have frequently been started concerning the *true nature* of *Christ*; some conceiving him to be "*very God of very God*," that is, *God himself*, if they mean any thing: others conceive him to be *God and man*, but in what sense we believe infinite wisdom itself could not explain to the comprehension of a finite understanding——Others conceive *Christ* to have been *mere man*, enlightened or inspired by God to a *superlative degree*, and disavow the *pre-existent* state of his soul or spirit. Touching the *two first* of these opinions, we have already given *our conceptions*, esteeming them enthusiastic, if not blasphemous; but respecting the supporters of *the third*, they shun (we fear) *Sylla*, and fall upon *Carybdis*.

115. A Treatise (which we never saw or heard of before we had closed our Second General Head, although published in 1767) intitled, "The true Doctrine of the New "Testament concerning *Jesus Christ* con-"sidered," contains a plausible chain of objections to his supposed *pre-existence*. Although

though in that book, and the appendix, we have the ſingular pleaſure of finding our ſentiments upon the evil tendency of the Athanaſian doctrine, and the true meaning and reading of the firſt chapter of St. *John*'s Goſpel, ſupported by ſo learned and judicious an advocate *for truth*; yet—we cannot avoid thinking that this author hurts the cauſe of Chriſtianity in a moſt tender part, by conteſting the pre-exiſtent ſtate of *Chriſt*, and thereby diveſting him of his *original divinity*, the criterion, the *ſine qua non* of his doctrines; for when he conſiders him as only *mere enlightened man*, he moſt certainly goes counter to the expreſs declarations of *Chriſt*, in many places of the Goſpels touching himſelf, his pre-exiſtency, and nature of his miſſion, as being a delegate *immediately* from heaven; but more particularly in St. *John*'s Goſpel, chap. iii. 16, 17, and 18th verſes. We concur in ſentiment with this writer, and feel very diſtinct ideas reſpecting the DEITY of the Father, and the *divinity* of the Son; but when he could without ſcruple admit, that *divinity* and *humanity may unite*, or rather, as the learned *Baxter* ſtates it, that God, by his omnipotency, can unite a ſpiritual being to any *material form* he pleaſes; we cannot conceive why he ſhould ſtumble at allowing the pre-exiſtence of the *divine Spirit of Chriſt*. The

 creation

creation and miſerable exiſtence of every mortal intelligent being, we have fully proved, can only be compatible with the juſtice of God, upon the ſuppoſition of the pre-exiſtent ſtate of their ſpiritual part or *ſoul*; then where lies the difficulty of ſuppoſing the pre-exiſtent nature of *Chriſt?* as the *firſt created*, *the firſt begotten* of God of *all celeſtial beings*, before all worlds, delegated by the Father to *unite for a time* with the mortal form of man, for the great purpoſe of ſalvation to a race of offending intelligent beings——Thus *Chriſt* may literally, with propriety, and without any myſtery or confuſion of ideas, be ſtiled and acknowledged THE SON OF GOD AND MAN, as he himſelf occaſionally uſes both thoſe titles.——When this learned and ingenious writer gives an unprejudiced hearing, and full force to the doctrines of the Metempſychoſis, and duly weighs the inſufficiency of every other human hypotheſis, to account for the *phenomena* of *our preſent exiſtence*, and indeed of *all nature*; he will, we flatter ourſelves, receive full conviction that his doubts and diſbelief of the pre-exiſtent ſtate and *original divinity* of *Chriſt*, were ill-founded, and not *the true doctrine of the New Teſtament*.

116. If

116. If *reaſon* and *religion* are deemed worthy a place in the argument, man has now the fulleſt conviction from *both*, of the true relation in which he ſtands to the whole brute creation, and that he can lay no rational claim to the power he has aſſumed for a multitude of ages paſt over ſome of their ſpecies; nor has he any the ſmalleſt juſtifiable pretence for the uſes to which he has converted others of them, murdering ſome for the gratification of his depraved unnatural appetites, ſubjecting others to the moſt cruel labors without humanity or remorſe, devoting others for his wanton ſport to premeditated deaths, attended with all the cruel and affecting circumſtances of *protracted terror*; training, exaſperating, aiding, and abetting others to bloody combats of death againſt one another of the *ſame ſpecies*; ſpiriting up and encouraging others of them, *of different ſpecies*, to diſcord, contention, and battle, worrying each other, ſometimes to death itſelf, for man's inhuman diverſion; impriſoning and diveſting others of the ſpecies of *that liberty* which was originally given to them by their Creator, upon a tenure equal with man's own; and this only for the ſake of a *trifling amuſement* and indulgence to the ear; exhauſting the ſtrength, and abridging the lives of multitudes of the moſt noble of the brute crea-

tion *in contentions of ſpeed*, for the baſe purpoſes of *iniquitous gain* and *worthleſs fame*, acquired not without the application of many cruel ruthleſs ſtripes, gaping wounds, and languid ſweats, that human pity, *if it had exiſtence*, would ſhudder at.

117. The above catalogue *of evils*, which man has hitherto, without ſcruple or feeling, wantonly loaded the brute creation with, we will ſuppoſe may be aſcribed to his having loſt ſight of *their original dignity*, and the *relation* they truly ſtand in to himſelf; and therefore this ignorance may, in ſome degree, be pleaded in extenuation of his guilt: but now he is fully evinced of *both*, he in future remains without excuſe, if he does not recede from practices that are neither warranted by reaſon, religion, juſtice, or the common dictates of humanity. The further to induce him to this worthy receſſion, we beg leave to remind him, that every brute is animated with *a ſoul* identical to *his own*, advancing only *in a progreſſive ſtate* TO MAN; and that he has no right either to haſten or retard *that progreſſion*, that being an act which God has reſerved to himſelf alone: GOD has ſaid,——"*Thou ſhalt do* NO *murder*," and man has had the boldneſs, either totally to diſregard this commandment, or by putting

his

his own construction upon it, has infringed it in every sense, where power gave him the means: how could we then expect mercy for the brute creation, when he has shewn none for his own species? But this is a kind of murder we shall not speak to here, intending in this place further to examine his pretensions *not only to murder, but to eat the animal beings*, and the fatal consequences of this transgression to the world, requesting our readers will have the goodness to advert to what has been already presented to them on this subject in our 102d and few following paragraphs. We know, that in this discussion we shall meet with potent enemies to contend with, no less than a most formidable train of all the sensual appetites and passions, but that shall not deter us; human reason, although long debased, and subjected to the dominion of *Circe*, is not quite extinct, and only wants to be roused by application of the *celestial Moly*, to shine forth in its native and original lustre.

118. Besides man's conceit of his right of dominion over the brute creation (which has been sufficiently refuted) he urges *two* other pleas in support of his practice of *killing and eating his fellow-creatures*; these he thinks are unanswerable——*The first* is the obvious course and destination of Providence,

whereby we fee that every race of the animal creation are in a perpetual ftate of war, and doomed to be a prey, the one to nourifh and fuftain the other *;—the fact, if laid down as a *general* pofition, may be admitted, but with large exceptions, as many tribes of quadrupeds are exempted from that general law of nature, as the horfe, the the cow, the deer, the goat, the fheep, &c. but allowing this plea to have its full force refpecting the carnivorous tribes of the brute creation, yet *man* cannot avail himfelf of this law; *they* deviate not from the line prefcribed them by the God of nature, but man, in becoming *a beaft of prey*, acts not only in violation of his order and rank in the fcale of beings, but alfo in oppofition to an exprefs interdict of God, as promulged in the Bramanical and Mofaic hiftory of his creation before cited; and indeed, upon a furvey of the natural conftruction of his form, the quadrupeds above fpecified might gorge and regale their appetites upon animal food with equal propriety as man, who cannot plead *the law of neceffity*, which carnivorous animals feem to be fubjected to for their daily fubfiftence.

119. Let us not, however, in our abundant zeal for the brute creation, be wanting

* Vide Part II. from page 77. to 86.

in our due applauſe to the amazing and unaccountable *moderation* and forbearance of man, in that he has not in *Europe* yet arrived, to what moſt certainly muſt be the higheſt perfection of good eating, *the fleſh of his own ſpecies*; which, from the nature of its regimen, and the repletion of animal ſalts and juices, muſt yield a much more exalted flavor, and higher enjoyment, than any other kind of *brutal fleſh* can poſſibly afford.—*Swift*, of ever witty and ſarcaſtic memory, was ludicrous on this ſubject; but we are quite ſerious, and think man's abſtinence from this *ſupreme indulgence* the more to be honored, and the more wonderful, as he is not without precedents for the practice, on the authentic records of *America*, and other *ſavage nations*; beſides——his virtue ſhines brighter in this *great ſelf-denial*, when he may with propriety urge very cogent *political* reaſons, that would fully juſtify his tranſplanting that *luſcious delicacy* and faſhion into *Europe*, to wit, the *increaſing ſcarcity* and *high price* of all animal food, both which evils would be effectually and ſpeedily averted from us, by the project of—KILLING AND EATING THE CONSUMERS; from which practice, the too great population of the human ſpecies would alſo be prevented. A conſideration which leads us to man's *ſecond plea* for killing and devouring the brute creation.

120. *The immenſe increaſe of the animal creation*, which it has been ſuppoſed would over-run the world, and endanger man's ſafety and exiſtence, has been urged as an unanſwerable *plea of neceſſity* for their deſtruction;—to ſay nothing of the wickedneſs of this argument, which directly and openly arraigns the wiſdom, goodneſs, and mercy of GOD, we will conſider the force of it, and hope to prove it as ill-grounded as the former; for, in the firſt place, ſuppoſing (although not allowing) the fact, it can only give a ſanction to man for killing, *but not for eating:* nor can this argument poſſibly be applied, even with the ſemblance of propriety, againſt any ſpecies of the brutes, but thoſe that are obviouſly obnoxious to him, and theſe ſhun his ſociety.——Any ſuperabundant increaſe of the *finny race* cannot poſſibly affect man's ſafety or exiſtence, yet he deſtroys and devours them in common with their terreſtrial and aerial brethren.——But to ſhow the fallacy of this plea, we find it levelled only againſt thoſe unoffending animals which man has deſtined *for his prey*, and no pretended inconvenience is felt from the increaſe

crease of those selected for our pleasure or our labor, as witness the elephant, the horse, &c.——But to cut this plea short, and divest it even of plausibility, let us appeal to facts, which set all reasoning at defiance;—let us cast our eyes back on the ancient extensive empire of *Indostan*, where, for a long succession of ages, to the late period of their subjection to *Tamerlane*, no animal was ever bereaved of life, but left to its natural decay and dissolution, and yet their increase was never found, or objected to as an evil, or obnoxious to man.—On the contrary, it is most evident, throughout the whole animal creation, man not excepted, that God has wisely adjusted the principles of decay in each, in a just proportion to their increase or prolific qualities, in such an equipoise, that the one shall not exceed the other, to the confusion or detriment of his works.—If we admit, that some parts may be overstocked, and that the increase may exceed the means for their support, yet this affords no plea or sanction for slaughtering and eating them;—since man has, without any authority from God or nature, doomed them to labor, to evade and set at nought that part of his sentence which decreed "*that he should till the ground by the* "*sweat of his own brow*," let him, in case of a superabundant increase, *as the least sinful*,

ful, export them to other regions that may ſtand in need of them for ſimilar purpoſes, in place of devoting them to death, for the gratification of his unnatural appetites.—— There may be one ſituation, and one only, wherein man can poſſibly, with ſeeming juſtice, deſtroy the animal creation; and that is, when there ſhould be ſuch an increaſe of thoſe ſpecies of ſimilar conſtruction with his own reſpecting maſtication, &c. that ſhould rob or diveſt him of that food which God and his own nature originally marked and pointed out for his ſole ſubſiſtence; in ſuch a caſe, provided he had no other means of freeing himſelf of them, he poſſibly might ſtand vindicated in killing, but *in no caſe* in eating them.——What has been above alledged reſpecting the empire of *Indoſtan,* may be as juſtly applied to other regions and people of early times, as we ſhall have occaſion to ſpecify below, where we purpoſe to enquire, when the vice of ſlaughtering and devouring the brute creation began, and conſider its fatal conſequences, *as one of the great roots of phyſical and moral evil in the world.* But before we proceed to this enquiry, it is neceſſary to obviate another plea in defence of this error, which juſts now ſtarts up, and arreſts our intended courſe.

121. Man,

121. Man, when hard preſſed, and at a loſs for rational argument (for he cannot eaſily and with a good grace give up the ſavory fleſh-pots of *Egypt)*, has advanced a *third plea* in ſupport of his practice, which he would alſo ſanctify into *a plea of neceſſity*, which is, that without the uſe of animal food, and vinous and ſpiritous potations, the human form could not be ſuſtained in full health and vigor.——Surely man cannot be in earneſt, when he urges this as argument, for not only the experience of nations, but daily inſtances in multitudes of individuals are againſt him.——The ſuperlatively wiſe and inſpired DANIEL, in his firſt chapter, exhibits to mankind a fine leſſon, which comes in point to invalidate this futile plea.——The King of *Babylon*, deſirous of having ſome youths of the royal *Hebrew* line trained up in his court, "*to ſtand* "*before the King*," he appointed them a daily proviſion of the *King's meat*, and *the wine* which he drank; but *Daniel*, anxious that neither himſelf nor the royal youths ſhould be defiled, rejected *the meat and wine*, and making an intereſt with the governor that was ſet over them, "beſeeched "him to give them *pulſe to eat*; *and water to* "*drink*;" the reſult was, that at the expiration of the time prefixed by way of experiment, "*their countenances appeared fairer*, "*and*

" *and fatter in flesh than all the children who*
" *had eat the portion of the King's meat.*"— Thus we humbly conceive that we have fairly driven man from every subterfuge, every retrenchment, which he has cast up in defence of the cruel and unnatural practice of *killing* and *eating* his fellow-brethren of the animal creation, without *any necessity*, *or other rational plea*, *for so doing*.

122. When, or in what period of the world, man fell into the fatal error of murdering and feeding upon his elder brethren of the creation, is difficult to fix with any precision, although we may with much probability conclude it had a very early rise; as it has been observed, man grows not wicked all at once, so we may rationally conjecture this vice became not general, until within the space of three thousand years back;—that copious fountain of wisdom and knowledge, that incessant advocate for the rationality and morals of the brute creation, the learned author of the Turkish Spy, recites many authorities in proof, that this vice was not practised in the *first times*, but was an innovation on the primitive manners of mankind; he honors the Brachmans of *India*, and seems to be a convert to the doctrine of the Metempsychosis; he stands amazed at the signal circumstances, pecu-

liar only to the SANSCRIT, and the four books of the law (*i. e. the Chartah Bhade of Bramah*), written in that language; he thinks it ſtrange that no hiſtory ſhould mention *ſo divine a ſpeech*, and draws his concluſion of the ſuperior antiquity of the Bramins, their language and books, to the reſt of the world,—"*in regard that they fall not* "*within any records, ſave their own.*"——He then, with great truth, remarks, that the people of *Indoſtan* are the only people in the world who have, in all ages to this day, paid a ſtrict obedience to that firſt injunction and law of GOD, *Thou ſhalt neither kill, nor eat thy fellow-creatures of the brute creation.* He alſo inſtances, that the primitive *Perſian* and *Egyptian* Magi abſtained from and prohibited this vice to their followers, and this abſtinence remained inviolate ſo long as they retained the pure theology which had been communicated to them by their neighbors the Bramins of *Indoſtan*. ——He alſo notes, that the ancient Druids of *Gaul* and *Britain*, who taught the doctrine of the Metempſychoſis, abſtained from killing and eating animal food, and remarks likewiſe, that the firſt people of the world made offerings to the gods only of the fruits and flowers of the earth, which has been, and is uniformly the practice of the people

ot

of *Indoſtan* to this time.—He recites, that the precepts of *Triptolemus* and *Draco*, the firſt law-givers of the *Athenians*, comprehended the whole ſyſtem of virtue and piety in practiſing theſe few following rules: "Let
" it be an eternal ſanction to the *Athenians*,
" to adore the immortal Gods, to revere the
" departed heroes, to celebrate their praiſe
" with ſongs, and the *firſt-fruits of the*
" *earth, and neither to kill man or beaſt*."

123. In whatſoever age this depravity took its riſe, it is plain it obtained not generally all at once, but by ſlow degrees; and as every *other* ſpecies of wickedneſs gained footing and flouriſhed in the world, ſo we may ſuppoſe this alſo grew to maturity with them, and became univerſal, except in the ſingle inſtance of a whole nation, marked above. The uſe of vinous, and afterwards ſpiritous potations, we conceive had a later riſe, and was a natural conſequent of an appetite previouſly vitiated by the unnatural reliſh of animal food; and we think it moſt probable, that both theſe vices firſt took poſſeſſion of man in ſome period of what *Bramah* calls the *Tirtah Jogue*, or ſecond age, immediately ſucceeding the *Suttee Jogue*, or age of truth and righteouſneſs; for it was in the *Tirtah*

Jogue * (which may be properly ſtiled the firſt age of evil) that the influence of *Moiſaſoor* or *Satan* brought about the *ſecond* defection of one-third of the angelic ſpirits; and as his power increaſed during the ſucceeding *Duapaar* and *Kolee Jogues* †, ſo we may rationally couclude the *two vices* under conſideration became univerſal (excepting the *Gentoos*) about the middle of the *Kolee Jogue* or age of corruption, that is, about three thouſand years ago: how it happened that the *Gentoos* alone, either never fell into the vice of killing and eating the animal beings, or were reclaimed from it, is eaſily accounted for, from God's poſitive injunctions againſt it ‡, delivered by the mouth and ſcriptures of *Bramah*; for as to the uſe of vinous and ſpiritous liquors, it ſhould ſeem that was a vice not in being at the period in which that inſpired legiſlator revealed his *Chartah Bhade Shaſtah* to the *Gentoos*, to wit, 4870 years ago, for if it had, it is moſt probable it would not have eſcaped his notice and prohibition;—and yet the *Gentoos* abſtain as religiouſly from the one vice as the other, probably from ſome poſitive injunctions laid upon them

* Vide Part II. p. 68 and 69.
† Ibid, p. 70 and 71.
‡ Ibid, p. 51 and 52.

in the *Insoff Bhade*, or fourth book of *Bramah*'s Shastah.

124. To give the devil his due, it must in justice be acknowledged, that the introduction of these two *first-rate vices* was a master-piece of politics in *Moisasoor or Satan*, who alone was capable of working so diabolical a change in rational intellectual beings. He had prescience enough to foresee, by reasoning from causes to effects, that if he succeeded in the attempt, he should be able in time to counteract and utterly circumvent the merciful intentions of GOD towards the delinquent spirits. To this he was stimulated by several different motives, all tending to the same end;—he considered them, from their persevering in penitence and holiness throughout the *Suttee Jogue*, as in a state of rebellion against himself, and with good reason, as they had acknowledged him for their King and Leader in heaven;—he had also, with grief and indignation observed, that during *that age* multitudes of them (on whose fidelity he had depended) had escaped out of his reach, and were advancing through the regions of purification towards their lost seats, and that probably the next age would leave him without any other subjects but those of *his*

own

own tribe, whoſe allegiance to him he knew was inviolable; therefore, effectually to guard againſt a farther revolt of his old aſſociates, he meditated the infernal ſcheme of tempting them to the uſe of animal food, and intoxicating drinks, as an infallible expedient that would fully anſwer all his diabolical purpoſes. For, *firſt*, he knew he ſhould thereby lead them into ſin and diſobedience, by a breach of an expreſs command and prohibition of their GOD. *Secondly*, he was ſenſible that thoſe unnatural aliments would inflame and exalt the deſires *of the fleſh*, above the rule and dominion *of the ſpirit*. *Thirdly*, he knew alſo, that by natural conſequence *diſeaſes* would enſue, that muſt aſſuredly *abridge* their *term of probation* in the form *of man*, which would be no inconſiderable point gained. *Fourthly*, his penetration made it obvious to him, that this *inflamed ſtate of the human body* (from the continued acceſſion of animal ſalts and juices, heated and fermented by the auxiliary force of ſpiritous liquors) would be propagated through the ſpecies; and that the ſure effects would be, their *giving birth* amongſt them to a train of monſtrous, unnatural, violent, and conſequently ungovernable paſſions, as luſts of every kind and ſpecies, ambition, avarice, envy, hatred, and malice, &c. that would regularly produce *a progeny* of concomitant actions and effects; as, invasions of property, contentions, wars, battles, murders, and sudden deaths. *Fifthly*, he foresaw a farther favorable consequence from the indulgence of these passions, as that they would, by the natural force of their operation, engage and confine their pursuits to the temporary sensual enjoyments and acquisitions of *this world only*, and cause them to lose sight of *the next*, as well as of *the means* by which they were destined to regain it. These deviations from the path marked out for them, *Satan* knew would in the end estrange their GOD from them, and that they and their posterity would become *his own*, from generation to generation.

125. It is worth enquiry, by what system of craft *Moisasoor, or Satan*, could possibly induce rational beings so widely to swerve from their obedience, and from their original nature and dignity, into that of lions, tigers, wolves, &c. beasts of prey; nay, to exceed them in every kind of vicious refinement, and to leave them so far behind in the race of luxurious, voluptuous gluttony, besides the *exalted invention* of either entirely divesting themselves of their senses and reason, or of turning them from their bias, by the licentious guzzle of wine and spirits;

an enchanting relifh and enjoyment, which the brutes have not yet arrived to, one fpecies of them only excepted, which approach in kind the neareft to our own, viz. the Satyr, Oronootan, Baboon, and others of the fame race, all of which (the firft excepted) we have feen fmoke and drink until they became as completely beafts *as man himfelf*; fo that man has not fo much caufe to plume himfelf upon this glorious acquifition, as he poffibly and vainly may have flattered himfelf withal.—But, not to lofe fight of our enquiry by any farther reflections on thefe grievous truths, fo degrading to humanity,—we may fuppofe, that *Satan*, having had experience that the angelic fpirits, in their fuperior and pre-exiftent ftate, had not been proof againft his artful feductions, began his operations, and exerted his influence, firft upon thofe who were appointed to prefide over the ceremonies of religious worfhip, rightly judging, that if he could corrupt thofe who had the lead on earth, the reft would fall an eafy prey; he was aware, that if he abruptly propofed the deftruction of their fellow-creatures, without fome fpecious plea, human nature might ftart at the propofition: he therefore cunningly fuggefted the fanctifying their murder by offering them up in facrifice, as a work that would be moſt acceptable to the Deity; he doubtleſs likewiſe inſinuated, they would thereby not only do a thing pleaſing to God, but alſo render a ſignal ſervice to their delinquent brethren, who they knew were impriſoned in the brute forms, the ſhortening whoſe lives would expedite their progreſſive advance to that of man, from which form alone they could regain their loſt ſtations in the celeſtial regions. That this was an argument *Satan* laid no ſmall ſtreſs on, appears obvious from this, that it has been frequently made uſe of by ſeveral ancient prieſts and philoſophers, *his faithful deputies*, in juſtification of the inhuman practice.—This great point gained, *Satan* met with little difficulty in prevailing on them to taſte; and thus by degrees the killing and eating the moſt innocent ſpecies of theſe devoted miſerable beings, became an eſtabliſhed *religious cuſtom* all over the world; a practice, ſay the Bramins, which the devil himſelf could *only* have forged.——Yet *Satan* thought himſelf not quite ſecure of his votaries, without playing an after-game that would infallibly work out their future perdition; therefore his next ſtep was to influence them to extend their *religious ſacrifices* to their *own ſpecies:* to bring them to this ſupreme pitch of wicked ſuperſtition, he he found ſome difficulty, but at length prevailed, by inſinuating, that they would thereby not only more effectually deprecate the diſpleaſure and vengeance of the gods, but alſo free the ſouls of thoſe who were thus devoted, from future tranſmigrations through the mortal brute forms of puniſhment and purgation.—If any of our readers doubt the addreſs and ſucceſs of *Satan* in this arduous attempt, we have only to recommend them to the peruſal of the hiſtories of the ancient *Phenicians*, *Tyrians*, and *Carthaginians*, who were all *ſhoots* from the *Chaldean ſtock*, and alſo the hiſtory of the *Canaanites* in our Old Teſtament.——*Satan* ſtill thinking his ſcheme defective, gave the finiſhing ſtroke to it, by ſuggeſting the practice of pouring out *libations* of wine to the gods, without which the ceremonies of religious ſacrifices would be imperfect; this obtained, he left them to themſelves, knowing, that as they had ſo readily been induced to eat of the one, they would of courſe make as licentious a uſe of the other; and that he ſhould, from the natural united effects of both, always find them in a proper ſtate to receive any diabolical impreſſions he ſhould in future ſuggeſt to them, by his own immediate operation on them, or by thoſe of his infernal agents:—and thus, although

though he had failed of acquiring *ſupreme worſhip* in heaven, he at length effectually obtained it on earth.

126. We may with probability conclude, that ſome ages (although not many) might have elapſed before the laity came in either for a bit or a ſup of thoſe religious ſacrifices; that theſe obſerving (by the inſtigation of *Satan)* how their prieſts *piouſly devoured them*, began to demur againſt ſupplying them with victims, unleſs they alſo came in for a ſhare, which at laſt they obtained; the prieſts ſtill reſerving the moſt delicious morſels for themſelves.——And thus, in proceſs of time, both prieſts and laity killed and eat the brute creation in common, without even *the pretence* of religious motives, or indeed any principle at all; a point which *Satan* foreſaw they would in the end arrive at, and the event confirmed the ſagacity of his judgment in forming a plan which at once afforded him a triumph over GOD *and man.*

127. Having above, we humbly conceive, made it manifeſtly appear, to the full conviction of every unprejudiced reader, that the *two vices* which we are combating have been, and ſtill are, the pernicious

roots

roots from which all moral evils ſprang, and continue to flouriſh in the world; permit us next to repeat, that (according to the ſhewing of the philoſophers, moraliſts, divines, and hiſtorians of all nations) *there has been an utter depravity in mankind in every part of the known earth, from the earlieſt records of time.* Let any caſuiſt aſſign any *other adequate cauſe* for this univerſal depravity and corruption of the ſpecies, that will account for this phenomenon, better than thoſe which we have above attributed it to, and we will moſt readily give up our ſyſtem;—*a cauſe* there muſt be ſomewhere, and that a general one too, that could produce ſuch *uniform effects.*——Divines point out no other cauſe than that we are undoubtedly under *the influence of the devil.* This we know as well as they, but they ſeem not to know *how* it happened that we came under that direction; all the learned of the world concur in the opinion that *there was a time* when *primitive man* was not under his dominion: the angels *continued good* for a long ſpace before they fell a ſacrifice to his ſeductions, and their own ambitious folly; and ſo they did again for an age, when doomed to animate mortal forms on earth, for their firſt tranſgreſſion; and they perſevered in angelic virtue until *Satan* projected the introduction of thoſe *two vices,*

 which

which he was ſenſible would infallibly work ſuch a change in the human body as would of courſe impair it, and conſequently that the free uſe, exerciſe, and operation of the *ſpirit's* intellectual powers of rectitude would be impeded, and liable to perverſion by foreign influence, which otherwiſe would have remained in full force and vigor, as is verified by many inſtances on record, where man, by abſtaining from theſe *capital vices,* has kept his ſoul in ſuch a ſtate as to reſiſt every effort *of Satan* to provoke him to ſin.

128. When the cauſe of any diſeaſe is diſcovered, it amounts to more than half a cure. Would man exert his intellectual powers, he would ſoon pull down what *Satan* has been ſo many ages erecting; his empire has acquired no ſtability but from our eaſy ſubmiſſion to his diabolical ſuggeſtions; and that in ſuch wiſe, that we can now hardly be ſaid to have any claim to that original free agency given to us, for the very purpoſe of withſtanding his influence; remove the cauſe, the effect ceaſes. When man returns to his natural, primitive, ſimple aliments, his inordinate deſires, his paſſions, and their direful iſſue, will as naturally ſubſide, as they roſe; then we may form a well-grounded hope of the renewal

renewal and reſtoration of the *primitive age* of purity and holineſs; that *halcyon age*, when man banqueted with innocence and content upon the delicious produce of his parent earth, without a thought of killing and eating his fellow animals;—that age, wherein the feathered tribe could in freedom and ſecurity range in their proper element without dread or apprehenſion of the cruel fowler;—when the roes and hinds, with the timorous hares, might gambol and ſcamper at pleaſure over the boundleſs plains, without the riſk of being ſcattered and drove, in protracted terrors and diſmay, to the mountains, rocks, and brakes for ſanctuary againſt the purſuit of the ruthleſs hunter;—when the ſcaly independent race enjoyed at large their watery courſe, without moleſtation, from the artful wiles of the inſidious angler;—when the ſea remained yet unexplored, and COMMERCE, that *bane* (falſely called the cement) of mankind, had not a being, and was not, as now, an inſtrument in the hands of *Satan* to excite the ſpecies to invaſions, fraud, and blood; the natural produce of the earth in every region ſupplied its offspring with all that was uſeful and neceſſary, becauſe men were ſtrangers to irregular deſires, and we have no *ſolid reaſon* to imagine its inhabitants were leſs numerous then, than now.

As

As the wickedneſs and unbounded violence of man brought on a rueful change on the face of the globe, ſo we might rationally hope and expect, that on an univerſal return to his *primitive goodneſs*, GOD would reſtore to him his habitation, in all its original beauty and *natural fertility*.——This happy reſtoration would man eaſily accompliſh, if he prevailed with himſelf to abſtain from theſe two capital vices, which were, as before obſerved, the parents of every other ſubſequent tranſgreſſion on earth;—JUSTICE would then return in freſh luſtre from her long baniſhment, accompanied by the lovely train of *temperance*, *harmony*, *reciprocal benevolence*, and *laſting peace*; HAGGARD DISEASE would be drove into a longer baniſhment than even *Juſtice* ſuffered, and (like her) only be known *by name*.——DEATH would be commanded to ſtand aloof, that man's happy term of probation on earth might be extended to a greater length, as a means for his future ſalvation.——Then, and then only, may we hope to ſee and feel the ſacred doctrines of *Chriſt*'s goſpel operate *univerſally* on mankind, by producing a general rectitude of morals and piety.——We are not ſo ſanguine as to expect that this wondrous change would be brought about in *one generation*, but the *next* would moſt ſenſibly experience

its

its happy effects, and *Satan* would ſoon find himſelf repulſed and baffled in all his cunning and deep planned machinations, and be obliged to retreat with diſgrace, and ſeek an empire in ſome other region of the univerſe.

129. Now, as it appears beyond a controverſy, that the *depravity* herein lamented began in the prieſthood, who firſt unhappily fell under the influence of *Satan*'s wicked ſuggeſtions; ſo it is undoubtedly incumbent on popes, patriarchs, cardinals, archbiſhops, biſhops, prieſts, paſtors, and rulers of every church on earth, to ſet the pious example of beginning a general reformation of theſe two execrable evils, the killing and eating the rational brute creation, and guzzling vinous, &c. potations, ———They would do well to conſider, that the perſevering in theſe vices themſelves, burdens *them* with a double weight of ſin, as being the firſt aggreſſors, and as being ſpecially commiſſioned to guard the morals, and point out the right road of worſhipping the Deity to the laity; conſiderations which, joined to their known aſſiduity and anxiety for the ſalvation of mankind, leaves us not the ſmalleſt room to ſuſpect, that they would heſitate a moment to ſet ſo laudable and eſſentially neceſſary a precedent.

dent. To one unſkilled in the workings of human nature, and the powerful ſway of the prince of the air, it may appear aſtoniſhing, that ſo learned and holy a body of men ſhould continue ſo long immerſed in ſuch groſs enormities;—but when we reflect, that the *(now human)* angelic ſpirit fell when it was more pure, and endued with more ſuperior and enlarged powers, let us ceaſe to wonder at its *errors* in its preſent degraded ſtate, and aim only at the correction of *them*.—As an encouragement to attempt and proſecute this great work (we may juſtly ſay) *of ſalvation*, we ſhall remark, that as the laity too readily followed the example of their ancient reverend teachers, ſo it may be reaſonably preſumed, they will as readily, in theſe our times, joyfully ſubſcribe to and ſupport their ſacerdotal leaders in the pious reformation of theſe unnatural and impious practices, as it would ſo manifeſtly inſure to them their *preſent*, as well as *future happy exiſtence*.

130. Before we quit this our Third General Head, we will, to enforce our arguments, take leave to preſent our readers with a lively picture of man's *primitive ſtate* in the age which we are laboring to reſtore him to; and alſo the progreſs of evil, ſuperſtition, and idolatry which *Satan* re-

ced

duced mankind to, after he had prepared them, *as above*, to receive any impreſſions he was pleaſed to meditate for their deſtruction.—Both theſe are drawn by an author profoundly ſkilled in every ſpecies of learning and wiſdom——" They went out and " in, ſlept and waked, labored and reſted, " in ſafety and quiet. Avarice, envy, and " injuſtice, had not as yet corrupted the " minds of mortals. The earth brought " forth corn, herbage, and fruits, without " the huſbandman's or gardener's labor. All " places abounded with plenty of *innocent* " refreſhments, and thoſe primitive inhabitants coveted no more. The cattle " and the bees afforded them milk and " honey, and the fountain-waters were generous as wine. This globe was a complete paradiſe, and no miſtaken zeal had " taught men *religiouſly to invade another's* " *rights, and in a pious fury to murder their* " *neighbors, in hopes of meriting heaven* " *hereafter.*——The law of nature was in " univerſal force. Every man purſued the " dictates of Reaſon, without hearkening " to religious ſophiſtry, and ſacred fables." ——" But——when (at *Satan*'s inſtigation) " the lucre of gold had corrupted men's " manners, and they, not contented with " the riches and ſweets which the ſurface " of the earth daily afforded them, had

" found

" found a way to descend into her bowels, " stung with an insatiable desire of hidden " treasures; then began injustice, oppres- " sion, and cruelty to take place. Men " made inclosures for themselves, and en- " compassed a certain portion of land, with " hedges, ditches, and pales, to fence them " from the invasions of others; for the " guilt of their own vicious inclinations " filled them with fears, and made them " jealous of one another. They built them- " selves strong holds, fortresses, castles, " and cities; and their terrors increasing " with their criminal possessions, they per- " suaded themselves that the very elements " would prove their enemies, if not pacified " by bribes and presents. Hence sprang " the first invention of altars and sacrifices, " and from these pannic fears of mortals, " the *gods* derived their pedigree; for one " built a temple to the Sun, another to the " Moon, a third to *Jupiter*, *Mars*, or the " rest of the planets. Some adored the " Fire, others the Water or Wind. Every " one set up to himself such a god as he " fancied would be propitious to him. " Thus error, being equally propagated " with human nature, they created an infi- " nite rabble of imaginary deities, paying " to those idols the supreme incommuni-

" cable

"cable honors due only to the Eternal "Eſſence, Father, and Source of all things."

Fourth General Head.

131. With our readers permiſſion, we will open this head with the following texts of *Bramah's* Chartah Bhade *,——"The "Eternal One ſpoke again and ſaid— "I have not with-held my mercy from "*Moiſaſoor*, *Rhaboon*, and the reſt of the "rebellious *debtah*;—but as they thirſted "for power, *I will enlarge their powers of* "*evil*;—they ſhall have liberty to *pervade* "*the eight boboons* of purgation and proba- "tion, and the delinquent *debtah* ſhall be "expoſed and open to the ſame temptations "that firſt inſtigated their revolt: but the "exertion of thoſe *enlarged powers* which "I will give to the rebellious leaders ſhall "be *to them* the ſource of aggravated guilt "and puniſhment; and the reſiſtance made "to their temptations by the perverted "*debtah*, ſhall be to me *the great proof* of "the ſincerity of their ſorrow and repent- "ance."——"The Eternal One ceaſ- "ed—And the faithful hoſt ſhouted forth "ſongs of praiſe and adoration, mixed with "grief and lamentation for the fate of their Fourth General Head.

* Vide Part II. p. 57.

"lapſed

" lapsed brethren.——They communed " amongst themselves, and with one voice, " by the mouth of *Bistnoo*, besought THE " ETERNAL ONE, that they might have " permission to descend occasionally to the " eight boboons of punishment, purgation, " and probation, to assume the form of " *Mhurd*, and by their presence, council " and example, guard the unhappy and " perverted *debtah*, against the further " temptations of *Moisasoor* and the rebel- " lious leaders.—THE ETERNAL ONE as- " sented, and the faithful heavenly bands " shouted their songs of gladness and thanks- " giving."

132. Before we proceed, it may to some appear necessary that we clear up a seeming contradiction in this part of Braman's scriptures.——It may be objected, that GOD, first by his sentence exposes the delinquent angels to the same temptations that influenced their revolt; and then, immediately after, permits the faithful host occasionally to descend, and guard them from the artful wiles of the tempters,——or in other words, to counteract his own decrees.— To reconcile this seeming absurdity, we have only to conceive that the faithful host foresaw, that the delinquents might not of themselves be able to withstand the superior faculties

faculties of the revolted leaders; who, it may rationally be ſuppoſed, were endued with higher powers in proportion to their original rank :—this circumſtance premiſed, we ſay, it is eaſy to imagine why GOD ſhould relent at the warm and pious interceſſion of his faithful angels, and aſſent to the auxiliary force petitioned for by the ſame interceſſion HE had before been prevailed upon to reverſe their firſt doom, and emerge them from their place of *utter darkneſs and anguiſh*, into a *pleaſing ſtate* of probation, comparatively conſidered; for, although they were ſentenced to a ſtate of degradation in their paſſage through the brute forms, yet being conſcious, from the ſentence pronounced to them by *Birmah*, that through theſe they ſhould arrive at a *form*, wherein they ſhould have powers to work out their reſtoration, their preſent ſtate muſt have appeared delectable to them, put in compariſon with the former, a ſtate of eternal deſpair and bitterneſs. Now, as the faithful hoſt had ſucceeded in the *firſt inſtance*, why ſhould they not in the ſecond?—They did.—Thus the ſeeming contradiction in the text vaniſhes, and at the ſame time conveys to us a uſeful and comfortable moral, to wit, that the prayers and ardent ſolicitations of *good beings* are not without their effect with a merciful deity.——The apprehensions too of the faithful host were well grounded; for even with their assistance, *Satan* proved an over-match for them both, and so continues to this day.

133. The visible or invisible ministration, or interposition of angelic beings in the concerns of mortals, is a doctrine which carries with it the sanction of the three great divine revelations, the *Shastah*, the *Old* and *New Testament*, as well as the concurring opinion of all mankind; and therefore we may justly rank it as one of the *primitive truths*, which had the most undoubted evidence for its birth and propagation in the *first times*.—From this doctrine (a relative of the Metempsychosis) flowed the first principle of the Manichean system originally broached by the *Persian* Magi, amongst other mutilated tenets of the *Chartah Bhade*;—the first principles of this *primitive truth* were simple and intelligible, but (in common *with the rest of the primitive truths)* mankind in process of time lost sight of it; and being unable to account for the mixture of *good* and *evil* which appeared in their existence, they rashly propagated the horrible doctrine of two absolute and independent divinities that governed the universe, each of diametrically opposite

 natures;

natures; not adverting, that a ſingle conſideration which preſented itſelf daily to them, was ſufficient to refute a doctrine which at once wickedly deſtroyed the very exiſtence of a Deity and Providence; whereas, had not *Satan* hoodwinked their underſtanding, they might have ſeen, that as no ſtate whatſoever could poſſibly be governed by two independent powers, without falling into anarchy and confuſion; ſo much leſs could the univerſe:—but from the cauſes above and elſewhere aſſigned, it is no wonder that mankind fell into a million of abſurdities, not leſs iniquitous than this.

134. The mixture of good and evil *in this world* flowed naturally from the *ſecond* angelic defection in the human form, as inevitable effects from adequate cauſes; for theſe beings were ſo ſtruck with the unexpected mercy of their Creator, in affording them a trial and term of probation, in a world replete with every beauty and accommodation beyond their deſert; that they continued truly ſenſible of that grace *for a ſpace*, diſtinguiſhed by the ancient poets and philoſophers by the title of the golden age, by *Bramah*, as the age of truth and holineſs; and it is reaſonable to believe, that during that period, many of them regained

their celeſtial habitations; and equally probable, that whilſt they continued in this ſtate of general contrition, neither natural or moral evil had a footing in this globe, but that the former commenced and kept pace with the latter; and it is a well grounded opinion of philoſophers and divines, that during the *primitive age*, this globe was not ſubject to thoſe convulſive viciſſitudes of ſtorms, earthquakes, deluges, &c. nor the animal forms to peſtilential or other diſeaſes, which moral evils produced at the beginning of the *ſecond age*, when the ſecond defection of the angelic beings under *mortal forms* took place as before noticed: then it was, that man began to kill and eat his brethren of the creation, the brute animals; and in proceſs of time to kill and eat one another;—then began contentions for property and power, which produced invaſions, murders, and every ſpecies of cruelty amongſt themſelves;—then began the contention between the elements by the deſignation of GOD, for the puniſhment of the ungrateful delinquents; and then alſo began the contention between the good and evil ſpiritual beings, the one laboring to recover them to their duty, the other to ſeduce them from it. Here we would ſtrenuouſly recommend to our readers the peruſal of the pious, forcible, and judicious

dicious reaſoning of the Rev. Mr. *Dean*, (before cited) in the firſt volume of his eſſay on the future lives of the brute creation, where he unanſwerably proves that moral tranſgreſſions were the cauſes of phyſical evils, although he ſeems a ſtranger to the *true reaſon, a priori, why they ſhould be ſo.*

135. The learned *Baxter* concurs with the Bramins, touching the exiſtence of evil ſpirits; and reaſon, joined to the conſideration of the goodneſs of God, naturally leads us to conclude, that if evil ſpirits have exiſtence and power, there muſt alſo be good ones.—His words are theſe: "The "*eaſtern* philoſophers aſſert, that there are "living beings exiſting ſeparate from mat-"ter; that they act in that ſtate upon our "bodies, and provoke our ſleeping viſions." —And he cites *Plutarch* in the inſtances of *Brutus* and *Dion*, ſaying, "We muſt own "with *the old philoſophers*, that there are "bad ſpirits who envy good men, and en-"deavour to ſtumble them, leſt going on "in the ways of virtue, they ſhould enjoy "a better lot than themſelves." And our learned divine adds in another place, "That "theſe *bad ſpirits are permitted* to excite "dreams that frequently degenerate into "awaking poſſeſſions, madneſs, idiotiſm, "&c. and by ſuch an *aſcendance, miſlead*

" *the soul*:"—From the same eastern sages, he might have known that there exist also *good spirits* who voluntarily endeavor to counteract the bad.

136. During the *primitive age*, it should seem that *Satan* and his associate leaders had small, if any influence in the world; he appears (like an able politician) only to wait for proper times and seasons to exert his abilities in:—he could not but know that the delinquents were now as much stunned with the unhoped-for mercy of GOD, as they had been before by his vengeance, and therefore that this could be no favorable juncture to operate upon them:—But he also knew (as is the case with all rebels) that mercy would have no long effect upon them; that the embers of rebellion in them were only smothered, but not extinguished; and that there was only wanting a proper period and occasion to blow them up, and make them blaze again with greater fury: he judged that they would in time (allured by the delicious enjoyments of their region of probation) forget both the torments and despairing anguish they had suffered in the *region of utter darkness*, as well as the mercy that had redeemed them from it; and he was perfectly right in his conclusion.——The

means

means this arch-traitor adopted to bring about his purposes of evil, both *natural and moral*, we have developed in our foregoing General Head, omitting one circumstance of encouragement as more properly applicable here—*Satan* and his leaders, although sensible that the powers of the faithful angelic beings they had to contend with, were equal with their own, yet they were not dismayed; knowing that the propensity to evil in the objects on whom their efforts were to be tried, would turn the balance in their favor.

137. It is most probable, that the earliest records that we have of the world, and the transactions of it, may be properly termed *modern times*, when put in comparison with those that preceded; at least we have no solid reasons, or certain guides, for our thinking otherwise. Howsoever the ancient records of the universe asserted to be in the possession of the *Indians*, *Chinese*, and *Egyptians*, stand discountenanced by the narrow and limited conjectures of the moderns, yet unprejudiced reason (as before hinted) recoils at the supposition of the world's being in the *juvenile state* given to it by the chronologers of *Europe*; when, from all its interior and external phænomena, it appears to stand on its last legs, or rather sup-

ported only on its crutches;—*Herodotus* was certainly a wiſe man, and although he recites many extravagant legends of the *Egyptian* prieſts, yet it is eaſy to diſtinguiſh by his manner of tranſmitting them to poſterity, what he really had ſufficient grounds to credit, and what to laugh at, as fabulous: amongſt the former, is *the antiquity of their records*;——if theſe extended eighteen thouſand years back from the period in which he wrote, then who knows what revolutions in ſtates, empires, learning, arts and ſciences may not have happened in the times preceding *their records? all thoſe phænomena, like birds of paſſage,* taking their flight from one region to ſettle for a time in another; or, to purſue our ſimile in a different ſpecies of thoſe animals, diving and ſinking in one place to riſe in another far diſtant; as we have obſerved to have happened *to them all*, within the period of our ſcanty and imperfect chronicles: and yet, ſcanty as they are, it is from *theſe alone*, we are enabled to form a rational ſurmiſe, or judge with any preciſion of the paſt; *from theſe* then we are ſupported in ſaying, that *the foundation* of every known empire, kingdom, and ſtate of the world, was *originally laid in blood and carnage*; and by theſe roſe to the ſummit of their greatneſs, and by theſe fell to perdition.

138. On

138. On a retroſpect into authentic hiſtory, we ſurvey the fatal and ſanguinary iſſue of the civil wars of all nations; wherein thoſe allied by the moſt ſacred ties, engaging on different parties, cut the throats of each other, and gloried in the ſacrifice.——Let us next take a view of the lamentable effects of invaſion, from the Pagan and idolatrous *Seſoſtris*, to the Chriſtian *Spaniard*'s invaſion of *Peru* and *Mexico*, in the proſecution of which laſt only, no leſs than twenty millions of unoffending people were ſlaughtered without mercy.——Let us obſerve the horrid concomitants of thoſe contentions, impiouſly ſtiled, *religious wars*; wherein religion, intended to correct our morals, and eſtabliſh peace on earth, has been made the ſtalking-horſe, to cover the perpetration of the moſt cruel and atrocious crimes, dictated by ambition, and an inſatiable thirſt for dominion and property; witneſs the progreſs of the *Koran*, eſtabliſhed by fire and ſword throughout the greateſt part of the world, the cruſades, (let us not call them Chriſtian) and the endleſs contentions between the profeſſors of Chriſtianity themſelves, and the dire maſſacres they have been the cauſe of;—religious wars had no exiſtence in the annals of antiquity; this was a ſpecies of wickedneſs reſerved for later, and more enlightened times, introduced

troduced by the perverſion of *Chriſt*'s goſpel.—Let us laſtly conſider the diſmal effects of *all wars*, even to the preſent hour, and the univerſal depravity of man; and then ſee if we can find any *adequate cauſe* for theſe horrible enormous *effects*, than that above aſſigned, namely, *the influence of Satan*, under which the whole race of angelic delinquent human beings unhappily fell, at the cloſe of the *primitive age*; a dominion he has preſerved ever ſince over the ſpecies, a very few individuals in every age and every region excepted, who have nobly withſtood his wicked machinations, and utmoſt efforts, to pervert them; a conſideration which amounts to proof, that *all might* partake of this celeſtial triumph *if they would*, by joining the exertion of their *own powers* with the faithful angelic beings, who are ever at their call; for we have no more cauſe to doubt their exiſtence and activity, than we have to doubt thoſe of the air and wind, although inviſible to us.

139. God, conſcious that he has endowed us with ſufficient powers of reſiſtance, abandons us to ourſelves; and it is by the neglect of thoſe powers that ſtill *man goes on as the devil drives him*, and muſt neceſſarily ſo continue, until he again, by the full exertion of his divine intellectual faculties, recovers

covers that purity he possessed in the primitive age; the full exertion of those powers he can only acquire, *by restoring the body, and its plastic juices, to their primitive natures*, thereby freeing the soul from those impeding chains which he himself has forged for her; the *sure means* for accomplishing this great end, and setting *Satan* at defiance, we have already pointed out; until then, we remain entangled in the snares and nets of the devil, and, like other animals so caught, shall persist in biting, scratching, worrying and murdering one another to the end of time.——Here we beg leave to dissent from the too generally received opinion, that the ancient and modern heroes, conquerors, leaders of battles and invasion, allies of death and the devil, so much celebrated in story (as your *Sesostrises*, *Semiramises*, *Cyruses*, *Crœsuses*, *Cambyses*, *Dariuses*, *Xerxes*, *Alexanders*, *Cæsars*, *Mahommeds*, and a very long &c. &c. &c.), were or are instruments, or a scourge in the hands of God for the chastisement of mankind, because we think there appears *no necessity* for such an interposition; nor can we bring ourselves to believe that God ever did, or does consent, to those furious massacres of the species, recorded in the annals of the world, and perpetrated to this day: why should

we

we be driven to ſo unneceſſary a concluſion, when we ſee, that the genius of man, by the guidance of *Satan*, is quite adequate to the purpoſe? nor have we a doubt, but that he takes ſpecial care, firſt to infuſe into his hero a proper diſpoſition for blood and conqueſt, and then places a *prime leader of his own* at his elbow, to keep him ſteady, and proof againſt the horrid and piercing groans, ſhrieks, and cries, of ſlaughtered parents, huſbands, and brothers, raviſhed wives and daughters, entertained at the ſame time with the heart-rending ſcreams of their expiring infants; for howſoever heroes and their blood-thirſty followers may, by cuſtom and practice, be inured to theſe *glorious ſcenes*, yet it might ſometimes ſo happen, that the feelings of humanity would ſtart up in their breaſt, and were they not immediately ſuppreſſed, *Satan*'s main purpoſe would be defeated; for the greater number of the ſpecies cut off ſhort *of their term of probation*, the farther his iniquitous end is anſwered; and therefore he never fails to excite to murder upon every favorable occaſion, no matter of what kind, whether of man or brute;——we likewiſe think it moſt probable, that, upon extraordinary incidents, where he might have doubts of the addreſs or influence of a *deputy*,

puty, he did ſome of the *firſt-rate heroes* the honor of accompanying them *himſelf* in their expeditions, particularly *Cyrus*, *Alexander*, *Cæſar*, *Mahommed*, and *Fernando Cortez*, with other captains both of ancient and modern date, needleſs to mention.——Reſpecting the deſtruction of *Babylon*, ſo minutely foretold by the prophets *Jeremiah* and *Iſaiah*, where " their young men and " their hoſt were to be utterly cut off by " the ſword, their houſes ſpoiled, their " wives and virgins raviſhed, thoſe in the " womb not ſpared, and their children's " brains daſhed out againſt the ſtones be- " fore their eyes;"——if we allow the prophets to have been juſtly inſpired in the circumſtances of this deſolation, yet they certainly were miſtaken as to the *firſt mover of it*, and, by ſome egregious error or other, deprived *Satan* of the honor of this glorious enterprize.

140. By what has been ſaid, and with a reference to the Metempſychoſis, it need not appear ſtrange, that the world has at all times been equally populous, reſpecting both man and beaſt, or very nearly ſo; for ſo few of the delinquent ſpirits in every age have tranſmigrated to heaven, that they have been hardly miſſed on earth.——Here, we know, will be objected to us *Moſes*'s account of

of the deluge, and the new propagation of all the animal ſpecies, from the ſtock which *Noah* ſaved in the ark.——To this we ſay, that there have been many ſolid arguments urged againſt the univerſality of *Moſes*'s deluge, which have never been refuted to the full ſatisfaction of inquiſitive reaſon.—It is true, we have *Moſes*'s *ipſe dixit* for the deſtruction of all, in whoſe noſtrils were the breath of life; but how came it to paſs, that a race of animals, as numerous, if not more ſo, than thoſe of the earth, eſcaped his notice ſo far, as not even to be worthy the mention, namely, the fiſhes of the ſeas and rivers? in their noſtrils were ſurely the breath of life. But the cauſe of *Moſes*'s ſilence reſpecting them is obvious; he knew the difficulty of conceiving how their deſtruction could be accompliſhed in their proper element, on which the moſt tremendous ſtorms and hurricanes are matters of ſport and paſtime to them; therefore he took the wiſer part in paſſing them over in ſilence, as having no exiſtence in the ſcale of beings. This conſideration proves, that whatſoever the deluge might have been, the deſtruction of the animal creation *was not univerſal*; then ſuffer us to aſk, in juſtice to the reſt of the devoted animals, what exemption this peculiar race was intitled to, that they did not participate in the general

wreck?

wreck?—God's juſtice, mercy, and providence are equal to all, "a ſparrow falls not "to the ground unnoticed of him"—therefore it ſhould ſeem, that the ſpirits animating the inhabitants of the waters, ſhould at that period have been *leſs guilty* than the other terreſtrial ſpecies; but that that might not have been the caſe, we ſhall ſhew preſently, and demonſtrate, that the ſeeming partial favor of Providence for that race can be only accounted for from the doctrine of the Metempſychoſis.

141. Let us ſuppoſe, for argument-ſake only (making a large allowance for the liberal genius of travellers), that every nation in the world retains a tradition of a deluge, yet this by no means invalidates the opinion that that of *Moſes* was only local and partial.——Men had ſinned, although probably not in equal degree, nor at the ſame period of time, in every region of the habitable world, and therefore all might merit the chaſtiſement of God, ſome at one time, and ſome at another; therefore why may we not ſuppoſe, that he was pleaſed to make uſe of a ſimilar mode of puniſhment to them all at different periods:—thus, in our own times, we ſee ſome nations ſuffer under earthquakes, ſtorms, inundations, and peſtilences,

ſtilences, &c. at one time, and others at another; and thus all nations may have retained a tradition of a deluge; univerſal as to each particular, but ſtrictly and properly ſpeaking, local only.—On this probable ſurmiſe we need no longer puzzle ourſelves with the difficulty of peopling *America* either with man or beaſts, or any of thoſe numerous iſlands which lie very far detached from any continent, and yet at their firſt diſcovery were found populous and flouriſhing in both.——But leaving this diſputed point of the univerſality of *Moſes*'s deluge, as many others have done before us, juſt as we found it, and as one of thoſe occult events in which mankind will never univerſally concur, we will ſuppoſe it to have been preciſely and minutely as *Moſes* has deſcribed it.

142. Then it follows, that the ſouls of every being were ouſted of their mortal habitation for a ſpace, except thoſe which animated the marine forms. Now, by *Moſes*'s ſhewing, GOD attributes no evil or wickedneſs to any of the brute creation; *nor* to the myriads of *infant innocents* ſtruggling under the bitter pangs of death in that dreadful cataſtrophe; and yet *theſe* ſuffered indiſcriminately, and in common with *guilty man.*

Now,

Now, ye divines, philosophers, sages, and moralists of the world! account for this general and undistinguished ruin of animal life, consistent with our ideas of *a just* and *merciful* God, upon any other hypothesis than that of the *Metempsychosis of Bramah*, and ye shall be to us more than our *Magnus Apollo*.—On the principles of this doctrine alone, those two divine attributes of the Deity stand confessed, and vindicated, whether applied to an universal, or partial deluge on the earth, or to any other marks of his displeasure:—death, to which man was doomed at the deluge, was no more than he was subject to before; but the destruction being so general, made it more signal: the measure of man's iniquity was more than full, it ran over; and God seemed determined, at one tremendous blow, to try if terror would not in future operate more powerfully upon them than his goodness had done. The brutes, animated by the same delinquent spirits, although under other mortal forms, had been equally guilty in their former transmigration of man, and therefore justly suffered; the infant human race were taken off, and the term of the spirits probation, with that of their parents, cut short, as the severest stroke of God's displeasure to man.——The fish, although exempted for the present from their share of the general calamity, yet partook of its consequences equal with the rest, in their future course of transmigration through other mortal forms, from the dire change in the nature of this habitable globe, whose delightful surface became rugged and inhospitable; its pure circumambient atmosphere, so essential to health and longevity, became vitiated; which, with other new and injurious phenomena in nature, contributed to shorten the date of animal life.——Then pestilence, famine, earthquakes, tempests, inundations, &c. became instruments in the hands of God for the chastisement of the delinquent spirit's second apostacy: and thus man brought upon himself accumulated *natural evils*, in consequence of his moral transgressions; oppression, war, ambition, and their cruel effects, in the hands of those spoilers of mankind *called heroes*, were instigated, as before shewn, by *another mover*.

143. We have said above, that the cutting short man's *term of probation* was the severest stroke of God's displeasure; for he alone knows how many direful vicissitudes, and variety of irksome forms the *delinquent soul* must pass through, before it receives the grace of re-entering the *human form*, for a new combat betwixt vice and virtue.——The *Egyptians*, according to *Herodotus*, fix the

the precise term of three thousand years between the *spirit*'s banishment from the human form, and its regaining that *state of probation*, from which only they can hope to transmigrate to heaven. In this opinion they were followed by *Pythagoras*, who averred his spirit animated the mortal form of *Euphorbus*, slain at the siege of *Troy* — The Bramins affix no precise space of time for the completion of this event; and teach only, that the *delinquent spirit* passes through eighty-eight mortal forms, *the species* appointed by GOD alone; so that, according to this doctrine, the space may be long or short, in proportion to the longevity or quick decay (consistent with the common course of nature) of the mortal bodies it is doomed to animate. That the determined space assigned by the *Egyptians*, was void of any solid foundation, and an innovation on the original doctrine of the Metempsychosis, appears from the consideration of the uncertain term between the dissolution of the human form, and the spirit's being allowed the grace of re-entering *any mortal form at all*:——Thus THE ETERNAL ONE, speaking in the text of *Bramah*, part 2d, p. 55.——" But it shall be,——that if
" the rebellious *debtah* do not benefit of my
" favor in the eighty-ninth transmigration
" of *mhurd* (man) according to the powers

" wherewith I will inveſt them ;——thou,
" *Sieb*, ſhalt return them *for a ſpace* into the
" *onderah*, and from thence, after a time
" which *I ſhall appoint*, *Biſtnoo* ſhall re-
" place them in the loweſt *boboon* of puniſh-
" ment and purgation *for a ſecond trial*:—
" and in this wiſe *ſhall they ſuffer*, until, by
" their repentance and perſeverance in good
" works during their eighty-ninth tranſmi-
" gration of *mhurd*, they ſhall attain the *ninth*
" *boboon*, even the firſt of the ſeven boboons of
" *purification*.—For it is decreed, that the
" rebellious *debtah* ſhall not enter the *mahah*
" *ſurgo*, nor behold my face, until they have
" paſſed the eight *boboons* of *puniſhment*, and
" the ſeven *boboons* of *purification*."—Now
it is moſt rational to conclude, that the term, or ſpace and degree of the ſpirit's ſufferings, both before it is permitted to enter any mortal body, and during its impriſonment therein, are (conformable to infinite juſtice and mercy) proportioned to its greater or leſſer degree of guilt, in its *lapſed ſtate of probation in the human form*.——This being the caſe, how greatly incumbent is it not on mankind, to exert with vigor that portion of God's divine ſpirit with which he is endowed, that he may riſe from this *gracious ſtate of trial*, to thoſe manſions of bliſs ſtill kept open for him; the more eſpecially as he has a moral certainty, that ſhould his own

powers

powers (from impeding causes to which he stands self-subjected) prove insufficient, there is *an invisible angelic aid* ready to second and support his pious endeavors.

FIFTH AND LAST GENERAL HEAD.

144. It may be remarked, that there are *two* points of *Bramah*'s doctrine, respecting the state of the spirit, after the dissolution of the human body; *the first*, its residence *for a space in the onderah*, the seat of darkness and anguish, before it is suffered to animate any mortal form at all;—*The second*, its state of purification, when by a life of purity and virtue, during its previous state of *probation*, it ceases from its mortal transmigrations.——We need not expatiate on the temporal pecuniary trade and advantages the church of *Rome* makes of *the first* of these doctrines; the leaders of that church will answer before a supreme and *infallible* judge, for that, and the multitude of other gross and extravagant principles of faith, by which they pervert the pure doctrines of Christ, and mislead the people committed to their charge; from whom the true God, and his worship, are as effectually obscured, as ever they were from the *Canaanites*, *Egyptians*, and *Tyrians* of old. Fifth General Head.

—But this by the bye; nor ſhould we have been provoked to theſe reflections, had we not ſo lately been an eye-witneſs of the corruptions, idolatries, vicious parade, and legerdemain of that mother-church of *Europe*.——That there is an intermediate ſtate of the ſpirit's purification between its deliverance from the human body, and its admiſſion to the preſence of God, is the opinion of all divines and philoſophers; and countenanced by the Chriſtian ſyſtem: no wonder then, that theſe two points of doctrine ſhould have ſo univerſally obtained, when it appears, that they hold a rank amongſt the *primitive truths*, revealed to the apoſtate angels, when doomed to take the mortal forms upon them, and are conſequently relative tenets of the Metempſychoſis.

145. The doctrine of the ſpirit's purification is evidently founded on the rational concluſion, that its various and many defilements contracted in the fleſh, render it an object unworthy of admiſſion to God, or of the ſociety of thoſe pure beings who had not known pollution, until it undergoes a perfect depuration; to accompliſh which, it was neceſſary it ſhould paſs through *ſeven regions* or ſtages of purification, according to the text of *Bramah*:

matter

matter, we know, when groſsly ſoiled, cannot be ſufficiently cleanſed *at once*; but will require the frequent reiteration of the ſame proceſs; and thus we may conceive of the ſoul: but why preciſely *Seven* gradations of cleanſings, we will not pretend to explain, nor is it a matter of much importance.—It is reaſonable to imagine, that the ſpirit's paſſage through theſe *ſeven* pure regions is retarded, or expedited, in proportion to the ſtains it had contracted during its abode in the fleſh, and the degree of its *original* tranſgreſſion; for we have no ſolid reaſon for thinking, that the apoſtate angels all equally ſinned; the *firſt movers* to ſedition and rebellion being certainly *moſt culpable*. —That *ſeven* was a myſtical number with all antiquity appears beyond all doubt: GOD reſted on the *Seventh day* according to *Moſes*; the univerſe is divided by aſtronomers into *ſeven* primary planets; the *ſeven* angels, and the *ſeven* vials of the Revelations; the *ſeven* wiſe men; the *ſeven* wonders of the world; the *ſeven* diviſions, or *parts of the world*, according to *Zoroaſter*, ſpecified in the voyage of the curious, and induſtrious *Monſieur de Perron*; wherein the reader, if he has nothing better to do, may amuſe himſelf with the rhapſodies, and theological dreams of that legiſlator of the *Perſians*; and when he has done, we dare promiſe him he will not find either his heart or his underſtanding much enlightened:—The *ſeven* heavens, and the *heaven of heavens* ſo frequently mentioned by the Jewiſh *Rabbis*, and by *Mahommed*, and the *Arabian* doctors, ſo correſpondent with *Bramah*'s *ſeven celeſtial regions of purification*, and the *mahah ſurgo*, or ſupreme heaven; and it is pretty plain, that *Mahommed*, whoſe olio, or hodge-podge of religion, was compoſed from every ſyſtem then extant, borrowed his *ſeven* heavens, and *heaven of heavens*, from the *Bramins*.

146. Reſpecting the diſſolution or deſtruction of the univerſe, or fifteen boboons of puniſhment and purification, *Bramah*'s doctrine differs from all others; in that he teaches, the deſtruction of the *firſt eight* will *precede* that of the *laſt ſeven*; at the deſtruction of the *firſt*, he marks the final day of judgment, but his text will ſpeak better for him than we can.——" When " all was huſhed! THE ETERNAL ONE " ſaid—It ſhall be—that, when the ſpace " of time, which I have decreed for the " duration of the *Dunneahoudah*, and the " ſpace which my mercy has allotted for " the probation of the *fallen debtah*, ſhall " be accompliſhed by the revolutions of " the *four Joques*—in that day, ſhould there

"be any of them, who, *remaining reprobate*, have not passed the *eighth boboon* of punishment and probation, and have not entered the *ninth boboon*, even the first boboon of purification;——thou, *Sieb*, shalt, armed with my power, CAST THEM INTO THE ONDERAH FOR EVER.——And thou shalt then destroy the eight boboons of punishment, purgation and probation, and THEY SHALL BE NO MORE.—And thou, *Bistnoo*, shalt yet for a space preserve the *seven boboons of purification*, until the *debtah*, who have benefited of my grace and mercy, have *by thee* been purified from their sin:—and in the day when that shall be accomplished, and they are restored *to their state*, and admitted to my presence,—*thou, Sieb*, shalt then destroy *the seven boboons of purification*, and—THEY SHALL BE NO MORE."——Thus, according to *Bramah*, as GOD has constructed the first eight regions for the reception, punishment, and probation of the apostate angels; so, when the term allotted for *its* duration, and *their* trial, expires, and the remaining reprobates are plunged into the place of darkness and anguish, these eight regions becoming useless, their form is destined for destruction, whilst the other seven are yet to be preserved for the gracious purposes expressed in the text.

147. This

147. This partial destruction of part of the universe carries nothing with it, incongruous to the wisdom and goodness of God, but rather exalts both.——Of all the numerous spheres or subdivisions of the fifteen primary boboons of *Bramah*, fabricated for the reception of the myriads of apostate beings, no mortal can know how many still exist in their original form, or what changes they may not have undergone;—many of them scattered through the vast expanse, may have been long (for aught we know to the contrary) reduced to their primitive *chaos*, without being missed by us, notwithstanding our busy, prying, artificial optics, to explore what does not belong to us; which researches only afford us futile matter of conjecture, whereon to found imaginary planetary systems; the one exploded, as soon as birth is given to another with more plausible appearances; thereby drawing off man's wisdom and attention from matters of more immediate and important concern to him.—Man has nothing to do in this world, if he keeps his talents properly employed, *but to explore himself*, and secure his immortal part (at its exit from the body) from future mortal chains, either in the brute or human forms.——Had that profusion of wisdom, and divine powers in man, which has in

all ages been squandered away in the pursuit of non-essentials, been applied to its proper objects; the *primitive truths* of his salvation would not have lain so long hid from him, nor he so long been a stranger to his real state and relative nature.

148. The ancient *Gentoos* celebrated the aniversary of their birth with solemn fasts and thanksgiving, succeeded by a feast of joy: this they did, upon the pious reflection, that the spirit had ceased from its transmigrations through the brute forms, and had attained to its state of probation in man; and upon this principle it was, that they celebrated in like manner the birth of their children.——We likewise celebrate the birth of our children, and theirs, and our own anniversaries; but alas! in a very different manner, and upon very different considerations;—the man who celebrates a *birth-day*, upon any other principle than that of the Metempsychosis, does it either from the incentives of folly, pride, self-love, and vanity, or from interested views of succession; motives, all most unworthy of a rational being: for man, *abstractedly considered*, has, GOD knows, little cause for pluming himself, or celebrating and rejoicing for an event which introduces him into a life fraught with many evils, inevitable, or

of

of his own procuring; ſo that the beſt of us would more ſenſibly commemorate the day of his nativity, as the poet *Dryden* makes *Marcus Antonius, in double pomp of ſadneſs*; but,—— when we conſider the ſame event with a retroſpect to the Metempſychoſis, and behold an *offending angelic being* freed from the brutal mortal chains, and entering into a ſtate wherein, by progreſſive degrees, he arrives to the full exerciſe of his divine intellectual powers, and is enabled thereby to re-aſcend to thoſe regions of bliſs, which he had too juſtly forfeited,——then he may with well-grounded reaſon annually celebrate ſo gracious an incident with pious praiſe and thankſgiving, and temperate ſocial joy and feſtivity; whether ourſelves, or any connected to us, are the objects:——otherwiſe, a ceremonial of this kind muſt appear to every *thinking being*, an empty parade of vainglory; and a mark of unaccountable infatuation, repugnant to common ſenſe.

CONCLUSION.

149. We have now, candid reader, brought our five General Heads to a cloſe; in the diſcuſſion of which, our chief aim has been the reſtoring to mankind thoſe eſſential PRIMITIVE TRUTHS, on which his real ſtate and nature originally exiſted, and ſtill exiſts; and on a due regard to which, his temporal and ſpiritual happineſs ever did, and ever muſt depend;—but yet, our taſk is not finiſhed; it remains, that we diſcipline the principal ſubjects of our labor, and draw them together in one compact body, that they may thereby acquire more ſtrength and influence than they poſſibly can, ſcattered as they are, at ſuch a diſtance from each other, as the nature of our diſquiſition required: it is alſo requiſite that we obviate ſome objections and difficulties attending our general ſyſtem, which have not yet been noticed, although we know they will ſtart up againſt us, in prejudiced, narrow, and ſelf intereſted minds;—but *theſe* are no leſs the objects of our benevolence, than the more enlarged and enlightened: we ſhall then

then conclude with a few perſuaſive reflections, that will naturally riſe from our ſubject.

150. With all humility we conceive, that we have proved beyond the power of refutation, 1ſt, That *original ſin* took its riſe in heaven, and that we have no grounds to look for it in the tranſgreſſions of *Adam* and *Eve*, or any where elſe.——2dly, That man and beaſt are either animated by the apoſtate angels, or,—that they are nothing —a mere vegetative portion of matter in the creation, and that their exiſtence at all, as intelligent beings, can only rationally be accounted for, *from the pure doctrine of the Metempſychoſis*.——3dly, That the brute creation was not made either for the uſe or dominion of man, in the ſenſe he has been pleaſed to adopt and practiſe.—4thly, That man, by murdering and eating the brute animals, was guilty of a manifeſt violation of his creator's commands, and of his own original nature.——5thly, That thoſe unnatural violations, with the auxiliary force of intoxicating potations, proved the ſource *on earth* of all evil, both phyſical and moral; producing the ſecond defection from GOD of the angelic delinquents in their mortal form of probation in man, and thereby affording *Satan* an open field, and full ſcope,

for

for all his diabolical purposes against the species.—6thly, That man has *no chance* for setting Satan at defiance, and for subduing the universal depravity of the species, and restoring piety and morals, and consequently *no chance* for salvation, but by putting a total stop to those two (or rather three, including murder) primary vices:—cut off the root, and the branches will necessarily perish; hereby the *primitive age* would be restored, and a reform in morals would probably restore also the globe to its pristine beauty and natural fertility as before urged.—7thly, That it rests on *the Clergy* of all nations to begin this general reform, for reasons before given.

151. We are sensible that there are many tribes amongst the inhabitants of every kingdom on the globe, who will be more deeply affected than others, should our general system of reducing mankind to their primitive regimen take place. Upon the return of moral rectitude into the world, laws would become useless, and consequently lawyers, and their mischievous train of retainers, will have no employment.—— Physicians and their coadjutors, upon the restoration of the human body to its original nature, will, in the second generation

at

at least, have no friendly disease for their support.--Wine-merchants, distillers, brewers, vintners, dealers in spiritous liquors, cooks, (those dangerous instruments of luxury, disease and death) and butchers, &c. will all be turned a-drift, and be forced to seek for other means of subsistence. When we become, *bona fide*, Christians, the art and destructive practice of war would cease to be the bane of mankind, and the inoffensive brute creation; and a numerous race of able-bodied beings, who have hitherto been employed only to work out the perdition of the species, would contribute to their support and maintenance, by being employed in the cultivation of the lands of the state they belong to; a work they would most certainly prefer to the trade of spilling the blood of their fellow-creatures, *they know not why*, or in support of the tyranny and wanton ambition of others.

152. Respecting the first of the two learned professions, it has long been the opinion of wise men, *that laws*, which were at first intended for the security of *property* and *peace*, are, by a strange fatality in the course of human affairs, become the greatest cause of manifold grievances to the subjects of all nations, and the great fomentors *of discord*: the

the caufe of this general perverfion is beft known to the learned profeffors; whilft the effects are felt only by their clients: and yet we think it is no very difficult tafk to account for, and explain this feeming paradox.——That there is a litigious, craving, Satanic fpirit in man, that too generally takes the rule and guidance of his actions, we believe no one will be hardy enough to difpute with us: this unhappy difpofition is encouraged by the chicane of the laws, and the addrefs of *making black appear white, and white black*; but far be it from us to impute thefe evils to the profeffors of the law, or to any defect in the laws themfelves, which can only be juftly applied in the firft inftance to the client's litigioufnefs, who defervedly fuffers when *that fpirit* will not allow him to fubmit the decifion of any matters in difpute to two or three of his rational neighbors. The one half of mankind fubfift and grow opulent by the ftupidity, wickednefs, and folly of the other: man is man's natural prey; and he that has the beft talents will be beft fed.——Be this as it may, we think, when our fyftem takes place, mankind will not fuffer any great lofs by the demolition of this learned tribe.——It is faid of a wife Emperor, when on a vifit to this and a neighboring kingdom, where he attended *the courts of justice*, "that "he declared he had but two lawyers in "his kingdom, and that he would *hang up* "*one of them as soon as he got home.*" Our historians record one of our parliaments that obtained the title of *the holy parliament*, because——*there was not one lawyer that had a seat in it.*——But these are sentiments and suggestions most unworthy, and can be only excused by the savageness and barbarity of those times.

153. Touching the second of the learned professions, it has ever been a moot point, whether it has not, at all times, and in all nations, been rather injurious than beneficial to mankind; and it has been esteemed a mark of the best regulated governments, where the fewest of this tribe have been tolerated: but this must have been in barbarous times too.

154. With regard to the next six tribes upon the list, and their confederates, we, in Christian charity, congratulate them upon the inexpressible joy and comfort they must experience, upon the near prospect of being freed from that daily load of guilt which must oppress and be a heavy weight upon their consciences, *for poisoning their fellow-*

fellow-ſubjects: an unhappy neceſſity this, which they labor under, in order to ſuit their liquors and eatables to the vitiated taſte of their cuſtomers.——As the profeſſors of theſe *crafts* are generally men ſkilled in *cunning devices*, we earneſtly recommend them to turn their genius to the improvement of their country's manufactures and agriculture, in which neceſſary branches hands are wanting: moving in theſe ſalutary ſpheres, they would become an univerſal benefit and honor to their country; whereas hitherto they have only been the dangerous inſtruments of deſtruction to their ſpecies.——But now, they will (ſome of them at leaſt) be the happy inſtruments of increaſe in every ſpecies of grain, ſo eſſential to the life of man; and thereby make ſome atonement for the immenſe quantities conſumed in fiery diſtillations, compoſitions, and potations, calculated for no other purpoſe but to burn out, *with wicked ſpeed*, the thread of human life.

155. Reſpecting *the butchers*, who merit a paragraph to themſelves, as being a tribe for whom we find ourſelves more deeply concerned than for all the reſt put together, becauſe——*humanity* and *tender feelings* being their peculiar characteriſtic, what muſt they not endure, at finding themſelves under

 der

der the fatal neceſſity of daily, nay hourly, ſhedding torrents of innocent blood, to gratify the unnatural appetites of man?——We ſolemnly proteſt, that we think there are no ſpecies of mankind more the objects of commiſeration;——we have known many of the moſt conſcientious among them deeply and piouſly lament, that ever *the trade* of killing and butchering the animal creation was transferred from *the prieſthood*, by whom it was firſt ſet up.——But we truſt the time is not far diſtant, when we ſhall be able to felicitate their being relieved from their *ſanguinary taſk*, for which we are moſt ſenſible they entertain a well-rooted and righteous averſion:——when that happy day arrives, we warmly recommend to them *to turn bakers*, for which *craft* an increaſe of profeſſors will be much wanted; and, to atone in ſome degree for the deluges of innocent blood they have ſpilt, we earneſtly intreat that they will put a ſtop——*to the adulteration of bread*, that neceſſary ſtaff of life.——In recompence for the preſent difficulties and inconveniencies which every one of theſe tribes will be liable to at their firſt ſetting off from their old track, we will ſtart one ſuggeſtion of comfort, which will be applicable to them all, and to all mankind;——whatſoever property they may be poſſeſſed of when our general ſyſtem commences,

commences, it will be preſerved to them for the noble purpoſes of ſupport for themſelves and families, and to diſtribute in acts of charity and benevolence to their poor neighbors: for now they will no longer be under the temptation, nor be ſtimulated to any deſire of gormandizing and guzzling their ſubſtance away in what is too commonly, but erroneouſly, termed *good living* and *good fellowſhip*; terms vague and unmeaning, as we hourly ſee them the ſource of the deepeſt miſeries to multitudes of individuals, whom we behold reduced from opulence to penury and want by this mode of *evil living* and *evil fellowſhip*.

156. Having thus obviated and removed, we hope to the ſatisfaction of our readers, the few foregoing difficulties which ſeemed to obſtruct our concluſion, we think it neceſſary to add, *that woman, that great mover of man*, whoſe *true* characteriſtics are ſobriety, mercy, delicacy, and tenderneſs, will prove the ſtrongeſt ſupport to the Reverend Clergy in the reform of thoſe two (three we ſhould ſay again) deadly vices we are meditating to aboliſh; and this for many other reaſons than barely the conſideration of thoſe amiable qualities juſt enumerated, although theſe cannot fail of their due influence.——On the principles of the Metempſychoſis

tempſchoſis they will have a purer enjoyment and amuſement in their favorite animals, when it proceeds from, not only rational, but pious motives; an intellectual felicity they have never yet taſted——in this way;——they will have the unſpeakable pleaſure of imagining, upon ſolid grounds, that the ſpirits which *now* animate their favorite lap-dogs, cats, parrots, ſquirrels, monkies, &c. &c. *heretofore* animated the form of a beloved friend, tender parent, huſband, brother, child, lover, &c. and their extravagant (and now irrational) fondneſs for theſe animals will then appear to be founded on principle:——mankind alſo, by their humane example, will cheriſh the brute creation, and become their defenders, in place of murdering them for ſport and paſtime, and then devouring them; a ſport and paſtime ſtill *more inhuman.*

157. We have hitherto ſpoken to mankind in general, but we now, with all humility and deference, addreſs ourſelves to the inhabitants of GREAT BRITAIN and IRELAND, but more particularly to their clergy of every denomination.——As you, Moſt Reverend, Right Reverend, and Reverend Sirs, are juſtly celebrated for your profound learning and abilities; and (what is much more to your honor and glory) diſtinguiſhed

ſtinguiſhed for the ſanctity of your lives and manners above any body of prieſthood in the known world; ſo it is the more incumbent on you *to ſtand forth to that world*, as the firſt champions for the univerſal reſtoration of morals; and by your example to ſuppreſs *three capital vices*, which are the only incentives to debauchery of every ſpecies, in every rank of mankind; the great fountain from which the torrent of immorality overflows all bounds, and muſt ſoon overwhelm us all, unleſs the timely check of ſome powerful dam be erected againſt it.——This has been the language of all times; divines have preached, moraliſts have wrote for ſucceſſive ages, but all in vain: immorality ſtill acquired freſh force. Is not the reaſon of this failure moſt obvious?—the *direful cauſes* of this general depravity have never been attended to.——The ſoul (as before urged) reaſons, and moves in conformity to the preſent ſtate of the organs and fluids of the body which it animates, and from which it receives its powers of action: this is evident from frequent inſtances of idiotiſm and inſanity: when the organs and fluids are vitiated, and reduced to any unnatural ſtate, the ſoul loſes, in a proportionate degree, its freedom and rational active powers; their influence on each other is invariable and re-

 ciprocal:

ciprocal: hence it is, that mankind by the uſe of *unnatural aliment*, may be juſtly ſaid to have been in one uninterrupted *ſtate of delirium* from the expiration of *the primitive age*; therefore it is no wonder that all reaſoning is caſt away upon beings whoſe intellectual faculties are diſordered, and in no capacity of receiving it:——mankind muſt be firſt brought to their ſenſes, before reaſon, or your pious exhortations, Reverend Sirs, can poſſibly operate upon them; but this once accompliſhed, they will then be open to every ſalutary diſcipline both of divines and moraliſts: but this moſt deſireable ſtate can be only obtained by the immediate prohibition of all animal food, and intoxicating drinks, as before often (but not too often) forcibly urged: until this is done, the daily marks of GOD's diſpleaſure, in his viſitations of peſtilences, ſtorms, inundations, famines, and earthquakes, brought to our very doors, and your ſpiritual remonſtrances will have none effect.——This being manifeſtly the caſe, and as the indulgence of any ſenſual appetites ought not to ſtand in competition with the preſent and future ſalvation of the ſouls committed to your care and guidance, you will, Moſt Reverend, Right Reverend, and Reverend Sirs, no longer give a ſanction by your practice

tice to daily murders and vices, which have proved the bane of mankind in all ages, to the preſent hour; but nobly ſuſtain the ſuperior character you have ſo worthily acquired, by preſenting yourſelves as the firſt great example of reformation.

158. As it has evidently been the general courſe of GOD's providence, *that a righteous nation ſhall be happy*, it is no marvel that the inhabitants of the globe ſhould have been, from the earlieſt accounts of time to the preſent, plunged in diſtractions, and viſited by dire calamities; for none have been righteous, no not one; at leaſt to perſeverance.——The whole continued hiſtory of the *Jews* affords a ſtriking inſtance in point: whilſt they walked in righteouſneſs, *they proſpered and were happy*; when they deviated from that path, they were puniſhed, by GOD's withdrawing from them his immediate protection, and leaving them a prey to their enemies, which we conceive to be his uſual mode of puniſhment; for, as to the portrait of him exhibited by *Moſes*, *Jeremiah*, *Iſaiah*, *Samuel*, and others of the prophets, who repreſent him as a being ſubject to the paſſions of *revenge*, *wrath*, *hatred*, and *violence*; we cannot help concluding they exceeded their commiſſions, and *humanized* their GOD to an unpardonable

able degree, to cover their own ſanguinary diſpoſitions and views: therefore we cannot prevail on ourſelves to pay a compliment to the veracity of thoſe prophets, at the expence of our GOD;——for we cannot conſiſtently conceive that GOD can be endued with any paſſions but thoſe of *love* and *pity*, without derogating from his *divine nature*: when he finds it neceſſary to puniſh us for our offences, in hopes of turning us to our duty, it is not done from motives of *revenge* and *wrath*, but thoſe of *love*; accompanied by commiſeration for our blindneſs and folly——whom the Lord loveth he chaſtiſeth.——In the above predicament ſtood the *primitive Hindoos*, who ſubſiſted for a long ſeries of ages in holineſs, peace, tranquillity, and happineſs; but in proceſs of time, although they ſtill kept themſelves free from the ſtains of murdering and eating their fellow-creatures, and the uſe of faſcinating drinks; yet, by blending idolatrous worſhip with that due only to the true GOD, and their neglect of the *primitive truths* bequeathed to them by their inſpired prophet and legiſlator *Bramah*; they, in the end loſt the protection of GOD, who gave them up a prey to inteſtine diviſions, and to the Mahommedan invaders. Thus alſo it is recorded of the primitive *Scythians*, whoſe extreme purity in morals and manners procured them the protection of GOD, but a deviation from that state of purity left them at last open to the successful invasions of many nations.——These signal instances, with many more which might be cited to the same purpose, prove, that no nation can expect or hope to prosper, or be happy, but by *persevering* in righteousness; and that the stake, although great, may be easily won.

159. Piety and Virtue, with tears and loud laments, call out for a reform throughout all the earth!——Reformation must begin somewhere.——*Europe*, the most enlightened portion of it at present, presumptuously usurps the title of CHRISTIAN, until she exert all her powers to effect this great work:——the way is cleared for her, ——the reign of superstition and fanaticism are nearly extinct,——the *cursed spirit* of religious persecution (that wicked weapon in the hands of *Satan*) *is laid*,——philosophy has enlarged the minds of the superior ranks of people, and a dawn of unprejudiced reason begins to shine upon the inferior, leaving them open to the reception of truth, when conveyed to them free from unintelligible mysteries.——*Great Britain* stands in the first rank of religious reformers; she has now an opportunity of taking the lead to *Europe* in the reform and restoration of morals.

rals.——All reforms which men may meditate in matters of religion, are purely ideal and vague; and will prove, alas! no reform at all, but a mere pretence to one, without a reform in morals; as faith without works will aſſuredly ſtand us in little ſtead.——*Great Britain* and her reſpectable clergy have it now in their power to ſhine forth in celeſtial luſtre, *a new ſtar of guidance* and inſtruction to *Europe*; and, by the reflection of her example, to enlighten the reſt of the world:—in order to this, we moſt anxiouſly recommend the conſideration of this moſt important of all ſubjects TO THE BEST OF KINGS AND MEN, and to the Legiſlature and people of *Great Britain* and *Ireland* in general; but——our firſt hope reſts on the pious example and preaching of our Moſt Reverend, Right Reverend, and Reverend Paſtors: by their unwearied endeavors, we doubt not but we ſhall ſoon ſee effectually (although not literally) verified, the ſpirit of that remarkable prophecy of the famous wandering *Jew*, recorded in the Turkiſh Spy, which conveys a ſuggeſtion ſo greatly honorable to the Britiſh nation *.

160. As a reform in ſpiritual matters (as above hinted) without a previous reform of

* Vide Turkiſh Spy, vol. vii. p. 216.

morals,

morals, as the ſtate of human nature now ſtands, is, as it were, beginning at the wrong end of things; ſo, when our Reverend Clergy obſerve, that, by a return to *natural* aliments, the return of reaſon and morals make a rapid progreſs amongſt their countrymen; then will be the happy time to make a thorough reform in the ceremonials and principles of religious worſhip; for then, and not before, will they be in a proper frame of mind to receive it; their bodies being temperate and cool, their ſouls will not be inflamed nor excited to irregular and violent paſſions or deſires; but in their place calm and unclouded reaſon and rectitude will take the rule.——Our Reverend Paſtors will then doubtleſs aboliſh, not only the uſe of the *Athanaſian* Creed, but the *Nicene* alſo, and correct that commonly called The Apoſtles.——They will pay ſome regard to the injunctions of *Chriſt*, who ſays, "But when ye pray, do not uſe *vain* "*repetitions*, as the *Heathens do*, for they "think they ſhall be heard *by much ſpeak-* "*ing*," and cut ſhort the tedious tautology and worrying of the Deity in the courſe of the Liturgy, and leave not the ſmalleſt ſemblance of polytheiſm in any part of our worſhip.——They will ſtudiouſly garble the unintelligible *Thirty-nine Articles of Faith*,

Faith, and correct the modes of *ordination* and *abſolution*; and no longer ſwear to the belief and obſervance of tenets which they neither can, or do believe or obſerve; nor preſume to be endued with *powers* which they know they have not, and which they alſo know belong to no being on earth.—— Theſe, and many more dregs of Paganiſm and Popery, which we ſtill erroneouſly retain, *they* will aſſuredly caſt away from us; and thus—on the whole, we ſhould become a new people: by quick gradations the pure ſpirit of *Chriſt*'s doctrines would take root in our hearts; *power* would no longer conſtitute the *rule of juſtice*; the *primitive truths* and the *primitive age* would be reſtored; mankind, who has from that period hitherto been, by nature, principle, and practice, *very devils*, would revert to a perfect ſenſe of their original dignity and angelic ſource, and no longer diſgrace it; all jarring ſects would be reconciled; peace and harmony would return to the earth; an effectual ſtop would be put to the carnage of man and brute; and *all united*, would produce *a ſure and happy tranſmigration to eternity*.—— Great Britain and Ireland would blaze out as *the torch of righteouſneſs* to all the world; her nations would proſper; her people be happy; their *pious flame* would be

caught

caught by their neighboring ſtates, and from thence be ſpread over the face of the whole earth; and THE KINGDOM OF SATAN WOULD BE NO MORE.

161. We are moſt ſenſible, that in this age of diſſipation, infidelity, and ſenſuality, our labors and ſyſtem will be deemed by the diſſolute and unthinking part of mankind, utterly chimerical and impracticable: be it ſo; it is not from thoſe we expect a reform: our hopes reſt on the efforts of the many, who, although they ſwim with the current of vice, have yet *at heart* a reverence for the ſublime truths of religion and morality, and would gladly join in ſtemming the tide, howſoever they are, by a fatal complacence, borne down by the prevailing torrent of folly and faſhion: would *theſe* but exert their powers in the cauſe of virtue; *thoſe* would ſoon be aſhamed of being out of *the mode*.——The marks of the divine diſpleaſure which hovers round us are tremendous! we know not how ſoon they may light upon us; therefore let us, by a general reform, effectually deprecate the "peſtilence that walketh in darkneſs," and thereby excite our GOD to "give his "angels charge over us."

162. Thus

162. Thus we have finiſhed a Diſſertation, begun from no other motives *but the glory of God, and the preſent and future good of all mankind, and the reſt of the animal intelligent beings:*——it muſt be allowed that our attempt is laudable, howſoever imperfect the execution.——And now we take our final leave of the Public, to whom ſome apology is due, for the tardy performance of our engagement, owing to unavoidable hindrances, as, bad health, a neceſſity for change of climate, &c.

163. We could have ſwelled the ſize of our book with the addition of many more learned quotations and notes, from ancient and modern productions, to illuſtrate and ſupport our ſyſtem; but, as we benefit not ourſelves in any ſhape by the ſale of our publications, ſo we have ſtudiouſly avoided taxing the Public for the emolument of our bookſeller.

164. Before we put an abſolute FINIS to our work, we think ſome apology is alſo due to thoſe individuals amongſt our readers, who, either from a weak mind, hard head, or ſoft and tender conſcience, may poſſibly be offended with ſome parts of our doctrines which bear a tendency ſo diametrically oppoſite to the ſenſual paſſions and

and appetites of one claſs, and to others ſo repugnant to the *opinions* they have imbibed in the early ſtages of life, which they have been taught to cheriſh, and look upon as orthodox and eſtabliſhed articles *of faith:*— to ſuch we only recommend, that they would endeavor to enlarge their intellectuals, by diveſting their ſouls of *all prejudice*, and thinking for themſelves; and then we reſt aſſured that we ſhall ſtand exculpated from *all intention* of offence.——We have already had occaſion, more than once, to aſſert, that our great and leading motive for this Eſſay was the *revival* of the PRIMITIVE TRUTHS, as the only ſure baſis for the reſtoration of morals and true religion; and with this principle we cloſe: conceiving, at the ſame time, that our laudable endeavors muſt ſhare the ſame fate with thoſe of others (much more equal to a taſk of this nature) and prove abortive of the end propoſed, whilſt a common error in the political inſtitutes of all nations ſubſiſts, namely, the proviſion of penal laws for the public puniſhment OF VICE, without eſtabliſhing laws for the encouragement and public reward of VIRTUE.——The principles of ſhame, and thirſt of applauſe, ſo firmly implanted in every human breaſt, ſeem to have been utterly neglected, whilſt they might, in the hands of a wiſe legiſlator or adminiſtration, be converted to the moſt ſalutary purpoſes of every well-governed ſtate. ——Some *univerſal cauſes* there muſt be, why every age proves more depraved than the laſt: ſome of the moſt fatal we have occaſionally marked in the body of our work, but the political error above noticed is not amongſt the leaſt—The tendency of all human laws ſeems calculated, not to make mankind *better*, but to prevent their growing *worſe:* how ineffectual all penal laws have proved to anſwer this partial purpoſe, every day's experience evinces; and yet we perſevere without varying our ſyſtem, although thereby we tacitly give up the cauſe of humanity; declaring in effect, that *human nature* is incapable of amendment, without trying whether in fact it is ſo, or not.——God himſelf has pointed out a ſhort inſtitute of laws for man's example, which man has never yet followed; he has decreed *puniſhment* for ſin, and *rewards* for righteouſneſs: man puniſhes evil actions, but rewards not good ones, by any eſtabliſhed laws: herein God proves himſelf a *juſt judge*, and man ſhews himſelf an *unjuſt one*, by leaving virtuous actions to their own reward in this life, in the breaſt only of the poſſeſſor, which, *in general*, proves but a weak excitement to univerſal practice.—All government is ſuppoſed to have taken its riſe from parental authority: although the juſt parent, in imitation of God, chaſtiſes the

the faults of his children, yet he rewards them for being good, notwithſtanding duty, and their own intereſt, prompt them to be ſo, for their own ſakes.—Hence it is moſt obvious, that in the eſtabliſhed laws of all nations, legiſlators have deviated from the invariable œconomy of GOD, as well as from the firſt maxims of human government in the world, in puniſhing crimes, without eſtabliſhing laws, either *pecuniary* or *honorary*, or both, for the reward and encouragement *of virtue*, in whatſoever objects or lights ſhe may appear.—Herein *alſo*, we would ſtimulate the legiſlature of our country *to take the lead* to *Europe:* let virtue be *honored* and *rewarded* by authority, and vice would ſoon fall into diſeſteem, as *unprofitable*.

We make no apology to the Public for the *matter* of our Eſſay, but as many inadvertencies may have eſcaped us in the execution, reſpecting want of ſtrict connection, diction, &c. for theſe we rely on the good-nature and indulgence of the learned world:—we have wrote from the full conviction of our heart and underſtanding; therefore, ſhould our ſtile ſometimes appear too dogmatic and dictatorial, we hope (the cauſe conſidered) candor will kindly overlook it.

Milford Haven, near Haverford Weſt,
South Wales, 1ſt Nov. 1770.

F I N I S.